NAGA VARMMA'S KARNATAKA BHASHA-BHUSHANA

NAGA VARMMA'S KARNATAKA BHASHA-BHUSHANA

The oldest grammar extant of the language

Edited

WITH AN INTRODUCTION

By

LEWIS RICE, M.R.A.S.,

Director of Public Instruction

GYAN

Published by

GYAN

Gyan Publishing House
5, Ansari Road
Daryaganj, New Delhi-110002
Phone: 011-47034999, 9811692060
E-mail: books@gyanbooks.com

Distribution Network
gyanbooks.com
India, USA, Canada, UK, Australia, France

ISBN : 978-81-212-3799-4 (PB)
First Published, 1884

2nd Impression 2020

Printed at: Gyan Press, Delhi.

Naga Varmma's Karnataka Bhasha-Bhushana
Author: Lewis Rice

CONTENTS.

INTRODUCTION.

I. Nâga Varmmâ and his Works.

Nâga Varmmâ is the oldest grammarian of the Kannaḍa or Karṇâṭaka (so called Canarese) language whose works are now extant, though by no means the earliest author in that language. Whether he had any predecessors in formulating the rules of its grammar we have no knowledge. The only standard writers on Kannaḍa grammar that came after him were Kês'i Râjâ, who was about half a century or more later, and Bhaṭṭâkalaṅka Deva, who probably belonged to the commencement of the 17th century.

Though Nâga Varmmâ's exact date is not specifically given, yet, from the authors he quotes, it can safely be decided that he was flourishing at the latest in the first twenty years of the 12th century. He traces his descent from a Brahman family of the Kauṇḍiṇya gotra, residing at the city of Vengi in the Vengi country (the modern Krishna district), and was the first-born son of Veṇṇamayya and Pôḷikabbe or Pôtikabbe.* He was evidently a Jaina, but would seem to have written under certain S'aiva influence. In connection with what we know of the history of his fellow-countryman Pampa, it may be conjectured that Nâga Varmmâ left Vengi on embracing the Jaina faith, and settled in some part of the Karṇâṭa territory which was subject to the sway of the Western Châḷukya kings: in all probability somewhere in the neighbourhood of the present Shimoga, Dharwad and Bellary districts.†

This view is borne out by a consideration of the political changes which had taken place at Vengi at the period referred to, in conjunction with the allusions

---

*His genealogy in full is thus given :—In the Vengi vishaya, one of the best in the world, among its chief seven grâmas, was the beautiful Vengi-paḷu. In it dwelt the learned and honorable Veṇṇamayya, skilled in the Vedas, an ornament to the Kauṇḍiṇya gotra. That distinguished Brahman's wife was Kauṇḍikabbe. They had a son Dâmamayya, whose wife was Kundakabbe. Of these two the first-born son was Veṇṇamayya, honoured by Brahmans, walking in the path of Manu, acquainted with all elegant arts, versed in the laukika and vaidika s'âstras, a great linguist (*anekâksharan*). His wife, filled with devotion to her husband, was Pôḷikabbe. To them was Nâga Varmmâ the first born son.

† Possibly at Poḷalu, the modern Hoḷalu, on the Tungabhadra, in the west of Bellary district. See sûtra 175.

found in our author to the ruling powers of his day. In 1063 the kingdom of Vengi, which for upwards of 450 years before had been governed by the kings of the Eastern Châḷukya dynasty, had passed, partly by conquest and partly by matrimonial alliance, into the possession of Râjendra Chôḷa, and for about half a century onwards a succession of Chôḷa kings continued to rule over it. But the word Chôḷa only once occurs in Nâga Varmmâ, while on the other hand all his sympathies seem to be with the Western Châḷukya and Ganga kings, whose names he freely introduces into the examples under his rules. And the single instance in which he directly refers to the government under which he was living, though not very definite, yet seems clearly to point to deliverance from a country subject to invasion and revolution.

> Aṛanam pâḷiyumam pudungoḷisikonḍ î bhûmiyum bhûmipan |
> nere yôḷg endum iḷâtaḷam baḷevudakk oḷgûlam utkiḷvaram |
> baṛanam pinguge—

"May the king be happily united with this land, protected from Yama and the edge of the sword. That the land may prosper, be the inroads (lit. foot-soles) of uprooters and famine ever turned back."

Moreover, that he was very intimately acquainted with the Kannaḍa literature of his time needs little proof, for his writings abound with evidence of it Now we know that in and about the regions bordering on the Tungabhadra, and especially at Puligeṛe, Huligeṛe or Pulikara-nagara (the modern Lakshmesvara in the Dharwad district), which in the 10th century was the capital of a subordinate Châḷukya prince, was then concentred the chief literary activity directed to the cultivation of the Kannaḍa language. And at a later age, or in the 12th century, this part of the country seems to have been included in the Ganga principality which had then been established, also under Châḷukya supremacy, with its capital at Kurugôḍ, a little north of Bellary. There is, further, reason to suppose that Nâga Varmmâ was specially intimate and perhaps a co-worker with Guṇa Varmmâ, whom he designates Bhuvanaika Vîra. But this is no literary title; and from inscriptions we learn that it belonged to the Ganga prince Udayâditya, who was the chief general and minister of the Châlukya king Bhuvanaika Malla (reigned 1069—1076), and who subsequently became governor of the Banavase Twelve Thousand (the modern Shimoga district) with adjoining tracts. Udayâditya is likewise the name of an author, and he would thus be identical with Guṇa Varmmâ, the Bhuvanaika Vîra and friend of Nâga Varmmâ.

Other precise grounds for the date assigned to Nâga Varmmâ are the following. He quotes Naya Sena by name, and that in a sûtra of the present grammar; in an integral portion therefore of the text. Now Naya Sena has supplied us with 1115 as the date of his own work. Again, it is worthy of note that Nâga Varmmâ, in naming the authorities consulted for his dictionary, does not mention Hemachandra who died in 1172; an omission which is unaccountable had they been contemporary. It is also clear beyond doubt that

Nâga Varmmâ preceded Kês'i Râjâ, whose period is that of Basava, the founder of the Lingâyit sect in about 1165. The question is thus narrowed within very close limits, and we are shut up to the conclusion that Nâga Varmmâ lived during the latter part of the 11th and first quarter of the 12th centuries.

His compositions, so far as they are known to us, are the following: in what order they were published is uncertain, but the first is quoted in the next three.

1. Kâvyâvalôkana;
2. Chhandô'mbudhi;
3. Karṇâṭaka Bhâshâ Bhûshaṇa;
4. Vastu Kôs'a;
5. Kâdambari.

The *Kâvyâvalôkana* is a work on the art of poetry, forming a handbook of rules for Kanna'a metrical composition. The sûtras are in Kannaḍa verse, and copiously illustrated by stanzas in the same language, either of original composition or more generally quotations from former or contemporary poets. The author in some of his opening lines says—

Kavigaḷg idu kai-gannaḍi ।
kavitege bâḷ-modal udâtta vâg-devateg ud-।
bhava-hêtu kôs'a-gṛiham ene ।
bhuvanadoḷ idu paredu nilpud ond achchariye ॥

"Being a hand-mirror for poets, the source of prosperity to poetry, the cause of birth to the bountiful speech-goddess, a treasure-house of terms—is it a wonder if this should shine and endure in the world?"

The work is in 5 *adhikaraṇas*, sub-divided into *prakaraṇas*. The former are named respectively:—i. S'abda-smṛiti; ii. Kâvyamalavyâvṛitti; iii. Guṇa-vivekam: iv. Rîti-krama-rasa-nirûpaṇam; v. Kavi-samayam. The 1st chapter contains an epitome of the grammar of the language and is in 6 sections, entitled—1. Samjnâ prakaraṇam; 2. Sandhi p.; 3. Nâma p.; 4. Samâsa p.; 5. Taddhita p.; 6. Âkhyâta p. The 2nd chapter has 2 sections—1. Pada-padârtha-sandhi-dôsha p.; 2.? Sâra-vichâra p. The 3rd chapter is in 3 sections, named—1. Mârga-dars'anam; 2. S'abdâlankâra-nirṇayam; 3. Arthâlankâram. They seem collectively to form what their author calls the Kavi-râja-mârga: this he describes to be the system prevailing in Southern India (dakshiṇa-dês'a-varti) as distinguished from that of the North (Vaidarbha-Gauḍa-mârga-bhêda). The remaining chapters appear not to be sub-divided, but it is unfortunate that notwithstanding every effort for several years no complete copy has been met with of this interesting and important work.*

The *Chhandô'mbudhi* is the only existing authority on Kannaḍa chhandas or prosody.† It is also written in Kannaḍa, in the form of verses addressed by

* Arthâlankâram has been lately published by itself at Mysore, edited by B. Mallappa of the Maharaja's College.

† Published at Mangalore in 1875, edited by the Rev. F. Kittel.

Nâga Varmmâ to his wife, the verses being so composed as themselves to furnish examples of the rules to be illustrated. He professes to have taken as his guide the sûtras of Pingala, the work on Sanskrit prosody. He appears however also to have followed another Pingaḷa, the author of sûtras for Prâkrit prosody. But though these served as guides, the arrangement and most of the nomenclature of his work are his own, which also unlike theirs is metrical. It is divided into 5 *âs'vâsas* preceded by a *pîṭhike* or introduction. The 1st and 2nd treat of Akshara gaṇas, and are named—i. Samjnâdhikâram; ii. Sama-vṛitta vivaraṇam. The 3rd and 4th treat of Mâtrâ gaṇas; and the 5th of Kannaḍa Mâtrâ gaṇas. The following statement of his views on the classification of Indian languages is of interest.

Samskṛitam Prâkṛitam Apabhrams'am Pais'âchikam emba mûṟu vare bhâshegaḷol puṭṭuva Draviḍ-Ândhra-Karṇâṭak-âdi shaṭ-panchâs'at sarvavishaya bhâshâ-jâtigaḷ akkum.

"Born in the three and a half languages—Sanskrit, Prâkrit, Apabhrams'a and Pais'âchika—are the Draviḍa (Tamil), Ândhra (Telugu), Karṇâṭaka (Kannaḍa) and other the various languages of all the fifty-six countries." The lists of these chapanna dês'as or 56 countries of Indian geography vary considerably in different works: most of them include the known countries but are eked out with names of more or less mythical regions.

The *Karṇâṭaka Bhâshâ Bhûshaṇa* is the present work—a Karṇâṭaka Vyâkaraṇa or grammar, in Sanskrit sûtras, after the manner of Pâṇini. The sûtras are accompanied by a vṛitti or explanatory gloss, by the author, also in Sanskrit. To this more particularly it would appear the name Karṇâṭaka Bhâshâ Bhûshaṇa applies, though the whole work is also so called. For the colophon runs—

Karṇâṭaka-sûtra-vṛittau tad Bhâshâ-Bhûshaṇa-nâmani I

while at the end of each parichchheda we have—

Iti Karṇâṭaka-Vyâkaraṇa-vrittau Bhâshâ-Bhûshaṇe, &c.

On the other hand one version omits the words Vyâkaraṇa-vrittau. Under each rule are given numerous examples and some quotations from authors, of whom Pampa, Naya Sena, Haripâla and Guṇa Varmma are mentioned by name. An account of these will be found further on. The present edition is a recension formed from the collection of three *ôle* or palmyra leaf copies, which have been distinguished as A—the text—B and C. They are all Jain copies and therefore the more likely to be genuine reproductions of the original. Lingâyit and Brâhman versions however also exist*, which are marked chiefly by alteration of all sectarian names and ascriptions in the examples to such as are agreeable to those forms of faith. These various readings I have given for what they are worth in

* While this is going through the press, a Brahman version in the Kannada character has appeared at Mysore, got up in poor style, edited by Pustakam Alasingalâchâri, who may thus claim to be the first publisher of the work, never before printed.

an appendix though they can at no time have formed a part of the work as it came from its author. The latter is divided into 10 *parichchhedas*, of which the names are.—1. Samjnâ vidhânam; 2. Sandhi v.; 3. Vibhakti v.; 4. Kâraka v.; 5. S'abda-rîti v.; 6. Samâsa v.; 7. Taddhita v.; 8. Âkhyâta-niyama v.; 9. Avyaya-nirûpaṇa v.; 10. Nipâta v. With the view of making it available for consultation by European scholars this edition has been printed in the Roman character, as well as in Kannaḍa for local use.

The *Vastu Kôs'a* is a Samskṛita-Karṇâṭa nighaṇṭu or dictionary, composed in many artificial metres, giving the meanings of Sanskrit words used in Kannaḍa. In its compilation our author states that he made use of Vararuchi, Halâyudha, S'as'vata, Amarakôs'a and other authorities. The work contains Ekârtha, Nânârtha and Sâmânya kâṇḍas.

The *Kâdambarî* is a close rendering into Kannaḍa of Bâṇa's celebrated romance of the same name in Sanskrit.*

The foregoing list will show the importance of Nâga Varmmâ's works for the study of the language. That writings of such value should have been allowed to lie so long neglected is I fear chiefly to be attributed to sectarian prejudice; but political changes, and the vicissitudes of the Kannaḍa speaking countries under the dominion of Mahrattas and of Muhammadans, have doubtless had no in-considerable share in putting a virtual stop to scholarly cultivation of the language.

In accordance with the prevailing fashion of his day Nâga Varmmâ assumes various *noms de plume* by which he is indiscriminately quoted or referred to in the works of others. The principal are Kavi Râja and Kavi Râja Hamsa, but he also calls himself Nâki, Nâkiga or Pinâki.

II. The Kannada Language.

Kannaḍa—the Karṇâṭaka of the Sanskrit pandits and the Canarese of European writers—is one of the family of South Indian languages of which Telugu, Tamiḻ and Malayâlam are the other principal representatives. But Karṇâṭaka as a generic term embraces both Kannaḍa and Telugu, which have the same written character, and by implication the various dialects of the former, which, so far as reduced to writing, also employ that character. The name Kannaḍa may be a *tadbhava* formed from Karṇâṭa, the derivation of which is unknown. But a probable origin has been suggested by Dr. Gundert in *kare nâḍu*, the "black country", referring to the black cotton soil which characterises the plateau f the southern Dekhan in which this language is spoken.† The form Karṇâṭaka

---

*I do not of myself know this to be a work by Nâga Varmmâ, but I am confidently assured of it by competent native scholar.

† Mr. C. P. Brown has tried to discover a clue to the derivation of Kannada from the name of Canada, the British Dominion in North America, which according to him is a word unknown to the aborigines. But the results are somewhat blank, for he professes to have found that it means *ca nada*, "we have nothing."

looks adjectival, but the *Vis'ragunádars'ana*, a work more than 200 years old derives it from *karṇa* and *aṭaka*, which is explained in the Mackenzie Mss. as meaning "passing to the ears" of all men, and hence applied to "this honoured and renowned country." Whatever its origin, the term is of considerable antiquity, as it occurs at the beginning of the 5th century in Varâhamihira.

Kannaḍa is spoken throughout the west of the Nizam's Dominions, the South Mahratta country, the Ceded Districts, Canara, Mysore and Coimbatore. A line drawn from Bidar in the Nizam's Dominions due south to the junction of the Bhavânî with the Kâvêri, and thence westwards through Coimbatore by the base of the Western Ghats to the coast a little north of Mangalore, with one drawn from Bidar south-west through Sholapur and Kolhapur round the east of the Goa territory to about Honavar on the coast, will in a general way indicate the region occupied by the Kannaḍa language.

The following dialects of Kannaḍa are also spoken within the same tracts;

Koḍagu, Kuḍagu or Coorg, in the country of that name.

Tuḷu or Tuḷuva in South Canara.

Tuda or Toda, by the race of that name in the Nilgiris.

Kota, by the tribe so called in the Nilgiris.

Baḍaga, by the people bearing that name in the Nilgiris.

The numbers of the races speaking Kannaḍa and its dialects are estimated at about ten millions.

From the works of authors and from inscriptions there may be distinguished three stages of the language,—Pûrvada Haḷe Kannaḍa, the former or Primitive Old Canarese, Haḷe Kannaḍa or Old Canarese, and Hosa Kannaḍa, the new or modern Canarese now current.* Pûrvada Haḷe Kannaḍa is described by Wilks as the language of Banavasi, the ancient capital of the Kadambas, to the north-west of the Mysore country, a city which is mentioned in the *Mahawanso* as one to which a Buddhist missionary was sent in the 3rd century B. C., and is also named by Ptolemy in the 2nd century A. D. This early form of the language may be said to have continued in use to the end of the 7th century. From the 8th to the 14th century was the Haḷe Kannaḍa period, and that during which the language was brought to a high state of cultivation by a succession of gifted writers of the Jaina faith. They refer to the language preceding their time as Haḷe Kannaḍa, and denominate what they used as Hosa Kannaḍa, though it is what is now understood by us as Haḷe Kannaḍa. Hence the necessity for discriminating the three stages as above specified; but the limits assigned to them are not to be taken absolutely, and the periods in different parts of the Kannaḍa region may be found to overlap or run into one another.

* The different forms of these names are Paḷe Kannaḍa or by euphony Paḷe Gannaḍa, Haḷe Kannaḍa or Haḷe Gannaḍa, and Posa Kannaḍa or Posa Gannaḍa, Hosa Kannaḍa or Hosa Gannaḍa.

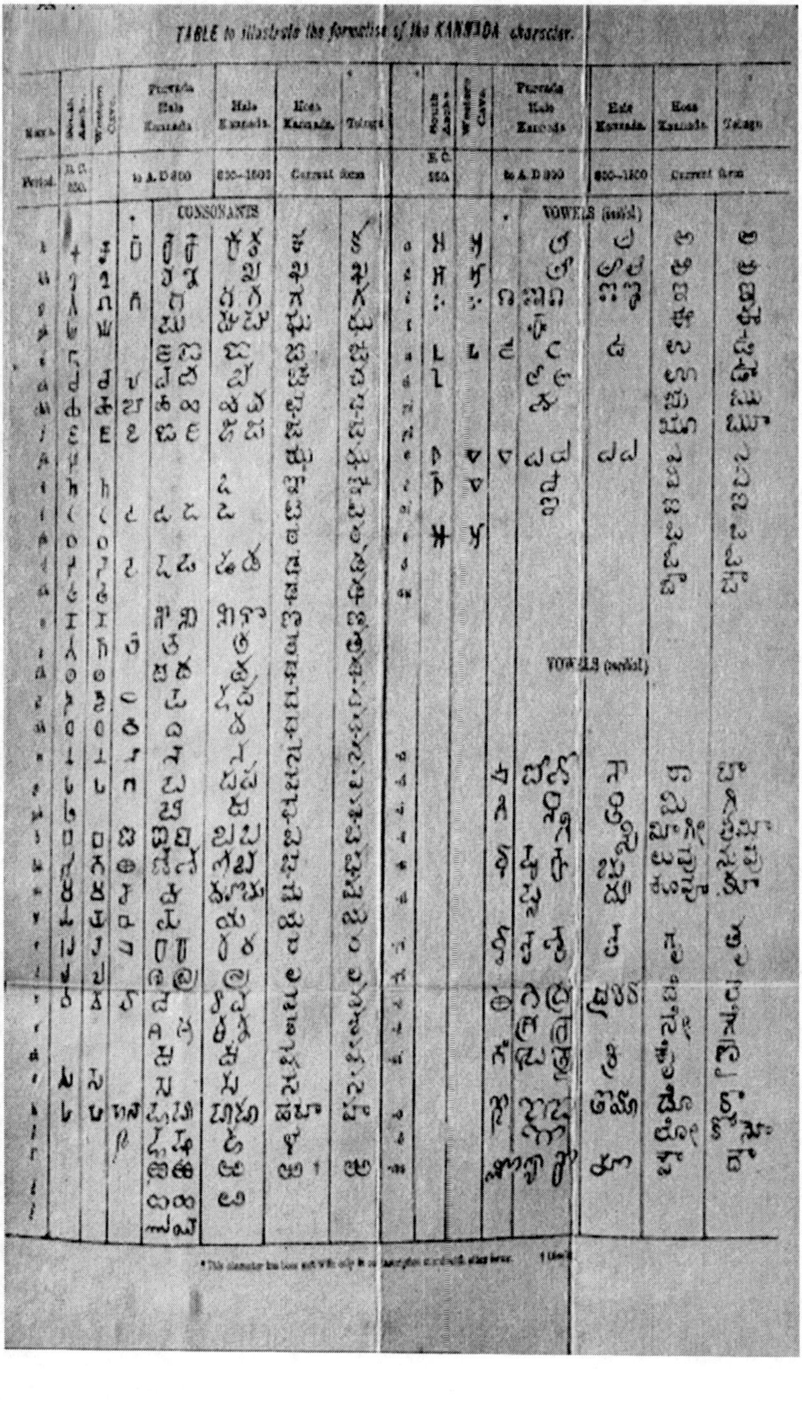

TABLE to illustrate the formation of the KANNADA character.
Period.
Purvada Hale Kannada
Hale Kannada.
Hosa Kannada.
Telugu
to A.D 800
800–1500
Current form
CONSONANTS
VOWELS (initial)
VOWELS (medial)

The written character which is common to Kannaḍa and Telugu, and which spread over the south and was carried even to Java, is derived, through that of the cave inscriptions of Western India, from the south Asʼoka character, or that in which the Girnar inscription of Asʼoka's edicts is written, belonging to about 250 B. C. Previous to this date no specimens of writing have been discovered in India. But it has recently been announced that Professor Sayce has deciphered some Babylonian tablets in the British Museum as old as the 7th century B. C. written in an Aramaic character which appears to be the source of the south Asʼoka.* "It may be accepted as a scientific fact" says Mr. Cust "that all the characters used in the East Indies can sooner or later be traced back to the Asʼoka inscriptions, and through them to the Phœnician alphabet, and thence backwards to the hieratic ideographs of the old kingdom of Egypt, and thence to the venerable hieroglyphics of the fourth dynasty." † The period assigned to this dynasty is 2,450 B. C.‡

The Kannaḍa character as used in inscriptions shows a decided transition in the 9th and 15th centuries in the shape of those letters which have undergone change, thus marking the Púrvada Haḷe Kannaḍa and the Haḷe Kannaḍa periods, and the growth of the Hosa Kannaḍa character. The accompanying table illustrates the prevalent forms of the letters at the different periods.

By European writers the group of languages which includes Kannaḍa is called the Dravidian family. The distinctive features of this family, as stated by Mr. Cust, are "that in its gender it distinguishes between rational and irrational objects: it has an oblique form for many of its nouns: it specialises the meaning of a root by the use of formatives: it modifies the root itself to convey different meanings and relations: it has a negative voice."

"The Dravidian languages" says Dr. Caldwell "occupy a position of their own, between the languages of the Indo-European family and those of the Turanian or Scythian group—not quite a midway position, but one considerably nearer the latter than the former. The Scythian family to which on the whole the Dravidian languages may be regarded as most nearly allied is the Finnish or Ugrian, with some special affinities as it appears to the Ostiak branch of that family; and this supposition derives some confirmation from the fact brought to light by the Behistun tablets that the ancient Scythic race by which the greater part of Central Asia was peopled prior to the irruption of the Medo-Persians belonged not to the Turkish, or to the Mongolian, but to the Ugrian stock."

On the other hand Dr. Pope has advocated the Indo-European relationship of the Dravidian languages on the ground "of deep-seated and radical affinities between them and the Celtic and Teutonic languages." But Dr. Caldwell replies

---

* *Academy*, 17 June 1882.

† *Mod. Lang. of the East Indies*, 19.

‡ Rawlinson's *Herodotus*, II, 341.

that "of all the members of the Indo-European family the Celtic is that which appears to have most in common with the Scythian group, and especially with the languages of the Finnish family, languages which may possibly have been widely spoken in Europe previously to the arrival of the Celts."

"The Dravidian tongues" writes Professor Whitney "have some peculiar phonetic elements, are richly polysyllabic, of general agglutinative structure, with prefixes only, and very soft and harmonious in their utterance: they are of a very high type of agglutination, like the Finnish and Hungarian... Excepting that they show no trace of the harmonic sequence of vowels, these languages are not in their structure so different from the Scythian that they might not belong to one family with them, if only sufficient correspondences of material were found between the two groups."

The native grammarians as a rule deduce all the Indian languages from Sanskrit through one or other of the Prákrits. Nâga Varmmâ, who was as far as we know the earliest Kannaḍa grammarian, assumes, as we have seen above,* the existence in India of three and a half mother languages—Samskṛita, Prâkṛita, Apabhrams'a and Paisâchika—from which sprung the fifty-six daughter languages—Drâviḍa, A'ndhra, Karṇâṭaka, &c. According to him the original Kannaḍa alphabet probably did not contain the lingual and dental vowels (*ṛi*, *ṛî*, *ḷri*, *ḷrî*) and the aspirated consonants which now assimilate it to the Sanskrit alphabet. On the other hand it has some characteristic letters not contained in Sanskrit. Thus, among the vowels Kannaḍa has both a short and a long form of *e* and *o*, while Sanskrit has only the long form. And in addition to the Sanskrit consonants, Kannaḍa has *ḷa*, *ṟa* and *ḻa*. The first of these only is now in use† and corresponds with the lingual *ḷa* of Vedic Sanskrit. The other two are obsolete, though the *ṟa* is still used in Telugu. The date of the disappearance from Kannaḍa literature of *ḻa* is about the 13th century, while *ṟa* was disused after the 18th century.

Modern Kannaḍa, as in current use for literary purposes, comprises four classes of words—*tatsama*, pure Sanskrit words; *tadbhava*, Sanskrit words changed to suit the language; *dês'ya*, indigenous words; and *grâmya*, provincialisms. To these a later classification adds *anyadês'ya*, foreign words. But, from the standard authorities among the earlier cultivators of the language, it is evident that Kannaḍa was not dependent upon Sanskrit as an aid in composition, but was quite self-sufficient and well adapted for independent use as a vehicle for the expression of thought. A knowledge of Sakkada, as Sanskrit was called in Kannaḍa—considered to be a *tadbhava* formed from the word Samskrita—was the necessary mark of a scholar, and the special attention paid to the cultivation of the learned language was no doubt combined with a corresponding disregard

---

* p. iv.

† An example in the *Karnâṭaka S'abdânus'âsana* quaintly says:—Kannaḍigar ḷa-kâraman oḷambattar.

for the vernacular, as we see perhaps even more in our own day. From this cause imported expressions have largely come into use, especially through the writings of Brahmans, who venerate the sacred language, and in fact of that alone may be said to make a study. But such was not the case in the best age of Kannada literature. The Jains who were its cultivators were not behindhand in their knowledge of Sanskrit; but they advocated purism in the use both of Kannada and of Sakkada, and condemned the mongrel composition of those who, professing to write in the former, were too indolent or too careless to perfect themselves in it and attempted to make up for their deficient knowledge of Kannada by an indiscriminate resort to Sanskrit.

Thus, Naya Sena, who is referred to as an authority even by Nâga Varmmâ, says—

Posa-Kannaḍadim vyâva- |
rṇṇisuvem sat-kritiyam endu Kannaḍamam chin- |
tisi kûḍalârad akkaṭa- |
misukada-Sakkadaman ikkuv avanum kaviyê ||

Sakkadamam pê|vare nere-
Sakkadamam pê|ge s'uddha-Kannaḍadoḷu tan- |
d ikku-ud î Sakkadangaḷa |
takkude berasalke ghṛitamumam tailamumam ||

"Is he a poet who, saying I will write a good poem in Hosa Kannaḍa, being unable to think of Kannaḍa words, uses incongruous Sanskrit that will not squeeze in? If he write Sanskrit, let him write entirely in Sanskrit; but to bring these Sanskritisms and thrust them into pure Kannaḍa—will it do to mix ghi and oil?"

Nâga Varmmâ, too, in an example which also occurs in Kês'i Râjâ, has the following:—

Paḷe-Gannaḍada padangoḷe |
koḷe-Sakkadamam taguḷchi ṟn-eḍam uttum |
meḷasam gôd ant ire pê- |
ḷv aḷi-gavigaḷa kavite budharan erdeg oḷisugume ||

"If into Haḷe Kannaḍa verses they stick in corrupt Sanskrit, that a clever deaf man would discern—as if pepper were like wheat—can the poetry of such ruination-poets please the heart of the wise?"

So also Ponna, whose real name was Savaṇa, prides himself on the ability to write in both Sakkada and Kannaḍa, whence his cognomen of Ubhaya Kavi Chakravartti:—

Yeraḍ edege vappanam mach- |
charisuvanum nuḍigo Sakkaḍam Kannaḍam em- |
b eraḍum kaviteya balmige |
beraḷ ettidan iḷeyoḷ î Kuruḷgala Savaṇam ||

"Lest any should bear malice for his precision in language of two kinds, by his ability in both Sakkada and Kannaḍa poetry he caused the finger to be raised (indicating him as number one, without a second) * throughout the world, this Kuruḷgaḷa Savaṇa."

Likewise Aggaḷa calls himself *Ubhaya-kavitâ-vis'âradhan*, skilled in both kinds of poetry.

In those old inscriptions, moreover, which display the most literary skill, separate verses in Sanskrit and in Kannaḍa are interspersed with one another according to the opportunities afforded by the theme, in such a way as greatly to heighten the general effect.

Kes'i Râjâ, in the concluding stanza of the *S'abdamaṇidarpaṇa*, lays down the following as the standard of good Kannaḍa.

> Gamaka-samâsadim ṟa-ḷa-kuḷakshaḷadim s'ruti-sahya-sandhiyim |
> samuchitamâgi barpa sati-saptamiyim sama-Samskṛit-ôktiyim |
> va-ma-ha-pa-bhêdadim virahit-âvyaya-Samskṛita- lingadim pado- |
> ttama-s'ithilatvadim yati-vilanghanadind aridalte Kannaḍam ||

"With energetic compounds, with distinction of ṟa, ḷa and ḷa, with euphonious combinations, moving fitly along (*i. e.* in harmony with the subject); from the use of the locative-infinitive, from apt Sanskrit vocables†, from marking the distinction between va, ma, ha, and pa, from (?) the absence of Sanskrit gerunds and genders‡, from the gliding consonants of well chosen words, from precision in rhyme:—is it not by these that Kannaḍa is known?"

III. Kannaḍa Literature.

The first cultivators of the Kannaḍa language for literary purposes were the Jains, and down to about A. D. 1300 we have none but Jaina authors. For about two centuries they were succeeded principally by Lingâyit and S'aiva writers, and from about 1500 date the Brahmanical and Vaishnava works. There were

---

* Such is the evident meaning of the poet; but for interesting light upon this phrase, showing, when taken in conjunction with the claims he sets up as given in the notice of him farther on, a not unlikely allusion to Kâlidâsa, see Sir E. Clive Bayley on *the Genealogy of Modern Numerals*, (J. R. A. S., Jan. 1883, p. 4) and Mr. Fleet on *The Ring Finger*, (*Ind. Ant.*, iv, 85). In reckoning the "nine gems" of Vikramâditya's court on the fingers, Kâlidâsa was always reckoned first (on the little finger of the left hand), but no one was counted on the next (or ring finger) because none of his contemporaries could be reckoned as even second to him: this finger was *anâmika*, without a name.

† Under his sûtra 80, *sama-Samskṛita* is exemplified as referring to names, such as Kâma, Bhîma, Râma, Soma, Nârada, Nârâyaṇa, &c.

‡ This phrase also is illustrated by his sûtra 80, which runs as follows:—

> Samudita sankhyâvyaya-rahi- | tam enisi vartipa nighaṇṭuvina nâma-padô- |
> ttama-varṇa-prakṛitigaḷam | sama-Samskṛita-vesaṟan iṭṭu lingam mâḷpar ||

subsequently occasional publications by Jains but most of the literature of the later period originated with the other sects.

The leading characteristic of the Jain earlier works is that they are *champu kâvyas,* or poems in a variety of composite metres, interspersed with paragraphs in prose. The Lingâyits brought into use the *ragaḷe* and *shaṭpadi* metres of the more modern works. While the most recent compositions are in *yaksha gâna* metre, and some in prose only.

It would appear that the chief impulse under which the language attracted the special attention of scholars to its systematic study and culture was coincident with the break up of the Ganga power that resulted from the capture of Talakâḍu by the Chôḷas, who thence extended their conquests till possessed of the Eastern Châlukya territory of Vengi, whence two or three of the most prominent early Kannaḍa authors derive their origin.

But it must not hastily be concluded that no literary effort was put forth in an earlier phase of the language; for one form which the persecutions under Kumârila Bhaṭṭa, and later under S'ankarâcharya in the 8th century, took was the destruction of Buddhist and Jain literature. It was on the occasion of S'ankara's casting such works into the waters of the Tungabhadra—so the story goes—that one book was observed to keep floating and could not be made to sink. On examination it proved to be the Amara Kos'a, which, being thus as it were evidently destined to be immortal, was suffered to live.

The earliest notices that have come to light of local authorship are contained in the inscriptions of the Ganga kings, who ruled over the south of the Mysore country and adjoining regions from about the end of the 2nd century to the end of the 9th. From this source we get the following particulars* :—

A. D.

c. 240. ***Mâdhava Râja*** wrote a treatise or commentary on the rules of adoption (*dattaka-sûtra-vṛittch-praṇetâ, dattaka-sûtra-vyâkhyâ-praṇetâ*).

c. 470. ***Avinîta*** wrote a commentary on 15 cantos of the Kirâtârjunîya (*Kirâtârjunîya-pañchadas'a-sargga-ṭîkâkâro*). This celebrated poem by Bhâravi is in 18 cantos.

Next, in an inscription of the Chaḷukya kings we have mention of—

634. ***Ravikîrtti***, a poet whose fame equalled that of Kâḷidâsa and Bhâravi (*kavitâs'rita-Kâḷidâsa-Bhâravi-kîrttih*).

Resorting now to the evidence derived from literature, we glean the following information. Where actual or approximate dates are given it is believed that they may be relied on, but the time and place of those authors to whom no

* The information relating to the Jain period, never before published, is taken from articles recently contributed by me to the Journal of the Royal Asiatic Society, London.

dates are assigned may require re-adjustment as our knowledge of the subject increases. A special difficulty in these investigations has arisen from the variety of names which one author assumes or by which he was known.

? 650. ***Samanta Bhadra***—named together with Kavi-parimeshṭi and Pûjyapâda, invariably in this order, by Pampa, Ponna, Naya Sena and several other old poets, as forming the earliest and most distinguished trio among the authors who preceded them. A Châḷukya inscription of the 11th century speaks of Samanta Bhadra as famous for his poetical skill. The following works are ascribed to him:—*Devâgama-stotra*, *Nyâya-nis'chaya-vârttikâlankâra*, *Uktyânus'âsana*, *Bhâshâ-manjarî*, *Chintâmaṇi-ṭippaṇi*, *Ashṭa-sahasra-ṭippaṇi*, *Ratna-karaṇḍaka*.

? 670. ***Kaviparimeshṭi***—always, as above stated, mentioned between Samanta Bhadra and Pûjyapâda. The name is no doubt a *nom de plume*, and we shall find that the assumption of such names became a regular fashion among poets and was carried to extravagant lengths. His real name has not been discovered nor any account of his works.

690. ***Pûjyapâda*** is specially known for his skill in *s'abda s'âstra* or as a grammarian, but he is referred to as a poet along with the two preceding, as above described. A Châḷukya inscription records a grant made in 729 to a pandit who had been his house-disciple. On this ground Pûjyapâda may be placed at the end of the 7th century. The following works are attributed to him:—*Jainendra-nyâsa*, *Pâṇini-s'abdâvatâra*, *Kârikâvṛitti*, *Surasa-sangraha*, *Sarvvârtha-siddhi*.*

788. ***Akalanka***, *Akalanka Chandra*, is mentioned by Pampa, Ponna, and others, and is named in an old inscription as excelling in *tarka s'âstra*. According to Wilson, he was a Jain from S'ravaṇa Belgoḷa, who, at the date given, disputed with the Buddhists in the presence of Hemas'îtala, king of Kânchî, and defeating them, procured their banishment to Kandy in Ceylon. Ponna styles him the *jaya-vâdi*, and Nâgachandra states that "at the radiance of the moonlight of his speech the Digambara *chakora* rejoiced and the lotus of opponent speakers shut up."† Kamalabhava, describing

---

* There are reasons for supposing that he was the author of the *Jainendra-vyâkaraṇa* itself, and that he also bore the name of *Devanandi*.—See *Ind. Ant.* xii, 20. The following quotations are there given by Mr. Pathak in support of these statements:—

From the *Dharma-parikshe*.

Bharadim Jainendramam bhâsuram enal oredam Pâṇinîyakke ṭîkum |
baredam Tatvârthamam ṭippaṇadin aripidam yantra-mantrâdi s'âstro-|
tkaramam bhû-rakshan-ârtham virachisi jasamum tâḷdidam vis'va-vidyâ-|
bharaṇam bhavy-âliy-ârâdhita-pada-kamalam Pûjyapâdam vratîndram ||

From the *Nandi-sangha-gurvâvaḷi*.

Yas'ah-kîrttir yas'o-nandî Devanandi mahâ-yatih |
S'ri-Pûjyapâd-âparâkhyo guṇanandi guṇâkarah ||

† Akalanka-chandra vâk-chan-| drikeyin dhavaḷise Digambara-s'rî-bhavya |
prakara-chakôram nalidudu | mukuḷitav âyt anyavâdi-vadanâmbhôjam ||

the effect of his eloquence, says *itara-mata-vâdi-mano-nayanam mugidudu.* The following are said to be works by him :—*Devâgama-sûtra-nyâsa, Pramâṇa-ratna-pradîpa.*

—*Vidyânanda*, *Vâdi Vidyânanda*, is mentioned by Naya Sena. His period is not known. The following works bear his name :—*S'lokavârttik-âlankâra, Âpta-mîmâmsa-nyâsa.*

941. *Pampa*, *Hampa*, *Kavitâguṇârṇava*, *Guru Hampa*, *Purâṇa Kavi*, *Sukavijanamanomanasottamsa Hamsa*, *Sujanottamsa Hamsa Râja.* By these and other names is this distinguished poet referred to, with whose publications a great impulse seems to have been given to the study of Kannaḍa. From his first work, the *Âdi Purâṇa*, we learn that he was born in 902. But his second work, called *Vikramârjuna Vijaya* or the *Pampa Bhârata*, which established his fame, tells us that both were written in the same year, 941. His genealogy is thus given. In the Bengi maṇḍala was a beautiful town named Vengi; connected with which were the agrahâras of Koṭṭûru, Niḍuguṇḍi and Vikramapura. The last, which was the chief of these, was renowned as the residence of Mânava (or Mâdhava) Somayâji, of the Vatsa gotra. His son was Abhimâna-chandra, whose son was Komarayya, whose son was Abhirâma Deva Râya. He, believing the Jina faith to be superior to that of the Brahmans, became a Jaina; and his son, distinguished as Kavitâguṇârṇava, was Pampa.* Other poets having related the Bhârata at great length, some excelling in description and some in the narrative, all the pandits agreed that Pampa was the one who could do justice to it without sacrificing any of the story. On their petition he made the attempt; and taking his king as Arjuna, crowned him as the hero.

The following is a summary of the account of this royal patron. In the sky of the Chaḷukya vamsa, Yuddha Malla shone as its moon. And he ruled over a $1\frac{1}{4}$ lakh country (*sa-pâda-laksha-kshitiyam*) His son was Ari Kesari, who, with the ministers of the Bange vishaya, penetrated into the kingdom of Nirupama Deva, and inscribed his fame on all the points of the compass. He had two sons, the chief of whom was Narasimha Bhadra Deva. This Narasinga's eldest son was Dugdha Malla; whose eldest son was Baddiga. He was skilled in forty-two modes of warfare, and obtained the name of Sôlada Gaṇḍa (invincible champion). As if seizing a crocodile, he entered into the water and proudly seized Bhima. To Baddiga was born Yuddha Malla, whose son was Narasimha. His guru was Subhadra muni. Erapa having gone over to the

* The statement in the original is as follows :—

Jâtiyoḷ ellam uttamaḍa jâtiya vipra kulange nambal ê ।
mâto Jinêndra dharmamame valam dôre dharmmadoḷ endu nambi sa- ।
jjâtiyan uttarôttarame mâḍi negaḷchidan int ilâtana vi- ।
khyâtiyan âtan âtana magam negaldam Kavitâguṇârṇavam ॥
Pampam.

Lâḷas asking them for an estate, this Kali Narasimha offered him a much better manḍala, and confirmed it with a strong promise. He subdued the chiefs of the seven Mâlala (?); and plucked from the Gûrjara Râja's arms the goddess of victory, whom, though desirous of keeping, he had held too loosely. The Mahipâla fled as if struck by thunderbolts, staying neither to eat, nor rest, nor pick himself up; while Narasimha pursuing, bathed his horse at the junction of the Ganges and established his fame. His queen was Chandrâmane. To them was born Ari Kesari Râja. He protected Vijayâditya, who took refuge with him on being attacked by Sakala Chakravartti named Gujjiga (or Gojjiga). Finding that in the four matters—bounty, valour, conquest, fame—he excelled even Baddiga and Narasimha, Guṇârṇava made that Ari Kesari his hero, and identifying him with Arjuṇa, undertook this poem.

So powerful was the effect of his poetry, that by means of it, in the war of his own king of the Jôḷa country*, he enabled him to win the very crowns of the hostile chiefs†. And Ari Kesari, taking him as a friend, directed him to write this *itihâsa kathe*, which he finished in one year; and the king rewarded him with the village of Dharma-uram, situated in the Bachche Sâsira (or Thousand) as a *s'âsana agrahâra*, which he re-named Sâram. In the pith (*tiruḷa*) of the Kannaḍa of Puligere, the royal city, did he write, naturally and without effort‡; thus his Bhârata and Âdi Purâṇa put all former poems under their feet §. Resolved, while doing his secular duty on the one hand, and his Jaina religious duties on the other, that he would essay for the good of the world to write the Bhârata and the Âdi Purâṇa, he completed the one in six months, and the other in three months. For these works, like Vyâsa, he got the name of Purâṇa Kavi; and they were read by all classes of people, by servants as well as by the greatest poets.

Such is the account, full of incident, that Pampa gives of himself and of his times. The following works are also said to be by him:—*Laghu Purâṇa*, *Pârs'vanâtha Purâṇa*, *Paramâgama*.

---

* It would appear as if we had here direct evidence of the position of the Jôḷa or Jôṛa country mentioned in the travels of the Chinese pilgrim Hiwen Thsang, the identification of which has exercised the ingenuity of many commentators without any satisfactory solution. If Dharma-uram be the modern Dharmavaram in the Bellary district, the Jôḷa territory would perhaps include the Dharvad and Bellary districts, as far as Karnul, close to which General Cuningham has pointed out the existence of an old Joram or Jorampur.

† Kavite negalteyam nirisi Jôḷada pâḷe nijâdhinâthan â- I
havadoḷ arâti nâyakara paṭṭave sârisi sanda pempu bhû- I
bhuvanadoḷ âḍugum belage mikk abhimânada mâtu kîrttiyam I
virarisi sandan êm kaviyo sat kaviyô Kavitârguṇârṇavam II

‡ Râja sudhâni puṭavaha I
sâjada Puligereya tiruḷa Kannaḍadoḷ nir- I
vyâjad esakadoḷu pudid a- I
nd ôjeya balav iniya kavite Pampana kavite II

§ Munnina kabbaman ellam ikki meṭṭidavu.

—*Asaga*, is named by Ponna and Kesi Râja, the former of whom claims to be a hundredfold better as a Kannaḍa poet (*Kannaḍa kaviteyoḷ Asagan-gam nûrmmaḍi*). Asaga and Agasa denote a washerman*. There is a *Varddha-mâna-svâmi-kâvya* by him, but this is in Sanskrit.

c. 950. ***Jinachandra***, is mentioned by Ponna as a contemporary and the author of *Pûjyapâda charita*. He is described as the equal of Akalanka and a new Samanta Bhadra.

c. 950. ***Ponna***, *Bonna*, *Ponniga*, *Ponnimayya*, *Kavi-chakravartti*, *Ubhaya-kavi-chakravartti*, *?S'ânti Varmmâ*. Such are the names by which he is referred to in literature, but his real name was *Savaṇa*, *Kuruḷgaḷa Savaṇa*, *Sarvva Deva*, *?Sarvva Varmmâ*, as given by himself in the *S'ânti Purâṇa*. From this, and from Ranna's work, the following particulars have been obtained regarding him:—In Pangunûru, a town of the Kamme des'a† in the Vengi maṇḍala, dwelt a chief Brahman (*dvijonnata*) named Nâgamayya, of the Kauṇḍiṇya gotra, celebrated for his learning, the equal of Yajnavalkya. "In his heart was born the Jina mata"—that is, he became a Jaina. His wife was Nâgiyabbe, and they had two sons—Mallapa and Ponnamayya—who rose to be distinguished ministers and generals under the Châlukya king Tailapa (reigned 973—997). In Mallapa was united all learning, with skill in state policy, horsemanship, bravery, shelter for those who took refuge with him, good fortune and religion. Pandits and poets considered his house as their *tavarmmane* (the home of their birth). The word he uttered in the king's assembly never proved false, hence throughout all countries was he believed. The brave Mallapa blessed the Bhû-vallabha, saying "You shall obtain a son and a victory," and called upon all present to hear. Ponna was all modesty, brave as mount Mandara, in ability (?) Ajanna, in justice the son of Dharma. Having the qualities of Baladeva and Vâsudeva, of Râma and Lakshmaṇa, the history of Mallapa and Ponnamayya threw into the shade that of Bhîma and Arjuṇa.

On the *paroksha* (or death) of their guru Jinachandra Deva, these two, in commemoration of the event, caused Ponniga to write a purâṇa, which they published through all the world. This was the *S'ânti Purâṇa*, which its author styles the *Purâṇa Chûḍâmaṇi*. For his superiority over all other poets

---

* But in selecting this poet with whom to measure Himself in Kannaḍa, as he does with Kâlidâsa in Sakkada (see next page), Ponna may indicate an acquaintance with the author of similar sounding name, Asanga, under whom a revival of Buddhist literature took place, and who is supposed to have been contemporary with Kâlidâsa, their period being about 550 A. D.—See the Renaissance of Sanskrit Literature in Max Müller's *India—what can it teach us ?* pp. 290, 302 ff.

† The large class of Smârta and Mâdhva Brahmans in Mysore called *Kamme*, seem to have no knowledge of the origin of their name. They all speak Kannaḍa except a few who use Telugu. The *Kammaḍe Kamme* are found chiefly in the eastern division. The *Ulcha* or *Urcha Kamme*, in the south and east: the *Bobbûru Kamme*, in the south and west. Pangunûru might be the modern Punganûru, capital of a Zamindari of the same name in North Arcot, but this would bring the limits of Vengi further south than is generally supposed.

in command of both Kannaḍa and Sakkada, he received the title of *Ubhaya Kavi Chakravartti* from the king Krishṇa * (perhaps, though this is uncertain, the Raṭṭa or Râshṭrakûṭa king, also known as Nirupama and Akâlavarsha, ruling in 945). In Kannaḍa poetry he was a hundred-fold of Asaga, and in Sanskrit poetry a hundred-fold of Kâḷidâsa of old, while in arrangement (*rachane*) he was four-fold both combined.† He denounces the poets of the day as merely copying old works and proclaiming them as their own. Though they professed to write in the three languages and a half ‡, everything was stolen from others; but throughout the kingdom of letters (*akkarada râjya*) not a child could say this, even in play, of the Kavi Chakravartti.§ From these unstinted praises, and the notices of him in other poets, there must be further writings by this author. But with regard to the *S'ânti Purâṇa*, it appears that on the death of Mallapa, his daughter Attiyabbe, in commemoration of the event, and that the work he had caused to be written might not be lost to the world, had a thousand copies made at her own expense. Mallapa for his filial piety had been called *ammana bhakta*; and she by this act perpetuated in the family the name of *tande bhakta*.

—Châmuṇḍa Râya, ? *Ganga-bhûshaṇa*, author of the *Châmuṇḍa Râya Purâṇa*. Ranna's patron bore this name, but whether he was the same person is not known. There is also by a *Châuṇḍa Râyâ*, a work called *Abhinava Das'a-kumâra-charita*.

983. **Ranna**, *Kavi Ratna, Abhinava Kavi-chakravartti*—is named by Nâgachandra and Mangarasa. He was the author of the *Ajita Tîrthakara Purâṇa*, in which he gives many particulars regarding himself and Ponna, who was a generation before him. Ranna was of the Balegâra kula, that of the bangle-sellers, and a sun to the Vanik kula (the Vais'yas). He was born in the year Saumya (949) in Muduvaḷalu, a village of the Jambukhaṇḍi Seventy, in the Beḷugare Five Hundred. This Beḷugare or Beḷugaḷe nâḍ was to the north of a stream flowing into the "big river" at Arekegaṭṭa, to the south of Taddavâḷi. (Most likely the reference is to Mudhoḷ and the Jamkhanḍi

---

* Bhuvanada Kannaḍa Sakkada I kavigaḷ sale sâle sôle Saṇayang ittam I
savivêṭam Ubhaya-kavi cha- I kravartti-vesaram nijâbhitôshṇam Krishṇam II

† Kannaḍa kavitèyoḷ Asagan- I gam nûr mmaḍi rêkheg aggaḷam Sakkadadoḷ I
munulla Kâḷidâsangam nûrmma- I ḍi nâlmaḍi rachaneyoḷ Kuruḷgaḷa Savaṇam II See note, p. xv.

‡ The reference probably is to the three and a half languages mentioned in Nâga Varmma. See above, pp. iv, viii.

§ Yosayade pûḷdu keṭṭa paḷe-gabbaman âvagam emmav endu bâ- I
jisi perargg ittud allade bahu-s'rutam embinam ekkalâvanam I
posayipa kammayippa samakaṭṭuva binnaṇam ill adakke ran- I
jisav erdegoḷḷav îgaḍina kabbiga-vanligaḷ ondavindigaḷ II

Nôḍire pêḷva mûru vare bhâshegaḷam perar-arthamam perar I
mâḍida dés'iyam perara binnaṇamam perar ôjeyam tadam I
mâḍuva kaḷvu koḷva khaḷar ikkema kabbiga-gaḷḷar endu kû- I
s âḍisad âgad akkarada râjyadoḷ i Kavi-chakravarttiyâ II

jaghir in the Belgaum district, where the Gatprabha flows to the Krishna). His mother was Abbalabbe, his father Janavallabhendra ; and he had three elder brothers—Bh[illegible]ḍabâhu, Rêchanna and Gunimâramaiyya. His guru was Ajitasenâchârya, and his lord was Châûṇḍa Râya. His wives were Jakki and Sânti, by whom he had a son Râya and a daughter Attiyabbe.

The circumstances under which his work was written may be thus summarised. Of Mallapa and Ponnimayya (previously mentioned in the account of Ponna) the latter was treacherously attacked by Gomindira, but without so much as disturbing the scarf he wore, he smote the invader and put an end to his pride. The victor then retired to the banks of the Kâvêrî and there went to *sura loka*. This looks as if he may have been severely wounded. Mallapa, on the other hand, "Apratima Malla, the protected by the Châḷukyas," lived to become a chief minister under Âhava Malla Deva (Satyâsraya, who ruled 997—1008). He took to wife Kabbe, the daughter of Nâgiyabbe and Nâgamayya (these are also the names of his own father and mother), and they had five sons—Guṇḍamaiyya, Eḷamaiyya, Ponnamaiyya, Âhava Malla and Valla—and two daughters—Attiyabbe and Guṇḍamabbe. The eldest son, Guṇḍa, gained a victory over Gonara and thus did credit to his father. The two daughters were given in marriage to Nâga Deva, the son of Dalla, a favourite minister of the king's ; and Attiyabbe bore a son called Paḍuvaḷa Taila. Nâga Deva, surnamed Haivatsa Râja, Môraṭa Malla, bee at the lotus-feet of Âhava Malla Deva, distinguished himself in the Komara war (or war with the Komaras), rushing like a lion upon these people of another faith (*anya mata*). The king, who was witness of his bravery, made him a chamupati : in a subsequent battle he defeated the army of Panchala ; and also by command of Ballaha pursued after Mallama from Karahaṭa. Thus having gained great glory, he went to *sura-loka*.

Then Guṇḍamabbe, thinking within herself that the fate of a woman is either to follow her lord or to take *Jina dikshe*, came to Attiyabbe, and with folded hands said, "You have a brave and distinguished son. You remain. I beg leave to go with Nâga Deva." Thus having besought her, she embraced her husband and was consumed in his funeral fire. This her faithfulness is worthy of celebration and her observance of the rite was a glory to the *mahâsati* Guṇḍamabbe. The apsaras were filled with disappointment to lose so handsome a man, and the pair were in *nirvâṇa loka*.*

Attiyabbe then said to herself, "My younger sister in one moment passed through the fire to her lord. I being the elder must for many days consume in the fire of hardship and fasting." Thus fasting, the protection of her offspring, and giving of charity preserved her alive ; and she acquired the fame

* I am not aware that the practice of *sati* among the Jains has been noticed before, though religious suicide, or *sallêkhana* as it was called, was common enough, as shown in the inscriptions at S'ravaṇa Belgoḷa published by me in the *Indian Antiquary*, II, 265, 322.

that no one in the world was equal to the mother of Paḷava'a Tailapa, the Nûrmmaḍi Taila. She made 1,500 Jina images of gold and jewels, and for each of them made bells, shrines, golden lamps, splendid robes and rich triumphal arches. Her son Paḷava'a Taila, also called Anniga Deva, was instructed in all wisdom by Nemichandra muni, his disciple Kânûrggaṇa Tilaka, and the learned Ayyapayya; and rose to be a commander of the emperor's army.

It was by desire of Attiyabbe, whom he calls the Dâna-chintâmaṇi, that Ranna wrote this poem, which he styles the *Purâṇa-tilaka*, his ambition being that it should endure as long as the Âdi Purâṇa and the S'ânti Purâṇa. As among kings Taila was a help to the independent emperor Raṇa Jaya, so among poets was Kavi Ratna a help to poetry. Being an emperor in the empire of poetry, he received the name of Kavichakravartti Ranna. Among numerous other praises of Pampa and Ponna, he says—"Through the fortunate poet Pampa was the glory of the language spread abroad, and shining with his qualities none are superior to Ubhaya Kavi Chakravartti and Abhinava Kavi Chakravartti. Among poets the two former are the most meritorious, the two latter the most successful; two of them only are fortunate—Kavitâguṇârṇava and Kaviratna The Âdi Purâṇa and the Ajita Purâṇa being composed by them, the flag of the Dvija vams'a (Brahmans) and the flag of the Vais'yas were Pampa and Ratna. As Pampa and Ponniga were honoured in the........* Râjya, so was Kavi Ratna, the Ubhaya Kavi, in the Châḷukya Râjya. Like the accepted dictum of the *Jainendra*, and the dictum of the *S'abdânus'âsana*, being well acquainted with both grammars, were the words of Kavi Ratna celebrated. The three histories he wrote were like the three jewels, namely, *Paras'urâma-charita*, *Chakres'vara-charita*, and *Ajita-tîrthes'vara-charita*." The latter concludes with the announcement that it was finished in S'aka 915, the year Vijaya. There is also said to be a *Sâhasa-Bhîma-vijaya* by *Kavi Ratna*. Likewise a *Bharates'vara-charitra* (see the *Chakres'vara-charita* above mentioned) and *Aparâjita-s'ataka* by *Ratnakara*.

c. 990. ***Nemichandra***, *Kavirâja-kunjara*. The exact date of this author is not known, but he is probably to be identified with the tutor of Taila mentioned above by Ranna. Mangarasa calls him *Angika Nemi*, and mentions his poem—the *Lîlâvati*, a *s'ṛingâra kâvya*. The poetry is of a high order, but the work fully maintains the profession of its erotic character. The hero and heroine are prince Kandarpa Deva and the princess Lîlâvati. The former belonged to Jayantipura, an old name of Banavasi. The author praises Samanta Bhadra, Akalanka, Pûjyapâda† and Ranna as follows:—

* It is a great disappointment that I cannot supply this name, which it would have been of the highest interest to clearly know. The word in the M.S. is at the end of a leaf and is unfortunately broken off. Every endeavour to get another copy has been unsuccessful.

† This is the only instance in which Kaviparimeshṭi is not mentioned between Samanta Bhadra and Pûjyapâda.

Yannage Samanta-Bhadrane kavis'varôl sa-kal-Âkalanka-De-|
vane vara-vada-vidyaro'asêsha-visêshaka-pûjya-Pûjyapâ-|
dane pada-vâkya-kôvidarol aty-abhinûtana-Rannar appam a- |
tt ina kavi-vâdi-s âbdikarol âg enitt ullodam alkar ullodam ||

" To me Samantra Bhadra among the chief poets, the sweet toned Akalanka Deva among the most eloquent speakers, the universally honoured Pûjyapâda among those skilled in verse and prose, the most recent Ranna, a master among poets, speakers and grammarians—being such, they have my affection."

——***Gajânkus'a***, named by Naya Sena, and ***Gajaga***, named by Kes'i Râja, may be the same.

1060—88. ***Bilhana***—was *vidyâpati* at Kalyâṇa to the Châḷukya king Vikrama, who reigned 1076—1127. He wrote the *Vikramânka Deva Charita* or *Vikramânka-kâvya*, a poem recounting the adventures of his patron.* He was born in Kashmir, in a learned family of Madhyades'i Brahmans. His father, Jyeshṭhakalas'a, wrote a commentary on the *Mahâbhâshya*. His mother was Nâga Devî, and his elder and younger brother were both poets. After finishing his education in Kashmir, Bilhaṇa visited various royal cities and sacred places in Hindustan, and coming to the south, having travelled as far as Râmes'vara, finally settled at Kalyâṇa under the royal patronage as above stated. It seems probable that he left Kashmir not later than 1065, and wrote this poem at an advanced age, about 1085. The following are also said to be works by this author—*Panchâs'ikha*, *Râmacharita* or *Râmastuti*, and? *Alankâra-s'âstra*.

—***Gunabhadra*** is mentioned by Nâga Varmmâ. He was the author of *Uttara Purâṇa*: also of *Âtmânus'âsana*.

c. 1070. ***Guṇachandra***—is mentioned by Naya Sena, who says that his feet were worshipped by the king Bhuvanaika Malla (reigned 1069 to 1076). The works assigned to him are *Pârs'vâbhyudaya* and *Mâghanandis'vara*.

—***Gunanandi*** referred to by Kes'i Râja may be the same as one of the preceding.

—***Haripâla*** is quoted by Nâga Varmmâ and Bhaṭṭâkalanka. Nothing more is known of him. But there is a *Dharma-s'armâbhyudaya* by a *Harichandra*.

c. 1070—1100. ***Guṇa-varmmâ***—is praised by Naya Sena. Nâga Varmmâ styles him *Bhuvanaika Vira*, a name befitting a warrior rather than a poet. Kes'i Râja describes him as the author of a *Harivams'a*. The title Bhuvanaika Vira seems to identify him with *Udayâditya* (also the name of an author), the Ganga prince who was the chief minister and a successful general under the Châḷukya king Bhuvanaika Malla (reigned 1069—1076), and subsequently governor of the Banavase Twelve Thousand. The celebrated Jain temple

* Published at Bombay, edited by Dr. G, Bühler, C. I. E.

of the Gangas at Lakshmes'var was probably erected by him. Other works by this author are *Pushpadanta Purâṇa* and *Devachandra-prabha-stotra.**

1115. ***Naya Sena,***—is named by Nâga Varmmâ in one of his sûtras. He describes himself as *Digambara Dâsa*, and was the author of *Dharmmâmṛita*, which he styles the *Kâvya-ratna.*† He wrote it at Muḷugunda (perhaps the present Mulgund in the Dharwar district), and finished it in Saka 1037, the year Nandana. Extracts have already been given from him showing that he was an advocate for purism in the use of Kannaḍa. The following is the testimony he bears to his predecessors:—

> Asagana dés'i Ponnana mahônnati-vetta beḍangu Pampan ond |
> as'adrus'am app apûrvva rasa-bhâva Gajânkus'an oḷpu-vettu ran- |
> jisuva sad-arttha-dṛishṭi Guṇa-varmmana jâṇ Kavi-Ratṇan ôje s'ô- |
> bhise nelas ikke dhâruṇi manam goḷe mat kṛitiyoḷ nirantaram ||

"Asaga's style, Ponna's majestic skill, Pampa's unequalled taste, Gajânkus'a's depth of meaning, Guṇa Varmma's knowledge, Kavi Ratṇa's manner—may all these be ever united in my poem."

——***S'amba Varmmâ,*** mentioned by Nâga Varmmâ, and ***S'ankha-Varmmâ,*** mentioned by Rudra Bhaṭṭa, are probably the same person, the letters *kh* and *b* being easily mistaken for one another. Beyond the names nothing more is known.

c. 1070—1120. ***Nâga Varmmâ,*** *Kavi Râja, Kavirâja Hamsa,* the earliest grammarian of the Kannaḍa language whose works have come down to us. Author of *Kâvyâvalôkana, Chhando'mbudhi, Karṇâṭaka Bhâshâ Bhûshaṇa, Vastu Kôs'a* and *Kâdambari.* For full particulars regarding him see Part I of the present Introduction.

c. 1120. ***Bâna***—was the author of the *S'rî Harsha Charita,* a life of Harsha Varddhana of Thânesar, who came to the throne in 1088. *Sumano-Bâṇa,* described as a poet, whose daughter was the mother of Kes'i Râja, may have been the same person.

—***Mallikârjuna,*** the father of Kes'i Râja, and a poet. He is said to be the author of *Chhôra-kathe,* the adventures of two princes, Somas'ekhara and Chitras'ekhara, in the disguise of robbers. According to tradition the principal scene of their exploits was Nilâvati-paṭṇa, the present Nirgunda in the Chitaldroog District.

—***Kumudêndu*** is mentioned by Devachandra as having written a *Kumudêndu Râmâyaṇa.*

—***Mâghanandi*** is stated by Kamalabhava, whose guru he was, to have been Kumudendu's disciple; and by Devachandra to have written a *Râma-kathe.* There is a *Padârtha-sâra* by an author of this name.

* Wilson says Guṇa Varmma "is considered to have been contemporary with Vira Ballâḷa Râya."
† There is also said to be a *Dharmmâmṛita* by *Asadhara.*

—**Bâlachandra** was the guru of Nâgachandra, and a story about him in Kamalabhava is given below. His works are said to be *Tatva-ratna-dîpika* and *Prâbhritaka-traya-vyâkhyâna*; also *S'râvakâchâra*.

1158. **Nâchi Râja** was the author of *Nâchirâji*, a commentary in Kannaḍa on the *Amara Kos'a*. His date is based on an inscription.

c. 1170. **Nâgachandra**, *Abhinava Pampa*, the author of the *Râmachandra Charita Purâṇa*, known as the *Pampa Râmâyaṇa*,* also of *Mallinâtha Purâṇa*, and of a little treatise on morals called *Jinamuni-tanayâ*, with which words each stanza concludes.† There is also an *Ârâdhana nîti* by *Chandrakîrtti*, which is probably to be assigned to this author. No particulars are given by him of his personal history, but he praises Samanta Bhadra, Kaviparimeshṭi, Pûjyapâda and Akalanka Chandra, also Pampa, Ponna and Ranna, naming the purâṇa written by each. The only guide to his period is that his guru was Bâlachandra muni. Of a muni of this name Kamalabhava relates that the king Simhana, though his tutor was Vinayendra brati, was as great a fool as an elephant (*hasti-mûrkhan*) and filled with pride: yet he was publicly compelled to do obeisance to Bâlachandra muni. Taking this Simhana to be the prince of that name among the Yâdava kings of Devagiri, who came to the throne in 1210, and the muni to be the same as one named in a grant made 20 years earlier to a disciple, the date in the margin has been conjecturally given. That it is not far out is further proved by Nâgachandra's mention as a contemporary of S'rutakîrtti, who it will be seen below was guru to Aggaḷa. Of our author Karṇapârya says—"In writing poems Ponna may almost compare with Nava Pampa, and no one before or after has excelled these. Though later in date (*adyatara*), yet being praised as master (*dore*) of the oldest poets, great was the fame that Nâgachandra obtained." Devachandra says—"Among those who have written Sanskrit and Kannaḍa poems Nâgachandra was distinguished for his skill."

c. 1170. **S'rutakîrtti** was Aggaḷa's guru. Nâgachandra says that "he cut off the wings of his opponents with the *syâd vâda* weapon in the same manner as Devendra smote off the wings of the mountains." Also that he was the author of a *Râghava Pânḍaviya*. He appears moreover to have written a *Jina-stuti*.

c. 1175. **Vîranandi** is named in Nâgachandra. A work called *Chandraprabha kâvyamâla* is ascribed to him.

1189. **Aggaḷa**, *Argaḷa Deva*, was the author of the *Chandraprabha Purâṇa*, which he finished in S'aka 1111, the year Saumya. He was of the Mûla sangha, Dêsi gaṇa, Pustaka gachcha and Kundakundânvaya. His father

* This work has been published by me at Bangalore, with an Introduction and Analysis.

† According to Wilson the author in this work is called *Chandra-kirtti-chitti*, a native of Champa.

was S'ântis'a and his mother Vâchâmbikâ. He specially invokes S'rî Chandraprabha of Ningales'vara-pura and S'ruta kirtti muni, apparently his guru, and styles himself *Ubhaya-kavitâ-vis'âradan*, learned in both poetries. In regard to his work, which he styles the *Kriti-ratna*, he says—

> Nayadim Pampan oraldu nirmmisida Ponnam pritiyim pêḷda bha- I
> ktiyin â Ratna kavis'varam sameda tat kâvya trayakkam jaga I
> trayamum mum beleyâgi pôyt ene balikk âm pêḷda Chandraprabhô-I
> daya vistâri yenippa kâvyav id amûlyatvakke pakk âgade ||

"That which Pampa beautifully composed, and Ponna told with affection, and Ratna Kavi related with devotion—those three poems beforehand absorbed the value of the three worlds: the *Chandraprabhôdaya* which I related afterwards, must it not therefore remain invaluable?"

As an *Aggaḷa Lîlâvatî* is mentioned in other works, it would appear that he must have written a poem of this name also.

——***Chandrabhaṭṭa*** is named by Kes'i Râja. There is a *Gomaṭṭis'vara-pratishṭha-charitra* by a *Chandraya Kavi*.

——***Manasija*** mentioned in Kes'i Râja is perhaps identical with **Chittaja** mentioned in the following lines by Îs'vara—

> . . . . . Pampanam I
> Chittaja-Nâga Varmma-sudhiyam kavi-Kes'ava-Ranna-mukhyaram I
> chittadoḷ iṭṭu pôḷve kṛitiyam vibudhar mana-mechchutirppanam ||

"Keeping in mind Pampa, the learned Chittaja and Nâga Varmmâ, the chief of poets Kes'ava and Ranna, I will write a poem pleasing to the wise."

——***S'rîvijaya***, also mentioned by Kes'i Râja.

c. 1160—1200. ***Kes'i Râja***, *Kes'ava*, author of the *S'abda-maṇi-darpaṇa*, the oldest grammar of the language written in Kannaḍa itself.* He was a Jain, and quotes from "Gajaga, Guṇanandi, Manasija, Asaga, Chandrabhaṭṭa, Guṇa Varmmâ, Srivijaya, Honna and Hampa." His father was Mallikârjuṇa and his mother the daughter of the poet Sumano-Bâṇa. He styles himself *Yâdava-kaṭakâchârya*, âchâri of the Yâdava army, or as we might say "chaplain to the forces." The period of the Yâdava kings of Devagiri extends from 1188 to 1312. On the other hand, in the *Basava Purâṇa*, finished in 1369, a Kes'i Râja is described as a devoted S'aiva at Kalyâṇa in the time of Bijjala and of Basava who founded the Lingâyit sect about 1165. Our author indeed is claimed by the Lingâyits and mentioned with special approval by subsequent writers of that sect. He may therefore possibly have embraced the new faith, but there is no trace of it in this work. From inscriptions we learn

* Published at Mangalore and Bangalore.

that there was a Kes'ava or Kes'i Râja, descended from a Brahman family of the Bhâradvaja gotra, who came to be Herggade Dandanâyaka of the Banavase Twelve Thousand under the king Bijjala, and held that office down to 1160 at least. In making a gift to a temple in 1157, he was at the unusual pains of providing for *Kannada-akshara-sikshe-ghalige*, learned men to teach Kannada letters. Whether these several persons of this name were identical with the author is not clear. The *S'abda-mani-darpana* is in verse, and gives the following as the names of his other works:—*Chôla-pâlaka-charita*, *Subhadrâharana*, *Prabodha-chandra*, *Kirâta*. None of these has been obtained as yet.

——***Bandhu Varmma*** is mentioned by Mangarasa. He was the author of *Harivams'âbhyudaya*, and *Jivasambôdhane*.

——***Janna***, *Jannuga*, ?*Janârddana*, is praised by Kamalabhava and by Mangarasa, the latter of whom states that he wrote the *Anantanâtha charita*.

c. 1200. ***Kamalabhava***, the author of a *S'ântis'ara Purâna*, not to be confounded with Ponna's work of like name, which is in 12 âs'vâsas, whereas the present one is in 16. Kamalabhava has the appearance of being an assumed name. He was of the Dês'i gana, the Postaka gachcha and the Kondakundânvaya. His guru was Mâghanandi. As he mentions Aggala, and also relates the story before given (under Nâgachandra) of how the prince Simhana was compelled to reverence Bâlachandra muni, his period would be about 1200. He praises Samanta Bhadra, Kaviparimeshti and Pûjyapâda, and bears the following testimony to his predecessors:—

> Jina-samaya-prakâs'a-krita sat-kavi Hampana pempuvetta Hon-|
> nana kavi Nâgachandrana negalteya Rannana sanda Bandhu Va-|
> rmmana budha Nêmichandrana jagan nuta Jannana ranjip Agga'a-|
> yyana kriti saundarî subhagam âvagam irkke madîya kâvyadôl ||

"Those luminaries of the Jina congregation, the true poet Hampa, the famous Honna, the poet Nâgachandra, the celebrated Ranna, the great Bandhu Varmma, the learned Nemichandra, the world-praised Janna, the famous Aggala—may the beauties of all their poems for ever dwell in mine."

c. 1220. ***Karnaparya***, *Kannapa*, *Karnama*, *Karna Varmmâ*. was the author of *Nêminâtha Purâna*, and is mentioned as such by Mangarasa. He wrote it for Vijayâditya, son of Govarddhana, king of Kilekila durga (apparently in the Kolhapur country) and a devoted adherent of the Srâvaka dharmma. Vijayâditya's wife was Sonnala Devî, and his younger brother Lakshmana. The latter having expressed a wish that some one should relate the history of Nêmi Jinêndra, Karnapârya undertook it, also including therein the Harivams'a and the Kuruvams'a. His praise of Nâgachandra or Nava Pampa has already been quoted.

——***Dharani Pandita***, *Dharani-dharendra*, wrote *Bijjala Râya charita* and *Varângana charita*.

c. 1225. ***Mangarasa**, Manga Râja*, the author of a *Harivams'a* or *Nêmi Jinês'a Sangati*, in which he describes himself as the son of Vijayêndra Râja, prabhu of Kallubaḷḷi. His notices of former authors are specially valuable from his naming their works. The following poets are mentioned by him as having written Kannaḍa champu kâvyas, namely, Pampa, Ranna, Guṇa Varmmâ, Jannuga, Naya Sena,* Ponna, Nâgachandra, Kaṇṇapa, Angika Nêmi, and Bandhu Varmmâ. Other works ascribed to this author are *Manmatha charitra*, an account of Pradyumna, the son of Krishṇa and Rukmini; *Samyaktva Kaumudi*, a collection of tales as to their adoption of the Jain faith related by Arhaddâsa and his eight wives, overheard by Udiṭodaya Râja; *Karṇâṭa S'abda-manjari.*

——***Amrita nandi***, author of *Dhanvantari nighanṭu* or *Akârâdi nighanṭu*, a vocabulary of medical terms; also of a work on composition.

c. 1300. ***Vidyanâtha*** wrote the *Pratâparudriya.*

——***Ganes'vara***, author of *Sâhitya-sanjivana.*

——***Kâma***, *Kavi-kâma*, wrote a work on composition. S'âlva speaks of the *Nâga Varmmâ-Kavikâmâdi-mârga.*

From this period † the Jains, who had hitherto had the field entirely to themselves, appear only now and then among Kannaḍa authors, their place being taken by Lingâyit writers till 1508, when Brahmanical works make their appearance with the Kannaḍa translation of the Mahâ Bhârata. It is not difficult to account for the disappearance from the arena of literature about this time of the Jains, who for centuries had proved themselves such pre-eminent scholars and the enlightened cultivators of the Kannaḍa language. The decline of their political power led to their withdrawal from literary pursuits. The conversion of the Hoysaḷa king Biṭṭi Ballâḷa from Jainism to the religion of Vishnu by Râmânujâchâri in 1117, whence he took the name of Vishnu Varddhana by which he is more familiarly known in history, was the first blow to Jaina influence. The foundation of the Lingâyit faith by Basava about 1160, and the assassination in 1165 of the Kalachurya king Bijjala, with the final overthrow

---

* By a singular error he names Ranna instead of Naya Sena as the author of *Dharmma charita*. The error probably arose from Ranna being called Kavi Ratna and the *Dharmmâmṛita* being called Kâvya Ratna.

† The following is a miscellaneous list of Jain works and authors whose place I am unable to determine.

Varddhamâna Purâṇa	by	Vâṇi-vallabha.
Nâga-kumâra-charitra	"	Bâhu Bali kavi.
Arddha Nemi Purâṇa	"	Kavi-mano-gehi-dipa.
Gumaṭa svâmi-charitra } *Loka-svarûpa* }	"	Chandramaṇi.
Prakriya-niti-vâkyâmṛita	"	Soma Deva Sûri.
Vidagdha-mukha-mandana (a book of riddles)	"	Dharma Dâsa.
Haya-lakshana-s'âstra (a book on horses)	"	Padmaṇṇa Paṇḍita
Buddhi-sâgara-charitra		
Vajrabâhu-kathe		
Triloka-s'ataka.		

about 1190 of the Kalachuryas, completed the subversion of the predominance the Jains had hitherto enjoyed in the Kannada countries. They had now to give way to the votaries of S'iva and Vishnu, especially to the Jangamas as representing the former; and in the reign of Krishna Râya of Vijayanagar the Brahmans came more prominently to the front.

The following is an approximate list of authors who contributed to Kannada literature in the modern period.*

c. 1290. ***Harîs'vara***, *Hampe Haripam*, a Lingâyit, who wrote in *ragale* metres. He is said in the *Channa Basava Purâna* to have been the chief of the *karnikas* or revenue accountants at Halebidu. When king Ballâla asked for his accounts, he seems to have excused himself by saying that the *kadata*† caught fire from a lamp in the temple of Virûpâksha and was burnt. He was consequently compelled to retire to that temple, situated in Pampâ kshetra (on the Tungabhadra). There he wrote the *Girijâ-kalyâna*‡ and *S'iva-gana*, and there ended his days. He was also the author of *Nambiyannana Ragale*, a work containing 37 *ragale* stories of Lingâyit saints, the first being Nambiyanna: this seems the reason why the book is popularly known by the above title, for it bears no specific name given by its author. There is also a *Mahâdeva Ragale* said to be by *Harihares'vara*.

c. 1300. ***Râghava***, *Râghavânka*, a Lingâyit, who wrote in *shatpadi* metres and claims to have invented them. According to the *Râghavânka charitra* he was the disciple of Haris'vara, being a son of the latter's sister Rudrâni by Mahâdeva Bhatta. He was born at Hampe or Pampâ-pura in the Kuntala dês'a on the banks of the Tungabhadra. He first recited the *Haris'chandra kâvya* at the court of Deva Râja in Pampâ-pura; but this gave such great offence to his guru, who was his uncle, that he devoted himself thenceforward to *Somanâtha satkâvyas*. He visited Hoysala nagara to see Kere Padmarasa, the minister of king Narasimha, and there encountered a Vaishnava named Tribhuvana Tâta, whom he confuted and converted to a Vîra S'aiva. On returning to Hampe, he heard that there were bad poets (*kukavi*) at the court of Rudra Pratâpa of Orungal, called eka-, dvi-, tri-sandhâgrâhis. Whereupon he proceeded there, was well received by the king, and established his superiority by composing a *Vîres'vara kathe*. After this, his guru directed him to go to Belur, where he ended his days, and Padmarasa (the minister) erected a tomb for him. He seems also to have written *Âdayyana* (or *Ândayyana*) *kathe*; and the original of the *Anubhava-s'ikhâmani* is said to have been by him. There is also a *Siddharâmes'vara-kathe* by this author.

* In much of the information regarding the Lingâyit literature I follow the Revd. F. Kittel.

† Cloth covered with a composition of charcoal and gum, and made up in the form of a folding book; used by merchants, shopkeepers and others for writing accounts and records on. It is written on with potstone, like a slate.

‡ There is a *Girijâ-kalyâna* in yaksha gâna metre by *Ganges'a*.

c. 1300. ***Somes'vara***, *Somes'a*, *Somanâtha Kavi*, the author of *Somes'vara S'ataka*, verses on morality, in *mattebhavikrîḍita* metre: also of *Gaṇa-sahasra-nâma*, the thousand names of the Pramatha gaṇa, Rudra gaṇa and Bhakta gaṇa. He is said to have been an Ârâdhya Brahman from Pâlkurike in the Godâvari district, but became a Lingâyit and wrote the *Basava Purâṇa* in Telugu. His linga was at Puligiri-nagari (the modern Hulikal paṭṇa) and he died at Kaḷḷeya. There is an *Akrûra-charitra* by a *Somanâtha*.

c. 1300. ***Harabhakta*** was a Lingâyit mendicant of Anekanjanûr, and was the author of a *Veda-bhâshya*.

c. 1330. ***S'iva Kavi***, *S'iva Kavîs'a*, apparently wrote a version of the *Basava Purâṇa*. He is described as belonging to Bâlachandra-nagara, but lived at one time at Bâyi-bidiri, probably Bidar in the Nizam's dominions. There is a *Sirumana kathe* by an author of this name, who seems however much later. Also *Paramârtha-prakâsika* by a *S'iva Yogi*.

1369. ***Bhîma Kavi***, author of the generally received *Basava Purâṇa* in Kannaḍa, composed in *shaṭpadi* metre. He was the son of S'iva Kavi, and his work is dated 1369.

——***S'ankara***, an Ârâdhya Brahman, who wrote a *Basava Purâṇa* in Sanskrit.

——***Mallaṇârya***, *Malhaṇa*, *Mallaṇâchâri*, was a native of Gubbi in the Tumkur district. He wrote *Viras'aivâmrita*, *S'ivabhaktara Purâṇa*, and *Bhâvachintâratna* or *Satyendra Chôḷa kathe*, the latter based on a Tamil itihâsa by Piḷḷe Naynâr. Our author also wrote a *Râmastavarâja* in Telugu. There is also a *Purâtana-ragaḷe* by him.

——***Kavi Bomma***, *Brammaya Kavi*. These two have been taken to be identical and may have been Jains. The former was the author of *Chaturâsya Nighaṇṭu*. The latter wrote *Jinadattu-Râya-Charitra* and *Dvâdas'ânuprekshu*. He may further be the *Brahma Deva*, author of *Samaya parikshe*. There was also a *Kumâra Bammarasa* who wrote a *Sanatkumâra charitra*.

——***Singi Râja***, *Singi Râjâchârya*, author of *Mala Basava charitra* or *Hara-kathâ-s'aradhi*, containing stories similar to those of the Basava and Channa Basava purânas.

1398. ***Abhinava Manga Râja***, author of the *Manga Râja Nighaṇṭu* or *Kavi Mangâbhidâna*, a valuable dictionary in Kannaḍa verse on the plan of the Amara Kos'a, giving the Kannaḍa meanings of Sanskrit words commonly used in the language. He describes himself as of the Kanne (? Kamme) kula and Vis'vâmitra gotra. He wrote under the patronage of Timmârya Râmarasa and by the blessing of S'as'ipura Somes'a. The nighaṇṭu is dated S'aka 1320, the year Bahudhânya. In it he professes to copy Nâga Varmmâ's Nighaṇṭu. He also styles himself *Abhinava Bâlasarasvati Manga Râja* and

Bûlas'ârade Manga Râja. Another work called *Chintâmaṇi pratipada* is said to be by him.

c. 1460. ***Châma arasa,*** a Lingâyit who wrote the *Prabhulinga-lîle*, a life of Prabhulinga, also called Prabhu deva, Allama prabhu and Gohes'-vara linga, who was an incarnation of S'iva's gaṇanâtha, and born as the son of Nirahankâra and Sujnâni. To try him, Pârvatî caused her tâmasa guṇa or Mâye to be born as the daughter of Mohini Devi and king Mamakara Prabhu of Banavase-pura in the Beḷavala des'a. But Allama withstood her temptations, obtained the linga of Anumisha, was seated by Basava on the s'ûnya pîṭha at Kalyâṇa, and finally died at S'ris'aila a little before Basava. Our author lived at the court of Prauḍha Râya of Vijayanagar (reigned 1451—1465), and his work was translated into Telugu by Pidupati Somayya, and into Tamil by S'ivaprakâsa Des'ika.

——***Linga,*** *Guru Linga, Lingana*, author of the *Kabbigara Kaipiḍi* (poets' handle), 100 verses in shaṭpadi, containing a vocabulary of Sanskrit and Kannaḍa words; written, as he states, to aid in understanding the former chief S'iva-kavis. The author, who was the son of a Brahman named Virûpâksha (an author of this name occurs in 1585), and a worshipper of the Virûpâksha linga at Pampâ-pura, became the first minister of the Râya of Uggehaḷḷi (? in Manjarabad). Other works ascribed to him are *Bhikshatana Kâvya*, and *Chôḷa sangatya.* There was also a ***Mahâlinga*** who wrote *Ashṭavarṇa tilaka*; and a ***Basava-Linga,*** who wrote the *S'ivâdhikya Purâṇa.* These may be identical persons. (See also infra p.   for a Basava Linga.)

c. 1480. ***Tôṭa Ârya,*** *Tôṭa Siddhalinga, Tôṭa Yati, Siddhes'a*, author of the *S'abda-manjari*, a vocabulary of Sanskrit and Kannaḍa words, in 120 shaṭpadi verses. From the *Channa Basava Purâṇa* it appears that with the accession in 1479 of Narasa to the Vijayanagar throne, the influence of the Vîras'aivâchâra had to give way to that of the anâchâra, the Vaishṇava faith. At that time Niranjana Gaṇes'vara was born in the person of our author as the son of Gosala Channa Basaves'vara, and was called Siddhes'a. He retired to the garden (*tôṭa*) of Kaggere, where his S'iva dhyâna made him famous, and thence he received the names given above.

1508. ***Kumâra Vyâsa,*** the assumed name of a Brahman who translated the first 10 parvas of the *Mahâ Bhârata* into Kannaḍa in shaṭpadi metre. His real name seems to have been *Nâraṇappa*, the gauḍa of Kôḍivâḷa. He dedicated his work to the god Vîra Nârâyaṇa of Gadagu in the Dharvad district, and wrote it about the time of the coronation of Krishna Râya, king of Vijayanagar (reigned 1508—1530). This seems to be the earliest Brahmanical work in the Kannaḍa language.

c. 1510. ***Timmana,*** translator of the remaining parvas, called the *Krishṇa Râja Bhârata.* The preface states that when Krishṇa, the son of Narasa, ruling in glory and happiness, had heard the Bhârata kathâ, addressing his poets he said to Timmaṇa, the son of the great poet Bhânu,—"Kumâra Vyâsa has already well composed ten parvas. Do thou relate the remaining parvas of the Bhârata." Whereupon Timmaṇa, the son of Bhânu bhaṭṭa, according to the instruction of the king, composed the rest of the work in the same metre (*bhâmini shaṭpadi*).

——***Îsvara Kavi***, *Abhinava Kes'i Râja*, *Abhinava Kes'ava*, author of the *Kavijihvâbandhana*, a work on prosody, in which he teaches the use of "the *vaḍi* according to the Ândhra mârga, as it is used only in Telugu." The work is in 4 chapters, which treat respectively of i. Gaṇas; ii. Prâsu and Vaḍi; iii. Aksharas; iv. Alankâra. It is written in verse, chiefly in *kanda* and *samavṛitta* metres.

——By an author unknown, but probably at about this time, was made the Kannaḍa version of the *Panchatantra*.

1538. ***Purandara***, *Viṭhala* of Pandaripura, a Vaishṇava dâsa who wrote a number of *Vaishṇava Dâsarapada*, or hymns in praise of Vishnu, in ragaḷe metre. He appears to have lived at Vijayanagar during the reign of Achyuta Râya (reigned 1530—1542) and to have died in 1564.

c. 1540. ***Kanaka***, *Kanaka Dâsa*, *Kanaka Râjottama*, a Vaishṇava dâsa, perhaps of the same period. He is said to have been a Beḍa, and belonged to Kâginele. His principal work was *Mohana-taranginị*, written in ragaḷe metre. It contains puranic stories about suras, asuras and Krishṇa, professing to be related by the author to his wife. He also wrote a *Krishṇa charitra* and *Krishṇa-bhakti-sâra*.

1585. ***Virûpâksha Paṇḍita***, a Lingâyit, who wrote the *Channa Basava Purâṇa*, dated 1585, in shaṭpadi metre. His guru was Siddha Vires'a of the Hiri maṭha at Vidyânagara, who, he says, became the guru of 700 vara khalindaras (Muhammadan faqirs), went to Makhya (Mecca), caused rain (*maḷe*) to fall at a time of drought, was reverenced by the Suritâṇa (*i. e.* the Sultan) and hence was called *Maḷe Malles'a*. This author may also have written *Tribhuvana-tilaka*.

c. 1590. ***Kumâra Vâlmîki***, the assumed name of the author of the *Torave Râmâyaṇa*, a Kannaḍa version of Vâlmiki's work. It is in shaṭpadi metre, and dedicated to the god Narasimha of Torave in the Sholapur district, whence its name. The opening lines praise "Kumâra Vyâsa, the author of the beautiful Kannaḍa Bhârata."

c. 1590. ***Châṭu Viṭhalanâtha***, *? Gopinâtha*, author of the Kannaḍa version of the *Bhâgavata Purâṇa*, written in shaṭpadi metre. Also by a *Viṭhala* there is a work called *Vidagdha chûḍâmaṇi*.

c. 1595. ***Venkaya Ârya***, *Hari Dâsa*, author of the *Krishṇa-lîlâbhyudaya*, an epitome of the 10th skanda of the Mahâ Bhâgavata, in shaṭpadi verses, dedicated to the god Venkaṭa S'auri (the Krishṇa of Tirupati).

Our author was descended from a Brahman family of Kadagatûr, in the Penugoṇḍa country. His grandfather was a devoted Vaishṇava, of northern Kannada origin, of the Jâmadagnâvatsa gotra, and disciple of Madhva muni. His father was Venkârya Timma, his mother Seshâmbe, his younger brother Nârâyaṇa.

c. 1595. ***Adris'a appa,*** author of the *Prauḍha-Râya-charitra* in shaṭpadi verses. It contains S'aiva stories professing to be related to Prauḍha Râya of Vidyânagara by his minister Jakkanârya to overcome his supposed leaning towards Vaishnavism, and containing more detailed accounts of legends briefly alluded to in the Basava Purâṇas. Our author was a disciple of Maḷe Malles'a, and the son of Aṇṇa appa, a desâyi of the Kollâpura paragaṇe in the Bijapura prânta.

——***Abhinava Vâdi Vidyânanda,*** a Jaina swâmi who made a collection of extracts from the old poets, called *Kâvya Sâra,* so arranged as to illustrate the several sentiments of poetry. His date is unknown, but he may belong to the 16th century.

——***Devottama*** was the author of *Nânârtha ratnâkara,* a Samskṛita-Karṇâṭa vocabulary, based upon Nâga Varmma's *Abhidânârtha* and (? Mangarasa's) *S'abda-manjari.* He was a Jaina, and of the dvija vams'a. His period is unknown.

——***Devachandra,*** *Devachandra Dvija, Vibudhendu,* a Jaina who wrote two prose works, the *Râmakathâvatâra* and the *Râjâvali kathe.* He may be identical with the preceding, or a totally different person, living at quite another period, whether ancient or modern.* In the first work he states that he kept Abhinava Pampa's poem before him as a guide, and gives some information about former Jaina writers of the Râmâyaṇa story, among whom he names Châmuṇḍa Râya, Nâgachandra, Mâghanandi, Kumudendu, and Naya Sena.

——***Vṛitti vilâsa,*** a Jaina who was the author of *S'âstra-sâra* and of *Dharma-parikshe.* His date is quite unknown.

1604. ***Bhaṭṭâkalanka Deva,*** *S'ri Bhaṭṭâkalanka,* a Jaina who was the author of the *Karṇâṭaka S'abdânus'âsana,* an exhaustive grammar of the language in Sanskrit sûtras, after the manner of Pâṇini, with a commentary, also in Sanskrit, called *Bhâshâ Manjari,* and a further voluminous commentary on the latter, in the same language, called *Manjari Makaranda,* the whole after the manner of the Mahâbhâshya. The work is dated in S'aka 1526, the year S'ubhakrit. It is divided into 4 pâdas, and professes to be an independent authority (*svopâjña*). To a Bhaṭṭâkalanka are also ascribed *Ashṭâs'ti, Pratishṭâ-kalpa, Râjavârttikâlankâra.*

c. 1650. ***Nanja Kavi,*** *Nanjaya,* was the author of *Kanṭhîrava Narasa Râja charitre,* the exploits of this king of Mysore, who ruled 1638 to 1658; also of *Kapota Vâkya.*

---

* See below, under Varâha Timmappa, for a Vibudhendu.

——*Nanjunda Kavi* wrote the *Kumâra Râma charitra*, an account of Kumâra Râma, the son of Kampila Râya of Hosadurga near Vijayanagar, who gained great distinction as a military leader under Pratâpa Rudra of Warankal. This author may be identical with the foregoing. His work has been rendered into Telugu as *Râma-nâtha-kathâ.*

——*Govinda Vaidya,* author of *Kanṭhirava Narasa Râja Vijaya,* the conquests of the above named king of Mysore (ruled 1638—1658).

c. 1650. *Nijaguṇa Yogi,* an Ârâdhya Brahman, who is mentioned by Shaḍakshara Deva. He was the author of several works, namely, *Kaivalya paddhati*, consisting of *ragaḷe* songs, in the Vaishnava dâsa manner, on yoga, &c.; *Anubhava-sâra* ; *Paramânubhava-bodhe* ; *Paramârtha Gîte*, instructions in Vedânta given by a guru to his disciple, in a variety of *lalita ragaḷe* ; *Purâtana tripadi*, verses in this measure on the 63 purâtanas or S'aiva saints ; *Viveka-chintâmaṇi*, a champu work containing a S'aiva concordance of the vedas, puraṇas, &c. This work has been translated into Tamil.

——*Chikka Nanjesa, Chikka Nanjaya,* author of *Râghavânka charitra*, an account of the poet Râghava (see above, p. xxv), written in *shaṭpadi* verse. The author was a disciple of Panchavaṇṇige Siddha Nanjes'a, guru of Pûvallipura (Hubbaḷḷi in Dharvad). Among others of his predecessors he mentions Châmarasa and Tôṇṭa ârya.

——*S'ântes'a Linga,* a guru under whom was written the *S'ivakathâmṛita sâra*, a Lingâyit version of the *Brahmottara Purâṇa*, written in shaṭpadi verse.

——*Sahajânanda,* author of *Bhaktirasâyana*, prayers in shaṭpadi verse. His guru was Sachchidânanda, probably the first S'ringeri guru of that name, who was consecrated 1622 and died 1663.

1657. *Shaḍakshara Deva,* a Lingâyit, and author of the celebrated *Râja-S'ekhara-Vilâsa*, which divides with the *Jaimini Bhârata* the honour of being the most highly esteemed poem in Kannaḍa. It is dated as above. Except a few ragaḷe verses, it is written in the champu style of the best period. The subject is the adventures of Râja S'êkhara, son of the king Satyendra Chôḷa of Dharmavatipura, as recounted in the *Bhâvachintâratna* of Mallanârya (see above, p. xxvi). Our author belonged to Yelandur, a Jaghir in the south of Mysore, and was the disciple of Chikka Vîra, who was the disciple of Revaṇa Sidda des'ika, of the Danugûr maṭha, to the south of Bangalore. He lived and wrote under royal patronage as head of the Virakta maṭha at Bidar in the Nizam's dominions, and died at Yelandur. His other works in Kannaḍa were *Vṛishabhendra-Vijaya*, written in 1671, and *S'abara-S'ankara vilâsa.* But he also wrote *Kavi karṇa rasâyana*, *Bhaktâdhikya* and *S'ivâdhikya* in Sanskrit.

c. 1678. *Ranganâtha,* S'rî Ranga, wrote the *Anubhavâmṛita*, a popular treatise on pantheism, in shaṭpadi verse. His father was Mâlinga of the Saha vâsi family: his guru, Sahajânanda (see above, p. xxx), and he was a devoted worshipper of the Mallikârjuṇa linga of S'rigiri or S'ris'aila.

c. 1670. ***Channaiya*** wrote the *Deva Râja Vijaya*, a poem containing the genealogy of the Mysore Râjas and the history of Dodda Deva Râja (ruled 1659—1672), with his defeat of S'ivappa Nâyak of Bednur in the attempt made by the latter to restore S'rî Ranga Râya, the last representative of Vijayanagar, who had fled to him for refuge.

——***Chikka Deva Râja***, one of the most distinguished of the Mysore kings, who reigned 1672 to 1704. His early youth was passed at Yelandur, where he formed an intimacy with a Jaina named Vis'hâlâksha Pandit, who adhering to him in confinement and exile, was partly instrumental in gaining for him the succession to the throne, and became his first prime minister. Chikka Deva Râja was the author of *Gîta-gopada* and *S'esha-dharma*.

c. 1685. ***Tirumalaiyangâr***, *Tirumalâchârya*, wrote *Chikka Deva Râja yas'obhûshaṇa*, *Chikka Deva Râja Vijaya*, *S'esha Kalânidhi*, and *Apratima Vîra charitram*, a work on rhetoric. When the Yelandur pandit, Chikka Deva Râya's minister as above stated, was assassinated, he with his dying breath recommended this author, who was a Brahman, as his successor, and the king appointed him accordingly.

——***Chikkopâdhyâya*** was also a mantri to Chikka Deva Râja, and wrote the following works:—*Rukmângada charitre*, *S'uka Saptati*, *Yâdavagiri mâhâtmya*, *Venkaṭagiri charitre*, *Kâmanḍaki nîti*, *Divya-suvi Mahâ-prabandha*.

1689. ***Rudra***, *Rudra Bhaṭṭa*, author of *Jagannâtha Vijaya*, consisting of stories about Kṛishṇa. According to tradition he wrote this work with the intention of eclipsing the reputation acquired by the Lingâyit poet Shaḍakshara Deva (see supra, p. xxx). The latter, when already famous as the author of *Râja S'ekhara Vilâsa* and *Vṛishabhendra Vijaya*, came to a Brahman agrahâra, and was received with such distinction, that Rudra Bhaṭṭa, offended at the honour shown to a heretic, resolved to outdo him in poetry, and produced the *Jagannâtha Vijaya*. But an assembly of the learned, having examined the respective works, decided that Rudra Bhaṭṭa's was not superior: he was therefore compelled to yield up his pretensions to Shaḍakshara Deva, who generously restored to him his titles. Rudra, in keeping with the above tradition, and possibly aided by S'âlva (see infra, p. xxxii), mentions only Jains as his predecessors, namely, S'ankha-Varmmâ, S'ânti-Varmmâ, Guṇa-Varmmâ, Manasija, Karṇama, Pampa, Chandra-bhaṭṭa, Ponnamayya and Gajânkus'a. He seems also to have written *Rasakalike* and *Viraktara Kâvya*.

1691. ***Lakshmîs'a***, author of the *Jaimini Bhârata*, the most admired and popular poem in the Kannaḍa language, which reputation it shares with the *Râja S'ekhara Vilâsa*. The author was a Brahman of the Bhâradvaja gotra, belonging to Devapura, the modern Devanur in the Banavar taluq of Kadur District. His father's name was Aṇṇama. No more information regarding himself is contained in his work, where he modestly introduces himself merely as—

Sad-vinuta-Karṇâṭa-kavi-chûta-vana-Chaitra Lakshmîs'an emb ôrvanu I

"One, Lakshmîs'a, spring to the mango grove of the justly praised Karṇâṭa poets." There has been much discrepancy in the dates assigned to him. The Devanur sthala purâṇa puts him in 1137, while Wilson says that he dedicated his work to Vira Ballâḷa, who reigned from 1191 to 1211 or later. But the *vârdhika shaṭpadi* metre indicates a more modern period for the work; and a continuation of the tradition above given regarding Rudra Bhaṭṭa seems to be decisive as to its exact date. Lakshmîs'a, it is said, was Rudra's friend, and hearing of his defeat as above related, resolved to wipe out this disgrace of the Brahmans. He accordingly composed his *Jaimini Bhârata*, of which the assembly of the learned so highly approved, that they conferred on him the title of *Karṇâṭa-kavi-chûta-vana-Chaitra*, engraved on a plate of gold. *

c. 1695. ***S'âlva***, a Jaina, author of the *Rasaratnâkara*, a Kannaḍa work on dramatic composition. It is in 3 chapters:—1. S'ṛingâra-prapancha; 2. Rasa-vivaraṇa; 3. Nâya-nâyikâ vivaraṇa. He refers as his authorities to Amṛita-nandi, Rudra Bhaṭṭa, Vidyânâtha, Hemachandra, Nâga Varmmâ, Kavi Kâma, Udayâditya, Gaṇes'vara, &c.

---

* These traditions are embodied in certain *Kavi-charitra-padyas*, for the following extracts from which I have to thank Siddhânti Subrahmaṇya S'âstri, Kannaḍa Pandit in the Madras Presidency College, who formerly obtained them from his preceptor Ranga Pandit.

S'iva-kalâbda-S'aka S'ukla-varsha Mâ- I
dhava-sit Ârka-dina Jîva-vâradoḷ I
bhavigaḷ ella vara Rudra Bhaṭṭanê I
kavi yanalk oredan ondu kâvyamam II

Arasal Jagannâtha-Vijayam enip â kabbi I
muru-dôsha-pûrṇa-parichitam âgil â kshaṇika I
varar adam Râja-S'êkhara-Vilâsake paḍiyan oreyadire Rudra Bhaṭṭam II
paribhavake guriyâdan endu sabhikar pêḷda I
pariy aritu karuṇadind â Shaḍakshara Deva I
birudugaḷ koṇḍu muguḷ ittu mannisi poredan ada hêḷi Lakshmîs'anu II

Hari-charitadim kûḍi Hari-mêdha-parva-kathe I
yoreda vârdhika-shaṭpadigaḷinda Jaiminiya I
vara-sûkti-tâtparya-bham-garbhitam ad âgi rasikarkaḷ anumôdisal II
pari-ariy-alankâra-rasa-bhâva-pushtiyim I
meredu duguṇ-êndu Kale parimit âbdada S'akadi I
Hari-vâra Kârtikad-asita panchamî Prajâpati S'aradi angam enalu II

Kannaḍa-kabbigar âtana I
mannisi Lakshmîs'an ôrvanê kavi-ratnam I
sannutan end uru-birudam I
chinnadi Kavi-chûta-Chaitran ene bared ittar II

1713. **Puttaiya**, *Nagarada Puttaiya*, author of the *Maisûru Arasugala Pûrvâbhyudaya*, a history of the Mysore kings which was one of the chief authorities used by Wilks for his History. The manuscript was saved from among those which Tipu Sultân had contemptuously ordered to be taken for boiling the *kulti* or gram for the horses.

——**Nishthûra Saniayya**, author of *S'abdamaṇidarpaṇa-vyâkhyâna*, a commentary on Kes'i Râja's work. He is a modern writer, and quotes from the *S'abdânus'âsana* and its commentaries.

——By an author unknown, living perhaps at this time, was written the *Akhaṇḍes'vara vachana*, also called the *Shaṭsthalâcharaṇa*, a Lingâyit work on sectarian topics.

c. 1760. **Varâha Timmappa**, wrote some *Vaishṇava-dâsa-pada*. His family seems to have been persecuted by Vibudhendu yati, and fled to Tirupati from Sâgara when the latter place fell into the hands of the Navâb (Haidar).

——**Nanja Râja**, or *Nanji Râja*, wrote *S'aiva dharma* and *S'ivabhakti mahâtmye*: also a *Harivams'a* and a *Linga Purâṇa*, both in prose. He is said to belong to Kalale.

——**Viṭhala**, *Abhinava Purandara*, also wrote *Vaishṇava-dâsa-pada*.

——**Madhva**, *Madhva Dâsa*, was another writer of *Vaishṇava-dâsa-pada*. He was also the author of *Abhimanyu kâḷaga* in ragaḷe metre, in which he praises Purandara Dâsa; and of *Chitrasena-kâḷaga-prasanga*, an episode of the Mahâ Bhârata, in yaksha gâṇa for recitation on the native stage. According to the latter work he belonged to Kuḍuma-pura (? Udupi).

1761. **Surâla**, a Jaina who was the author of *Padmâvati Devi kathe*, written in ragaḷe metre. He says that it was composed for Chennamma Devi of the râṇi-vâsa (queen's palace) of S'ri Chandras'ekhara Chikka Râya Chauṭa of Puttikâpura, perhaps Puttur near Mangalore. Representatives of the Chauṭa kings are still found on the Western coast: according to this author they are descended from the Kadambas.

1768. **Râmachandra**, was the author of *Anubhava s'ikhâmaṇi*, dated in the year Sarvadhâri. He seems to represent that the original of the work was composed by Râghava, the disciple of Hampe Harihara (see above, p. xxv), in s'ara shaṭpadi, and that he re-wrote it in bhâmini, vârdhika and s'ara shaṭpadis. His father bore the same name as himself, and was the karṇika of Kurutukôṭe in the Krutupura paragaṇe. His purohita was Bommi bhaṭṭa of Jaḍa Hebbaḷḷi, and he was a worshipper of the Virûpaksha linga at Hampe. His guru was Pedda arasa of the Gautama gotra, the Ângirasa Âyâsya pravara, and Baudhâyana sûtra of the Yajuh s'âkha; and his maternal uncle Govinda Sâmba, who was karṇika of Mayyûrapura, showed him the road to good poetry.

——About this time was composed the *Nala-charitra* in shatpadi by an author who seems to have been a worshipper of Channiga Râya of Varapura.

——Here also may come the *Nijalinga s'ataka*, consisting of shatpadi verses in praise of S iva, by an author whose linga was at Kadrubhavapura on the bank of the Tungabhadra.

——*Venka*, *Hampa Venka*, *Pradhâna Venkappa* of Râmapuri (in the Koratagiri taluq), wrote the *Sudhâ-lahari*, in 2 tarangas (or waves). It contains the story of Râdhâ and Krishna, and the author's professed object is to supersede the *Kâdambari* of Bâna. He says—"That being by Bâna (arrow), and this by one whose kula des'ika is Kodandapâni (bow in hand), as the bow is greater than the arrow, so is the work of Bâna lighter (*lâghava*) than this. Hitherto the ears of the learned have been filled with the kâdambari (toddy) juice; with this Sudhâ-lahari (stream of nectar) will I purify them." He also wrote *S ivashtapadi*, a work like the *Gita-Govinda*, but in praise of S iva. Also *Das'arûpaka*, illustrating the 10 kinds of dramatic poetry; and *Chid-advaita-bhâshya*, composed of sûtras with bhâshya on the advaita system of the Vallabhâchâryas. The *Pârvati-koravanji-kathe* in yaksha gâna is also by an author of similar name.

——***Lakshmi Nâranappa***, a Brahman of Mâgadi, was the author of *Gangâvatârana*, a champu work; and of *Vainateya s'ataka*, verses in praise of Garuda.

——***Sidda Vîranâchârya***, was the author of the *Anâdi-Vira-S'aiva-Sangraha*, a work in 27 prakaranas. The author reveres the Somes'a Linga of Aipura (Aihole in Dharwad).

——***Sâmbayya***, wrote *Karibhantana-kathe* and *Sârangadhara charitre*, both in yaksha gâna. He is described as the son of Siddhayya.

——***Bhîma Sena***, was the author of *Sûpa-s'âstra*, a work on cookery. He is described as of Virâta-nagari (Hangal in Dharwad).

——***Bâlâlochana***, made a version of *Battisu-puttale kathe*, the 32 stories relating to Vikramâditya told to Bhoja Râja by as many images which decorated the steps of his throne.

c. 1800. ***Sarvajna***, a Lingâyit who wrote the *Sarvajña vachana* in tripadi; also the *Sarvajña Kâlajñâna*, professing to be prophecy. He appears to have been the son of Basavarasa, a S'aiva Brahman of Mâsur in Dharwad, by a Mâlava widow whom he met at Ambalûr when returning from a pilgrimage.

——***Rangayya***, a Lingâyit who wrote a *Kumâra Râya charitra* (see above, p. xxx) in ragale metres. His father was Channa Bhujanga, a panchâla or artificer of the Kannada country, and he was a worshipper of the god Vighnarâja of Tagadûr (? near Talakâd).

——Here may be mentioned the *Gangâ-Gauri-samvâda* in ragale verses by an unknown author.

c. 1800. ***Channappa*** wrote the *S'iva-s'araṇa-lîlâmṛita*, a work in yaksha gâna verse, containing stories of Lingâyit saints. The author was an Ayya or Lingâyit priest of Niḍugal.

——About this time was written the *Mones'vara Purâṇa*, by an author who was a disciple of Gangâdhara guru, but professes to be ignorant of the rules of composition. The work is an account of the miracles of Mona, a Lingâyit saint who lived at Bijapur during the Muhammadan rule there.

c. 1810. ***Chidânanda,*** author of *Chidakhanḍânubhava-sâra* and of *Hari-bhakti-rasâyana*, both in shaṭpadi verse, on Vedânta subjects.

c. 1820. ***Chidânandâvadhûta,*** author of the *Jñâna-sindhu*, a work in shaṭpadi verse on Vedântism. He was the disciple of Chidânanda Bhârati (see foregoing), a guru of Ayodhyâ-pura on the banks of the Tunga-bhadra. If S ringeri be meant, the dates of Sachchidânanda Bhârati are 1770 to 1814, and of Abhinava Sachchidânanda Bhârati 1814 to 1817.

——***Krishṇa Râja,*** wrote the *Anubhava-rasâyana*, a prose tract on religious topics. Also *Châmunḍikâ-laghu-nighanṭu*.

1830. ***Venkaṭes'a Bhaṭṭa*** wrote the *Viṭhoba-charitra* or *Viṭhala charitra*, in *ragaḷe* verse, at Kundâpura on the Western coast.

c. 1840. ***S'ântayya,*** a Sârasvata Brahman of Gersappe (Kshemapura), who became Principal Sadr Amin at Mangalore, composed a number of prasangas in yaksha gâna metre for recitation on the native stage, taking for his subjects stories from the Bhârata and Râmâyaṇa. Some of these works are *Bhishma-parva*, *Droṇa-parva*, *Karṇa-parva*, *Ekâdas'i prasanga*, *Jarâsandha-kâḷaga*, *Suratha-Sudhanva-kâḷaga*, *Saubhadrâ-kalyâṇa*, *Sitâ-kalyâṇa*, *Sitâ-viyoga*, *Lavana-samhâra*, *Râvaṇa-digvijaya*.

The following is a miscellaneous list of works and authors whose place has not been determined :—

Jîvandhara-charitra	by	Bhâskara kavi.
Nannaya-charitra	"	Râma kavi.
Brahmaya-suvi	"	Râmayya.
Kâliyara-kâvya / *Dîpakali-charitra*	} "	Channa Males'a.
Bichchha-dâna	"	Kumâra Malayya.
Yama-Basavana kâlajñâna	"	Yamayya jñâni.
Sâkâra Siddhânta charitra	"	Nandikes'vara.
Anjanâ Devî charitre	"	Mâyaṇṇa cheṭṭi.
Yogaratnâkara	"	Brahma Jayakîrtti.
Kshapana-sâra.	"	Mâdhava-chandra.
Herûra hennina sangatya	"	Mahâdeva.
S'ivagaṇa-charitra	"	S'ântavîra des'ika.
Gurubhaktiyândara-charitra	"	Prâsa-bhûshaṇa.

Shadsthala-upades'a / *Prabhu-devara vachana*	} by	Kumâra Bangunâtha.
Vikrama-vilâsa	„	Vîra Râja.
Prahlâda-charitra	„	Narahari.
Suyoga-charitra	„	Guruprasâda (?).
Shadsthala-jñâna-sârâmṛita	„	Siddhes'vara Deva.

Rudra Bhârata.
Siddharâmaya-charita.
Râjendra-vijaya.
Gajendra-moksha.
Vidura-nîti.
S'ânti-gaṇes'vara sangatya.
Sat-guru-rahasya.
Shaḍsthala-tilaka.
Guru-bodhâmṛita.
Linga-charita.
Saundra-purâṇa.
Siddha-yoga-mâla.
Vijaya-kumâra kathe.
Svetângani kathe.
Vîrasangayyana sangatya.
Vetâla pancha-vims'ati kathe
Chikkaṇyana sangatya.
Bhairaves'vara kathe.
Hari kathâmṛita sâra.

Among more modern works may be named—

Tennâla Râmakṛishṇa hâsyarasa kathâ, stories of Tennâla Râmakṛishṇa, who was the court fool or jester to Kṛishṇa Râya of Vijayanagar (ruled 1508—1530) at the time that Appâji was mantri.

Hamsa vims'ati kathâ, 20 love tales by a swan.

Kṛishṇârjuna-dundume / *S'arana Basava ragaḷe* / *Saumini kathe*	} by	Basava Linga.
S'iva-bhakti-sâra	„	S'ivadhyâna Râmayya.
Kṛishṇa-pârijâta	„	Apparâla Tammaṇṇa of Raichor.

Hosa Gannaḍa nuḍi-gannadi, a grammar by Kṛishṇamâchâri, College Munshi at Madras.

Hanumad-vilâsa.
Lava-Kus'a-kâḷaga.
Kîchaka-samhâra.
S'iva-pârijâta.
S'ivarâtri kathe.
Sudhâma-charitra.
Subodhâmṛita.
Kalâvati-pariṇaya.

Sânanda gaṇes'vara kathe.

It would be difficult to make an exhaustive list up to the present date, but few original works now appear of literary importance. Republication of former writings that are popular chiefly occupies the attention of the presses. It has been part of my duty for several years annually to review the publications of Mysore, the principal country in which Kannaḍa works are printed. And my experience leads me to the opinion that (omitting notice of school books) the yaksha gâṇa stories from the Mahâ Bhârata, Râmâyaṇa and other similar works have been the most popular books of late years. Then follow religious verses embodying the *bhakti sâra* of different sects, *nâmâvaḷi* hymns in praise of particular deities, songs of Kṛishṇa and the milkmaids, with verses on *nîti sára* or morality. The various amusing stories about Tennâla Râmakrishṇa, and those told by the Betâḷa to Vikrama, and by the *puttaḷe* or images decorating his throne to Bhoja Râja, are steady favourites. In addition, a few works on astrology, omens, horoscopy, &c., seem to be in good demand. The *Jaimini Bhârata, Râja S'ekhara vilâsa* and other standard works, with the Lingâyit sectarian books, and Vedântic writings, command a fair sale.

But as an outcome of European education, a strong desire seems to have sprung up for dramatic works of a higher order than the yaksha gâna stories that have hitherto satisfied rustic audiences. This aspiration has found expression in the *Bhrânti-vilâsa* by Tirumalâchârya, adapted from Shakespeare's "Comedy of Errors"; and in the *Jayasimha Râja charitre,* adapted from Shakespeare's "Cymbeline." A translation has also been made of Kâlidâsa's *S'akuntalâ,* with the view of putting it on the stage in a manner approaching the European fashion. Attempts at novel writing too have begun.

Here this review of Kannaḍa literature from the earliest times may fitly be brought to a conclusion. No such complete statement has ever before been made public. The extent and range of this body of writings will doubtless excite surprse, so virtually unexplored has the field remained, and so little acquaintance is there with the resources of the language. The early excellence of the compositions and the modern decline will be patent to all. But interest is even now awakening in the mother tongue of the Kannaḍigas; while the Native State of Mysore, recently restored to its own rulers, has a special mission to discharge, in relation to the learned world of Orientalists in general and to Karṇâṭaka and South India in particular, in vindicating the claims and promoting a revival of the culture of its sonorous and expressive language. Should the furtherance of this object be in any degree stimulated or aided by the present investigation, the labour bestowed on these researches will not be without fruit.

LEWIS RICE.

BANGALORE,
September 1882.

Names of Authors, in alphabetical order.

Names of Works, in alphabetical order.

NÂGA VARMMÂ'S

KARṆÂṬAKA BHÂSHÂ BHÛSHAṆA.

[Invocation.]

Sarvajñam tad aham vande Parañjyotis tamo'paham ।
Pravṛittâ yan mukhâd devî sarva-bhâshâ-Sarasvatî ॥

[The Supreme Light (or Intelligence) do I adore, that All-knowing dispenser of the darkness (of ignorance), from whose mouth proceeded the goddess, the Sarasvatî of all languages.]

ನಾಗವರ್ಮ್ಮಕೃತ

ಕರ್ಣಾಟಕ ಭಾಷಾ ಭೂಷಣ.

ಮಙ್ಗಳ ಶ್ಲೋಕಃ ।

ಸರ್ವಜ್ಞಂ ತದಹಂ ವನ್ದೇ ಪರಂಜ್ಯೋತಿಸ್ತಮೋಪಹಂ ।
ಪ್ರವೃತ್ತಾ ಯನ್ಮುಖಾದ್ದೇವೀ ಸರ್ವಭಾಷಾ ಸರಸ್ವತೀ ॥

ತಾತ್ಪರ್ಯ ॥ ಸಕಲ ಭಾಷಾತ್ಮಕಳಾದ ಸರಸ್ವತೀ ದೇವಿಯು ಯಾರ ಮುಖದ ದೆಸೆಯಿಂದ ಪ್ರವರ್ತಿಸಿದಳೋ ಅಂಥಾ ಸರ್ವಜ್ಞನಾದಂಥಾ ಅಜ್ಞಾನವೆಂಬ ಅಂಧಕಾರವನ್ನ ಹೋಗಲಾಡಿಸುವಂಥಾ ಪ್ರಸಿದ್ಧನಾದಂಥಾ ಉತ್ಕೃಷ್ಟ ತೇಜೋರೂಪನಾದಂಥಾವನಿಗೆ ನಾನು ನಮಸ್ಕಾರವನ್ನ ಮಾಡುತ್ತೇನೆ.

(I. The Alphabet.)

Samjnâ Vidhânam.

Sûtra 1.—*Atha Karṇâṭaka-s'abda-siddhiḥ.*

Vṛitti.—*Atha s'abdo'yam âdau mâṅgalyârthaḥ* I *mâṅgalyâdîni s'âstrâṇi pradanta iti prasiddheḥ* I *adhikârârtho vâ* I *mayâ Karṇâṭaka-vishaya-s'abda-siddhir adhikriyata ity arthaḥ* I

[Here begin the rules of the Karṇâṭaka language.]

Sûtra 2.—*Akârâdayaḥ prasiddhâ varṇâḥ.*

Vṛitti.—*Akârâdayo varṇâ hakâra-paryavasânâḥ prasiddhâ eva veditavyâḥ* I *teshâm anâdi-kâla-prasiddhatvâd anyathâ nopadeshṭavyâḥ* I

[The letters (of the alphabet) from *a* to *ha* are well known (from time immemorial): it is unnecessary to repeat them.)*].

Sûtra 3.—*Teshv âdau chaturdas'a svarâḥ.*

Vṛitti.—*Teshv akârâdishu varṇeshv âdau chaturdas'a-vyavasthitâs'chatur das'a-varṇâs svara-samjñâ bhavanti* I *te ke* I *a â, i î, u û, ṛi ṛî, ḷri ḷṛî, e ai, o au.* I

[The first fourteen letters are vowels.]

---

೧. ಸಂಜ್ಞಾ ವಿಧಾನಂ.

ಸೂತ್ರ॥ ಅಥ ಕರ್ಣಾಟಕ ಶಬ್ದ ಸಿದ್ಧಿಃ ॥೧॥

ವೃತ್ತಿ॥ ಅಥ ಶಬ್ದೋ'ಯಮಾದೌ ಮಾಙ್ಗಲ್ಯಾರ್ಥಃ। ಮಾಙ್ಗಲ್ಯಾದೀನಿ ಶಾಸ್ತ್ರಾಣಿ ಪ್ರದನ್ತ ಇತಿ ಪ್ರಸಿದ್ಧೇಃ। ಅಧಿಕಾರಾರ್ಥೋ'ವಾ। ಮಯಾ ಕರ್ಣಾಟಕ ವಿಷಯ ಶಬ್ದ ಸಿದ್ಧಿರಧಿಕ್ರಿಯತ ಇತ್ಯರ್ಥಃ॥

ತಾತ್ಪರ್ಯ॥ ಮಙ್ಗಲಾನಂತರದಲ್ಲಿ ಕರ್ಣಾಟಕ ಲಕ್ಷಣದಲ್ಲಿ ಶಬ್ದಸಿದ್ಧಿ ಹೇಳಲ್ಪಡುತ್ತದೆ.

ಸೂತ್ರ॥ ಅಕಾರಾದಯಃ ಪ್ರಸಿದ್ಧಾ ವರ್ಣಾಃ ॥೨॥

ವೃತ್ತಿ॥ ಅಕಾರಾದಯೋ ವರ್ಣಾ ಹಕಾರ ಪರ್ಯ್ಯವಸಾನಾಃ ಪ್ರಸಿದ್ಧಾ ಎವ ವೇದಿತವ್ಯಾಃ॥ ತೇಷಾಮನಾದಿಕಾಲ ಪ್ರಸಿದ್ಧತ್ವಾದನ್ಯ ಥಾ ನೋಪದೇಷ್ಟವ್ಯಾಃ॥

ತಾತ್ಪರ್ಯ॥ ಅಕಾರ ಮೊದಲು ಹಕಾರ ಪರ್ಯ್ಯಂತವಾದ ಅಕ್ಷರಗಳು ಅನಾದಿಪ್ರಸಿದ್ಧಗಳಾಗಿರುವದರಿಂದ ಅವುಗಳನ್ನು ಪ್ರತ್ಯೇಕವಾಗಿ ಹೇಳ ಕೆಲಸವಿಲ್ಲ.

ಸೂತ್ರ॥ ತೇಷ್ವಾದೌ ಚತುರ್ದಶ ಸ್ವರಾಃ ॥೩॥

ವೃತ್ತಿ॥ ತೇಷ್ವಕಾರಾದಿಷು ವರ್ಣೇಷ್ವಾದೌ ಚತುರ್ದಶ ವ್ಯವಸ್ಥಿತಾಶ್ಚತುರ್ದಶ ವರ್ಣಾಸ್ಸ್ವರ ಸಂಜ್ಞಾ ಭವನ್ತಿ। ತೇ ಕೇ। ಅ ಆ ಇ ಈ ಉ ಊ ಋ ೠ ಌ ೡ ಎ ಐ ಒ ಔ॥

ತಾತ್ಪರ್ಯ॥ ಆ ಅಕ್ಷರಗಳಲ್ಲಿ ಮೊದಲು ಇರುವ ಹದಿನಾಲ್ಕು ವರ್ಣಗಳಿಗೆ ಸ್ವರಗಳೆಂದು ಸಂಜ್ಞೆ ಆಗಿದೆ.

---

* From what follows it appears that the original letters of the Kannaḍa alphabet were,
Vowels :—a á i í u ú e é ai o ó au. *Anusvâra* :—am. *Visarga* :—ah.
Consonants :—k g ṅ ch j ñ ṭ ḍ ṇ t d n p b m y r l v s h ḷ ṛ ḻ.

Sûtra 4.—*Eka-dvi-tri-mâtrâs te hrasva-dîrgha-plutâh.*

Vritti.—*Atra ta iti tach-chhabdopâdânam vyaktârtham* । *akârâdi-svara-vyaktâ ye varṇâ eka-dvi-tri-mâtrâs santah yathâ-sankhyam pratyekam pratyekam hrasva-dîrgha-pluta-samjñikâ bhavanti* । a1 â2 â3 *ity âdi sâmânyâpekshayâ sankhyâpi na virudhyate* ।

[Accordingly as they are of one, two, or three *mâtrâ* (quantity in metre), they are *hrasva* (short), *dirgha* (long), or *pluta* (prolonged). Thus *a1, â2, â3* &c.]

Sûtra 5.—*Ed-otau hrasvau cha.*

Vritti.—*Ekâraukârâv api kvachid bhâshâyâm hrasvau bhavatah* । *nityam sandhy-aksharâṇi dîrghânîty upades'âd idam vachanam* । *udâharaṇe* । *ele, êlakki, sele, sêle, ole, ôle* ।

[*E* and *o* have also a short form in this language (though in Sanskrit always long).]

Sûtra 6.—*Kâdayas trayas-trims'ad vyañjanâni.*

Vritti.—*Ka-kâra-prabhritayas trayas-trims'at-parimitâ ye varṇâh pratyekam te vyañjana-samjñâ bhavanti* । *te ke* । *ka-kârâdi ha-kârântâh* । *ka, kha, ga, gha, ṅa* । *cha, chha, ja, jha, ña* । *ṭa, ṭha, ḍa, ḍha, ṇa* । *ta, tha, da, dha, na* । *pa, pha, ba, bha, ma* । *ya, ra, la, va, s'a, sha, sa, ha* ।

[Beginning with *ka*, there are thirty three consonants.]

ಸೂತ್ರ ॥ ಏಕದ್ವಿತ್ರಿಮಾತ್ರಾಸ್ತೇ ಹ್ರಸ್ವದೀರ್ಘಪ್ಲುತಾಃ ॥ ೪ ॥

ವೃತ್ತಿ ॥ ಅತ್ರ ತ ಇತಿ ತಚ್ಛಬ್ದೋಪಾದಾನಂ ವ್ಯಕ್ತಾರ್ಥಂ । ಅಕಾರಾದಿ ಸ್ವರವ್ಯಕ್ತಾ ಯೇ ವರ್ಣಾ ಏಕದ್ವಿತ್ರಿ ಮಾತ್ರಾಸ್ಸನ್ತಃ ಯಥಾಸಂಖ್ಯಂ ಪ್ರತ್ಯೇಕಂ ಪ್ರತ್ಯೇಕಂ ಹ್ರಸ್ವ ದೀರ್ಘಪ್ಲುತ ಸಂಜ್ಞಿಕಾ ಭವನ್ತಿ । ಅ೧ ಆ೨ ಆ೩ ಇತ್ಯಾದಿ ಸಾಮಾನ್ಯಾಪೇಕ್ಷಯಾ ಸಙ್ಖ್ಯಾಪಿ ನವಿರುಧ್ಯತೇ ॥

ತಾತ್ಪರ್ಯ ॥ ಅಕಾರಾದಿಸ್ವರಗಳು ಒಂದು, ಎರಡು, ಮೂರು ಮಾತ್ರೆಗಳನ್ನುಳ್ಳದ್ದಾದಾಗ ಕ್ರಮವಾಗಿ ಹ್ರಸ್ವ ದೀರ್ಘ ಪ್ಲುತಗಳೆಂಬ ಸಂಜ್ಞೆಯನ್ನು ಪಡೆಯುತ್ತವೆ.

ಸೂತ್ರ ॥ ಏದೋತೌ ಹ್ರಸ್ವೌಚ ॥ ೫ ॥

ವೃತ್ತಿ ॥ ಏಕಾರೌಕಾರಾವಪಿ ಕ್ವಚಿದ್ಭಾಷಾಯಾಂ ಹ್ರಸ್ವೌ ಭವತಃ । ನಿತ್ಯಂ ಸನ್ಧ್ಯಕ್ಷರಾಣಿ ದೀರ್ಘಾಣೀತ್ಯುಪದೇಶಾದಿದಂ ವಚನಂ । ಉದಾಹರಣೆ ॥ ಎಲೆ, ಏಲಕ್ಕಿ । ಸೆಲೆ, ಸೇಲೆ । ಒಲೆ, ಓಲೆ ॥

ತಾತ್ಪರ್ಯ ॥ ಏಕಾರ ಓಕಾರಂಗಳು ಕರ್ನಾಟಕ ಭಾಷೆಯಲ್ಲಿ ಹ್ರಸ್ವಗಳಾಗುವವು । ಸಂಸ್ಕೃತದಲ್ಲಿ ಯಾವಾಗ್ಯೂ ದೀರ್ಘಗಳೇ ॥

ಸೂತ್ರ ॥ ಕಾದಯಸ್ತ್ರಯಸ್ತ್ರಿಂಶದ್ವ್ಯಂಜನಾನಿ ॥ ೬ ॥

ವೃತ್ತಿ ॥ ಕಕಾರ ಪ್ರಭೃತಯಸ್ತ್ರಯಸ್ತ್ರಿಂಶತ್ಪರಿಮಿತಾ ಯೇ ವರ್ಣಾಃ ಪ್ರತ್ಯೇಕಂ ತೇ ವ್ಯಂಜನ ಸಂಜ್ಞಾ ಭವನ್ತಿ । ತೇ ಕೇ । ಕಕಾರಾದಿ ಹಕಾರಾನ್ತಾಃ । ಕ ಖ ಗ ಘ ಙ । ಚ ಛ ಜ ಝ ಞ । ಟ ಠ ಡ ಢ ಣ । ತ ಥ ದ ಧ ನ । ಪ ಫ ಬ ಭ ಮ । ಯ ರ ಲ ವ ಶ ಷ ಸ ಹ ॥

ತಾತ್ಪರ್ಯ ॥ ಕಕಾರ ಮೊದಲಾಗಿ ಹಕಾರಂ ಕಡೆಯಾದ ಮೂವತ್ತ್ಮೂರು ಅಕ್ಷರಗಳು ವ್ಯಂಜನಗಳೆನ್ನಿಸುವವು.

Sûtra 7.—*Vargâs te mântâh pañcha-pañcha pañcha.*

Vṛitti.—*Te punah ka-kârâdayo mâvasânâ-varṇâh pañcha-pañcha-bhûtvâ pañchaiva varga-samjñâ veditavyâh* । *te ke* । *kakârâdi mântâh* । *ka kha ga gha ṅa ka-vargah* । *cha chha ja jha ña cha-vargah* । *ṭa ṭha ḍa ḍha ṇa ṭa-vargah* । *ta tha da dha na ta-vargah* । *pa pha ba bha ma pa-vargah* । *akâra ihochchâraṇârthah* ।

[Of these, five fives down to *ma* form five *vargas* (or groups).]

Sûtra 8.—*Anunâsikâs teshâm pañchamâh.*

Vṛitti.—*Teshâm pañcha-vargâṇâm ante vyavasthitâ ye varṇâh te anunâsika-samjñâ bhavanti* । *te ke* । *ṅa ña ṇa na mâh* ।

[The fifth letter of each is *anunâsika* (a nasal).]

Sûtra 9.—*Vibhâshayâ ya-va-lâh.*

Vṛitti.—*Ya-va-lâ ity ete varṇâh vibhâshayâ vikalpena anunâsika-samjñâ bhavanti* ।

Prayoga.—*Samyuta, sayyuta; yam lokam, yallokam; semve, seve; gâmve, gâve; kâmpam, kâpam*; kamlane kanaldu, kallane kanaldu; ity âdi* ।

[Before *ya*, *va*, or *la*, it may optionally combine with them.]

ಸೂತ್ರ ॥ ವರ್ಗಾಸ್ತೇ ಮಾನ್ತಾಃ ಪಂಚ ಪಂಚ ಪಂಚ ॥ ೭ ॥

ವೃತ್ತಿ ॥ ತೇ ಪುನಃ ಕಕಾರಾದಯೋ ಮಾವಸಾನಾ ವರ್ಣಾಃ ಪಂಚ ಪಂಚ ಭೂತ್ವಾ ಪಂಚೈವ ವರ್ಗಸಂಜ್ಞಾ ವೇದಿತವ್ಯಾಃ । ತೇ ಕೇ । ಕಕಾರಾದಿ ಮಾನ್ತಾಃ ॥ ಕ ಖ ಗ ಘ ಙ ಕವರ್ಗಃ । ಚ ಛ ಜ ಝ ಞ ಚವರ್ಗಃ । ಟ ಠ ಡ ಢ ಣ ಟವರ್ಗಃ । ತ ಥ ದ ಧ ನ ತವರ್ಗಃ । ಪ ಫ ಬ ಭ ಮ ಪವರ್ಗಃ । ಅಕಾರ ಇಹೋಚ್ಚಾರಣಾರ್ಥಃ ॥

ತಾತ್ಪರ್ಯ ॥ ಕಕಾರ ಮೊದಲಾಗಿ ಮಕಾರವೇ ಕಡೆಯಾಗಿವುಳ್ಳ ಇಪ್ಪತ್ತೈದಕ್ಷರಗಳು ಐದೈದಕ್ಷರಗಳುಳ್ಳವಾಗಿ ಐದು ವರ್ಗಗಳಾಗುವವು । ಇವುಗಳಿಗೆ ಕವರ್ಗ ಇತ್ಯಾದಿ ಹೆಸರುಗಳು ॥

ಸೂತ್ರ ॥ ಅನುನಾಸಿಕಾಸ್ತೇಷಾಂ ಪಂಚಮಾಃ ॥ ೮ ॥

ವೃತ್ತಿ ॥ ತೇಷಾಂ ಪಂಚವರ್ಗಾಣಾಂ ಅನ್ತೇ ವ್ಯವಸ್ಥಿತಾ ಯೇ ವರ್ಣಾಃ ತೇ ಅನುನಾಸಿಕ ಸಂಜ್ಞಾ ಭವನ್ತಿ । ತೇ ಕೇ । ಙ ಞ ಣ ನ ಮಾಃ ॥

ತಾತ್ಪರ್ಯ ॥ ಆ ವರ್ಗಗಳ ಐದನೇ ಅಕ್ಷರಗಳು ಅನುನಾಸಿಕಗಳೆನ್ನಿಸುವವು.

ಸೂತ್ರ ॥ ವಿಭಾಷಯಾ ಯವಲಾಃ ॥ ೯ ॥

ವೃತ್ತಿ ॥ ಯವಲಾ ಇತ್ಯೇತೇ ವರ್ಣಾಃ ವಿಭಾಷಯಾ ವಿಕಲ್ಪೇನ ಅನುನಾಸಿಕ ಸಂಜ್ಞಾ ಭವನ್ತಿ ॥
ಪ್ರಯೋಗ ॥ ಸಂಯುತ, ಸಯ್ಯುತ । ಯಂಲೋಕಂ, ಯಲ್ಲೋಕಂ । ಸೆಂವೆ, ಸವೆ । ಗಾಂವೆ ಗಾವೆ । ಕಾಂಪಂ, ಕಾಪಂ । ಕಂಲನೆ ಕನಲ್ದು, ಕಲ್ಲನೆ ಕನಲ್ದು । ಇತ್ಯಾದಿ ॥

ತಾತ್ಪರ್ಯ ॥ ಯಕಾರ ವಕಾರ ಲಕಾರಗಳು ವಿಕಲ್ಪವಾಗಿ ಅನುನಾಸಿಕಗಳೂ ಆಗುವವು ನಿರನುನಾಸಿಕಗಳೂ ಆಗುವವು ।

---

* This example seems doubtful.

Sûtra 10.—*La-ra-ḍair eva ḷa-ṟa-ḻâḥ.*

Vritti.—*Prayatnâs'rayât la-ra-ḍaire va ḷa-ṟa-ḻa iti des'îyâkshare bhavanti* । *teshâm vibhâshayâ prithak prithak prayoga niyamârtham ayam ârambhaḥ* । *tad yathâ* । *mole, moḷe ; kale, kaḷe ; more, moṟe ; koḍe, koḻe ; kaḍal, kaḻal* । *ity âdi* । *Samskṛta padeshu teshâm aikyam eva* । *salilam, saḷilam ; khaḍgam, khaḷgam* ।

[Ḷa, ṟa, ḻa* in indigenous words stand for *la, ra, ḍa.* (Their use is optional.)]

Sûtra 11.—*Nâtra prâyeṇa vargâṇâm dritîya chaturthâḥ.*

Vritti.—*Asmin Karṇâṭaka-vishaye vargâṇâm dvitîya-chaturtha-varṇâḥ kha gha chha jha ṭha ḍha tha dha pha bha ity ete prâyeṇa na vidyante* । *prâyeṇeti vachanât saṅkhyânukaraṇâdau dṛs'yante* । *tat katham* ।

Prayoga.—*Saṅkhyâyâm:—irchhâsiram, ênchhâsiram, nûrchhasiram* । *anukaraṇe :—ghaṇane, ghaḷilene, chiṭhilene, dhummane, ḍhoṅkane, dhôpene, bhôṅkene* । *âdi grahaṇâd anyatrâpi* । *ghaḷiyam, jhaḷam, ḍhaḷam, bhâram, ḍhoṅkaram, ṭhakku, ṭhôḷike* ।

[The second and fourth letter of each *varga* (*i. e.* the aspirated consonants) were perhaps not in the language originally.]

ಸೂತ್ರ ॥ ಲರಡೈರೇವ ಳ ಱ ೞಃ ॥ ೧೦ ॥

ವೃತ್ತಿ ॥ ಪ್ರಯತ್ನಾಶ್ರಯಾತ್ ಲರಡೈರೇವ ಳ ಱ ೞ ಇತಿ ದೇಶೀಯಾಕ್ಷರೇ ಭವನ್ತಿ । ತೇಷಾಂ ವಿಭಾಷಯಾ ಪೃಥಕ್ ಪೃಥಕ್ ಪ್ರಯೋಗ ನಿಯಮಾರ್ಥಮಯಮಾರಮ್ಭಃ । ತದ್ಯಥಾ । ಮೊಲೆ, ಮೊಳೆ । ಕಲೆ, ಕಳೆ । ಮೊರೆ, ಮೊಱೆ । ಕೊಡೆ, ಕೊೞೆ । ಕಡಲ್, ಕೞಲ್ । ಇತ್ಯಾದಿ । ಸಂಸ್ಕೃತಪದೇಷು ತೇಷಾಮೈಕ್ಯಮೇವ । ಸಲಿಲಂ, ಸಳಿಲಂ । ಖಡ್ಗಂ, ಖಳ್ಗಂ ॥

ತಾತ್ಪರ್ಯ ॥ ಲ ರ ಡ ಯಂಬಕ್ಷರಗಳಿಗೆ ಳ ಱ ೞ ಯಂಬಕ್ಷರಗಳು ಆದೇಶವಾಗಿ ದೇಶ್ಯ ಪದಗಳಲ್ಲಿ ಪ್ರಯೋಗಿಸುವದು.

ಸೂತ್ರ ॥ ನಾತ್ರ ಪ್ರಾಯೇಣ ವರ್ಗಾಣಾಂ ದ್ವಿತೀಯ ಚತುರ್ಥಾಃ ॥ ೧೧ ॥

ವೃತ್ತಿ ॥ ಅಸ್ಮಿನ್ ಕರ್ಣಾಟಕ ವಿಷಯೇ ವರ್ಗಾಣಾಂ ದ್ವಿತೀಯ ಚತುರ್ಥ ವರ್ಣಾಃ ಖ ಘ ಛ ಝ ಠ ಢ ಥ ಧ ಫ ಭ ಇತ್ಯೇತೇ ಪ್ರಾಯೇಣ ನ ವಿದ್ಯನ್ತೇ । ಪ್ರಾಯೇಣೇತಿ ವಚನಾತ್ ಸಂಖ್ಯಾನುಕರಣಾದೌ ದೃಶ್ಯನ್ತೇ । ತತ್ಕಥಂ ।

ಪ್ರಯೋಗ ॥ ಸಂಖ್ಯಾಯಾಂ ॥ ಇರ್ಛಾಸಿರಂ । ಏಂಛಾಸಿರಂ । ನೂರ್ಛಾಸಿರಂ ॥ ಅನುಕರಣೇ ॥ ಘಣನೆ । ಘಳಿಲನೆ । ಛಿಠಿಲನೆ । ಧುಮ್ಮನೆ । ಢೊಂಕನೆ । ಧೋಪನೆ । ಭೋಂಕನೆ ॥ ಆದಿಗ್ರಹಣಾದನ್ಯತ್ರಾಪಿ ॥ ಘಳಿಯಂ । ಝಳಂ । ಢಳಂ । ಭಾರಂ । ಢೊಂಕರಂ । ಠಕ್ಕು । ಠೋಳಿಕೇ ॥

ತಾತ್ಪರ್ಯ ॥ ಈ ಕರ್ಣಾಟಕ ಭಾಷೆಯಲ್ಲಿ ವರ್ಗಗಳ ಎರಡನೇ ನಾಲ್ಕನೆಯ ವರ್ಣಗಳಾದ ಖ ಘ ಛ ಝ ಠ ಢ ಥ ಧ ಫ ಭ ಎಂಬೀವರ್ಣಂಗಳು ಇಲ್ಲ. ಆದರೇ ಸೂತ್ರದಲ್ಲಿ ಪ್ರಾಯೇಣ ಎಂಬ ಪದವಿರುವದರಿಂದ ಸಂಖ್ಯೆ ಅನುಕರಣ ಮುಂತಾದವುಗಳಲ್ಲಿ ಕಾಣಲ್ಪಡುವವು. ಮುಂತಾದವುಗಳಲ್ಲಿ ಯಂದದ್ದರಿಂದ ಇನ್ನೂ ಕೆಲವು ಪದಗಳಲ್ಲಿ ಬರುವವು.

---

* Of these three letters two are now obsolete : *ḻa* (ೞ) disappears from written compositions after about the 13th century, and *ṟa* (ಱ, represented in Nâgari inscriptions by ഥ) after about the 18th century. The remaining letter *ḷa*, (ಳ, represented by the Vedic ळ) a cerebral, continues as an essential and characteristic letter of the Kannaḍa language. This is indicated by one of the examples under a rule in the *Karṇâṭaka Śabdânus'âsana* which runs as follows :—*Kannaḍigar ḷa-kâraman oḍambaṭṭar,* the Kannaḍigas (or Canarese people) adopted the letter *ḷa.*

Sûtra 12.—*S'a-shau cha.*

Vṛitti.—*S'a-sha-kârau drâv apy asmin Karṇâṭaka-vishaye na staḥ* ।

Prayoga.—*S'as'i, sasi ; s'is'u, sisu ; vesham, vêsam ; sesham, sêsam* ।

[Nor *s'a* and *sha.*]

Sûtra 13.—*Ṛikârâdayas chatvâras svarâs' cha.*

Vṛitti.—*Ṛi ṛî ḷṛi ḷṛî ity ete chatvâras svara-samjñikâs' cha asmin Karṇâṭaka-bhâshântare na santi* ।

Prayoga.—*Ṛishi, risi ; ṛiṇam, riṇam ; vṛishabha, basava ; evam âdi* ।

[Nor the four vowels from ṛi (*ṛi, ṛî, ḷṛi, ḷṛî*)]

Sûtra 14.—*Anusvâro binduḥ.*

Vṛitti.—*Kara-taḷa-nikshipta nistulodâtta *muktâphalânukâri bindur anusvâra-samjño bhavati* । *kevalasyâsya bindoḥ prayogâbhâvâd akâras sannidhîyate* । *am ity âdi* ।

[*Anusvâra* is an open dot (resembling a faultless pearl).]

ಸೂತ್ರ ॥ ಶಷೌಚ ॥ ೧೨ ॥

ವೃತ್ತಿ ॥ ಶಷಕಾರೌ ದ್ವಾವಪ್ಯಸ್ಮಿನ್ ಕರ್ಣಾಟಕ ವಿಷಯೇ ನ ಸ್ತಃ ॥

ಪ್ರಯೋಗ ॥ ಶಶಿ, ಸಸಿ । ಶಿಶು, ಸಿಸು । ವೇಷಂ, ವೇಸಂ । ಶೇಷಂ, ಸೇಸಂ ॥

ತಾತ್ಪರ್ಯ ॥ ಈ ಕರ್ಣಾಟಕ ಭಾಷೆಯಲ್ಲಿ ಶಷ ಕಾರಂಗಳು ಮಿಲ್ಲ ॥ ಹ್ಯಾಗೆಂದರೆ ಶಶಿ ಎಂಬುದಕ್ಕೆ ಸಸಿ ಯೆಂದಾಗುವದು, ಆದರೆ ಶಶಿ ಯೆಂದು ತತ್ಸಮ ಪದ ಪ್ರಯೋಗವೇ ಆಗುವಲ್ಲಿ ಶಷಕಾರಂಗಳುಂಟೆಂದು ತಿಳಿಯಬೇಕಾದದ್ದು.

ಸೂತ್ರ ॥ ಋಕಾರಾದಯಶ್ಚತ್ವಾರಸ್ಸ್ವರಾಶ್ಚ ॥ ೧೩ ॥

ವೃತ್ತಿ ॥ ಋ ೠ ಌ ೡ ಇತ್ಯೇತೇ ಚತ್ವಾರಸ್ಸ್ವರ ಸಂಜ್ಞಿಕಾಶ್ಚ ಅಸ್ಮಿನ್ ಕರ್ಣಾಟಕ ಭಾಷಾನ್ತರೇ ನ ಸನ್ತಿ ॥

ಪ್ರಯೋಗ ॥ ಋಷಿ, ರಿಸಿ । ಋಣಂ, ರಿಣಂ । ವೃಷಭ, ಬಸವ । ಏವಮಾದಿ ॥

ತಾತ್ಪರ್ಯ ॥ ಋ ೠ ಌ ೡ ಎಂಬೀ ನಾಲ್ಕು ಸ್ವರಗಳು ಈ ಕರ್ಣಾಟಕ ಭಾಷೆಯಲ್ಲಿಲ್ಲ.

ಸೂತ್ರ ॥ ಅನುಸ್ವಾರೋ ಬಿನ್ದುಃ ॥ ೧೪ ॥

ವೃತ್ತಿ ॥ ಕರತಲನಿಕ್ಷಿಪ್ತ ನಿಸ್ತುಲೋದಾತ್ತ *ಮುಕ್ತಾಫಲಾನುಕಾರಿ ಬಿನ್ದುರನುಸ್ವಾರಸಂಜ್ಞೋ ಭವತಿ ॥ ಕೇವಲಸ್ಯಾಸ್ಯ ಬಿನ್ದೋಃ ಪ್ರಯೋಗಾಭಾವಾದಕಾರಸ್ಸನ್ನಿಧೀಯತೇ । ಅಂ ಇತ್ಯಾದಿ ॥

ತಾತ್ಪರ್ಯ । ಬಿನ್ದುವೆಂತಲೂ ಅನುಸ್ವಾರವೆಂತಲೂ ಸೊನ್ನೆಗೆ ಹೆಸರು. ಬಿಂದು ಮಾತ್ರಕ್ಕೆ ಪ್ರಯೋಗವಿಲ್ಲದ್ದರಿಂದ ಅಂಕಂ ಎಂದು ಇದನ್ನು ತಿಳಿಸುತ್ತಾರೆ. ॥

---

* In B the vritti begins here.

* ದ್ವಿ ॥ ಮುಕ್ತಾ ಎಂಬಪದರಿಂದ ಪ್ರಾರಂಭವಾಗುತ್ತದೆ.

Sûtra 15.—*Sa upary-adhas tâch-cha visargah.*

Vritti.—*Sa eva bindur upary-adhas'-cha vyavasthito visarga-samjño bhavati* । *ah kah ity âdi* ।

[Two such dots one above the other are *visarga*.]

Sûtra 16.—*Vibhaktyantam padam.*

Vritti.—*Nâmâkhyâta vibhaktyantam yachchhabda rûpam tat pada samjñam bhavati* ।

Prayoga.—*Kaiyvolam diradante sasiyind esedattu* । *ity âdi* ।

[An inflected word is *pada*.]

Sûtra 17.—*Paraspara sannikarshas samhitâ.*

Vritti.—*Vis'ishṭânâm varṇânâm anyonya-sannikarshas samsleshas samhitâ sandhir ity uchyate* ।

[The union of letters is *sandhi*.]

Iti Karṇâṭaka-vyâkaraṇa-vrittau Bhâshâ-bhûshaṇe Samjñâ-vidhânam nâma prathamah parichchhedah* ।

ಸೂತ್ರ ॥ ಸ ಉಪರ್ಯಧಸ್ತಾಚ್ಚ ವಿಸರ್ಗಃ ॥ ೧೫ ॥

ವೃತ್ತಿ ॥ ಸ ಏವ ಬಿನ್ದುರುಪರ್ಯಧಶ್ಚ ವ್ಯವಸ್ಥಿತೋ ವಿಸರ್ಗ ಸಂಜ್ಞೋ ಭವತಿ ॥ ಅಃ ಕಃ ಇತ್ಯಾದಿ ॥

ತಾತ್ಪರ್ಯ ॥ ಅದೇ ಸೊನ್ನೆಯನ್ನು ಮೇಲೆಯೂ ಕೆಳಗೂ ಇಟ್ಟರೆ ಅದಕ್ಕೆ ವಿಸರ್ಗವೆಂಬ ಸಂಜ್ಞೆಯು ॥ ಅಃ ಎಂಬ ಇತ್ಯಾದಿ ॥

ಸೂತ್ರ ॥ ವಿಭಕ್ತ್ಯನ್ತಂ ಪದಂ ॥ ೧೬ ॥

ವೃತ್ತಿ ॥ ನಾಮಾಖ್ಯಾತ ವಿಭಕ್ತ್ಯನ್ತಂ ಯುಚ್ಛಬ್ದರೂಪಂ ತತ್ಪದ ಸಂಜ್ಞಂ ಭವತಿ ॥

ಪ್ರಯೋಗ ॥ ಕೈಯ್ವೊಲಂ ದಿವದಂತೆ ಸಸಿಯಿಂದೆಸೆದತ್ತು । ಇತ್ಯಾದಿ ॥

ತಾತ್ಪರ್ಯ ॥ ನಾಮವಿಭಕ್ತಿ ಯಾಗಲಿ ಆಖ್ಯಾತವಿಭಕ್ತಿಯಾಗಲಿ ಕಡೆಯಾಗುಳ್ಳ ಶಬ್ದಕ್ಕೆ ಪದವೆಂದು ಸಂಜ್ಞೆ ॥

ಸೂತ್ರ ॥ ಪರಸ್ಪರ ಸನ್ನಿಕರ್ಷಸ್ಸಂಹಿತಾ ॥ ೧೭ ॥

ವೃತ್ತಿ ॥ ವಿಶಿಷ್ಟಾನಾಂ ವರ್ಣಾನಾಮನ್ಯೋನ್ಯ ಸನ್ನಿಕರ್ಷಸ್ಸಂಶ್ಲೇಷಸ್ಸಂಹಿತಾ ಸನ್ಧಿರಿತ್ಯುಚ್ಯತೆ ॥

ತಾತ್ಪರ್ಯ ॥ ವರ್ಣಗಳನ್ನು ಪರಸ್ಪರವಂಪರೆ ಬಂದರೊಳಗೊಂದನ್ನು ಕೂಡಿಸುವದು ಸಂಧಿಯನ್ನಿಸುವದು ॥

ಇತಿ ಕರ್ಣಾಟಕ ವ್ಯಾಕರಣ ವೃತ್ತೌ* ಭಾಷಾಭೂಷಣೇ ಸಂಜ್ಞಾ ವಿಧಾನಂ ನಾಮ ಪ್ರಥಮಃ ಪರಿಚ್ಛೇದಃ ॥

---

* In P, the words *vyâkaraṇa-vrittau* are omitted in the concluding sentence of every chapter

* ದ್ವಿತೀಯ ಪ್ರತಿಯಲ್ಲಿ ವ್ಯಾಕರಣ ವೃತ್ತೌ ಎಂಬುದು ಇಲ್ಲ.

(II. Union of Letters.)

Sandhi Vidhânam.

Sûtra 18.—*Sandhau.*

Vṛitti.—*Sandhâv-ity-ayam-adhikâraḥ ita uttaram yad vivakshyate tat punas sandhau bhavatîty avagantavyam* ।

["In sandhi" to be understood with each of the following rules.]

Sûtra 19.—*Svare svarasya lopaḥ.*

Vṛitti.—*Svare parato'vasthite pûrva-svarasya lopo bhavati* ।

Prayoga.—*Enna-arasam, ennarasam; enna-âḷdam, ennâḷdam; munnu-iravam, munniravam; kûrtu-iravam, kûrtiravam.*

[A final vowel in uniting with a following initial vowel is omitted.]

Sûtra 20.—*Prakṛiter ud-etoḥ.*

Vṛitti.—*Siddhe vidhir ârabhyamâṇo niyamârtho' yam yogaḥ* । *prakṛites sambandhinas svarasya lopo yadi syât ukâra-ekârayor eva nânyasya* । *svarâdhikârâder hrasva-lopo-niyamyate na punaḥ prakṛiteḥ* ।

Prayoga.—*Mâtu-ellam, mâtellam; lêsu-ellam, lêsellam; nâlige-uḷvane bâḷgum, nâliguḷvane bâḷgum* ।

[Also final *u* and *e* of radical forms.]

---

೨. ಸನ್ಧಿ ವಿಧಾನಂ.

ಸೂತ್ರ ॥ ಸನ್ಧೌ ॥ ೧೮ ॥

ವೃತ್ತಿ ॥ ಸನ್ಧಾವಿತ್ಯಯಮಧಿಕಾರಃ ಇತ ಉತ್ತರಂ ಯದ್ವಿವಕ್ಷ್ಯತೇ ತತ್ಪುನಸ್ಸನ್ಧೌ ಭವತೀತ್ಯವಗನ್ತವ್ಯಂ ॥

ತಾತ್ಪರ್ಯ ॥ ಇದು ಅಧಿಕಾರ ಸೂತ್ರ, ಮುಂದೆ ಹೇಳಲ್ಪಡುವ ವಿಧಾನಗಳು ಸಂಧಿಯಲ್ಲಿ ಆಗುತ್ತವೆಂದು ತಿಳಿಯತಕ್ಕದ್ದು ॥

ಸೂತ್ರ ॥ ಸ್ವರೇ ಸ್ವರಸ್ಯ ಲೋಪಃ ॥ ೧೯ ॥

ವೃತ್ತಿ ॥ ಸ್ವರೇ ಪರತೋಽವಸ್ಥಿತೇ ಪೂರ್ವಸ್ವರಸ್ಯ ಲೋಪೋ ಭವತಿ ॥

ಪ್ರಯೋಗ ॥ ಎನ್ನ-ಅರಸಂ, ಎನ್ನರಸಂ । ಎನ್ನ-ಆಳ್ದಂ, ಎನ್ನಾಳ್ದಂ । ಮುನ್ನು-ಇರವಂ, ಮುನ್ನಿರವಂ । ಕೂರ್ತು-ಇರವಂ, ಕೂರ್ತಿರವಂ ॥

ತಾತ್ಪರ್ಯ ॥ ಸ್ವರಕ್ಕೆ ಸ್ವರ ಪರವಾದರೆ ಪೂರ್ವ ಸ್ವರಕ್ಕೆ ಲೋಪವಾಗುವದು.

ಸೂತ್ರ ॥ ಪ್ರಕೃತೇರುದೇತೋಃ ॥ ೨೦ ॥

ವೃತ್ತಿ ॥ ಸಿದ್ಧೇ ವಿಧಿರಾರಭ್ಯಮಾಣೋ ನಿಯಮಾರ್ಥೋಽಯಂ ಯೋಗಃ । ಪ್ರಕೃತೇಸ್ಸಮ್ಬನ್ಧಿನಸ್ಸ್ವರಸ್ಯ ಲೋಪೋ ಯದಿ ಸ್ಯಾತ್ ಉಕಾರಏಕಾರಯೋರೇವ ನಾನ್ಯಸ್ಯ । ಸ್ವರಾಧಿಕಾರಾದೇರ್ಹ್ರಸ್ವ ಲೋಪೋ ನಿಯಮ್ಯತೇ ನ ಪುನಃ ಪ್ರಕೃತೇಃ ॥

ಪ್ರಯೋಗ ॥ ಮಾತು-ಎಲ್ಲಂ, ಮಾತೆಲ್ಲಂ । ಲೇಸು-ಎಲ್ಲಂ, ಲೇಸೆಲ್ಲಂ । ನಾಲಿಗೆ-ಉಳ್ವನೆ ಬಾಳ್ಗುಂ, ನಾಲಿಗುಳ್ವನೆ ಬಾಳ್ಗುಂ ॥

ತಾತ್ಪರ್ಯ ॥ ಸ್ವರೇ ಸ್ವರಸ್ಯ ಲೋಪಃ ಎಂಬ ಸೂತ್ರದಿಂ ಸಿದ್ಧವಾಗಿದ್ದಾಗ್ಯೂ ನಿಯಮಾರ್ಥವಾಗಿ ಈ ಸೂತ್ರವನ್ನು ಹೇಳಿ ಇದೆ. ಪ್ರಕೃತಿ ಎಂದು ಹೆಸರುಳ್ಳ ಶಬ್ದದ ಉಕಾರ ಎಕಾರಂಗಳಿಗೆ ಮುಂದೆ ಸ್ವರಪರವಾದರೇ ಮೊದಲ ಸ್ವರಕ್ಕೆ ಲೋಪವಾಗುವದು.

Sûtra 21.—*Na nâma-bhâga-pradhvamse.*

Vṛitti.—*Yasmin nâma-bhâga-pradhvamso bhavati tasmin ukâraikârayor lopo na bhavati* ।

Prayoga.—*Paṭu-ivam, paṭuyivam ; gâḷu-ivaḷ, gâḷuyivaḷ ; âse-oḍḍu, aseyoḍḍu ; kudure-akku, kudureyakku ; paḍe-idu, paḍeyidu* ।

[But not if it destroys the sense.]

Sûtra 22.—*Â-î-varṇaikâraikârebhyo yaḥ.*

Vṛitti.—*Âkârâd îkârâd ekârâd aikârâch-cha yakâro vyavadhâyako bhavati* । *varṇa-grahaṇe savarṇa-grahaṇam* । *kâra-grahaṇe kevala-grahaṇam* । *takâro dîrgha nirdes'ârthaḥ* ।

Prayoga.—*Â-eḍe, âyeḍe ; s'rî-eḍe, s'rîyeḍe ; kavi-ar, kaviyar ; naḍe-endu, naḍeyendu ; rai-oḍavittu, raiyoḍavittu* ।

[An initial vowel following upon final *á, í, é, ai* (or their short forms), *y* comes between.]

Sûtra 23.—*Akârântâch-châvadhâraṇârtha e.*

Vṛitti.—*Akârântâchchhabda-rûpâd avadhâraṇârtha ekâre pare yakâro vyavadhâyako bhavati* ।

Prayoga.—*Âtana-ê, âtanayê ; avaḷa-ê, avaḷayê* ।

[When a word ending in *a* takes *é* emphatic, *y* comes between.]

ಸೂತ್ರ ॥ ನ ನಾಮಭಾಗ ಪ್ರಧ್ವಂಸೇ ॥ ೨೧ ॥

ವೃತ್ತಿ ॥ ಯಸ್ಮಿನ್ ನಾಮ ಭಾಗಪ್ರಧ್ವಂಸೋ ಭವತಿ ತಸ್ಮಿನ್ ಉಕಾರೈಕಾರಯೋರ್ಲೋಪೋ ನಭವತಿ॥

ಪ್ರಯೋಗ ॥ ಪಟು-ಇವಂ, ಪಟುಯಿವಂ । ಗಾಳು-ಇವಳ್, ಗಾಳುಯಿವಳ್ । ಆಸೆ-ಒಡ್ಡು, ಆಸೆಯೊಡ್ಡು । ಕುದುರೆ-ಅಕ್ಕು, ಕುದುರೆಯಕ್ಕು । ಪಡೆ-ಇದು, ಪಡೆಯಿದು ॥

ತಾತ್ಪರ್ಯ ॥ ಎಲ್ಲಿ ನಾಮಭಾಗ ಪ್ರಧ್ವಂಸೆಯಾಗುತ್ತದೆಯೋ ಅಲ್ಲಿ ಪ್ರಕೃತಿಯ ಉಕಾರ ಎಕಾರಗಳಿಗೆ ಲೋಪವಿಲ್ಲ.

ಸೂತ್ರ ॥ ಆ ಈ ವರ್ಣೈಕಾರೈಕಾರೇಭ್ಯೋ ಯಃ ॥ ೨೨ ॥

ವೃತ್ತಿ ॥ ಆಕಾರಾದೀಕಾರಾದೇಕಾರಾದೈಕಾರಾಚ್ಚ ಯಕಾರೋ ವ್ಯವಧಾಯಕೋ ಭವತಿ । ವರ್ಣಗ್ರಹಣೇ ಸವರ್ಣಗ್ರಹಣಂ। ಕಾರಗ್ರಹಣೇ ಕೇವಲ ಗ್ರಹಣಂ । ತಕಾರೋ ದೀರ್ಘನಿರ್ದೇಶಾರ್ಥಃ ॥

ಪ್ರಯೋಗ ॥ ಆ-ಎಡೆ, ಆಯೆಡೆ । ಶ್ರೀ-ಎಡೆ, ಶ್ರೀಯೆಡೆ । ಕವಿ-ಅರ್, ಕವಿಯರ್ । ನಡೆ ಎಂದು, ನಡೆಯೆಂದು । ರೈ-ಒದವಿತ್ತು, ರೈಯೊದವಿತ್ತು ॥

ತಾತ್ಪರ್ಯ ॥ ಆಕಾರ ಈಕಾರ ಏ ಐ ಕಾರಗಳಿಗೆ ಪರವಾದರೇ ಯಕಾರ ಬರುತ್ತದೆ. ಆಯೆಂದದ್ದರಿಂದ ಸವರ್ಣವಾದ ಅಕಾರ ಈ ಯೆಂದದ್ದರಿಂದ ಸವರ್ಣವಾದ ಇಕಾರವೂ ಗ್ರಹಿಸಿಯಿವೆ ಯೆಂದರಿಯುವದು.

ಸೂತ್ರ ॥ ಅಕಾರಾನ್ತಾಚ್ಚಾವಧಾರಣಾರ್ಥ ಏ ॥ ೨೩ ॥

ವೃತ್ತಿ ॥ ಅಕಾರಾನ್ತಾಚ್ಛಬ್ದರೂಪಾದವಧಾರಣಾರ್ಥ ಏಕಾರೇ ಪರೇ ಯಕಾರೋ ವ್ಯವಧಾಯಕೋ ಭವತಿ ॥

ಪ್ರಯೋಗ ॥ ಆತನ-ಏ, ಆತನಯೇ । ಅವಳ-ಏ, ಅವಳಯೇ ।

ತಾತ್ಪರ್ಯ ॥ ಅಕಾರಾನ್ತದ ಶಬ್ದಕ್ಕೆ ಅವಧಾರಣಾರ್ಥಕವಾದ ಏ ಯೆಂಬುದು ಪರವಾದರೆ ಇದಕ್ಕೆ ಯಕಾರ ಬರುತ್ತದೆ.

Sûtra 24.—*Vo ṛi-varṇebhyaḥ.*

Vṛitti.—*Okârântâd aukârântâd ukârântad ṛikârântâch-cha vakâro vyavadhâyako bhavati* ǀ

Prayoga.—*Kuḍu-uḍu, kuḍuvuḍu ; manu-ina, manuvina ; pû-ina, pûvina ; hôtṛi-ê, hôtṛiyê ; gô-ina, gôvina ; glau-am, glauvam* ǀ

[An initial vowel following upon final *ó, au, u* or *ṛi, v* comes between.]

Sûtra 25.—*Ed-odanta-nipâtâs svare prakṛityâ.*

Vṛitti.—*Ekârântâ okârântâs' cha ye nipâtâs te svare prakṛityâ bhavanti* ǀ

Prayoga.—*Elê idâvuḍu, arê yaḍeyôḷ, ayyô akaṭa, ohô irali iddante irkkum* ǀ

[Interjections ending in *é* or *ó* do not form *sandhi* with a vowel following.]

Sûtra 26.—*Vis'aṅkâvadhâraṇayoḥ.*

Vṛitti.—*Vis'aṅkâyâm avadhâraṇe cha vartamânâs' s'abdâḥ svare pare prakṛityâ bhavanti* ǀ

Prayoga.—*Âneyô adriyô ; ahiyô'rajjuô ; akkumê ? âgadu ; poravanê âḷvam ; kûrpanê âptam* ǀ

[When doubt or emphasis are expressed there is no *sandhi*.]

ಸೂತ್ರ ‖ ವೋ ವೃವರ್ಣೇಭ್ಯಃ ‖ ೨೪ ‖

ವೃತ್ತಿ ‖ ಓಕಾರಾನ್ತಾದೌಕಾರಾನ್ತಾದುಕಾರಾನ್ತಾದೃಕಾರಾನ್ತಾಚ್ಚ ವಕಾರೋ ವ್ಯವಧಾಯಕೋ ಭವತಿ ‖

ಪ್ರಯೋಗ ‖ ಕುಡು-ಉದು, ಕುಡುವುದು ǀ ಮನು-ಇನ, ಮನುವಿನ ǀ ಪೂ-ಇನ, ಪೂವಿನ ǀ ಹೋತೃ-ಏ, ಹೋತೃವೇ ‖ ಗೋ-ಇನ, ಗೋವಿನ ǀ ಗ್ಲೌ-ಅಂ, ಗ್ಲೌವಂ ‖

ತಾತ್ಪರ್ಯ ‖ ಓ ಔ ಉ ಋ ಕಾರಾನ್ತಗಳು ಪರವಾದಾಗ ವಕಾರ ಆಗುತ್ತದೆ.

ಸೂತ್ರ ‖ ಏದೋದನ್ತ ನಿಪಾತಾಸ್ಸ್ವರೇ ಪ್ರಕೃತ್ಯಾ ‖ ೨೫ ‖

ವೃತ್ತಿ ‖ ಏಕಾರಾನ್ತಾ ಓಕಾರಾನ್ತಾಶ್ಚ ಯೇ ನಿಪಾತಾಸ್ತೇ ಸ್ವರೇ ಪ್ರಕೃತ್ಯಾ ಭವನ್ತಿ ‖

ಪ್ರಯೋಗ ‖ ಎಲೇ ಇದಾವುದು ǀ ಅರೇ ಎಡೆಯೋಳ್ ǀ ಅಯ್ಯೋ ಅಕಟ ǀ ಓಹೋ ಇರಲಿ ಇದ್ದಂತೆ ಇರ್ಕ್ಕುಂ ‖

ತಾತ್ಪರ್ಯ ‖ ಸ್ವಭಾವವಾಗಿ ಏಕಾರಾನ್ತ ಓಕಾರಾನ್ತಗಳಾದ ನಿಪಾತ ಶಬ್ದಂಗಳು ಸ್ವರಪರವಾದರೆ ಸಂಧಿಯಾಗವು.

ಸೂತ್ರ ‖ ವಿಶಙ್ಕಾವಧಾರಣಯೋಃ ‖ ೨೬ ‖

ವೃತ್ತಿ ‖ ವಿಶಙ್ಕಾಯಾಮವಧಾರಣೇ ಚ ವರ್ತಮಾನಾಶ್ಶಬ್ದಾಃ ಸ್ವರೇ ಪರೇ ಪ್ರಕೃತ್ಯಾ ಭವನ್ತಿ ‖

ಪ್ರಯೋಗ ‖ ಆನೆಯೋ ಅದ್ರಿಯೋ ǀ ಅಹಿಯೋ ರಜ್ಜುಓ ǀ ಅಕ್ಕುಮೇ ಆಗದು ǀ ಪೊರವನೇ ಆಳ್ವಂ ǀ ಕೂರ್ಪನೇ ಆಪ್ತಂ ‖

ತಾತ್ಪರ್ಯ ‖ ವಿಶಜೆ ಯಲ್ಲಿಯೂ ಅವಧಾರಣದಲ್ಲಿಯೂ ಸ್ವರಪರವಾದರೆ ಸಂಧಿಯಾಗುವದಿಲ್ಲ.

Sûtra 27.—*Plutâs' cha.*

Vṛitti.—*Tri-mâtrâ ye varṇâs te cha svare pare prakṛityaiva tishṭhanti* ।

Prayoga.—*Elê aṇṇâ3, itta bâ3; kukkû kû3 yendu kôḷi kûgitt âgaḷ* ।

[Also a final *pluta* (prolonged vowel) forms no *sandhi* with a following initial vowel.]

Sûtra 28.—*Varga-prathamânâm tṛitîyâs* samâsottara-padâdau.*

Vṛitti.—*Varga-prathamâksharâṇâm samâsottara-padâdau vartamânânâm teshâm tṛitîyâ varṇâ bhavanti* ।

Prayoga.—*Haḷe-Kannaḍam, HaḷeGannaḍam; âḷi-kabbam, âḷigabbam; ken-taḷir, kendaḷir; bân-tore, bândore* ।

[When the second member of a compound word begins with the first letter of a *varga* (a surd), it is exchanged for the third of the same *varga* (a sonant).]

Sûtra 29.—*Nâdishṭa-rephât.*

Vṛitti.—*Âdes'a-vihitât pariṇâmino rephât tasmât parabhûtânâm tṛitîyâ na bhavanti* ।

Prayoga.—*Mâr-koral, mârkoral; mâr-tale, mârtale; mâr-paḍe, mârpaḍe* ।

[But not when the first member ends in *r*.]

ಸೂತ್ರ ॥ ಪ್ಲುತಾಶ್ಚ ॥ ೨೭ ॥

ವೃತ್ತಿ ॥ ತ್ರಿಮಾತ್ರಾ ಯೇ ವರ್ಣಾಸ್ತೇ ಚ ಸ್ವರೇ ಪರೇ ಪ್ರಕೃತ್ಯೈವ ತಿಷ್ಠನ್ತಿ ॥

ಪ್ರಯೋಗ ॥ ಎಲೇ ಅಣ್ಣಾ೩ ಇತ್ತಬಾ೩ । ಕುಕ್ಕೂ ಕೂ೩ ಎಂದು ಕೋಳಿ ಕೂಗಿತ್ತಾಗಳ್ ॥

ತಾತ್ಪರ್ಯ ॥ ಪ್ಲುತಗಳಿಗೆ ಸ್ವರಪರವಾದರ ಸನ್ಧಿಯಾಗುವದಿಲ್ಲ.

ಸೂತ್ರ ॥ ವರ್ಗಪ್ರಥಮಾನಾಂ ತೃತೀಯಾ* ಸ್ಸಮಾಸೋತ್ತರಪದಾದೌ ॥ ೨೮ ॥

ವೃತ್ತಿ ॥ ವರ್ಗಪ್ರಥಮಾಕ್ಷರಾಣಾಂ ಸಮಾಸೋತ್ತರ ಪದಾದೌ ವರ್ತಮಾನಾನಾಂ ತೇಷಾಂ ತೃತೀಯಾ ವರ್ಣಾ ಭವನ್ತಿ ॥

ಪ್ರಯೋಗ ॥ ಹಳೇ-ಕನ್ನಡಂ, ಹಳೆಗನ್ನಡಂ । ಆಳಿ-ಕಬ್ಬಂ, ಆಳಿಗಬ್ಬಂ । ಕೆನ್-ತಳಿರ್, ಕೆಂದಳಿರ್ । ಬಾನ್-ತೊರೆ, ಬಾಂದೊರೆ ॥

ತಾತ್ಪರ್ಯ ॥ ಸಮಾಸದ ಪರಪದದ ಆದಿಯಲ್ಲಿದ್ದ ವರ್ಗ ಪ್ರಥಮಾಕ್ಷರಗಳಿಗೆ ಆದರದರ ವರ್ಗ ತೃತೀಯಾಕ್ಷರಗಳಾಗುವವು ॥

ಸೂತ್ರ ॥ ನಾದಿಷ್ಟರೇಫಾತ್ ॥ ೨೯ ॥

ವೃತ್ತಿ ॥ ಆದೇಶವಿಹಿತಾತ್ಪರಿಣಾಮಿನೋ ರೇಫಾತ್ ತಸ್ಮಾತ್ಪರಭೂತಾನಾಂ ತೃತೀಯಾ ನ ಭವನ್ತಿ ॥

ಪ್ರಯೋಗ ॥ ಮಾರ್-ಕೊರಲ್, ಮಾರ್ಕೊರಲ್ । ಮಾರ್-ತಲೆ, ಮಾರ್ತಲೆ । ಮಾರ್-ಪಡೆ, ಮಾರ್ಪಡೆ ॥

ತಾತ್ಪರ್ಯ ॥ ಆವರ್ಗ ಪ್ರಥಮಾಕ್ಷರಗಳು ಆದೇಶದಿಂದ ಬಂದ ರೇಫೆಗೆ ಪರವಾದರೆ ಆದರದರ ವರ್ಗತೃತೀಯಾಕ್ಷರಗಳು ಬರುವದಿಲ್ಲ.

---

* In B the sûtra ends here.

* ದ್ವಿ ॥ ಸಮಾಸೋತ್ತರ ಪದಾದೌ ಎಂಬುದು ಇಲ್ಲ

Sûtra 30.—*Cha-ṭa-vargayos' cha.*

Vṛitti—*Cha-ṭa-vargayoh prathamâksharayos' cha sva-tritiyau na bhavatah* ।

Prayoga.—*Kaḍuchannam, kaḍuchâgi, ûrachalli, mâtaṭepparam, posaṭoppige, posaṭaṅkam, mâṇiṭekke, kaḷaṭippaṇam* ।

[Nor when the first letter of the second member is of the *cha* or *ṭa varga.*]

Sûtra 31.—*Svara-ya-ra-lebhyo bahuḷam vah pavargasya.*

Vṛitti—*Svarât yakârât rephât lakârât parasya pavargasya bahuḷam vakârâdes'o bhavati* ।

Prayoga.—*Posa-pesar, posavesar; eḷe-bidir, eḷevidir; mai-besam, maivesam; kal-bâḷe, kalvâḷe ; pul-mane, pulvane; nîr-pâvu, nîrvâvu* ।

Bahuḷa-grahaṇât krachin-na bhavati । *Prayoga* । *naḍubênu, uḍumôlam, kemmugil, pâlmosar, balmugaḷ, kârmugil* ।

[An initial letter of the *pa varga* becomes *v* in uniting with a final vowel, *y*, *r*, or *l*. But not always.]

ಸೂತ್ರ ॥ ಚಟವರ್ಗಯೋಶ್ಚ ॥ ೩೦ ॥

ವೃತ್ತಿ ॥ ಚಟವರ್ಗಯೋಃ ಪ್ರಥಮಾಕ್ಷರಯೋಶ್ಚ ಸ್ವತೃತೀಯೌ ನ ಭವತಃ ।

ಪ್ರಯೋಗ ॥ ಕಡುಚನ್ನಂ । ಕಡುಚಾಗಿ । ಊರಚಲ್ಲಿ । ಮಾತಟೆಪ್ಪರಂ । ಪೊಸಟೊಪ್ಪಿಗೆ । ಪೊಸಟಂಕಂ । ಮಾಣಿಟೆಕ್ಕೆ । ಕಳಟಿಪ್ಪಣಂ ॥

ತಾತ್ಪರ್ಯ ॥ ಚಟ ವರ್ಗಗಳ ಪ್ರಥಮಾಕ್ಷರಗಳಿಗೂ ಸಮಾಸ ಪರಪದದಲ್ಲಿ ಅವುಗಳ ತೃತೀಯಾಕ್ಷರಗಳಾಗವು ॥

ಸೂತ್ರ ॥ ಸ್ವರಯರಲೇಭ್ಯೋ ಬಹುಳಂ ವಃ ಪವರ್ಗಸ್ಯ ॥ ೩೧ ॥

ವೃತ್ತಿ ॥ ಸ್ವರಾತ್ ಯಕಾರಾತ್ ರೇಫಾತ್ ಲಕಾರಾತ್ ಪರಸ್ಯ ಪವರ್ಗಸ್ಯ ಬಹುಳಂ ವಕಾರಾದೇಶೋ ಭವತಿ ॥

ಪ್ರಯೋಗ ॥ ಪೊಸ-ಪೆಸರ, ಪೊಸವೆಸರ । ಎಳೆ-ಬಿದಿರ, ಎಳೆವಿದಿರ । ಮೈ-ಬೆಸಂ, ಮೈವೆಸಂ । ಕಲ್-ಬಾಳೆ, ಕಲ್ವಾಳೆ । ಪುಲ್-ಮನೆ, ಪುಲ್ವನೆ । ನೀರ್-ಪಾವು, ನೀರ್ವಾವು ॥

ಬಹುಳ ಗ್ರಹಣಾತ್ಕ್ವಚಿನ್ನ ಭವತಿ ॥ ಪ್ರಯೋಗ ॥ ನಡುಬೇನು । ಉಡುಮೋಲಂ । ಕೆಂಮುಗಿಲ್ । ಪಾಲ್ಮೊಸರ । ಬಲ್ಮುಗಳ್ । ಕಾರ್ಮುಗಿಲ್ ॥

ತಾತ್ಪರ್ಯ ॥ ಸ್ವರ ಯಕಾರ ರೇಫ ಲಕಾರಗಳಿಗೆ ಪರವಾದ ಪವರ್ಗಕ್ಕೆ ವಿಕಲ್ಪವಾಗಿ ವಕಾರವಾಗವದು. ಬಹುಳ ಸ್ವೀಕಾರದಿಂದ ಕೆಲವೆಡೆಗಳಲ್ಲಾಗದು.

Sûtra 32.—*Vyañjanâd ala-yât sasya chah.*

Vṛitti.—*La-ya-kâra-varjita-vyañjanât paratas sakârasya chakârâdes'o bhavati* ।

Prayoga.—*Nuṇ-saram, nuṇcharam ; in-saram, iñcharam ; ôr-savaḍi, ôrchavaḍi* ।

Bahuḷam ity anuvartate tatah kvachin na bhavati । *Prayoga* । *kaṇ-sôlam, kaṇsôlam ; kîḷ-sari, kîḷsari* ।

[An initial *s* becomes *ch* in uniting, with any final consonant but *y* or *l*. But not always]

Sûtra 33.—*Kvachij-jatvam.*

Vṛitti.—*Tâdṛis'asya sakârasya kvachij-jatvam jakâro bhavatity arthah* ।

Prayoga.—*Mun-sûr, muñjûr ; mun-sulige, muñjulige ; pon-sarige, poñjarige; mun-seragu, muñjeragu ; kaṇ-soḍar, kaṇjoḍar* ।
Ala-yâd iti kim । *mêlsari, pôlsari, maisônku, kaisôre, bâyisavi* ।

[In some cases it becomes *j*.]

ಸೂತ್ರ ॥ ವ್ಯಞ್ಜನಾದಲಯಾತ್ಸಸ್ಯ ಚಃ ॥ ೩೨ ॥

ವೃತ್ತಿ ॥ ಲಯಕಾರ ವರ್ಜಿತ ವ್ಯಞ್ಜನಾತ್ ಪರತಸ್ಸಕಾರಸ್ಯ ಚಕಾರಾದೇಶೋ ಭವತಿ ॥

ಪ್ರಯೋಗ ॥ ನುಣ್-ಸರಂ, ನುಣ್ಚರಂ । ಇನ್-ಸರಂ, ಇಂಚರಂ । ಓರ್-ಸವಡಿ, ಓರ್ಚವಡಿ ॥
ಬಹುಳಮಿತ್ಯನುವರ್ತತೇ ತತಃ ಕ್ವಚಿನ್ನ ಭವತಿ ॥ ಪ್ರಯೋಗ ॥ ಕಣ್-ಸೋಲಂ, ಕಣ್ಸೋಲಂ ।
ಕೀಳ್-ಸರಿ, ಕೀಳ್ಸರಿ ॥

ತಾತ್ಪರ್ಯ ॥ ಲಕಾರ ಯಕಾರಗಳಲ್ಲದೆ ನಿಂತ ವ್ಯಂಜನಗಳಿಗೆ ಪರವಾದ ಸಕಾರಕ್ಕೆ ಚಕಾರವಾಗುವದು. ಬಹುಳವೆಂಬ ವಿಕಲ್ಪ ಸ್ವೀಕಾರದಿಂದ ಕೆಲವು ಕಡೆಯಾಗದು.

ಸೂತ್ರ ॥ ಕ್ವಚಿಜ್ಜತ್ವಂ ॥ ೩೩ ॥

ವೃತ್ತಿ ॥ ತಾದೃಶಸ್ಯ ಸಕಾರಸ್ಯ ಕ್ವಚಿಜ್ಜತ್ವಂ ಜಕಾರೋ ಭವತೀತ್ಯರ್ಥಃ ॥

ಪ್ರಯೋಗ ॥ ಮುನ್-ಸೂರ್, ಮುಂಜೂರ್ । ಮುನ್-ಸುಲಿಗೆ, ಮುಂಜುಲಿಗೆ । ಪೊನ್-ಸರಿಗೆ, ಪೊಂಜರಿಗೆ ।
ಮುನ್-ಸೆರಗು, ಮುಂಜೆರಗು । ಕಣ್-ಸೊಡರ್, ಕಣ್ಜೊಡರ್ ।
ಅಲಯಾದಿತಿ ಕಿಂ ॥ ಮೇಲ್ಸರಿ । ಪೋಲ್ಸರಿ । ಮೈಸೋಂಕು । ಕೈಸೋರೆ । ಬಾಯಿಸವಿ ॥

ತಾತ್ಪರ್ಯ ॥ ಕೆಲವೆಡೆಯೊಳು ವ್ಯಂಜನಗಳಿಂದ ಪರವಾದ ಸಕಾರಕ್ಕೆ ಜಕಾರವಾಗುವದು ॥

Sûtra 34.—*Saṅkhyâyâm chhatvam.*

Vṛitti.—*Saṅkhyâ-vishaye vartamânasya la-ya-rahita-vyañjanâd uttarasya sakârasya chhakârâdes'o bharati* ।

Prayoga.—*Mûvattir-sâsiram, mûvattirchhâsiram ; ippattâr-sâsiram, ippattârchhâsiram ; padinêṇ-sâsiram, padinêṇchhâsiram ; eṇ-sâsiram, eṇchhâsiram* ।

Ala-yâd iti kim । *nâlsâsiram, aisâsiram* ।

[In numerals it becomes *chh*.]

Sûtra 35.—*Na-ṇa-la-ya-ḷâ drih svare hrasva-pûrvâh.*

Vṛitti.—*Hrasvâkshara-pûrvakâh na-ṇa-la-ya-ḷa-kârâh svare pare dvirbhâvam âpadyante* ।

Prayoga.—*Pon-uḷḷavane kulînam, ponnuḷḷavane kulînam; pon-alli, ponnalli ; chitrada peṇ-ante vôl, chitrada peṇṇante vôl ; maṇ-ellam, maṇṇellam ; kal-ellam, kallellam ; pal-ellam, pallellam ; nel-ellam, nellellam ; maiy-oḷage maiyyoḷage ; kaiy-alli, kaiyyalli ; muḷ-uḷḷa, muḷḷuḷḷa* ।

Hrasva pûrva iti kim । *tân-endum, tânendum, ; jâṇ-indam, jâṇindam ; mêl-ârgam, mêlârgam ; bây-âram, bâyâram ; kêḷ-îtam, kêḷîtam* ।

[An initial vowel in uniting with final *n*, *ṇ*, *l*, *y* or *ḷ* preceded by a short vowel, doubles them. But not when they are preceded by a long vowel.]

ಸೂತ್ರ ॥ ಸಙ್ಖ್ಯಾಯಾಂ ಛತ್ವಂ ॥ ೩೪ ॥

ವೃತ್ತಿ ॥ ಸಙ್ಖ್ಯಾವಿಷಯೇ ವರ್ತಮಾನಸ್ಯ ಲ ಯ ರಹಿತ ವ್ಯಞ್ಜನಾದುತ್ತರಸ್ಯ ಕಾರಸ್ಯ ಛಕಾರಾದೇಶೋ ಭವತಿ ॥

ಪ್ರಯೋಗ ॥ ಮೂವತ್ತಿರ್-ಸಾಸಿರಂ, ಮೂವತ್ತಿರ್ಛಾಸಿರಂ । ಇಪ್ಪತ್ತಾರ್-ಸಾಸಿರಂ, ಇಪ್ಪತ್ತಾರ್ಛಾಸಿರಂ । ಪದಿನೇಣ್-ಸಾಸಿರಂ, ಪದಿನೇಣ್ಛಾಸಿರಂ । ಎಣ್-ಸಾಸಿರಂ, ಎಣ್ಛಾಸಿರಂ ॥
ಅಲಯಾದಿತಿ ಕಿಂ ॥ ನಾಲ್ಸಾಸಿರಂ । ಐಸಾಸಿರಂ ॥

ತಾತ್ಪರ್ಯ ॥ ಲಕಾರ ಯಕಾರ ವ್ಯತಿರಿಕ್ತವಾದ ವ್ಯಂಜನಗಳಿಂದ ಪರವಾದ ಸಕಾರಕ್ಕೆ ಲೆಖ್ಖದೆಣಿಕೆಯನ್ನು ನುಡಿಯುವಲ್ಲಿ ಛಕಾರವಾಗುವದು.

ಸೂತ್ರ ॥ ನಣಲಯಳಾ ದ್ವಿಃ ಸ್ವರೇ ಹ್ರಸ್ವಪೂರ್ವಾಃ ॥ ೩೫ ॥

ವೃತ್ತಿ ॥ ಹ್ರಸ್ವಾಕ್ಷರಪೂರ್ವಕಾಃ ನಣಲಯಳಕಾರಾಃ ಸ್ವರೇ ಪರೇ ದ್ವಿರ್ಭಾವಮಾಪದ್ಯನ್ತೇ ॥

ಪ್ರಯೋಗ ॥ ಪೊನ್-ಉಳ್ಳವನೆ ಕುಲೀನಂ, ಪೊನ್ನುಳ್ಳವನೆ ಕುಲೀನಂ । ಪೊನ್-ಅಲ್ಲಿ, ಪೊನ್ನಲ್ಲಿ । ಚಿತ್ರದ ಪೆಣ್-ಅಂತೆವೋಲ್, ಚಿತ್ರದ ಪೆಣ್ಣಂತೆವೋಲ್ । ಮಣ್-ಎಲ್ಲಂ, ಮಣ್ಣೆಲ್ಲಂ । ಕಲ್-ಎಲ್ಲಂ, ಕಲ್ಲೆಲ್ಲಂ । ಪಲ್-ಎಲ್ಲಂ, ಪಲ್ಲೆಲ್ಲಂ । ನೆಲ್-ಎಲ್ಲಂ, ನೆಲ್ಲೆಲ್ಲಂ । ಮೈಯ್-ಒಳಗೆ, ಮೈಯ್ಯೊಳಗೆ । ಕಯ್-ಅಲ್ಲಿ ಕೈಯ್ಯಲ್ಲಿ । ಮುಳ್-ಉಳ್ಳ, ಮುಳ್ಳುಳ್ಳ ॥

ಹ್ರಸ್ವ ಪೂರ್ವ ಇತಿ ಕಿಂ ॥ ತಾನ್-ಎಂದುಂ, ತಾನೆಂದುಂ । ಜಾಣ್-ಇಂದಂ, ಜಾಣಿಂದಂ । ಮೇಲ್-ಆರ್ಗಂ, ಮೇಲಾರ್ಗಂ । ಬಾಯ್-ಆರಂ, ಬಾಯಾರಂ । ಕೇಳ್-ಈತಂ, ಕೇಳೀತಂ ॥

ತಾತ್ಪರ್ಯ ॥ ಹ್ರಸ್ವಾಕ್ಷರಗಳು ಮೊದಲೊಳುಳ್ಳ ನಣಲಯಳಕಾರಗಳಿಗೆ ಸ್ವರಪರವಾದರೇ ಇವು ದ್ವಿತ್ವಗಳಾಗುವವು. ದೀರ್ಘಾಕ್ಷರಗಳು ಮೊದಲೊಳುಳ್ಳ ನಣಲಯಳಕಾರಗಳಿಗೆ ಸ್ವರಪರವಾದರೆ ದ್ವಿತ್ವಗಳಾಗವು.

Sûtra 36.—*Nânekâkshara-pade.*

Vṛitti.—*Hrasva-pûrvepi dvi-tryâdi-svara-sampanne pade vyavasthitâ na-ṇa-la-ya-ḷa-kârâh svare pare dvirbhâvam nâpadyante* ।

Prayoga.—*Pavaṇ-uṇṭu, pavaṇuṇṭu*; **konar**-*ellam, konarellam*; *s'craṇ-ellam, s'craṇellam* ।

[And not in dissyllables or polysyllables.]

Sûtra 37.—*Avyayeshu.*

Vritti.—*Avyaya-s'abdeshu vartamânâh na-ṇa-la-ya-ḷa-kârâh svare pare dvirbhâvam nâpadyante* ।

Prayoga.—*Smarana vôl-îtam, smarana vôlîtam* ।

[Nor in indeclinables.]

Iti Karṇâṭaka-vyâkaraṇa-vrittau Bhâshâ-bhûshaṇe Sandhi-vidhânam nâma dvitîyah parichchhedah* ।

ಸೂತ್ರ ‖ ನಾನೇಕಾಕ್ಷರಪದೇ ‖ ೩೬ ‖

ವೃತ್ತಿ ‖ ಹ್ರಸ್ವ ಪೂರ್ವೇಽಪಿ ದ್ವಿತ್ರ್ಯಾದಿ ಸ್ವರಸಮ್ಪನ್ನೇ ಪದೇ ವ್ಯವಸ್ಥಿತಾ ನಣಲಯಳಕಾರಾಃ ಸ್ವರೇ ಪರೇ ದ್ವಿರ್ಭಾವಂ ನಾಪದ್ಯನ್ತೇ ‖

ಪ್ರಯೋಗ ‖ ಪವಣ್-ಉಂಟು, ಪವಣುಂಟು । ಕೊನರ್-ಎಲ್ಲಂ, ಕೊನರೆಲ್ಲಂ । ಕರಣ್-ಎಲ್ಲಂ, ಕರಣೆಲ್ಲಂ ‖

ತಾತ್ಪರ್ಯ ‖ ಹ್ರಸ್ವಾಕ್ಷರಗಳು ಮೊದಲೊಳುಳ್ಳವಾದಾಗ್ಯೂ ಅನೇಕಾಕ್ಷರಗಳುಳ್ಳ ಪದದಲ್ಲಿನ ನಣಲಯಳಕಾರಗಳಿಗೆ ಸ್ವರಪರವಾದರೆ ಇವುಗಳಿಗೆ ದ್ವಿತ್ವವಾಗದು.

ಸೂತ್ರ ‖ ಅವ್ಯಯೇಷು ‖ ೩೭ ‖

ವೃತ್ತಿ ‖ ಅವ್ಯಯ ಶಬ್ದೇಷು ವರ್ತಮಾನಾಃ ನಣಲಯಳಕಾರಾಃ ಸ್ವರೇ ಪರೇ ದ್ವಿರ್ಭಾವಂ ನಾಪದ್ಯನ್ತೇ ‖

ಪ್ರಯೋಗ ‖ ಸ್ಮರನ ವೋಲ್-ಈತಂ, ಸ್ಮರನ ವೋಲೀತಂ ।

ತಾತ್ಪರ್ಯ ‖ ಅವ್ಯಯ ಶಬ್ದಗಳಲ್ಲಿರುವ ನಣಲಯಳಕಾರಗಳಿಗೆ ಸ್ವರ ಪರವಾದರೆ ದ್ವಿತ್ವವಾಗದು.

ಇತಿ ಕರ್ಣಾಟಕ ವ್ಯಾಕರಣ ವೃತ್ತೌ* ಭಾಷಾಭೂಷಣೇ ಸನ್ಧಿ ವಿಧಾನಂ
ನಾಮ ದ್ವಿತೀಯಃ ಪರಿಚ್ಛೇದಃ ‖

---

* See note p. 7.

* ೭ನೇ ಪುಟವನ್ನು ನೋಡಬೇಕು.

(III. Declension.)

Vibhakti Vidhânam.

Sûtra 38.—*Arthavad akriyáráchi kṛidantam cha liṅgam.*

Vṛitti.—*Kriyâvâchino'nyad arthavach-chhabda-rûpam kṛitpratyayântam cha liṅga-samjñam bhavati* ।

[The primary suffix of a word having meaning but not used as a verb, denotes gender.]

Sûtra 39.—*Tato vibhaktayah.*

Vṛitti.—*Tasmâl-liṅga-samjñât parâ vibhaktayo hy utpadyante* । *tâstu* ।

[The case termination follows after that of gender.]

Sûtra 40.—*M-am-im-kay-ar-ad-ôḷ.*

Vṛitti.—*M, am, im, ke, ar, ad, ôḷ iti kramena sapta vibhaktayo jñâtavyâh.*

Prayoga.—*Nelam, nelanam, nelanim, nelakke, neladattaṇim, nelada, neladôḷ* ।

[*M, am, im, ke, ar, ad, ol,* taken in order, are the seven cases (or case terminations.]

---

೩. ವಿಭಕ್ತಿ ವಿಧಾನಂ.

ಸೂತ್ರ ॥ ಅರ್ಥವದಕ್ರಿಯಾವಾಚಿ ಕೃದನ್ತಂ ಚ ಲಿಙ್ಗಂ ॥ ೩೮ ॥

ವೃತ್ತಿ ॥ ಕ್ರಿಯಾವಾಚಿನೋಽನ್ಯದರ್ಥವಚ್ಛಬ್ದರೂಪಂ ಕೃತ್ಪ್ರತ್ಯಯಾನ್ತಂ ಚ ಲಿಙ್ಗಸಂಜ್ಞಂ ಭವತಿ ॥

ತಾತ್ಪರ್ಯ ॥ ಅರ್ಥವುಳ್ಳದ್ದಾಗಿ ಕ್ರಿಯಾವಾಚಕವಲ್ಲದೆ ವರ್ತಿಸುವ ಕೃತ್ಪ್ರತ್ಯಯಾನ್ತ ಶಬ್ದವನ್ನು ಲಿಂಗವೆನ್ನುವರು.

ಸೂತ್ರ ॥ ತತೋ ವಿಭಕ್ತಯಃ ॥ ೩೯ ॥

ವೃತ್ತಿ ॥ ತಸ್ಮಾಲ್ಲಿಙ್ಗಸಂಜ್ಞಾತ್ಪರಾ ವಿಭಕ್ತಯೋ ಹ್ಯುತ್ಪದ್ಯನ್ತೇ ॥ ತಾಸ್ತು ॥

ತಾತ್ಪರ್ಯ ॥ ಆ ಲಿಂಗದ ಮೇಲೆಯಿಂದ ಪರವಾಗಿ ವಿಭಕ್ತಿಗಳಾಗುವವು.

ಸೂತ್ರ ॥ ಮಮಿಮ್ಕಯರದೋಳ್ ॥ ೪೦ ॥

ವೃತ್ತಿ ॥ ಮ್ । ಅಮ್ । ಇಮ್ । ಕೆ । ಅರ್ । ಅದ್ । ಓಳ್ । ಇತಿ ಕ್ರಮೇಣ ಸಪ್ತ ವಿಭಕ್ತಯೋ ಜ್ಞಾತವ್ಯಾಃ ॥

ಪ್ರಯೋಗ ॥ ನೆಲಂ । ನೆಲನಂ । ನೆಲನಿಂ । ನೆಲಕ್ಕೆ । ನೆಲದತ್ತಣಿಂ । ನೆಲದ । ನೆಲದೋಳ್ ॥

ತಾತ್ಪರ್ಯ ॥ ಮ್ । ಅಮ್ । ಇಮ್ । ಕೆ । ಅರ್ । ಅದ್ । ಓಳ್ । ಎಂಬವು ಕ್ರಮವಾಗಿ ಪ್ರಥಮಾದಿ ಸಪ್ತ ವಿಭಕ್ತಿಗಳೆಂದಱಿವುದು.

Sûtra 41.—*Dvitva-bahutvayor gaḷ âdau.*

Vritti.—*Tâsâm vibhaktînâm âdau dvitva-bahutva-vishaye gaḷ-âgamo bhavati* ।

Prayoga.—*Kaṇgaḷ, kaṇgaḷam, kaṇgaḷim, kaṇgaḷge, kaṇgaḷattaṇim, kaṇgaḷa, kaṇgaḷôḷ* ।

[In the dual and plural they are preceded by *gaḷ*.]

Sûtra 42.—*Sarvanâma-guṇavachanânâm avu tad ante.*

Vritti.—*Sarvanâmnâm guṇavachanânâm cha dvitva-bahutve vivakshite teshâm ante vibhaktishu parâbhûtâsu avu bhavati* ।

Prayoga.—*Adu, idu, udu, âvudu, elladu, peratu, peradu, ên, ete sarvanâma-s'abdâḥ* । *oḷḷitu, mellitu, beṭṭitu, ity-âdayo guṇavâchaka-s'abdâḥ* ।

Prayoga । *ellavu, ellavam, ellavarim, ellavargge, ellavarattaṇim, ellavara, ellavarôḷ* । *guṇavachane* । *iniyavu, iniyavam, iniyavarim, iniyavarkke, iniyavarattaṇim, iniyavara, iniyavarôḷ, ity âdi* ।

[But in pronouns and adjectives by *avu*.]

ಸೂತ್ರ ॥ ದ್ವಿತ್ವ ಬಹುತ್ವಯೋರ್ಗಳಾದೌ ॥ ೪೧ ॥

ವೃತ್ತಿ ॥ ತಾಸಾಂ ವಿಭಕ್ತೀನಾಮಾದೌ ದ್ವಿತ್ವ ಬಹುತ್ವ ವಿಷಯೇ ಗಳಾಗಮೋ ಭವತಿ ॥

ಪ್ರಯೋಗ ॥ ಕಣ್ಗಳ್ । ಕಣ್ಗಳಂ । ಕಣ್ಗಳಿಂ । ಕಣ್ಗಳ್ಗೆ । ಕಣ್ಗಳತ್ತಣಿಂ । ಕಣ್ಗಳ । ಕಣ್ಗಳೋಳ್ ॥

ತಾತ್ಪರ್ಯ ॥ ದ್ವಿವಚನ ಬಹುವಚನಗಳಲ್ಲಿ ಆ ವಿಭಕ್ತಿಗಳ ಆದಿಯೊಳಗೆ ಗಳ್ ಎಂಬುದು ಆಗಮವಾಗುತ್ತದೆ ಅಂದರೆ ಬರುತ್ತದೆ.

ಸೂತ್ರ ॥ ಸರ್ವನಾಮ ಗುಣವಚನಾನಾಮವು ತದನ್ತೇ ॥ ೪೨ ॥

ವೃತ್ತಿ ॥ ಸರ್ವನಾಮ್ನಾಂ ಗುಣವಚನಾನಾಂ ಚ ದ್ವಿತ್ವ ಬಹುತ್ವೇ ವಿವಕ್ಷಿತೇ ತೇಷಾಮನ್ತೇ ವಿಭಕ್ತಿಷು ಪರಾಭೂತಾಸು ಅವು ಭವತಿ ॥

ಪ್ರಯೋಗ ॥ ಅದು । ಇದು । ಉದು । ಆವುದು । ಎಲ್ಲದು । ಪೆರತು । ಪೆರದು । ಏನ್ । ಏತೇ ಸರ್ವನಾಮ ಶಬ್ದಾಃ । ಒಳ್ಳಿತು । ಮೆಲ್ಲಿತು । ಬೆಟ್ಟಿತು । ಇತ್ಯಾದಯೋ ಗುಣವಾಚಕ ಶಬ್ದಾಃ ॥

ಪ್ರಯೋಗ ॥ ಎಲ್ಲವು । ಎಲ್ಲವಂ । ಎಲ್ಲವರಿಂ । ಎಲ್ಲವರ್ಗ್ಗೆ । ಎಲ್ಲವರತ್ತಣಿಂ । ಎಲ್ಲವರ । ಎಲ್ಲವರೋಳ್ ॥ ಗುಣವಚನೇ ॥ ಇನಿಯವು । ಇನಿಯವಂ । ಇನಿಯವರಿಂ । ಇನಿಯವರ್ಕ್ಕೆ । ಇನಿಯವರತ್ತಣಿಂ । ಇನಿಯವರ । ಇನಿಯವರೋಳ್ ॥ ಇತ್ಯಾದಿ ॥

ತಾತ್ಪರ್ಯ ॥ ಸರ್ವನಾಮಗಳಿಗೂ ಗುಣವಾಚಕಗಳಿಗೂ ದ್ವಿವಚನ ಬಹುವಚನ ವಿವಕ್ಷಣೆ ಮಾಡುವಲ್ಲಿ ವಿಭಕ್ತಿ ಪ್ರತ್ಯಯಗಳಿಗೆ ಪೂರ್ವದಲ್ಲಿ ಅವು ಎಂಬುದು ಬರುತ್ತದೆ.

Sûtra 43.—*Strî-purusha-vâchishv ir-ar-dir-vir krachit.*

Vritti.—*Strî-purusha-vâchakeshu s'abdeshu vartamânânâm vibhaktînâm âdau krachit ir ar dir vir ity ete gaḷ âpavâdâs san nirdis'yante* |

Prayoga.—*Peṇḍir, taṭṭir, sallar, tammandir, tâyindir, aṇṇandir, tanderir* | *atra gaḷ api krachid bharati* | *magaḷ, aiyaṅgaḷ, appaṅgaḷ* | *krachid ubhayam cha* | *mâvaṅgaḷ, mâvandir, atteḡaḷ, attevir, ity âdi* |

[Words relating to men and women take *ir, ar, dir* or *vir* in some cases, instead of *gaḷ*. In some cases both.]

Sûtra 44.—*Svârthe'tah kaḷ.*

Vritti.—*Atah ebhyah param svârthe kaḷ bharati* |

Prayoga.—*Paṇḍitarkaḷ, sutarkaḷ, richâra pararkaḷ* | *kevalâd api krachid bharati* | *makkaḷ, nâṭkaḷ, kôḷkaḷ.*

[In others of this class *kaḷ* is used.]

Sûtra 45.—*Saṅkhyâyâm vah.*

Vritti.—*Saṅkhyâ-vâchaka-s'abdât parâsâm vibhaktînâm âdau vakâro bharati* |

Prayoga.—*Ôrvaḷ, irvaḷ, mûvar* |

[When numerals, the case termination is preceded by *v.*]

ಸೂತ್ರ || ಸ್ತ್ರೀ ಪುರುಷ ವಾಚಿಷ್ವಿರರ್ದಿರ್ವಿರ್ಕ್ವಚಿತ್ ||೪೩||

ವೃತ್ತಿ || ಸ್ತ್ರೀ ಪುರುಷ ವಾಚಕೇಷು ಶಬ್ದೇಷು ವರ್ತಮಾನಾನಾಂ ವಿಭಕ್ತೀನಾಮಾದೌ ಕ್ವಚಿತ್ ಇರ್ ಅರ್ ದಿರ್ ವಿರ್ ಇತ್ಯೇತೇ ಗಳಪವಾದಾಸ್ಸನ್ನಿರ್ದಿಶ್ಯಂತೇ ||

ಪ್ರಯೋಗ || ಪೆಂಡಿರ್ | ತಟ್ಟಿರ್ | ಸಲ್ಲರ್ | ತಮ್ಮಂದಿರ್ | ತಾಯಿಂದಿರ್ | ಅಣ್ಣಂದಿರ್ | ತಂದೆವಿರ್ | ಅತ್ರ ಗಳಪಿ ಕ್ವಚಿದ್ಭವತಿ || ಮಗಳ್ | ಐಯಂಗಳ್ | ಅಪ್ಪಂಗಳ್ | ಕ್ವಚಿದುಭಯಂ ಚ | ಮಾವಂಗಳ್, ಮಾವಂದಿರ್ | ಅತ್ತೆಗಳ್, ಅತ್ತೆವಿರ್ | ಇತ್ಯಾದಿ ||

ತಾತ್ಪರ್ಯ || ಸ್ತ್ರೀ ಪುರುಷವಾಚಕ ಶಬ್ದಗಳಲ್ಲಿನ ವಿಭಕ್ತಿಗಳ ಆದಿಯಲ್ಲಿ ಕೆಲವು ಕಡೆ ಇರ್, ಅರ್, ದಿರ್, ವಿರ್ ಎಂಬುವು ಗಳ್ ಎಂಬುವಕ್ಕೆ ಬದಲಾಗಿ ಬರುತ್ತವೆ. ಕೆಲವುಕಡೆ ಗಳ್ ಎಂಬುದೂ ಕೆಲವು ಕಡೆ ಎರಡೂ ಬರುತ್ತವೆ.

ಸೂತ್ರ || ಸ್ವಾರ್ಥೇ'ತಃ ಕಳ್ ||೪೪||

ವೃತ್ತಿ || ಅತಃ ಏಭ್ಯಃ ಪರಂ ಸ್ವಾರ್ಥೇ ಕಳ್ ಭವತಿ ||

ಪ್ರಯೋಗ || ಪಂಡಿತರ್ಕಳ್ | ಸುತರ್ಕಳ್ | ವಿಚಾರಪರರ್ಕಳ್ | ಕೇವಲಾದಪಿ ಕ್ವಚಿದ್ಭವತಿ | ಮಕ್ಕಳ್ | ನಾಟ್ಕಳ್ | ಕೋಳ್ಕಳ್ ||

ತಾತ್ಪರ್ಯ || ಇವುಗಳಲ್ಲದೆ ಇಂತ ಸ್ವಾರ್ಥದಲ್ಲಿ ಕಳ್ ಯೆಂಬುದು ಬರುತ್ತದೆ.

ಸೂತ್ರ || ಸಙ್ಖ್ಯಾಯಾಂ ವಃ ||೪೫||

ವೃತ್ತಿ || ಸಙ್ಖ್ಯಾವಾಚಕ ಶಬ್ದಾತ್ಪರಾಸಾಂ ವಿಭಕ್ತೀನಾಂ ಆದೌ ವಕಾರೋ ಭವತಿ ||

ಪ್ರಯೋಗ || ಓರ್ವಳ್ | ಇರ್ವಳ್ | ಮೂವರ್ ||

ತಾತ್ಪರ್ಯ || ಸಙ್ಖ್ಯಾವಾಚಕ ಶಬ್ದಕ್ಕೆ ಪರವಾದ ವಿಭಕ್ತಿಗಳಿಗೆ ಆದಿಯಲ್ಲಿ ವಕಾರಾಗಮವಾಗುತ್ತದೆ.

Sûtra 46.—*Ato'nusvârah prathamaika-vachanasya.*

Vritti.—*Akârântâl-lingât parasya* prathamâ-vibhakter eka-vachanasya anusvâro bhavati* |

Prayoga.—*Maram, dharmmam, dânam, evam âdi* |

[The first (nominative) case singular of words ending in *a*, becomes *anusvára*.]

Sûtra 47.—*Anyasmâl-lopah.*

Vritti.—*Anakârântâl-lingâd uttarasya prathamâ-vibhakter eka-vachanasya lopa eva syât* |

Prayoga.—*Hari, kari, nari, vidhu, vadhu, pitri, kere, tore* |

[In words not ending in *a*, it is omitted.]

Sûtra 48.—*Gunokter avâv upântyâvadheh.*

Vritti.—*Gunavachanasya s'abdasya avau pare upântyâvadher avayavasya lopas syât* |

Prayoga.—*Kariyavu, piriyavu, doddiyavu* | *bahulam ity anuvartate* | *doddidavu, ollidavu* |

[Adjectives, on taking *avu* (see 42), drop their last syllable. But in some cases not.]

ಸೂತ್ರ || ಅತೋ'ನುಸ್ವಾರಃ ಪ್ರಥಮೈಕವಚನಸ್ಯ || ೪೬ ||

ವೃತ್ತಿ || ಅಕಾರಾನ್ತಾಲ್ಲಿಙ್ಗಾತ್ಪರಸ್ಯ * ಪ್ರಥಮಾವಿಭಕ್ತೇರೇಕವಚನಸ್ಯ ಅನುಸ್ವಾರೋ ಭವತಿ ||

ಪ್ರಯೋಗ || ಮರಂ | ಧರ್ಮ್ಮಂ | ದಾನಂ | ಏವಮಾದಿ ||

ತಾತ್ಪರ್ಯ || ಅಕಾರಾನ್ತ ಶಬ್ದ ಪ್ರಥಮಾ ವಿಭಕ್ತಿಯ ಏಕವಚನಕ್ಕೆ ಅನುಸ್ವಾರವಾಗುತ್ತದೆ.

ಸೂತ್ರ || ಅನ್ಯಸ್ಮಾಲ್ಲೋಪಃ || ೪೭ ||

ವೃತ್ತಿ || ಅನಕಾರಾನ್ತಾಲ್ಲಿಙ್ಗಾದುತ್ತರಸ್ಯ ಪ್ರಥಮಾವಿಭಕ್ತೇರೇಕವಚನಸ್ಯ ಲೋಪ ಏವ ಸ್ಯಾತ್ ||

ಪ್ರಯೋಗ || ಹರಿ | ಕರಿ | ನರಿ | ವಿಧು | ವಧು | ಪಿತೃ | ಕೆರೆ | ತೊರೆ ||

ತಾತ್ಪರ್ಯ || ಅಕಾರಾನ್ತವಲ್ಲದ ಶಬ್ದಗಳ ಪ್ರಥಮಾ ವಿಭಕ್ತಿಯ ಏಕವಚನಕ್ಕೆ ಲೋಪವೇ ಆಗುತ್ತದೆ. ಅಂದರೆ ಪ್ರಕೃತಿಯೇ ನಿಲ್ಲುತ್ತದೆ. ಪ್ರತ್ಯಯವಿಲ್ಲವೆಂಬುವದು.

ಸೂತ್ರ || ಗುಣೋಕ್ತೇರವಾವುಪಾನ್ತ್ಯಾವಧೇಃ || ೪೮ ||

ವೃತ್ತಿ || ಗುಣವಚನಸ್ಯ ಶಬ್ದಸ್ಯ ಅವೌ ಪರೇ ಉಪಾನ್ತ್ಯಾವಧೇರವಯವಸ್ಯ ಲೋಪಸ್ಸ್ಯಾತ್ ||

ಪ್ರಯೋಗ || ಕರಿಯವು | ಪಿರಿಯವು | ದೊಡ್ಡಿಯವು || ಬಹುಳಮಿತ್ಯನುವರ್ತತೇ | ದೊಡ್ಡಿದವು | ಒಳ್ಳಿದವು ||

ತಾತ್ಪರ್ಯ || ನಲವತ್ತೆರಡನೇ ಸೂತ್ರದಿಂದ ಗುಣವಾಚಕಕ್ಕೆ ದ್ವಿತ್ವ ಬಹುತ್ವಗಳಲ್ಲಿ ಅವು ಬರಲಾಗಿ ಕಡೆಯ ವರ್ಣಕ್ಕೆ ಲೋಪವಾಗುವದು.

---

* In B *uttarasya*.

* ದ್ವಿ | ಲಿಙ್ಗಾದುತ್ತರಸ್ಯ ಎಂದು ಪಾಠವಿದೆ.

Sûtra 49.—*Sarvanâmnas tad-âder api.*

Vṛitti.—*Sarvanâma-samjñasya avau pare upântyasyâradher avu s'abdâdes cha lopo bhavati* ।

Prayoga.—*Avu, ivu, uvu, ellavu* ।

[Pronouns, on taking *avu*, drop their last syllable.]

Sûtra 50.—*Ad-antân-nâgamah pûrvasmin gaḷah.*

Vṛitti.—*Akârântâch-chhabda-rûpâd gaḷah pûrvasmin nakârâgamo bhavati* ।

Prayoga.—*Janaṅgal, hayaṅgal* । *bahuḷâdhikârât kvachid vikalpah* । *maraṅgaḷ, maragaḷ, phalaṅgaḷ, phalagaḷ* । *akârântâd iti kim* । *maḍigaḷ, manegaḷ, ûrgaḷ, sûlgaḷ* ।

[Words ending in *a*, take *n* before *gaḷ*. But not always.]

Sûtra 51.—*Svarâdau nâgamah pumsi.*

Vṛitti.—*Akârântât pulliṅgât svarâdi-vibhakti-gaṇe parato'vasthite nakârâgamo bhavati* ।

Prayoga.—*Arasanam kaṇḍar, sachivanam muñche, keḷeyana baladoḷ* ।

[Masculines ending in *a*, take *n* before a case termination beginning with a vowel.]

ಸೂತ್ರ ॥ ಸರ್ವನಾಮ್ನಸ್ತದಾದೇರಪಿ ॥ ೪೯ ॥

ವೃತ್ತಿ ॥ ಸರ್ವನಾಮಸಂಜ್ಞಸ್ಯ ಅವೌ ಪರೇ ಉಪಾನ್ತ್ಯಸ್ಯಾವಧೇರವುಶಬ್ದಾದೇಶ್ಚ ಲೋಪೋ ಭವತಿ ॥

ಪ್ರಯೋಗ ॥ ಅವು । ಇವು । ಉವು । ಎಲ್ಲವು ।

ತಾತ್ಪರ್ಯ ॥ ಸರ್ವನಾಮಕ್ಕೆ ಅವು ಬರಲಾಗಿ ಉ ಲೋಪವಾಗುವದು.

ಸೂತ್ರ ॥ ಅದನ್ತಾನ್ನಾಗಮಃ ಪೂರ್ವಸ್ಮಿನ್ ಗಳಃ ॥ ೫೦ ॥

ವೃತ್ತಿ ॥ ಅಕಾರಾನ್ತಾಚ್ಛಬ್ದರೂಪಾದ್ಗಳಃ ಪೂರ್ವಸ್ಮಿನ್ ನಕಾರಾಗಮೋ ಭವತಿ ॥

ಪ್ರಯೋಗ ॥ ಜನಂಗಳ್ । ಹಯಂಗಳ್ ॥ ಬಹುಳಾಧಿಕಾರಾತ್ಕ್ವಚಿದ್ವಿಕಲ್ಪಃ ॥ ಮರಂಗಳ್ । ಮರಗಳ್ । ಫಲಂಗಳ್ । ಫಲಗಳ್ ॥ ಅಕಾರಾನ್ತಾದಿತಿ ಕಿಂ ॥ ಮಡಿಗಳ್ । ಮನೆಗಳ್ । ಊರ್ಗಳ್ । ಸಾಲ್ಗಳ್ ॥

ತಾತ್ಪರ್ಯ ॥ ಅಕಾರಾನ್ತ ಶಬ್ದಕ್ಕೆ ಪರವಾಗಿ ದ್ವಿತ್ವ ಬಹುತ್ವಕ್ಕೆ ಬಂದ ಗಳ್ ಎಂಬದಕ್ಕೆ ಮೊದಲು ಪ್ರಕೃತಿಯ ಪರದಲ್ಲಿ ನಕಾರಾಗಮವಾಗುತ್ತದೆ. ಬಹುಳಾಧಿಕಾರದಿಂ ವಿಕಲ್ಪವೂ ಉಂಟು.

ಸೂತ್ರ ॥ ಸ್ವರಾದೌ ನಾಗಮಃ ಪುಂಸಿ ॥ ೫೧ ॥

ವೃತ್ತಿ ॥ ಅಕಾರಾನ್ತಾತ್ಪುಲ್ಲಿಙ್ಗಾತ್ಸ್ವರಾದಿ ವಿಭಕ್ತಿಗಣೇ ಪರತೋಽವಸ್ಥಿತೇ ನಕಾರಾಗಮೋ ಭವತಿ ॥

ಪ್ರಯೋಗ ॥ ಅರಸನಂ ಕಂಡರ್ । ಸಚಿವನಂ ಮುಂಚೆ । ಕೆಳೆಯನ ಬಲದೊಳ್ ॥

ತಾತ್ಪರ್ಯ ॥ ಅಕಾರಾನ್ತವಾದ ಪುಲ್ಲಿಙ್ಗ ಶಬ್ದದಲ್ಲಿ ಸ್ವರಾದಿಯಾಗಿರುವ ವಿಭಕ್ತಿಗಳು ಪರವಾದರೆ ಆ ವಿಭಕ್ತಿಗಳ ಸ್ವರದ ಮೊದಲಲ್ಲಿ ನಕಾರಾಗಮ ಬರುತ್ತದೆ.

Sûtra 52.—*Napumsaka-linge dah.*

Vritti.—*Napumsaka-linga-vishaye akârântât svarâdi-vibhakti-gane pare dakârâgamo bhavati* ।

Prayoga.—*Manadim bêgam, manadattanim bêgam, jaladôl tandam* ।

[Neuters similarly take *d*.]

Sûtra 53.—*Vibhâshâyâm amo ma-nau.*

Vritti.—*Dritiyaika-vachane napumsaka-lingâd akârântâd vibhâshâyâm makâra-nakârau bhavatah* । *Samskrita-s'abdasya makâra eva* ।

Prayoga.—*Kulamam, chalamam, nelamam, polamam, nelanam, polanam* ।

[In the second (accusative) case singular, they take *m* and *n*. If Sanskrit words, only *m*.]

Sûtra 54.—*Anusvârasya cha.*

Vritti.—*Padânte vartamânasyânusvârasya svare pare makâra-nakârâdes'au bhavatah* । *kvachid vakâras' cha* ।

Prayoga.—*Ivam adhika-balam, ivan-adhika-balam ; puravaram intidu, puravaran-intidu* ।

[A final *anusvâra*, uniting with an initial vowel, becomes *m* or *n* : sometimes *v*.]

ಸೂತ್ರ ॥ ನಪುಂಸಕ ಲಿಙ್ಗೇ ದಃ ॥ ೫೨ ॥

ವೃತ್ತಿ ॥ ನಪುಂಸಕ ಲಿಙ್ಗ ವಿಷಯೇ ಅಕಾರಾನ್ತಾತ್ಸ್ವರಾದಿ ವಿಭಕ್ತಿಗಣೇ ಪರೇ ದಕಾರಾಗಮೋ ಭವತಿ ॥

ಪ್ರಯೋಗ ॥ ಮನದಿಂ ಬೇಗಂ । ಮನದತ್ತಣಿಂ ಬೇಗಂ । ಜಲದೋಳ್ ತಂದಂ ॥

ತಾತ್ಪರ್ಯ ॥ ನಪುಂಸಕ ಲಿಙ್ಗದಲ್ಲಿ ವಿಭಕ್ತಿಗಳ ಸ್ವರದ ಮೊದಲಲ್ಲಿ ದಕಾರಾಗಮವಾಗುತ್ತದೆ.

ಸೂತ್ರ ॥ ವಿಭಾಷಾಯಾಮಮೋ ಮನೌ ॥ ೫೩ ॥

ವೃತ್ತಿ ॥ ದ್ವಿತೀಯೈಕವಚನೇ ನಪುಂಸಕ ಲಿಙ್ಗಾದಕಾರಾನ್ತಾದ್ವಿಭಾಷಾಯಾಂ ಮಕಾರನಕಾರೌ ಭವತಃ । ಸಂಸ್ಕೃತ ಶಬ್ದಸ್ಯ ಮಕಾರ ಏವ ॥

ಪ್ರಯೋಗ ॥ ಕುಲಮಂ । ಚಲಮಂ । ನೆಲಮಂ । ಪೊಲಮಂ । ನೆಲನಂ । ಪೊಲನಂ ॥

ತಾತ್ಪರ್ಯ ॥ ನಪುಂಸಕ ಲಿಙ್ಗದ ಅಕಾರಾನ್ತ ಶಬ್ದದ ದ್ವಿತೀಯೈಕವಚನಕ್ಕೆ ವಿಕಲ್ಪವಾಗಿ ಮಕಾರ ನಕಾರಗಳಾಗುವವು. ಸಂಸ್ಕೃತ ಶಬ್ದವಾಗಿದ್ದರೆ ಅದಕ್ಕೆ ಮಕಾರವೇ ಆಗುವದು.

ಸೂತ್ರ ॥ ಅನುಸ್ವಾರಸ್ಯ ಚ ॥ ೫೪ ॥

ವೃತ್ತಿ ॥ ಪದಾನ್ತೇ ವರ್ತಮಾನಸ್ಯಾನುಸ್ವಾರಸ್ಯ ಸ್ವರೇ ಪರೇ ಮಕಾರ ನಕಾರಾದೇಶೌ ಭವತಃ । ಕ್ವಚಿದ್ವಕಾರಶ್ಚ ॥

ಪ್ರಯೋಗ ॥ ಇವಂ ಅಧಿಕಬಲಂ, ಇವನಧಿಕಬಲಂ । ಪುರವರಂ-ಇಂತಿದು, ಪುರವರನಿಂತಿದು ॥

ತಾತ್ಪರ್ಯ ॥ ಪದಾನ್ತ್ಯದಲ್ಲಿನ ಸ್ವರಕ್ಕೆ ಸ್ವರಪರವಾದರೆ ಮಕಾರ ನಕಾರಗಳಾದೇಶಗಳಾಗುವವು. ಕೆಲವು ಕಡೆ ವಕಾರಾದೇಶವೂ ಉಂಟು.

Sûtra 55.—*Ukârântât tritîyâdishv in-âgamo bhavati.*

Vritti.—*Ukârântâl-lingât parâsu tritiyâdi-vibhaktishu in-âgamo bahuḷam bhavati* ǀ

Prayoga.—*Gururinim nîtijñam, manurinim migil, pempinoḷ sura-nagaram, guruvina manam* ǀ *bahuḷa-grahaṇât krachin na bhavati* ǀ *gurura matam, manura kulam* ǀ *bahuḷât krachin nityam* ǀ *maḍurinoḷ, gaḍurinoḷ, gururinoḷ, manurinoḷ* ǀ

[Words ending in *u*, take *in* before the third (instrumental) and remaining case terminations. But not always. In some cases it is essential.]

Sûtra 56.—*Ar ukârasya saṅkhyâ-sarvanâma-guṇavachaneshu.*

Vritti.—*Saṅkhyâ-sarvanâma-guṇavâchaka-vishaye vartamânasya s'abdasya sambandhina-ukârasya tritiyâdi-vibhakti-gaṇe pare ar-âdes'o bhavati* ǀ

Prayoga.—*Ondarim, eraḍarim, adarim, idarim, oḷḷidarim* ǀ

[Numerals, pronouns and adjectives similarly take *ar*.]

Sûtra 57.—*Dig-vâchibhyo'ṇ.*

Vritti.—*Dig-vâchakebhyas tritiyâdau pare ante aṇ bhavati* ǀ

Prayoga.—*Mûḍaṇim, paḍuvaṇim, baḍagaṇim, paḍuvaṇge, baḍagaṇge, teṅkaṇa des'eyim, baḍagaṇa des'eyim* ǀ

[Words relating to direction similarly take *aṇ*.]

ಸೂತ್ರ ॥ ಉಕಾರಾನ್ತಾತ್ತೃತೀಯಾದಿಷ್ವಿನಾಗಮೋ ಭವತಿ ॥ ೫೫ ॥

ವೃತ್ತಿ ॥ ಉಕಾರಾನ್ತಾಲ್ಲಿಙ್ಗಾತ್ಪರಾಸು ತೃತೀಯಾದಿವಿಭಕ್ತಿಷು ಇನಾಗಮೋ ಬಹುಳಂ ಭವತಿ ॥

ಪ್ರಯೋಗ ॥ ಗುರುವಿನಿಂ ನೀತಿಜ್ಞಂ । ಮನುವಿನಿಂ ಮಿಗಿಲ್ । ಪೆಂಪಿನೊಳ್ ಸುರನಗರಂ । ಗುರುವಿನ ಮನಂ ॥ ಬಹುಳ ಗ್ರಹಣಾತ್ಕ್ವಚಿನ್ನ ಭವತಿ ॥ ಗುರುವ ಮತಂ । ಮನುವ ಕುಲಂ ॥ ಬಹುಳಾತ್ಕ್ವಚಿನ್ನಿತ್ಯಂ ॥ ಮಡುವಿನೊಳ್ । ಗಡುವಿನೊಳ್ । ಗುರುವಿನೊಳ್ । ಮನುವಿನೊಳ್ ॥

ತಾತ್ಪರ್ಯ ॥ ಉಕಾರಾನ್ತ ಶಬ್ದಗಳಲ್ಲಿನ ತೃತೀಯಾದಿ ವಿಭಕ್ತಿಗಳಿಗೆ ಬಹುಳವಾಗಿ ಇನಾಗಮವಾಗುತ್ತದೆ. ಬಹುಳಾಧಿಕಾರದಿಂದ ಕೆಲವು ಕಡೆ ಇನಾಗಮವಿಲ್ಲ. ಕೆಲವು ಕಡೆ ಇನಾಗಮವು ನಿತ್ಯವು.

ಸೂತ್ರ ॥ ಅರುಕಾರಸ್ಯ ಸಙ್ಖ್ಯಾ ಸರ್ವನಾಮ ಗುಣವಚನೇಷು ॥ ೫೬ ॥

ವೃತ್ತಿ ॥ ಸಙ್ಖ್ಯಾ ಸರ್ವನಾಮ ಗುಣವಾಚಕ ವಿಷಯೇ ವರ್ತಮಾನಸ್ಯ ಶಬ್ದಸ್ಯ ಸಮ್ಬನ್ಧಿನ ಉಕಾರಸ್ಯ ತೃತೀಯಾದಿ ವಿಭಕ್ತಿಗಣೇ ಪರೇ ಅರಾದೇಶೋ ಭವತಿ ॥

ಪ್ರಯೋಗ ॥ ಒಂದರಿಂ । ಎರಡರಿಂ । ಅದರಿಂ । ಇದರಿಂ । ಒಳ್ಳಿದರಿಂ ॥

ತಾತ್ಪರ್ಯ ॥ ಸಂಖ್ಯಾವಾಚಕ ಸರ್ವನಾಮ ಗುಣವಾಚಕ ಶಬ್ದಗಳಲ್ಲಿನ ಉಕಾರಕ್ಕೆ ತೃತೀಯಾದಿ ವಿಭಕ್ತಿಗಳು ಪರವಾದಾಗ ಅರಾದೇಶವಾಗುತ್ತದೆ.

ಸೂತ್ರ ॥ ದಿಗ್ವಾಚಿಭ್ಯೋಽಣ್ ॥ ೫೭ ॥

ವೃತ್ತಿ ॥ ದಿಗ್ವಾಚಕೇಭ್ಯಸ್ತೃತೀಯಾದೌ ಪರೇ ಅನ್ತೇ ಅಣ್ಭವತಿ ॥

ಪ್ರಯೋಗ ॥ ಮೂಡಣಿಂ । ಪಡುವಣಿಂ । ಬಡಗಣಿಂ । ಪಡುವಣ್ಗೆ । ಬಡಗಣ್ಗೆ । ತೆಂಕಣ ದೆಸೆಯಿಂ । ಬಡಗಣ ದೆಸೆಯಿಂ ॥

ತಾತ್ಪರ್ಯ ॥ ದಿಗ್ವಾಚಕ ಶಬ್ದಗಳಿಗೆ ತೃತೀಯಾದಿ ವಿಭಕ್ತಿಗಳು ಪರವಾದರೆ ಅನ್ತ್ಯದಲ್ಲಿ ಅಣ್ ಎಂಬಾದೇಶವಾಗುತ್ತದೆ.

Sûtra 58.—*Vâl atah prathamâ-dvitîyayoh.*

Vritti.—*Akârântâd dig-vâchinah prathamâ-dvitîyayor al vâ bhavati* ।

Prayoga.—*Mûḍal, mûḍa, paḍuval, paḍuva, teṅkal, teṅka, baḍagal, baḍaga* ।

[But those ending in *a* take *al* in the first (nominative) and second (accusative) cases.]

Sûtra 59.—*Saptamyâm cha.*

Vritti.—*Saptamî-vibhaktau parâyâm akârântâd dig-vâchino vâ tad al bhavati* ।

Prayoga.—*Teṅkaliriddam, teṅkiriddam, vattaliriddam, vattiriddam* ।

[Also in the seventh (locative) case.]

Sûtra 60.—*Uta et.*

Vritti.—*Digvâchi-sambandhina-ukârasya saptamî-vibhaktau parâyâm ed bhavati* ।

Prayoga.—*Mêgiriddudu, keḷage pôdam, oḷage beḷagu, porage kattale* । *uta iti kim* । *ittal, attal, ettal* ।

[But *e* in this case when they end in *u*.]

ಸೂತ್ರ ॥ ವಾಲತಃ ಪ್ರಥಮಾದ್ವಿತೀಯಯೋಃ ॥ ೫೮ ॥

ವೃತ್ತಿ ॥ ಅಕಾರಾನ್ತಾದ್ದಿಗ್ವಾಚಿನಃ ಪ್ರಥಮಾದ್ವಿತೀಯಯೋರಲ್ವಾ ಭವತಿ ॥

ಪ್ರಯೋಗ ॥ ಮೂಡಲ್ । ಮೂಡ । ಪಡುವಲ್ । ಪಡುವ । ತೆಂಕಲ್ । ತೆಂಕ । ಬಡಗಲ್ । ಬಡಗ ॥

ತಾತ್ಪರ್ಯ ॥ ಅಕಾರಾನ್ತ ದಿಗ್ವಾಚಿ ಶಬ್ದಗಳ ಪ್ರಥಮ ದ್ವಿತೀಯೇ ವಿಭಕ್ತಿಗಳಿಗೆ ವಿಕಲ್ಪವಾಗಿ ಅಲ್ ಎಂಬಾದೇಶವಾಗುವದು.

ಸೂತ್ರ ॥ ಸಪ್ತಮ್ಯಾಂ ಚ ॥ ೫೯ ॥

ವೃತ್ತಿ ॥ ಸಪ್ತಮೀವಿಭಕ್ತೌ ಪರಾಯಾಮಕಾರಾನ್ತಾದ್ದಿಗ್ವಾಚಿನೋ ವಾ ತದಲ್ ಭವತಿ ॥

ಪ್ರಯೋಗ ॥ ತೆಂಕಲಿರ್ದ್ದಂ । ತೆಂಕಿರ್ದ್ದಂ । ವತ್ತಲಿರ್ದ್ದಂ । ವತ್ತಿರ್ದ್ದಂ ॥

ತಾತ್ಪರ್ಯ ॥ ಅಕಾರಾನ್ತ ದಿಗ್ವಾಚಕ ಶಬ್ದಕ್ಕೆ ಸಪ್ತಮೀ ವಿಭಕ್ತಿ ಪರವಾದರೆ ವಿಕಲ್ಪವಾಗಿ ಅಲ್ ಎಂಬದಾಗುತ್ತದೆ.

ಸೂತ್ರ ॥ ಉತ ಏತ್ ॥ ೬೦ ॥

ವೃತ್ತಿ ॥ ದಿಗ್ವಾಚಿ ಸಮ್ಬನ್ಧಿನ ಉಕಾರಸ್ಯ ಸಪ್ತಮೀ ವಿಭಕ್ತೌ ಪರಾಯಾಮೇದ್ಭವತಿ ॥

ಪ್ರಯೋಗ ॥ ಮೇಗಿರ್ದ್ದುದು । ಕೆಳಗೆ ಪೋದಂ । ಒಳಗೆ ಬೆಳಗು । ಪೊರಗೆ ಕತ್ತಲೆ ॥ ಉತ ಇತಿ ಕಿಂ ॥ ಇತ್ತಲ್ । ಅತ್ತಲ್ । ಎತ್ತಲ್ ॥

ತಾತ್ಪರ್ಯ ॥ ದಿಗ್ವಾಚಿ ಸಮ್ಬನ್ಧವಾದ ಉಕಾರಕ್ಕೆ ಸಪ್ತಮೀ ವಿಭಕ್ತಿ ಪರವಾದರೆ ಏಕಾರ ಬರುತ್ತದೆ. ಉಕಾರಕ್ಕೆಂಬದು ನಿತ್ಯಾರ್ಥಸೂಚಕಂ.

Sûtra 61.—* *Dam tṛitîyâyâḥ.*

Vṛitti.—*Tṛitîyâ-vibhakty-antasya s'abdasya tad ante dam bhavati* ‖

Prayoga.—*Dharmmadindam, dânadindam, dayeyindam, kuḍipindam* ‖

[*Dam* is added to the termination of the third (instrumental) case.]

Sûtra 62.—*Ed-antatâ cha.*

Vṛitti.—*Tṛitîyântasya s'abdasya ekârântatâ bhavati* ‖ *anusvâra-hînam kvachit kevalam daḥ* ‖

Prayoga.—*Adarinde, idarinda, yadṛichchheyinde, santushṭiyinda* ‖ *gadadinde bagedantâge Surendranim kramade kalyâṇa drayam* ‖

[Sometimes *de* is used, sometimes *da* without the anusvâra.]

Sûtra 63.—*Akârântâch-chaturthyâs tṛitîyo'nusvâra-pûrvah pumsi.*

Vṛitti.—*Akârântâl-lingât parasyâs' chaturthyâh pumsi tṛitîyo varṇo'nusvâra-pûrvo bhavati* ‖

Prayoga.—*Indrange, chandrange, narendrange, perange, magange* ‖

[In masculines ending in *a*, the fourth (dative) case termination is the third *varga* letter (*g*) preceded by anusvâra.]

ಸೂತ್ರ ‖ *ದಂ ತೃತೀಯಾಯಾಃ ‖ ೬೧ ‖

ವೃತ್ತಿ ‖ ತೃತೀಯಾವಿಭಕ್ತ್ಯಂತಸ್ಯ ಶಬ್ದಸ್ಯ ತದನ್ತೇ ದಂ ಭವತಿ ‖

ಪ್ರಯೋಗ ‖ ಧರ್ಮ್ಮದಿಂದಂ । ದಾನದಿಂದಂ । ದಯೆಯಿಂದಂ । ಕುಡಿಪಿಂದಂ ‖

ತಾತ್ಪರ್ಯ ‖ ಶಬ್ದದ ತೃತೀಯಾವಿಭಕ್ತಿಯ ಅಂತ್ಯದಲ್ಲಿ ದಂ ಎಂಬದು ಆಗುತ್ತದೆ.

ಸೂತ್ರ ‖ ಎದನ್ತತಾ ಚ ‖ ೬೨ ‖

ವೃತ್ತಿ ‖ ತೃತೀಯಾನ್ತಸ್ಯ ಶಬ್ದಸ್ಯ ಎಕಾರಾನ್ತತಾ ಭವತಿ । ಅನುಸ್ವಾರ ಹೀನಂ ಕ್ವಚಿತ್ಕೇವಲಂ ದಃ ‖

ಪ್ರಯೋಗ ‖ ಅದರಿಂದೆ । ಇದರಿಂದ । ಯದೃಚ್ಛೆಯಿಂದೆ । ಸಂತುಷ್ಟಿಯಿಂದ । ಗದದಿಂದೆ ಬಗೆದಂತಾಗೆ ಸುರೇಂದ್ರನಿಂ ಕ್ರಮದ ಕಲ್ಯಾಣದ್ವಯಂ ‖

ತಾತ್ಪರ್ಯ ‖ ಶಬ್ದದ ತೃತೀಯಾ ವಿಭಕ್ತಿಯ ಅನ್ತ್ಯದಲ್ಲಿ ಬರುವ ದಕಾರಕ್ಕೆ ಎತ್ವವಾಗುತ್ತದೆ. ಕೆಲವುಕಡೆ ಅನುಸ್ವಾರವಿಲ್ಲದೆ ದಕಾರ ಮಾತ್ರ ಬರುತ್ತದೆ.

ಸೂತ್ರ ‖ ಅಕಾರಾನ್ತಾಚ್ಚತುರ್ಥ್ಯಾಸ್ತೃತೀಯೋ'ನುಸ್ವಾರಪೂರ್ವಃ ಪುಂಸಿ ‖ ೬೩ ‖

ವೃತ್ತಿ ‖ ಅಕಾರಾನ್ತಾಲ್ಲಿಙ್ಗಾತ್ಪರಸ್ಯಾಶ್ಚತುರ್ಥ್ಯಾಃ ಪುಂಸಿ ತೃತೀಯೋ ವರ್ಣೋ'ನುಸ್ವಾರ ಪೂರ್ವೋ ಭವತಿ ‖

ಪ್ರಯೋಗ ‖ ಇಂದ್ರಂಗೆ । ಚಂದ್ರಂಗೆ । ನರೇಂದ್ರಂಗೆ । ಪೆರಂಗೆ । ಮಗಂಗೆ ‖

ತಾತ್ಪರ್ಯ ‖ ಅಕಾರಾನ್ತ ಪುಲ್ಲಿಂಗಶಬ್ದದ ಚತುರ್ಥೀವಿಭಕ್ತಿಯಲ್ಲಿನ ಕವರ್ಗದ ಮೂರನೇ ವರ್ಣವು ಪೂರ್ವದಲ್ಲಿ ಅನುಸ್ವಾರವನ್ನುಳ್ಳದ್ದಾಗುತ್ತದೆ.

---

* In B the sûtra begins with *ante.*

* ದ್ವಿ । ಅನ್ತೇ ಎಂಬದು ಸೂತ್ರಾದಿಯಲ್ಲಿ ಸೇರಿಸಿ ಇದೆ.

Sûtra 64.—*Vâ napumsakâd dvitvam.*

Vṛitti.—*Napumsaka-vishayâd akârântât paratra vyavasthitâyâs' chaturthyâh dvitvam vâ bhavati* ।

Prayoga.—*Kulakke, kulake ; chalakke, chalake; manakke, manake ; jauvanakke, jauvanake; matakke, matake* ।

[But in neuters ending in *a* it may optionally be doubled.]

Sûtra 65.—*S'eshât tṛitîyatvam.*

Vṛitti.—*Akârântâd anyasmâch-chheshâch-chhabdarûpât parasyâs' chaturthyâh tṛitîyatvam eva bhavati* ।

Prayoga.—*Matige, yatige, naḍuge, giḍuge, ûrge, nîrge* ।

[In all other words it becomes *ge.*]

Sûtra 66.—*Sarvanâmno'liṅgât ko vâ.*

Vṛitti.—*Aliṅgât sarvanâmnah parâyâs' chaturthî-vibhakteh pûrvah kakâro bhavati vâ* ।

Prayoga.—*Adakke, adake; idakke, idake* ।

[Save in neuter pronouns, which have *ke.*]

ಸೂತ್ರ ॥ ವಾ ನಪುಂಸಕಾದ್ದ್ವಿತ್ವಂ ॥ ೬೪ ॥

ವೃತ್ತಿ ॥ ನಪುಂಸಕವಿಷಯಾದಕಾರಾನ್ತಾತ್ಪರತ್ರ ವ್ಯವಸ್ಥಿತಾಯಾಶ್ಚತುರ್ಥ್ಯಾಃ ದ್ವಿತ್ವಂ ವಾ ಭವತಿ ॥

ಪ್ರಯೋಗ ॥ ಕುಲಕ್ಕೆ, ಕುಲಕೆ । ಚಲಕ್ಕೆ, ಚಲಕೆ । ಮನಕ್ಕೆ, ಮನಕೆ । ಜೌವನಕ್ಕೆ, ಜೌವನಕೆ । ಮತಕ್ಕೆ, ಮತಕೆ ॥

ತಾತ್ಪರ್ಯ ॥ ಅಕಾರಾನ್ತ ನಪುಂಸಕ ಲಿಙ್ಗದ ಚತುರ್ಥೀ ವಿಭಕ್ತಿಯ ಅನ್ತ್ಯ ವರ್ಣಕ್ಕೆ ವಿಕಲ್ಪವಾಗಿ ದ್ವಿತ್ವವಾದರೂ ಆಗುತ್ತದೆ.

ಸೂತ್ರ ॥ ಶೇಷಾತ್ತೃತೀಯತ್ವಂ ॥ ೬೫ ॥

ವೃತ್ತಿ ॥ ಅಕಾರಾನ್ತಾದನ್ಯಸ್ಮಾಚ್ಛೇಷಾಚ್ಛಬ್ದರೂಪಾತ್ಪರಸ್ಯಾಶ್ಚತುರ್ಥ್ಯಾಃ ತೃತೀಯತ್ವಮೇವ ಭವತಿ ॥

ಪ್ರಯೋಗ ॥ ಮತಿಗೆ । ಯತಿಗೆ । ನಡುಗೆ । ಗಿಡುಗೆ । ಊರ್ಗೆ । ನೀರ್ಗೆ ॥

ತಾತ್ಪರ್ಯ ॥ ಅಕಾರಾನ್ತವಲ್ಲದ ಇತರ ಶಬ್ದಗಳ ಚತುರ್ಥೀ ವಿಭಕ್ತಿಗೆ ತೃತೀಯಾಕ್ಷರವಾದ ಗೆ ಯೆಂಬುದೇ ಆಗುವದು.

ಸೂತ್ರ ॥ ಸರ್ವನಾಮ್ನೋ’ ಲಿಙ್ಗಾತ್ಕೋ ವಾ ॥ ೬೬ ॥

ವೃತ್ತಿ ॥ ಅಲಿಙ್ಗಾತ್ಸರ್ವನಾಮ್ನಃ ಪರಾಯಾಶ್ಚತುರ್ಥೀ ವಿಭಕ್ತೇಃ ಪೂರ್ವಃ ಕಕಾರೋ ಭವತಿ ವಾ ॥

ಪ್ರಯೋಗ ॥ ಅದಕ್ಕೆ, ಅದಕೆ । ಇದಕ್ಕೆ, ಇದಕೆ ॥

ತಾತ್ಪರ್ಯ ॥ ನಪುಂಸಕ ಸರ್ವನಾಮ ಶಬ್ದದ ಚತುರ್ಥೀ ವಿಭಕ್ತಿಗೆ ವಿಕಲ್ಪವಾಗಿ ಕಕಾರವಾಗುತ್ತದೆ.

Sûtra 67.—*Attaṇim tv-anusandheyah pañchamyâh.*

Vṛitti.—*Pañchamy-antasyâbhivyaktaye punas tad ante attaṇim ity anusandheyah* ।

Prayoga.—*Ûrattaṇim bandam, avanattaṇim bhayam, kereyattaṇim tandam* ।

[*Attaṇim* is added to distinguish the fifth (ablative) case termination.]

Sûtra 68.—*Dirghâdês'ash shashṭhyâ yatheshṭam.*

Vṛitti.—*Shashṭhy-antasya s'abdasya dirghâdes'ah kâmachârato vidhâtavyah* ।

Prayoga.—*Narendranâ parijanam, pêrmme dharmmadâ, lokam âkânteyâ* । *yatheshṭatvât kvachid dirgho na* । *madanana kaidu, chandrana kânti, vasantana sobagu* ।

[The final letter of the sixth (genitive) case may be long at will.]

Sûtra 69.—*Dvitîyântasya vâ svare.*

Vṛitti.—*Dvitîyâ-vibhakty-antasya svare pare dirgho vâ bhavati* ।

Prayoga.—*Haripâlasya prayogah* * । *kallân êridam, billân êrisidam* । *tathâ Guṇa-varmma-kaver Bhuvanaika-vîrasya prayogah* * । *vams'astha vṛittam* ।

Enitt enitt ambuja patra nêtreyâ ।
ghana stanaṅgaḷ baḷeyaḷ kirâteyâ ॥
Anitt anittam vanadoḷ vanê-charam ।
tanattu billân adan antu kisugum ॥ *iti* ॥

[When followed by a vowel, the termination of the second (accusative) case may become long.]

ಸೂತ್ರ ॥ ಅತ್ತಣಿಂ ತ್ವನುಸನ್ಧೇಯಃ ಪಞ್ಚಮ್ಯಾಃ ॥ ೬೭ ॥

ವೃತ್ತಿ ॥ ಪಞ್ಚಮ್ಯನ್ತಸ್ಯಾಭಿವ್ಯಕ್ತಯೇ ಪುನಸ್ತದನ್ತೇ ಅತ್ತಣಿಮಿತ್ಯನುಸನ್ಧೇಯಃ ॥

ಪ್ರಯೋಗ ॥ ಊರತ್ತಣಿಂ ಬಂದಂ । ಅವನತ್ತಣಿಂ ಭಯಂ । ಕೆರೆಯತ್ತಣಿಂ ತಂದಂ ॥

ತಾತ್ಪರ್ಯ ॥ ಪಂಚಮೀ ವಿಭಕ್ತಿಯು ಸ್ಪಷ್ಟವಾಗಿ ಕಾಣುವದಕ್ಕಾಗಿ ವಿಭಕ್ತಿಯ ಅಂತ್ಯದಲ್ಲಿ ಅತ್ತಣಿಂ ಎಂಬದನ್ನು ಸೇರಿಸಬೇಕು.

ಸೂತ್ರ ॥ ದೀರ್ಘಾದೇಶಷ್ಷಷ್ಠ್ಯಾ ಯಥೇಷ್ಟಂ ॥ ೬೮ ॥

ವೃತ್ತಿ ॥ ಷಷ್ಠ್ಯನ್ತಸ್ಯ ಶಬ್ದಸ್ಯ ದೀರ್ಘಾದೇಶಃ ಕಾಮಚಾರತೋ ವಿಧಾತವ್ಯಃ ॥

ಪ್ರಯೋಗ ॥ ನರೇಂದ್ರನಾ ಪರಿಜನಂ । ಪೆರ್ಮ್ಮೆ ಧರ್ಮ್ಮದಾ । ಲೋಕಮಾಕಾಂತೆಯಾ ॥ ಯಥೇಷ್ಟತ್ವಾತ್ಕ್ವಚಿದ್ದೀರ್ಘೋ ನ ॥ ಮದನನ ಕೈದು । ಚಂದ್ರನ ಕಾಂತಿ । ವಸಂತನ ಸೊಬಗು ॥

ತಾತ್ಪರ್ಯ ॥ ಶಬ್ದದ ಷಷ್ಠೀ ವಿಭಕ್ತಿಗೆ ಇಷ್ಟವಿದ್ದಲ್ಲಿ ದೀರ್ಘಾದೇಶ ಮಾಡಲಾಗುವದು. ಯಥೇಷ್ಟವೆಂದು ಸೂತ್ರಕಾರರ ತಾತ್ಪರ್ಯವಿರುವದರಿಂದ ಕೆಲವು ಕಡೆ ದೀರ್ಘವಿಲ್ಲ.

ಸೂತ್ರ ॥ ದ್ವಿತೀಯಾನ್ತಸ್ಯ ವಾ ಸ್ವರೇ ॥ ೬೯ ॥

ವೃತ್ತಿ ॥ ದ್ವಿತೀಯಾ ವಿಭಕ್ತ್ಯನ್ತಸ್ಯ ಸ್ವರೇ ಪರೇ ದೀರ್ಘೋ ವಾ ಭವತಿ ॥

ಪ್ರಯೋಗ ॥ ಹರಿಪಾಲಸ್ಯ ಪ್ರಯೋಗಃ * ॥ ಕಲ್ಲಾನೇರಿದಂ । ಬಿಲ್ಲಾನೇರಿಸಿದಂ ॥ ತಥಾ ಗುಣವರ್ಮ್ಮಕವೇರ್ಭುವನೈಕವೀರಸ್ಯ ಪ್ರಯೋಗಃ * ॥ ವಂಶಸ್ಥ ವೃತ್ತಂ ॥

ಎನಿತ್ತನಿತ್ತಂಬುಜ ಪತ್ರನೇತ್ರೆಯಾ ।
ಘನಸ್ತನಂಗಳ್ ಬಳೆಯಳ್ಕಿರಾತೆಯಾ ॥
ಅನಿತ್ತನಿತ್ತಂ ವನದೊಳ್ ವನೇಚರಂ ।
ತನತ್ತು ಬಿಲ್ಲಾನದನಂತು ಕೀಸುಗುಂ ॥ ಇತಿ ॥

ತಾತ್ಪರ್ಯ ॥ ದ್ವಿತೀಯಾ ವಿಭಕ್ತಿಯ ಅಂತ್ಯಕ್ಕೆ ಸ್ವರ ಪರವಾದರೆ ವಿಕಲ್ಪವಾಗಿ ದೀರ್ಘವಾದರೂ ಆಗುತ್ತದೆ.

---

* Not in C. Guṇa-varmma was the author of a *Harivams'a* in Kannaḍa.

* ತೃ ॥ ಈ ಪ್ರಯೋಗಗಳು ಇಲ್ಲ.

Sûtra 70.—*Saptamyâ alli vâ.*

Vritti.—*Linga-samjñâyâm nihitâyâm saptamyâs sthâne alliti vâ bhavati* ।

Prayoga.—*Manadalli, manadol; banadalli, banadol* ।

[The seventh (locative) case termination may optionally become *alli.*]

Sûtra 71.—*Âmantrage prathamaika-vachanasya lopah.*

Vritti.—*Âmantranârthe vihitasya prathamaika-vachanasya lopa eva bhavati* ।

Prayoga.—*Ele annâ, ele akkâ* ।

[The first (nominative) case of address (vocative) is without termination.]

Sûtra 72.—*Etvam vâ tad antasya.*

Vritti.—*Âmantranârthe vartamânasya prathamâ-vibhaktyaika-vachanasya etvam vâ bhavati* ।

Prayoga.—*Mâle malligeye, tâmbelere, kolane* । *vâ s'abdo'yam vyavasthita vibhâshâyâm vartamâno grihyate* । *atah ele deva, ele bhûpa* ।

[Or it may become e]

ಸೂತ್ರ ॥ ಸಪ್ತಮ್ಯಾ ಅಲ್ಲಿ ವಾ ॥ ೭೦ ॥

ವೃತ್ತಿ ॥ ಲಿಙ್ಗ ಸಂಜ್ಞಾಯಾಂ ನಿಹಿತಾಯಾಂ ಸಪ್ತಮ್ಯಾಸ್ಸ್ಥಾನೇ ಅಲ್ಲೀತಿ ವಾ ಭವತಿ ॥

ಪ್ರಯೋಗ ॥ ಮನದಲ್ಲಿ, ಮನದೊಳ್ । ಬನದಲ್ಲಿ, ಬನದೊಳ್ ॥

ತಾತ್ಪರ್ಯ ॥ ತ್ರಿಲಿಙ್ಗಗಳಲ್ಲಿಯೂ ಸಪ್ತಮೀ ವಿಭಕ್ತಿಗೆ ವಿಕಲ್ಪವಾಗಿ ಅಲ್ಲಿ ಯೆಂಬದಾಗುತ್ತದೆ.

ಸೂತ್ರ ॥ ಆಮನ್ತ್ರಣೇ ಪ್ರಥಮೈಕ ವಚನಸ್ಯ ಲೋಪಃ ॥ ೭೧ ॥

ವೃತ್ತಿ ॥ ಆಮನ್ತ್ರಣಾರ್ಥೇ ವಿಹಿತಸ್ಯ ಪ್ರಥಮೈಕ ವಚನಸ್ಯ ಲೋಪ ಏವ ಭವತಿ ॥

ಪ್ರಯೋಗ ॥ ಎಲೆ ಅಣ್ಣಾ । ಎಲೆ ಅಕ್ಕಾ ॥

ತಾತ್ಪರ್ಯ ॥ ಆಮನ್ತ್ರಣಾರ್ಥದಲ್ಲಿನ ಪ್ರಥಮೈಕ ವಚನಕ್ಕೆ ಲೋಪವೇ ಆಗುತ್ತದೆ.

ಸೂತ್ರ ॥ ಏತ್ವಂ ವಾ ತದನ್ತಸ್ಯ ॥ ೭೨ ॥

ವೃತ್ತಿ ॥ ಆಮನ್ತ್ರಣಾರ್ಥೇ ವರ್ತಮಾನಸ್ಯ ಪ್ರಥಮಾ ವಿಭಕ್ತ್ಯೈಕವಚನಸ್ಯ ಏತ್ವಂ ವಾ ಭವತಿ ॥

ಪ್ರಯೋಗ ॥ ಮಾಲೆ ಮಲ್ಲಿಗೆಯೆ । ತಾಂಬೆಲೆರೆ । ಕೊಳನೆ ॥ ವಾ ಶಬ್ದೋ'ಯಂ ವ್ಯವಸ್ಥಿತ ವಿಭಾಷಾಯಾಂ ವರ್ತಮಾನೋ ಗೃಹ್ಯತೇ । ಅತಃ ಎಲೆ ದೇವ । ಎಲೆ ಭೂಪ ॥

ತಾತ್ಪರ್ಯ ॥ ಆಮನ್ತ್ರಣಾರ್ಥದ ಪ್ರಥಮಾ ವಿಭಕ್ತ್ಯೈಕ ವಚನಕ್ಕೆ ಏತ್ವವಾದರೂ ಆಗುತ್ತದೆ. ವಾ ಶಬ್ದದಿಂದ ಎಲೆ ದೇವ ಎಲೆ ಭೂಪ ಇತ್ಯಾದಿ ವಿಭಾಷೆಯಲ್ಲಿನ ಪ್ರತಿಷೇಧಕ ದೃಷ್ಟಾಂತ ಸೂಚಕ ವಾಗುತ್ತದೆ.

Sûtra 73.—*Irâslesho gaḷah.*

Vṛitti.—*Sambodhana-vishaye dvitva-bahutve vartamânasya gaḷ-antasya irâslesho bhavati* ।

Prayoga.—*Daiyvaṅgaḷira, maraṅgaḷira, nandanaṅgaḷira, neṇṭargaḷira* ।

[In the vocative dual and plural, *gaḷ* is followed by *ira.*]

Sûtra 74.—*Dirghoktir Naya-senasya.*

Vṛitti.—*Sambodhanârthe vartamânasya sarvasyâpi s'abda-rûpasya Naya-sena-muner mate dîrgho bhavati* ।

Prayoga.—*Dêvâ binnapam, dêva binnapam; sugî, sugi; vidhû, vidhu; kântê kânte; giḷigaḷirâ, giḷigaḷira* ।

[According to Naya Sena*, the vocative termination should always be long.]

Iti Karṇâṭaka-vyâkaraṇa-vṛittau† Bhâshâ-bhûshaṇe Vibhakti-vidhânam nâma tritîyah parichchhedah ।

ಸೂತ್ರ ॥ ಇರಾಶ್ಲೇಷೋ ಗಳಃ ॥ ೭೩ ॥

ವೃತ್ತಿ ॥ ಸಮ್ಬೋಧನ ವಿಷಯೇ ದ್ವಿತ್ವ ಬಹುತ್ವೇ ವರ್ತಮಾನಸ್ಯ ಗಳನ್ತಸ್ಯ ಇರಾಶ್ಲೇಷೋ ಭವತಿ ॥

ಪ್ರಯೋಗ ॥ ದೈಯ್ವಂಗಳಿರ । ಮರಂಗಳಿರ । ನಂದನಂಗಳಿರ । ನೆಂಟರ್ಗಳಿರ ॥

ತಾತ್ಪರ್ಯ ॥ ಸಂಬೋಧನ ವಿಷಯದಲ್ಲಿ ದ್ವಿವಚನ ಬಹುವಚನಗಳಲ್ಲಿನ ಗಳನ್ತ್ಯಕ್ಕೆ ಇರ ಯೆಂಬುದು ಸೇರುತ್ತದೆ.

ಸೂತ್ರ ॥ ದೀರ್ಘೋಕ್ತಿರ್ನಯಸೇನಸ್ಯ ॥ ೭೪ ॥

ವೃತ್ತಿ ॥ ಸಮ್ಬೋಧನಾರ್ಥೇ ವರ್ತಮಾನಸ್ಯ ಸರ್ವಸ್ಯಾಪಿ ಶಬ್ದರೂಪಸ್ಯ ನಯಸೇನಮುನೇರ್ಮತೇ ದೀರ್ಘೋ ಭವತಿ ॥

ಪ್ರಯೋಗ ॥ ದೇವಾ ಬಿನ್ನಪಂ, ದೇವ ಬಿನ್ನಪಂ । ಸುಗೀ, ಸುಗಿ । ವಿಧೂ, ವಿಧು । ಕಾಂತೇ, ಕಾಂತೆ । ಗಿಳಿಗಳಿರಾ, ಗಿಳಿಗಳಿರ ॥

ತಾತ್ಪರ್ಯ ॥ ನಯಸೇನ ಮುನಿ ಮತಾನುಸಾರವಾಗಿ ಸಂಬೋಧನದಲ್ಲಿ ದೀರ್ಘವಾಗುತ್ತದೆ.

ಇತಿ ಕರ್ಣಾಟಕ ವ್ಯಾಕರಣ ವೃತ್ತೌ† ಭಾಷಾಭೂಷಣೇ ವಿಭಕ್ತಿ ವಿಧಾನಂ ನಾಮ ತೃತೀಯಃ ಪರಿಚ್ಛೇದಃ ॥

---

* Naya Sena was the author of *Dharmmâmṛita*, which he finished in A. D. 1115.

† See note p. 7. ೭ನೇ ಪುಟವನ್ನ ನೋಡಬೇಕು.

(IV. Uses of the Cases.)

Kâraka Vidhânam.

Sûtra 75.—*Atha kârakam nirûpyate.*

Vritti.—*Samjña-sandhi-vibhakti-niyam-ânantaram kartri-karma-karana-sampradân-âpâdâna-svâmy-âdhikaran-âkhyam kârakam yathâ kramam nirûpyate* |

[Here begin rules for the uses of the cases.]

Sûtra 76.—*Lingârtha-vachana-mâtre prathamâ.*

Vritti.—*Linge arthe vachane cha vishaye prathamâ vibhaktir bhavati* |

Prayoga.—*Linge:—Dêvam, nripam, nallam, nallaḷ, âlam, jalam* | *arthe:—uchcham, nîcham, uddam, biddam* | *vachana-mâtre:—ondanum, eradanum* |

[The first (nominative) case indicates gender, sense and number.]

Sûtra 77.—*Sambodhane cha.*

Vritti.—*Sambodhanam abhimukhî-karanam* | *asminn-arthe cha prathamâ vibhaktir bhavati* | *âmantrane prathamaika-vachanasya lopa* iti lopah* |

Prayoga.—*Nripendra* |

Etvam vâ tad-antasyety† etvam | *Prayoga* | *kânte, koḷane, vasantame* |

[The vocative shows the same of the object addressed. (The nominative is used for this).]

---

೪. ಕಾರಕ ವಿಧಾನಂ.

ಸೂತ್ರ ‖ ಅಥ ಕಾರಕಂ ನಿರೂಪ್ಯತೇ ‖ ೭೫ ‖

ವೃತ್ತಿ ‖ ಸಂಜ್ಞಾಸನ್ಧಿವಿಭಕ್ತಿನಿಯಮಾನನ್ತರಂ ಕರ್ತೃಕರ್ಮಕರಣಸಂಪ್ರದಾನಾಪಾದಾನ ಸ್ವಾಮ್ಯಾಧಿಕರಣಾಖ್ಯಂ ಕಾರಕಂ ಯಥಾಕ್ರಮಂ ನಿರೂಪ್ಯತೇ ‖

ತಾತ್ಪರ್ಯ ‖ ಸಂಜ್ಞಾ ಸನ್ಧಿ ವಿಭಕ್ತಿಗಳನ್ನು ಮೂರು ಪರಿಚ್ಛೇದಗಳಿಂದ ಯಥಾ ನಿಯಮವಾಗಿ ನಿರೂಪಿಸಿ ಈ ಕರ್ತೃ ಕರ್ಮ ಕರಣ ಸಂಪ್ರದಾನ ಅಪಾದಾನ ಸ್ವಾಮ್ಯ ಅಧಿಕರಣಗಳೆಂಬ ಕಾರಕಾರ್ಥ ಭೇದಗಳನ್ನು ಯಥಾಕ್ರಮವಾಗಿ ನಿರೂಪಿಸುತ್ತಾನೆ.

ಸೂತ್ರ ‖ ಲಿಙ್ಗಾರ್ಥವಚನಮಾತ್ರೇ ಪ್ರಥಮಾ ‖ ೭೬ ‖

ವೃತ್ತಿ ‖ ಲಿಙ್ಗೇ ಅರ್ಥೇ ವಚನೇ ಚ ವಿಷಯೇ ಪ್ರಥಮಾ ವಿಭಕ್ತಿರ್ಭವತಿ ‖

ಪ್ರಯೋಗ ‖ ಲಿಙ್ಗೇ ‖ ದೇವಂ । ನೃಪಂ । ನಲ್ಲಂ । ನಲ್ಲಳ್ । ಆಲಂ । ಜಲಂ ‖ ಅರ್ಥೇ ‖ ಉಚ್ಚಂ । ನೀಚಂ । ಉದ್ದಂ । ಬಿದ್ದಂ ‖ ವಚನಮಾತ್ರೇ ‖ ಒಂದನುಂ । ಎರಡನುಂ ‖

ತಾತ್ಪರ್ಯ ‖ ಲಿಙ್ಗದಲ್ಲಿಯೂ ಅರ್ಥದಲ್ಲಿಯೂ ವಚನದಲ್ಲಿಯೂ ಪ್ರಥಮಾ ವಿಭಕ್ತಿಯಾಗುವದು, ಅಂದರೆ ಇವುಗಳನ್ನೆಲ್ಲಾ ಪ್ರಥಮಾ ವಿಭಕ್ತಿಯೇ ವಿವಕ್ಷೆ ಮಾಡುತ್ತದೆಂಬುದು.

ಸೂತ್ರ ‖ ಸಮ್ಬೋಧನೇ ಚ ‖ ೭೭ ‖

ವೃತ್ತಿ ‖ ಸಮ್ಬೋಧನಮಭಿಮುಖೀಕರಣಂ । ಅಸ್ಮಿನ್ನರ್ಥೇ ಚ ಪ್ರಥಮಾ ವಿಭಕ್ತಿರ್ಭವತಿ । ಆಮನ್ತ್ರಣೇ ಪ್ರಥಮೈಕವಚನಸ್ಯ ಲೋಪ ಇತಿ ಲೋಪಃ ‖

ಪ್ರಯೋಗ ‖ ನೃಪೇಂದ್ರ ।

ಎತ್ವಂ ವಾತದನ್ತಸ್ಯೇತ್ಯೇತ್ವಂ ‖ ಪ್ರಯೋಗ ‖ ಕಾಂತೆ । ಕೊಳನೆ । ವಸಂತಮೆ ‖

ತಾತ್ಪರ್ಯ ‖ ಸಮ್ಬೋಧನೆಯಂದರೆ ಮಾತಾಡುವದಕ್ಕೆ ಮನುಷ್ಯನನ್ನು ತನ್ನ ಯದುರಿಗೆ ಮಾಡಿಕೊಳ್ಳುವಿಕೆ. ಅಂಥ ಅರ್ಥದಲ್ಲಿಯೂ ಪ್ರಥಮಾ ವಿಭಕ್ತಿಯಾಗುವದು. ೭೧ನೇ ಸೂತ್ರದ ಪ್ರಕಾರ ಲೋಪವೂ ೭೨ನೇ ಸೂತ್ರದ ಪ್ರಕಾರ ಎತ್ವವೂ ಆಗುವದು.

---

* This is the 71st Sûtra. † This is the 72nd Sutra.

Sûtra 78.—*Dvitîyâ karmaṇi.*

Vritti—*Yat kriyate tat karma* । *tach-cha nivartyam kâryam prâpyam vais'eshikam vishaya-bhûtam iti pañcha vidham* । *teshu dvitîyâ vibhaktir bhavati* ।

Prayoga—*Nivartyârthe :—maneyam mâḍidam* । *kâryârthe :—paḷupam kaḍidam* । *prâpyârthe :—ûran aiḍidam* । *vais'eshikârthe :—paṭṭaṇan aiḍidam* । *vishayârthe :—nêsaram nôḍidam* ।

Tad îpsitânîpsitatvena punar dvidhâ bhavati । *Prayoga* । *îpsitârthe :—kûḷan aṭṭam, bûḷam kûydam* । *anîpsitârthe :—pâvam dâṭidam, koraḍan eḍapidam* ।

[The second (accusative) case shows the object of an action. This is of five kinds accordingly as the object is one made or produced, acted on, reached, defined, or observed. These again are divided into objects of desire or of aversion.]

Sûtra 79.—*Kâlâdhvanor avichchhede.*

Vritti—*Kâle vâ adhvani vâ avichchhedaḥ kriyâ-vyâptis tatra dvitîyâ bhavati* ।

Prayoga—*Ondu varushan irddam, tiṅgaḷan ôdidam, ôrgâvudam paridam, jâvamam nidde-gaidam* ।

[Also duration of time or extent of space.]

ಸೂತ್ರ ॥ ದ್ವಿತೀಯಾ ಕರ್ಮಣಿ ॥ ೭೮ ॥

ವೃತ್ತಿ ॥ ಯತ್ಕ್ರಿಯತೇ ತತ್ಕರ್ಮ । ತಚ್ಚ ನಿವರ್ತ್ಯಂ ಕಾರ್ಯಂ ಪ್ರಾಪ್ಯಂ ವೈಶೇಷಿಕಂ ವಿಷಯಭೂತ ಮಿತಿ ಪಂಚವಿಧಂ । ತೇಷು ದ್ವಿತೀಯಾ ವಿಭಕ್ತಿರ್ಭವತಿ ॥

ಪ್ರಯೋಗ ॥ ನಿವರ್ತ್ಯಾರ್ಥೇ । ಮನೆಯಂ ಮಾಡಿದಂ । ಕಾರ್ಯಾರ್ಥೇ । ಪಳುಪಂ ಕಡಿದಂ । ಪ್ರಾಪ್ಯಾರ್ಥೇ । ಊರನೈದಿದಂ । ವೈಶೇಷಿಕಾರ್ಥೇ । ಪಟ್ಟಣನೈದಿದಂ । ವಿಷಯಾರ್ಥೇ । ನೇಸರಂ ನೋಡಿದಂ ॥

ತದೀಪ್ಸಿತಾನೀಪ್ಸಿತತ್ವೇನ ಪುನರ್ದ್ವಿಧಾ ಭವತಿ ॥ ಪ್ರಯೋಗ ॥ ಈಪ್ಸಿತಾರ್ಥೇ । ಕೂಳನಟ್ಟಂ । ಬೂಳಂ ಕೂಯ್ದಂ ॥ ಅನೀಪ್ಸಿತಾರ್ಥೇ । ಪಾವಂ ದಾಟಿದಂ । ಕೊರಡನೆಡಪಿದಂ ॥

ತಾತ್ಪರ್ಯ ॥ ಯಾವದು ಮಾಡಲ್ಪಡುತ್ತದೆಯೋ ಅದು ಕರ್ಮ । ಆಕರ್ಮವು ನಿವರ್ತ್ಯ, ಕಾರ್ಯ, ಪ್ರಾಪ್ಯ, ವೈಶೇಷಿಕ, ವಿಷಯೀಭೂತ ಯೆಂಬೈದು ವಿಧವಾಗಿ, ಇವು ಪುನಃ ಈಪ್ಸಿತ ಅನೀಪ್ಸಿತ ಯೆಂಬೆರಡು ಭೇದಗಳಾಗುತ್ತವೆ. ಇವುಗಳ ಭೇದವನ್ನುದಾಹರಣೆಗಳ ಮೂಲವಾಗಿ ಊಹಿಸುವದು.

ಸೂತ್ರ ॥ ಕಾಲಾಧ್ವನೋರವಿಚ್ಛೇದೇ ॥ ೭೯ ॥

ವೃತ್ತಿ ॥ ಕಾಲೇ ವಾ ಅಧ್ವನಿ ವಾ ಅವಿಚ್ಛೇದಃ ಕ್ರಿಯಾವ್ಯಾಪ್ತಿಸ್ತತ್ರ ದ್ವಿತೀಯಾ ಭವತಿ ॥

ಪ್ರಯೋಗ ॥ ಒಂದು ವರುಷನಿರ್ದ್ದಂ । ತಿಂಗಳನೋದಿದಂ । ಓರ್ಗಾವುದಂ ಪರಿದಂ । ಜಾವಮಂ ನಿದ್ದೆಗೈದಂ ॥

ತಾತ್ಪರ್ಯ ॥ ಕಾಲದಲ್ಲಿಯಾಗಲಿ ಮಾರ್ಗದಲ್ಲಿಯಾಗಲಿ ಕ್ರಿಯೆಯ ವ್ಯಾಪ್ತಿ ಅಂದರೆ ತೀರುವಿಕೆಯನ್ನು ಹೇಳುವದಕ್ಕೆ ದ್ವಿತೀಯೆಯಾಗುವದು.

Sûtra 80.—*Kartri-karaṇayos tritiyâ.*

Vritti.—*Yah kriyâm karoti sa kartâ* | *sâdhakatamam karaṇam* | *tasmin kartari-karaṇe cha vivakshite tritiyâ bhavati* |

Prayoga.—*Kartari:—Dêvadattanim mâḍalpaṭṭudu, Yajñadattanim pêḷalpaṭṭudu* | *karaṇe:—kuḍugôlim kuydam, paras'uvim kaḍidam* |

[The third (instrumental) case shows the agent or instrument of an action.]

Sûtra 81.—*Hetâv api.*

Vritti.—*Hetur-nâma nimittam* | *tasminn-arthepi tritiyâ vibhaktir bhavati* |

Prayoga.—*Ôlagadindam irddam, âjñeyinde bandam* |

[Also the cause.]

Sûtra 82.—*Sampradâne chaturthî.*

Vritti.—*Karmaṇâ kâraṇa-bhûtopâdhi-niyates savivakshitatvam sampradânam* | *tasminn-arthe chaturthî vibhaktir bhavati* |

Prayoga.—*Upâdhyâyange dakshiṇeyam koṭṭam, Brâhmaṇange gôvan ittam** |

[The fourth (dative) case shows the indirect object of an action.]

ಸೂತ್ರ ॥ ಕರ್ತೃಕರಣಯೋಸ್ತೃತೀಯಾ ॥ ೮೦ ॥

ವೃತ್ತಿ ॥ ಯಃ ಕ್ರಿಯಾಂ ಕರೋತಿ ಸ ಕರ್ತಾ । ಸಾಧಕತಮಂ ಕರಣಂ । ತಸ್ಮಿನ್ ಕರ್ತರಿ ಕರಣೇ ಚ ವಿವಕ್ಷಿತೇ ತೃತೀಯಾ ಭವತಿ ॥

ಪ್ರಯೋಗ ॥ ಕರ್ತರಿ । ದೇವದತ್ತನಿಂ ಮಾಡಲ್ಪಟ್ಟುದು । ಯಜ್ಞದತ್ತನಿಂ ಪೇಳಲ್ಪಟ್ಟುದು । ಕರಣೇ । ಕುಡುಗೋಲಿಂ ಕುಯ್ದಂ । ಪರಶುವಿಂ ಕಡಿದಂ ॥

ತಾತ್ಪರ್ಯ ॥ ಯಾವದು ಕ್ರಿಯೆಯನ್ನು ಮಾಡುತ್ತದೋ ಅದು ಕರ್ತಾ, ಕ್ರಿಯೆಗೆ ಸಾಧನಭೂತವಾದದ್ದು ಕರಣ, ಇವುಗಳನ್ನು ವಿವಕ್ಷೆ ಮಾಡುವಲ್ಲಿ ತೃತೀಯಾ ವಿಭಕ್ತಿ ಬರುತ್ತದೆ.

ಸೂತ್ರ ॥ ಹೇತಾವಪಿ ॥ ೮೧ ॥

ವೃತ್ತಿ ॥ ಹೇತುರ್ನಾಮ ನಿಮಿತ್ತಂ । ತಸ್ಮಿನ್ನರ್ಥೇಽಪಿ ತೃತೀಯಾ ವಿಭಕ್ತಿರ್ಭವತಿ ॥

ಪ್ರಯೋಗ ॥ ಓಲಗದಿಂದಮಿರ್ದ್ದಂ । ಆಜ್ಞೆಯಿಂದೆ ಬಂದಂ ॥

ತಾತ್ಪರ್ಯ ॥ ಹೇತುವಂದರೆ ನಿಮಿತ್ತ, ಅಂಥಾ ನಿಮಿತ್ತಾರ್ಥಕದಲ್ಲಿ ತೃತೀಯೆಯಾಗುವದು.

ಸೂತ್ರ ॥ ಸಮ್ಪ್ರದಾನೇ ಚತುರ್ಥೀ ॥ ೮೨ ॥

ವೃತ್ತಿ ॥ ಕರ್ಮಣಾ ಕಾರಣಭೂತೋಪಾಧಿನಿಯತೇಸ್ಸವಿವಕ್ಷಿತತ್ವಂ ಸಮ್ಪ್ರದಾನಂ । ತಸ್ಮಿನ್ನರ್ಥೇ ಚತುರ್ಥೀ ವಿಭಕ್ತಿರ್ಭವತಿ ॥

ಪ್ರಯೋಗ ॥ ಉಪಾಧ್ಯಾಯಂಗೆ ದಕ್ಷಿಣೆಯಂ ಕೊಟ್ಟಂ । * ಬ್ರಾಹ್ಮಣಂಗೆ ಗೋವನಿತ್ತಂ ॥

ತಾತ್ಪರ್ಯ ॥ ಕರ್ಮದೊಡನೆ ಕಾರಣ ಭೂತವಪ್ಪ ಪದವು ಸಮ್ಪ್ರದಾನವೆನಿಸುವದು. ಅದಕ್ಕೆ ಚತುರ್ಥೀ ವಿಭಕ್ತಿಯಾಗುತ್ತದೆ.

---

* This second example is given only in B.

* ದ್ವಿ ॥ ಈ ಪ್ರತಿಯಲ್ಲಿ ಮಾತ್ರ ಎರಡನೇ ಉದಾಹರಣೆ ಇದೆ.

Sûtra 83.—*Ruchi-hitershyâ-bhayeshu cha.*

Vṛitti.—*Ruchyâdishv api chaturthî bhavati* ।

Prayoga.—*Dêvadattaṅge mô.lakam ruchiyu, pas'uviṅge hitam triṇam, âryaṅge s'aṇasugam durjanam, pulig-añjugam janam* ।

[Also the object to which like, friendship, envy or fear is referred.]

Sûtra 84.—*Manyukarmaṇy-anâdare cha.*

Vṛitti.—*Kopa-kṛitye anâdare cha gamyamâne prâpyârthe chaturthî bhavati* ।

Prayoga.—*Avana pulge kashṭavâgi bagedam, âtana mâtan ond-aḍikege koḷvam* ।

[Or to which an act of anger or disrespect is referred.]

Sûtra 85.—*Namaskriyâ-svasty-âdishu cha.*

Vṛitti.—*Eshv artheshu cha chaturthî bhavati* ।

Prayoga.—*Devaṅge namaskâram geydam, arasaṅg-eragidam, prajeg-ellam svasti yakkum, bhadram s'âsanakke* ।

Âdi-s'abdât svâhâ-svadhâ-vaushaḍ-artheshu chaturthî bhavati । *Prayoga* । *Agni'ge svâhâ-kâram pitṛigaḷige svadhâ-kâram Indraṅge vaushaṭ-kâram priyam ; mallaṅge prati-mallam samartham* ।

[Or the object of an obei-ance or benediction, or of the ritual invocations *svâhâ, svadhâ, vaushaḍ.*]

ಸೂತ್ರ ॥ ರುಚಿಹಿತೇರ್ಷ್ಯಾಭಯೇಷು ಚ ॥ ೮೩ ॥

ವೃತ್ತಿ ॥ ರುಚ್ಯಾದಿಷ್ವಪಿ ಚತುರ್ಥೀ ಭವತಿ ॥

ಪ್ರಯೋಗ ॥ ದೇವದತ್ತಂಗೆ ಮೋದಕಂ ರುಚಿಯು । ಪಶುವಿಂಗೆ ಹಿತಂ ತೃಣಂ । ಆರ್ಯಂಗೆ ಶಣಸುಗಂ ದುರ್ಜನಂ । ಪುಲಿಗಂಜುಗಂ ಜನಂ ॥

ತಾತ್ಪರ್ಯ ॥ ರುಚಿ, ಹಿತ, ಈರ್ಷ್ಯವೆಂಬ ಹೊಟ್ಟೆಕಿಚ್ಚು, ಭಯವೆಂಬ ಅಂಜಿಕೆ, ಇವುಗಳಲ್ಲಿ ಚತುರ್ಥೀಯಾಗುವದು.

ಸೂತ್ರ ॥ ಮನ್ಯು ಕರ್ಮಣ್ಯನಾದರೇ ಚ ॥ ೮೪ ॥

ವೃತ್ತಿ ॥ ಕೋಪಕೃತ್ಯೇ ಅನಾದರೇ ಚ ಗಮ್ಯಮಾನೇ ಪ್ರಾಪ್ಯಾರ್ಥೇ ಚತುರ್ಥೀ ಭವತಿ ॥

ಪ್ರಯೋಗ ॥ ಅವನ ಪುಲ್ಗೆ ಕಷ್ಟವಾಗಿ ಬಗೆದಂ । ಆತನ ಮಾತನೊಂದಡಿಕೆಗೆ ಕೊಳ್ವಂ ॥

ತಾತ್ಪರ್ಯ ॥ ಕೋಪಕೃತ್ಯದಲ್ಲಿಯೂ ತಿರಸ್ಕಾರದಲ್ಲಿಯೂ ಚತುರ್ಥೀಯಾಗುತ್ತದೆ.

ಸೂತ್ರ ॥ ನಮಸ್ಕ್ರಿಯಾ ಸ್ವಸ್ತ್ಯಾದಿಷು ಚ ॥ ೮೫ ॥

ವೃತ್ತಿ ॥ ಏಷ್ವರ್ಥೇಷು ಚ ಚತುರ್ಥೀ ಭವತಿ ॥

ಪ್ರಯೋಗ ॥ ದೇವಂಗೆ ನಮಸ್ಕಾರಂ ಗೆಯ್ದಂ । ಅರಸಂಗೆರಗಿದಂ । ಪ್ರಜೆಗೆಲ್ಲಂ ಸ್ವಸ್ತಿಯಕ್ಕುಂ । ಭದ್ರಂ ಶಾಸನಕ್ಕೆ ॥

ಆದಿಶಬ್ದಾತ್ ಸ್ವಾಹಾಸ್ವಧಾವೌಷಡರ್ಥೇಷು ಚತುರ್ಥೀ ಭವತಿ ॥ ಪ್ರಯೋಗ । ಅಗ್ನಿಗೆ ಸ್ವಾಹಾಕಾರಂ ಪಿತೃಗಳಗೆ ಸ್ವಧಾಕಾರಂ ಇಂದ್ರಂಗೆ ವೌಷಟ್ಕಾರಂ ಪ್ರಿಯಂ । ಮಲ್ಲಂಗೆ ಪ್ರತಿಮಲ್ಲಂ ಸಮರ್ಥಂ ॥

ತಾತ್ಪರ್ಯ ॥ ನಮಸ್ಕಾರದಲ್ಲಿಯೂ ಸ್ವಸ್ತಿಯೆಂಬವದಲ್ಲಿಯೂ ಆದಿಶಬ್ದದಿಂದ ಸ್ವಾಹಾ ಸ್ವಧಾ ವೌಷಟ್ ಯೆಂಬಿವುಗಳ ಅರ್ಥದಲ್ಲಿಯೂ ಚತುರ್ಥೀಯಾಗುತ್ತದೆ.

Sûtra 86.—*Apâdâne pañchamî.*

Vṛitti.—*Apâdânam apanayah । tasmin vivakshite pañchamî bhavati* ।

Prayoga.—*Ûrattaṇim bandam, beṭṭadattaṇind iḷidam, puliyattaṇim bhayam, S'rîvîranattaṇim rakshaṇam** ।

[The fifth (ablative) case shows the object separated from.]

Sûtra 87.—*Sva-svâmi-sambandhe shashṭhî.*

Vṛitti.—*Asminn-arthe shashṭhî prayojyate* ।

Prayoga.—*Ennoḍane nâḍereyam, marada kombu, maleya piṇḍu, ponna gejje* ।

[The sixth (genitive) case denotes possession.]

Sûtra 88.—*Adhikaraṇe saptamî.*

Vṛitti.—*Âdhârârthe saptamî bhavati* ।

Prayoga.—*Nuḍivavaroḷ kaḍu jâṇam, kaligaḷoḷ meygali, nararoḷ uttamam, kaiyyoḷ kaṅkaṇam, toreyoḷ bîḷvam, neleyoḷ puṭṭirddam, puvvinoḷ kampu* ।

[The seventh (locative) case denotes location.]

ಸೂತ್ರ ॥ ಅಪಾದಾನೇ ಪಞ್ಚಮೀ ॥ ೮೬ ॥

ವೃತ್ತಿ ॥ ಅಪಾದಾನಮಪನಯಃ । ತಸ್ಮಿನ್ ವಿವಕ್ಷಿತೇ ಪಞ್ಚಮೀ ಭವತಿ ॥

ಪ್ರಯೋಗ ॥ ಊರತ್ತಣಿಂ ಬಂದಂ । ಬೆಟ್ಟದತ್ತಣಿಂದಿೞಿದಂ । ಪುಲಿಯತ್ತಣಿಂ ಭಯಂ । ಶ್ರೀವೀರನತ್ತಣಿಂ ರಕ್ಷಣಂ* ॥

ತಾತ್ಪರ್ಯ ॥ ಅಪಾದಾನವೆಂಬ ಅಪನಯಾರ್ಥದಲ್ಲಿ ಪಂಚಮೀವಿಭಕ್ತಿಯಾಗುತ್ತದೆ. ಅಪನಯವೆಂದರೆ ಅದೆಕೆಯಿಂದೆಂಬರ್ಥ.

ಸೂತ್ರ ॥ ಸ್ವಸ್ವಾಮಿಸಮ್ಬನ್ಧೇ ಷಷ್ಠೀ ॥ ೮೭ ॥

ವೃತ್ತಿ ॥ ಅಸ್ಮಿನ್ನರ್ಥೇ ಷಷ್ಠೀ ಪ್ರಯೋಜ್ಯತೇ ॥

ಪ್ರಯೋಗ ॥ ಎನ್ನೊಡನೆ ನಾಡೆರೆಯಂ । ಮರದ ಕೊಂಬು । ಮಲೆಯ ಪಿಂಡು । ಪೊನ್ನಗೆಜ್ಜೆ ॥

ತಾತ್ಪರ್ಯ ॥ ತನ್ನ ಸ್ವಾಮಿ ಸಮ್ಬನ್ಧಾರ್ಥದಲ್ಲಿ ಷಷ್ಠೀ ವಿಭಕ್ತಿ ಪ್ರಯೋಗಿಸಲ್ಪಡುತ್ತದೆ.

ಸೂತ್ರ ॥ ಅಧಿಕರಣೇ ಸಪ್ತಮೀ ॥ ೮೮ ॥

ವೃತ್ತಿ ॥ ಆಧಾರಾರ್ಥೇ ಸಪ್ತಮೀ ಭವತಿ ॥

ಪ್ರಯೋಗ ॥ ನುಡಿವವರೊಳ್ ಕಡುಜಾಣಂ । ಕಲಿಗಳೊಳ್ಮೆಯ್ಗಲಿ । ನರರೊಳುತ್ತಮಂ । ಕೈಯ್ಯೊಳ್ಕಂಕಣಂ । ತೊರೆಯೊಳ್ ಬೀಳ್ವಂ । ನೆಲೆಯೊಳ್ ಪುಟ್ಟಿರ್ದ್ದಂ । ಪುವ್ವಿನೊಳ್ ಕಂಪು ॥

ತಾತ್ಪರ್ಯ ॥ ಆಧಾರಾರ್ಥದಲ್ಲಿ ಸಪ್ತಮೀ ವಿಭಕ್ತಿಯಾಗುತ್ತದೆ.

---

* In C this is preceded by *svargadattaṇind iḷidam Varddhamânam.* B has *Kṛishṇanattaṇim rakshaṇam* instead of it.

* ಪಾ । ತೃ ॥ ಪ್ರತಿಯಲ್ಲಿ ಸ್ವರ್ಗದತ್ತಣಿಂದಿೞಿದಂ ವರ್ದ್ಧಮಾನಂ ಎಂದು ಇದೆ. ದ್ವಿ । ಪುಲ್ಲಿ ಕೃಷ್ಣನತ್ತಣಿಂ ರಕ್ಷಣಂ ಎಂದು ಇದೆ.

Sûtra 89.—*Nirdhâraṇe cha kriyayâ guṇena vâ.*

Vṛitti.—*Sajâtîyaugha kriyayâ guṇena vâ yâ nirdis'yate nirdhâryate tan-nirdhâraṇam* । *tatra vivakshite shashṭhî-saptamyau vibhaktî bhavataḥ* ।

Prayoga.—*Purusharoḷ kshattriyam s'ûram, nuḍivaroḷ kaḍu jâṇam (Akalaṅkam*), kavigaḷoḷ uttamam (Siddha-senam*), jñânigaḷa ballaham* ।

[Also distinction among those of the same class on account of conduct or character. (Both genitive and locative are used in this sense).]

Sûtra 90.—*Âsâm vyatyayo bahuḷam.*

Vṛitti.—*Âsâm sapta-vibhaktînâm bhâshâsu prâyeṇa vyatyâso† bhavati* । *yathâ :—*

[In composition the following differences arise in the use of the cases.]

Sûtra 91.—*Pañchamy-arthe tṛitîyâ.*

Vṛitti.—*Spashṭam* ।

Prayoga.—*S'ereyattaṇim barduṅkidam, s'ereyim barduṅkidam‡; mane-yattaṇim poramaṭṭam, maneyim poramaṭṭam* ।

[The third (instrumental) is used in the sense of the fifth (ablative).]

ಸೂತ್ರ ॥ ನಿರ್ಧಾರಣೇ ಚ ಕ್ರಿಯಯಾ ಗುಣೇನ ವಾ ॥ ೮೯ ॥

ವೃತ್ತಿ ॥ ಸಜಾತೀಯೌಘ ಕ್ರಿಯಯಾ ಗುಣೇನ ವಾ ಯಾ ನಿರ್ದಿಶ್ಯತೇ ನಿರ್ಧಾರ್ಯತೇ ತನ್ನಿರ್ಧಾರಣಂ। ತತ್ರ ವಿವಕ್ಷಿತೇ ಷಷ್ಠೀ ಸಪ್ತಮ್ಯೌ ವಿಭಕ್ತೀ ಭವತಃ॥

ಪ್ರಯೋಗ ॥ ಪುರುಷರೊಳ್ ಕ್ಷತ್ತ್ರಿಯಂ ಶೂರಂ । ನುಡಿವರೊಳ್ ಕಡುಜಾಣಂ (ಅಕಲಂಕಂ*) । ಕವಿಗಳೊಳುತ್ತಮಂ (ಸಿದ್ಧಸೇನಂ*)। ಜ್ಞಾನಿಗಳ ಬಲ್ಲಹಂ ॥

ತಾತ್ಪರ್ಯ ॥ ಸಜಾತೀಯಗಳಾದವುಗಳಲ್ಲಿ ಕ್ರಿಯೆಯಿಂದಲಾಗಲಿ ಗುಣದಿಂದಲಾಗಲಿ ಯಾವದು ನಿರ್ಧರಿಸಲ್ಪಡುತ್ತದೊ ಅದು ನಿರ್ಧಾರಣವು। ಅದರಲ್ಲಿ ಷಷ್ಠೀ ಸಪ್ತಮೀ ವಿಭಕ್ತಿಗಳೆರಡೂ ಪ್ರಯೋಗಿಸಲ್ಪಡುವವು.

ಸೂತ್ರ ॥ ಆಸಾಂ ವ್ಯತ್ಯಯೋ ಬಹುಳಂ ॥ ೯೦ ॥

ವೃತ್ತಿ ॥ ಆಸಾಂ ಸಪ್ತವಿಭಕ್ತೀನಾಂ ಭಾಷಾಸು ಪ್ರಾಯೇಣ ವ್ಯತ್ಯಾಸೋ† ಭವತಿ ॥ ಯಥಾ ॥

ತಾತ್ಪರ್ಯ ॥ ಈ ಯೇಳು ವಿಭಕ್ತಿಗಳಿಗೂ ಭಾಷೆಯಲ್ಲಿ ಪ್ರಯೋಗಿಸುವಾಗ ಪ್ರಾಯಕವಾಗಿ ವ್ಯತ್ಯಾಸವಾಗುತ್ತದೆ। ಅದು ಹ್ಯಾಗಂದರೆ :—

ಸೂತ್ರ ॥ ಪಞ್ಚಮ್ಯರ್ಥೇ ತೃತೀಯಾ ॥ ೯೧ ॥

ವೃತ್ತಿ ॥ ಸ್ಪಷ್ಟಂ ॥

ಪ್ರಯೋಗ ॥ ಶೆರೆಯತ್ತಣಿಂ ಬರ್ದುಂಕಿದಂ, ಶೆರೆಯಿಂ ಬರ್ದುಂಕಿದಂ‡ । ಮನೆಯತ್ತಣಿಂ ಪೊರಮಟ್ಟಂ, ಮನೆಯಿಂ ಪೊರಮಟ್ಟಂ ॥

ತಾತ್ಪರ್ಯ ॥ ಪಂಚಮೀ ವಿಭಕ್ತಿಯ ಅರ್ಥದಲ್ಲಿ ತೃತೀಯೆಯನ್ನು ಪ್ರಯೋಗಿಸುತ್ತಾರೆ.

---

* These names are in C only. † *Viparyâso* in B. ‡ This example not in C.

* ತೃ । ಯಲ್ಲಿ ಮಾತ್ರವೇ ಇದೆ. † ದ್ವಿ । ಯಲ್ಲಿ ವಿಪರ್ಯಾಸೋ ಎಂದು ಇದೆ.

‡ ತೃ । ಯಲ್ಲಿ ಮೊದಲನೇ ಉದಾಹರಣೆ ಇಲ್ಲ.

ûtra 92.—*Shashṭhy-arthe chaturthî.*

Shashṭhy-arthe vivakshite kvachich-chaturthî vibhaktih prayuj-

—*Neladereyam, nelakkereyam; Srîyadhîs'varam, Srîgadhîs'varam* *âtham**) ।

[The fourth (dative) in the sense of the sixth (genitive.)]

ûtra 93.—*Dvitîyârthe chaturthî.*

Dvitîyâyâm chaturthî bhavati ।

—*Bhû-tâpakke bigurtu Vishṇu paḍedam Matsyâvatârâṅkamam*† ।

[The fourth (dative) in the sense of the second (accusative).]

ûtra 94.—*Prathamârthe shashṭhî.*

Prathamâyâs-sthâne shashṭhî prayogah ।

—*Nîm bare Muramathana, nîm bare Madana*‡ ।

[The sixth (genitive) in the sense of the first (nominative).]

ûtra 95.—*Tritîyârthe saptamî.*

Spashṭam ।

—*Chaladind avane doreyâdam, chaladoḷ avane doreyâdam ; koḍali-* *dam, koḍaliyoḷ kaḍidam* ।

[The seventh (locative) in the sense of the third (instrumental).]

ಸೂತ್ರ ॥ ಷಷ್ಠ್ಯರ್ಥೇ ಚತುರ್ಥೀ ॥ ೯೨ ॥

ವೃತ್ತಿ ॥ ಷಷ್ಠ್ಯರ್ಥೇ ವಿವಕ್ಷಿತೇ ಕ್ವಚಿಚ್ಚತುರ್ಥೀ ವಿಭಕ್ತಿಃ ಪ್ರಯುಜ್ಯತೇ ॥
ಪ್ರಯೋಗ ॥ ನೆಲದೆರೆಯಂ, ನೆಲಕ್ಕೆರೆಯಂ। ಶ್ರೀಯಧೀಶ್ವರಂ, ಶ್ರೀಗಧೀಶ್ವರಂ (ಶಾಂತಿನಾಥಂ*) ॥
ತಾತ್ಪರ್ಯ ॥ ಷಷ್ಠ್ಯರ್ಥದಲ್ಲಿ ಕೆಲವು ವೇಳೆ ಚತುರ್ಥೀ ವಿಭಕ್ತಿಯು ಪ್ರಯೋಗಿಸಲ್ಪಡುತ್ತದೆ.

ಸೂತ್ರ ॥ ದ್ವಿತೀಯಾರ್ಥೇ ಚತುರ್ಥೀ ॥ ೯೩ ॥

ವೃತ್ತಿ । ದ್ವಿತೀಯಾಯಾಂ ಚತುರ್ಥೀ ಭವತಿ ॥
ಪ್ರಯೋಗ ॥ ಭೂತಾಪಕ್ಕೆ ಬಿಗುರ್ತು ವಿಷ್ಣು ಪಡೆದಂ ಮತ್ಸ್ಯಾವತಾರಾಂಕಮಂ† ॥
ತಾತ್ಪರ್ಯ ॥ ದ್ವಿತೀಯಾರ್ಥದಲ್ಲಿ ಚತುರ್ಥೀ ಬರುತ್ತದೆ.

ಸೂತ್ರ ॥ ಪ್ರಥಮಾರ್ಥೇ ಷಷ್ಠೀ । ೯೪ ॥

ವೃತ್ತಿ । ಪ್ರಥಮಾಯಾಸ್ಸ್ಥಾನೇ ಷಷ್ಠೀ ಪ್ರಯೋಗಃ ॥
ಪ್ರಯೋಗ ॥ ನೀಂ ಬರೆ ಮುರಮಥನ । ನೀಂ ಬರೆ ಮದನ ‡ ॥
ತಾತ್ಪರ್ಯ ॥ ಪ್ರಥಮಾರ್ಥದಲ್ಲಿ ಷಷ್ಠೀಯಾಗುತ್ತದೆ.

ಸೂತ್ರ ॥ ತೃತೀಯಾರ್ಥೇ ಸಪ್ತಮೀ ॥ ೯೫ ॥

ವೃತ್ತಿ ॥ ಸ್ಪಷ್ಟಂ ॥
ಪ್ರಯೋಗ ॥ ಚಲದಿಂದವನೆ ದೊರೆಯಾದಂ, ಚಲದೊಳವನೆ ದೊರೆಯಾದಂ। ಕೊಡಲಿಯಿಂ ಕಡಿದಂ, ಕೊಡಲಿಯೊಳ್ ಕಡಿದಂ ॥
ತಾತ್ಪರ್ಯ ॥ ತೃತೀಯಾರ್ಥದಲ್ಲಿ ಸಪ್ತಮೀ ಬರುತ್ತದೆ.

---

* Only in C.

† For this example C has *Bhû-tâpakke bigurtu bhûpa paḍedam râjyâdhikâritvamam.*

‡ C has only *bandan â bhûpana.*

* ತೃ । ಯಲ್ಲಿ ಮಾತ್ರ ಇದೆ.

† ತೃ । ಯಲ್ಲಿ ಭೂತಾಪಕ್ಕೆ ಬಿಗುರ್ತು ಭೂಪ ಪಡೆದಂ ರಾಜ್ಯಾಧಿಕಾರಿತ್ವಮಂ ಎಂದು ಇದೆ.

‡ ತೃ । ಬಂದನಾಭೂಪನ ಎಂದಿದೆ.

Sûtra 96.—*Jâtir ekavad bahvâkhyâyâm.*

Vritti—*Jâti-vâchaka-s'abdo bahutrâkhyâne eka-vachanavad bhavati bahulam* ।

Prayoga.—*Kariyavu, karigaḷavu ; kaî beḷadavu, kaigaḷ beḷadavu* । *bahuḷâdhikârât strî-purusha-vishaye kvachin na bhavati* । (*Brâhmaṇar bandar, sûḷeyar nakkar.**)

[Words relating to a kind or class having a plural signification are used in the singular ; but sometimes not, when they relate to men or women.]

Sûtra 97.—*Sankhyeye sankhyâsu cha.*

Vritti—*Sankhyeye sankhyâsv api vartamâno yas s'abdas sopy ekavad bharati vâ* ।

Prayoga.—*Des'e pattu, des'egaḷu pattu ; mûru nâlku, mûrugaḷu nâlku ; padinaidavar* ।

[Numerals remain in the singular.]

Sûtra 98.—*Bhâvavachanepi.*

Vritti—*Bhâvâkhyâyâm api vartamâno yas s'abdah sopy ekavad bhavati* ।

Prayoga.—*Kappu, biḷpu, taṇbu, pêrmme* । *bahuḷa-grahaṇât biḷpugaḷu* ।

[Also abstract nouns.]

Iti Karṇâṭaka-vyâkaraṇa-vṛittau† Bhâshâ-bhûshaṇe Kâraka-vidhânam nâma chaturthah parichchhedah ।

ಸೂತ್ರ ॥ ಜಾತಿರೇಕವದ್ಬಹ್ವಾಖ್ಯಾಯಾಂ ॥ ೯೬ ॥

ವೃತ್ತಿ ॥ ಜಾತಿವಾಚಕಶಬ್ದೋ ಬಹುತ್ವಾಖ್ಯಾನೇ ಏಕವಚನವದ್ಭವತಿ ಬಹುಲಂ ॥

ಪ್ರಯೋಗ ॥ ಕರಿಯವು, ಕರಿಗಳವು । ಕೈ ಬೆಳದವು, ಕೈಗಳ್ ಬೆಳದವು ॥ ಬಹುಳಾಧಿಕಾರಾತ್ ಸ್ತ್ರೀ ಪುರುಷ ವಿಷಯೇ ಕ್ವಚಿನ್ನ ಭವತಿ ॥

ತಾತ್ಪರ್ಯ ॥ ಜಾತಿವಾಚಕ ಶಬ್ದವು ಬಹುತ್ವವನ್ನು ಹೇಳುವದಾದರೆ ಬಹುಲವಾಗಿ ಏಕವಚನದಂತೆ ಆಗುತ್ತದೆ. ಬಹುಳಾಧಿಕಾರದಿಂದ ಸ್ತ್ರೀಪುಂ ವಿಷಯದಲ್ಲಿ ಕೆಲವು ವೇಳೆ ಆಗುವದಿಲ್ಲ. [ಬ್ರಾಹ್ಮಣರ್ ಬಂದರ್, ಸೂಳೆಯರ್ ನಕ್ಕರ್.*]

ಸೂತ್ರ ॥ ಸಙ್ಖ್ಯೇಯೇ ಸಂಖ್ಯಾಸು ಚ ॥ ೯೭ ॥

ವೃತ್ತಿ ॥ ಸಙ್ಖ್ಯೇಯೇ ಸಙ್ಖ್ಯಾಸ್ವಪಿ ವರ್ತಮಾನೋ ಯಶ್ಶಬ್ದಸ್ಸೋಪ್ಯೇಕವದ್ಭವತಿ ವಾ ॥

ಪ್ರಯೋಗ ॥ ದೆಸೆ ಪತ್ತು, ದೆಸೆಗಳು ಪತ್ತು । ಮೂರು ನಾಲ್ಕು, ಮೂರುಗಳು ನಾಲ್ಕು । ಪದಿನೈದವರ್ ॥

ತಾತ್ಪರ್ಯ ॥ ಯೆಣಿಸುವದರಲ್ಲಿ ಸಂಖ್ಯಾ ಸೂಚಕ ಪದಗಳು ವಿಕಲ್ಪವಾಗಿ ಏಕವಚನದಲ್ಲಿ ನಿಲ್ಲುತ್ತವೆ.

ಸೂತ್ರ ॥ ಭಾವವಚನೇಪಿ ॥ ೯೮ ॥

ವೃತ್ತಿ ॥ ಭಾವಾಖ್ಯಾಯಾಮಪಿ ವರ್ತಮಾನೋ ಯಶ್ಶಬ್ದಃ ಸೋಪ್ಯೇಕವದ್ಭವತಿ ॥

ಪ್ರಯೋಗ ॥ ಕಪ್ಪು । ಬಿಳ್ಪು । ತಣ್ಪು, ಪೆರ್ಮೆ ॥ ಬಹುಳ ಗ್ರಹಣಾತ್ ಬಿಳ್ಪುಗಳು ॥

ತಾತ್ಪರ್ಯ ॥ ಭಾವನಾಮವಾಚಕ ಶಬ್ದಗಳು ಬಹುಳವಾಗಿ ಯೇಕವಚನದಲ್ಲಿಯೇ ಪ್ರಯೋಗಿಸಲ್ಪಡುವವು. ಬಹುಳಾಧಿಕಾರದಿಂದ ಇದಕ್ಕೆ ವ್ಯತ್ಯಯವಾದ ಪ್ರಯೋಗವುಂಟು.

ಇತಿ ಕರ್ಣಾಟಕ ವ್ಯಾಕರಣ ವೃತ್ತೌ† ಭಾಷಾ ಭೂಷಣೇ ಕಾರಕ ವಿಧಾನಂ ನಾಮ ಚತುರ್ಥಃ ಪರಿಚ್ಛೇದಃ

---

* In C only.
* ತ್ರ । ಯಲ್ಲಿ ಮಾತ್ರವಿದೆ.

† See note p. 7
† ೭ನೇ ಪುಟವನ್ನ ನೋಡಬೇಕು.

(V. Forms of Words.)

S'abda-rîti Vidhânam.

Sûtra 99.—*Nin-ân-tân prathamâ-vibhaktau.*

Vritti.—*Ninn-enna-tannânâm yushmad-asmad-anyad-artha-prathamânâm nîn ân tân iti rûpâṇy anukrameṇa bhavanti* ।

Prayoga.—*Nîn irdde, âm bandc, tâm pôdam* ।

[*Nin, ân, tân* are the first (nominative) cases of *ninna, enna, tanna*; meaning thine, mine, his.]

Sûtra 100.—*Nina-ena-tanâs' chaturthyâs tritîyatvam châsyâh.*

Vritti.—*Ninn-enna-tanna-ity eteshâm punas' chaturthî-vibhaktau parato yathâ saṅkhyam nina-ena-tana-ity ete âdes'â bhavanti* । *asyâs' chaturthyâs tritîyatvam cha bhavati* ।

Prayoga.—*Ninage, enage, tanage* ।

[*Ninna, enna, tanna* in the fourth (dative) case take the form *nina, ena, tana*; and this fourth (dative) case is used in the sense of the third (instrumental).]

Sûtra 101.—*Dvi-bahvor nasya mah.*

Vritti.—*Dvitva-bahutve vivakshite eshâm nakârasya makârâdes'o bhavati* ।

Prayoga.—*Nîm, âm, tâm, nimage, yamage, tamage, nimma, emma, tamma, nimmoḷ, emmoḷ, tammoḷ* ।

[In the dual and plural their *n* becomes *m*.]

ಶಬ್ದರೀತಿ ವಿಧಾನಂ.

ಸೂತ್ರ ॥ ನೀನಾನ್ತಾನ್ಪ್ರಥಮಾವಿಭಕ್ತೌ ॥ ೯೯ ॥

ವೃತ್ತಿ ॥ ನಿನ್ನೆನ್ನತನ್ನಾನಾಂ ಯುಷ್ಮದಸ್ಮದನ್ಯದರ್ಥಪ್ರಥಮಾನಾಂ ನೀನ್ ಆನ್ ತಾನ್ ಇತಿ ರೂಪಾಣ್ಯನುಕ್ರಮೇಣ ಭವನ್ತಿ ॥

ಪ್ರಯೋಗ ॥ ನೀನಿರ್ದ್ದೆ । ಆಂ ಬಂದೆ । ತಾಂ ಪೋದಂ ।

ತಾತ್ಪರ್ಯ ॥ ಯುಷ್ಮತ್ ಅಸ್ಮತ್ ಅನ್ಯತ್ ಯೆಂಬರ್ಥವುಳ್ಳ ನಿನ್ನ ಎನ್ನ ತನ್ನ ಯೆಂಬವುಗಳ ಪ್ರಥಮಾ ವಿಭಕ್ತಿಗಳಿಗೆ ಕ್ರಮವಾಗಿ ನೀನ್, ಆನ್, ತಾನ್ ಯೆಂಬ ರೂಪಗಳಾಗುತ್ತವೆ.

ಸೂತ್ರ ॥ ನಿನಎನತನಾಶ್ಚತುರ್ಥ್ಯಾಸ್ತೃತೀಯತ್ವಂ ಚಾಸ್ಯಾಃ ॥ ೧೦೦ ॥

ವೃತ್ತಿ ॥ ನಿನ್ನೆನ್ನತನ್ನ ಇತ್ಯೇತೇಷಾಂ ಪುನಶ್ಚತುರ್ಥೀವಿಭಕ್ತೌ ಪರತೋ ಯಥಾಸಙ್ಖ್ಯಂ ನಿನ ಎನ ತನ ಇತ್ಯೇತೇ ಆದೇಶಾ ಭವನ್ತಿ । ಅಸ್ಯಾಶ್ಚತುರ್ಥ್ಯಾಸ್ತೃತೀಯತ್ವಂ ಚ ಭವತಿ ॥

ಪ್ರಯೋಗ ॥ ನಿನಗೆ । ಎನಗೆ । ತನಗೆ ॥

ತಾತ್ಪರ್ಯ ॥ ನಿನ್ನೆನ್ನ ತನ್ನ ಯೆಂಬವುಗಳಿಗೆ ಚತುರ್ಥೀ ವಿಭಕ್ತಿ ಪರವಾದರೆ ಕ್ರಮವಾಗಿ ನಿನ ಎನ ತನ ಯೆಂಬಾದೇಶವಾಗುತ್ತವೆ. ಈ ಚತುರ್ಥಿಗೇನೆ ಪುನಃ ತೃತೀಯತ್ವವೂ ಬರುತ್ತದೆ.

ಸೂತ್ರ ॥ ದ್ವಿಬಹ್ವೋರ್ನಸ್ಯ ಮಃ ॥ ೧೦೧ ॥

ವೃತ್ತಿ ॥ ದ್ವಿತ್ವಬಹುತ್ವೇ ವಿವಕ್ಷಿತೇ ಏಷಾಂ ನಕಾರಸ್ಯ ಮಕಾರಾದೇಶೋ ಭವತಿ ॥

ಪ್ರಯೋಗ ॥ ನೀಂ । ಆಂ । ತಾಂ । ನಿಮಗೆ । ಎಮಗೆ । ತಮಗೆ । ನಿಮ್ಮ । ಎಮ್ಮ । ತಮ್ಮ । ನಿಮ್ಮೊಳ್ । ಎಮ್ಮೊಳ್ । ತಮ್ಮೊಳ್ ॥

ತಾತ್ಪರ್ಯ ॥ ದ್ವಿವಚನ ಬಹುವಚನಗಳನ್ನು ವಿವಕ್ಷಿಸುವಲ್ಲಿ ಇವುಗಳಲ್ಲಿನ ನಕಾರಕ್ಕೆ ಮಕಾರಾದೇಶವಾಗುತ್ತದೆ.

Sûtra 102.—*Adu-idu-udûnâm ante va-tau pumsi.*

Vritti.—*Eteshâm prakriti-vis'esháṇâm pul-linga-vivakshâyâm sarvâsu vibhaktishu parabhûtâsv ante va-tau bhavataḥ* ।

Prayoga.—*Avam, ivam, uvam, avanam, ivanam, uvanam, âtam, îtam, ûtam, âtanam, îtanam, ûtanam* ।

[The roots of *adu, idu, udu*, on taking the masculine terminations of all the cases change their last syllable to *va* and *ta.*]

Sûtra 103.—*Vaḷ-ke-cha striyâm.*

Vritti.—*Tesham strîtva-vivakshâyâm sarvâsu vibhaktishu antyasya vaḷ-ke iti bhavataḥ* ।

Prayoga.—*Avaḷ, ivaḷ, uvaḷ, avaḷam, ivaḷam, uvaḷam, âke, îke, ûke, âkeyam, îkeyam, ûkeyam* ।

[For the feminine of all the cases to *vaḷ* and *ke.*]

Sûtra 104.—*Dîrghaḥ ka-tayoḥ.*

Vritti.—*Eteshâm eva ka-tayoḥ pûrva-svarasya dîrgho bhavati* । *pûrvokt-odâharaṇeshv eva spashṭam* ।

[The vowel is lengthened before *k* and *t.*]

ಸೂತ್ರ ॥ ಅದುಇದುಉದೂನಾಮನ್ತೇ ವತೌ ಪುಂಸಿ ॥ ೧೦೨ ॥

ವೃತ್ತಿ ॥ ಏತೇಷಾಂ ಪ್ರಕೃತಿವಿಶೇಷಾಣಾಂ ಪುಲ್ಲಿಙ್ಗವಿವಕ್ಷಾಯಾಂ ಸರ್ವಾಸು ವಿಭಕ್ತಿಷು ಪರಭೂತಾಸ್ವನ್ತೇ ವತೌ ಭವತಃ ॥

ಪ್ರಯೋಗ ॥ ಅವಂ । ಇವಂ । ಉವಂ । ಅವನಂ । ಇವನಂ । ಉವನಂ । ಆತಂ । ಈತಂ । ಊತಂ । ಆತನಂ । ಈತನಂ । ಊತನಂ ॥

ತಾತ್ಪರ್ಯ ॥ ಅದು ಇದು ಉದು ಯೆಂಬ ಪ್ರಕೃತಿಗಳ ಪುಲ್ಲಿಂಗದಲ್ಲಿ ಸರ್ವವಿಭಕ್ತಿಗಳೂ ಪರವಾಗುತ್ತಿರಲಾಗಿ ಅನ್ತದಲ್ಲಿ ವಕಾರ ತಕಾರಗಳಾಗುವವು.

ಸೂತ್ರ ॥ ವಳ್ಕೇಚಸ್ತ್ರಿಯಾಂ ॥ ೧೦೩ ॥

ವೃತ್ತಿ ॥ ತೇಷಾಂ ಸ್ತ್ರೀತ್ವವಿವಕ್ಷಾಯಾಂ ಸರ್ವಾಸು ವಿಭಕ್ತಿಷು ಅನ್ತ್ಯಸ್ಯ ವಳ್ಕೇ ಇತಿ ಭವತಃ ॥

ಪ್ರಯೋಗ ॥ ಅವಳ್ । ಇವಳ್ । ಉವಳ್ । ಅವಳಂ । ಇವಳಂ । ಉವಳಂ । ಆಕೆ । ಈಕೆ । ಊಕೆ । ಆಕೆಯಂ । ಈಕೆಯಂ । ಊಕೆಯಂ ॥

ತಾತ್ಪರ್ಯ ॥ ಅವುಗಳ ಸ್ತ್ರೀಲಿಂಗದಲ್ಲಿ ಸರ್ವ ವಿಭಕ್ತಿಗಳೂ ಪರವಾಗುತ್ತಿರಲಾಗಿ ಅನ್ತದಲಿ ವಳ್ ಕೆ ಯೆಂಬವುಗಳಾಗುವವು.

ಸೂತ್ರ ॥ ದೀರ್ಘಃ ಕತಯೋಃ ॥ ೧೦೪ ॥

ವೃತ್ತಿ ॥ ಏತೇಷಾಮೇವ ಕತಯೋಃ ಪೂರ್ವಸ್ವರಸ್ಯ ದೀರ್ಘೋ ಭವತಿ । ಪೂರ್ವೋಕ್ತೋದಾಹರಣೇಷ್ವೇವ ಸ್ಪಷ್ಟಂ ॥

ತಾತ್ಪರ್ಯ ॥ ಇವುಗಳಲ್ಲಿನ ಕಕಾರ ತಕಾರಗಳ ಪೂರ್ವ ಸ್ವರಕ್ಕೆ ದೀರ್ಘವಾಗುತ್ತದೆ. ಈ ವಿಷಯವು ಮೇಲಿನ ಉದಾಹರಣೆಗಳಿಂದಲೇ ಸ್ಪಷ್ಟವಾಗಿದೆ.

Sûtra 105.—*Strî-pumsayor vyatyâsah krachit.*

Vritti.—*Strî-linga-pul-lingayoh krachit karuṇopatyak-âbhilâshâdi-s'abdeshu viparyâso bhavati* ı

Prayoga.—*Karuṇam, upatyakam, abhilâshe* ı

[(Sanskrit) masculines and feminines, such as *karuṇa*, *upatyaka*, *abhilâsha*, change their form (as in the examples).]

Sûtra 106.—*Nityam kaḷatrâdau napumsakatvam.*

Vritti.—*Kaḷatra-prabhṛiti-s'abdeshu napumsakatvam nityam eva bhavati* ı

Prayoga.—*Idu kaḷatram, adu kûsu* ı

[*Kaḷatra*, &c., are always neuter.]

Sûtra 107.—*Âto laghur et.*

Vritti.—*Lingântasyâkârasya vibhaktishu para-bhûtâsu laghu-bhûta ekâro bhavati* ı

Prayoga.—*Vasudhâ, vasudhe ; chandrikâ, chandrike; vanitâ, vanite; dayâ, daye, ity âdi* ı

Akârasyâpi krachit ı *Prayoga* ı *Abhilâsha, abhilâshe ; udâharaṇa, udâharaṇe; darbha, darbhe** ı

[The final â (of Sanskrit words) becomes e short (also sometimes the final a).]

ಸೂತ್ರ ॥ ಸ್ತ್ರೀ ಪುಂಸಯೋರ್ವ್ಯತ್ಯಾಸಃ ಕ್ವಚಿತ್ ॥ ೧೦೫ ॥

ವೃತ್ತಿ ॥ ಸ್ತ್ರೀಲಿಙ್ಗಪುಲ್ಲಿಙ್ಗಯೋಃ ಕ್ವಚಿತ್ ಕರುಣೋಪತ್ಯಕಾಭಿಲಾಷಾದಿಶಬ್ದೇಷು ವಿಪರ್ಯಾಸೋ ಭವತಿ ॥

ಪ್ರಯೋಗ ॥ ಕರುಣಂ । ಉಪತ್ಯಕಂ । ಅಭಿಲಾಷೆ ॥

ತಾತ್ಪರ್ಯ ॥ ಸ್ತ್ರೀ ಲಿಙ್ಗ ಪುಲ್ಲಿಙ್ಗಗಳಲ್ಲಿ ಕೆಲವು ಕಡೆ ಕರುಣ ಉಪತ್ಯಕ ಅಭಿಲಾಷೆ ಇತ್ಯಾದಿ ಶಬ್ದಗಳಲ್ಲಿ ವ್ಯತ್ಯಯವಾಗುತ್ತದೆ.

ಸೂತ್ರ ॥ ನಿತ್ಯಂ ಕಳತ್ರಾದೌ ನಪುಂಸಕತ್ವಂ ॥ ೧೦೬ ॥

ವೃತ್ತಿ ॥ ಕಳತ್ರಪ್ರಭೃತಿಶಬ್ದೇಷು ನಪುಂಸಕತ್ವಂ ನಿತ್ಯಮೇವ ಭವತಿ ॥

ಪ್ರಯೋಗ ॥ ಇದು ಕಳತ್ರಂ । ಅದು ಕೂಸು ॥

ತಾತ್ಪರ್ಯ ॥ ಕಳತ್ರ ಮೊದಲಾದ ಶಬ್ದಗಳಿಗೆ ಯಾವಾಗಲೂ ನಪುಂಸಕತ್ವವು.

ಸೂತ್ರ ॥ ಆತೋ ಲಘುರೇತ್ ॥ ೧೦೭ ॥

ವೃತ್ತಿ ॥ ಲಿಙ್ಗಾನ್ತಸ್ಯಾಕಾರಸ್ಯ ವಿಭಕ್ತಿಷು ಪರಭೂತಾಸು ಲಘುಭೂತ ಏಕಾರೋ ಭವತಿ ॥

ಪ್ರಯೋಗ ॥ ವಸುಧಾ, ವಸುಧೆ । ಚಂದ್ರಿಕಾ, ಚಂದ್ರಿಕೆ । ವನಿತಾ, ವನಿತೆ । ದಯಾ, ದಯೆ । ಇತ್ಯಾದಿ ॥

ಅಕಾರಸ್ಯಾಪಿ ಕ್ವಚಿತ್ ॥ ಪ್ರಯೋಗ ॥ ಅಭಿಲಾಷ, ಅಭಿಲಾಷೆ । ಉದಾಹರಣ, ಉದಾಹರಣೆ । ದರ್ಭ, ದರ್ಭೆ* ॥

ತಾತ್ಪರ್ಯ ॥ ಸಂಸ್ಕೃತ ಆಕಾರಾನ್ತ ಶಬ್ದಕ್ಕೆ ವಿಭಕ್ತಿಗಳು ಪರವಾದರೆ ಲಘು ಏಕಾರವಾಗುತ್ತದೆ. ಕೆಲವು ಕಡೆ ಅಕಾರನ್ತ ಶಬ್ದಕ್ಕೂ ಲಘು ಏಕಾರವಾಗುವದುಂಟು.

---

* Not in C.

* ತ್ರಿ ॥ ಪುಲ್ಲಿ ಇಲ್ಲ.

Sûtra 108.—*Îd-ûtau hrasvau cha.*

Vṛitti.—*Liṅgântayor îkârokârayoḥ hrasvau bhavatas' s'abdau vâkyâlaṅkâre* ǀ

Prayoga.—*Pakshî, pakshi ; nadî, nadi; nârî, nâri; vadhû, vadhu; Sarayû, Sarayu,* evam âdi* ǀ

[Final *î* and *û* become short.]

Sûtra 109.—*Naikâkshara-pade.*

Vṛitti.—*Â-î-û-ity ekâksharam yat padam tasmin eteshâm hrasvo na bhavati* ǀ

Prayoga.—*Û, jyâ, s'rî, hrî, bhrû* ǀ

[But final *â*, *î*, *û* are not shortened in monosyllables.]

Sûtra 110.—*Dhâtos tṛi-s'abdasya vâraḥ.*

Vṛitti.—*Dhâtor vihitasya tṛi-s'abdasya ar-âdeso bhavati vâ* ǀ

Prayoga.—*Kartâram, kartṛi ; bhartâram, bhartṛi *; dhâtâram, dhâtṛi ; hôtâram, hôtṛi** ǀ

[The *tṛi* of a Sanskrit root may become *ar*.]

ಸೂತ್ರ ॥ ಈದೂತೌ ಹ್ರಸ್ವೌ ಚ ॥ ೧೦೮ ॥

ವೃತ್ತಿ ॥ ಲಿಙ್ಗಾನ್ತಯೋರೀಕಾರೋಕಾರಯೋಃ ಹ್ರಸ್ವೌ ಭವತಶ್ಶಬ್ದೌ ವಾಕ್ಯಾಲಂಕಾರೇ ॥

ಪ್ರಯೋಗ ॥ ಪಕ್ಷೀ, ಪಕ್ಷಿ । ನದೀ, ನದಿ । ನಾರೀ, ನಾರಿ । ವಧೂ, ವಧು । ಸರಯೂ, ಸರಯು । ಏವಮಾದಿ ॥

ತಾತ್ಪರ್ಯ ॥ ಸಂಸ್ಕೃತ ಈಕಾರ ಊಕಾರಾನ್ತ ಶಬ್ದಗಳಿಗೆ ಕನ್ನಡ ವಿಭಕ್ತಿಗಳು ಪರವಾದರೆ ಹ್ರಸ್ವವಾಗುತ್ತವೆ.

ಸೂತ್ರ ॥ ನೈಕಾಕ್ಷರಪದೇ ॥ ೧೦೯ ॥

ವೃತ್ತಿ ॥ ಆ ಈ ಊ ಇತ್ಯೇಕಾಕ್ಷರಂ ಯತ್ಪದಂ ತಸ್ಮಿನ್ ಏತೇಷಾಂ ಹ್ರಸ್ವೋ ನ ಭವತಿ ॥

ಪ್ರಯೋಗ ॥ ಊ । ಜ್ಯಾ । ಶ್ರೀ । ಹ್ರೀ । ಭ್ರೂ ॥

ತಾತ್ಪರ್ಯ ॥ ಆ ಈ ಊ ಯೆಂಬ ಸ್ವರಗಳುಳ್ಳ ಯೇಕಾಕ್ಷರ ಪದಗಳಲ್ಲಿ ಹ್ರಸ್ವವಾಗುವದಿಲ್ಲ.

ಸೂತ್ರ ॥ ಧಾತೋಸ್ತೃಶಬ್ದಸ್ಯ ವಾರಃ ॥ ೧೧೦ ॥

ವೃತ್ತಿ ॥ ಧಾತೋರ್ವಿಹಿತಸ್ಯ ತೃಶಬ್ದಸ್ಯ ಅರಾದೇಶೋ ಭವತಿ ವಾ ॥

ಪ್ರಯೋಗ ॥ ಕರ್ತಾರಂ, ಕರ್ತೃ । ಭರ್ತಾರಂ, ಭರ್ತೃ* । ಧಾತಾರಂ, ಧಾತೃ । ಹೋತಾರಂ, ಹೋತೃ* ॥

ತಾತ್ಪರ್ಯ ॥ ಸಂಸ್ಕೃತದ ತೃ ಶಬ್ದಕ್ಕೆ ವಿಕಲ್ಪವಾಗಿ ಅರಾದೇಶ ಬರುತ್ತದೆ.

---

* Not in C.

* ತೃ ॥ ಪ್ರತಿಯಲ್ಲಿ ಇಲ್ಲ.

Sûtra 111.—*Rânto Vedhasi vidhâtuh.*

Vritti.—*Vidhâtri-s'abdasya Vedhasy arthe rânto bhavati* ।

Prayoga.—*Vidhâtram, Vidhâtam* ।

[*Vidhâtri* when applied to Brahma has the termination *ra*.]

Sûtra 112.—*Aro'nyatra.*

Vritti.—*Anyatra kriyâ-vâchino dhâto rikârântasya ar-âdes'o bhavati* ।

Prayoga.—*Pitar, pitrigal, bhrâtaram, bhrâtrigal* ।

[Except in the root of a verb, the terminal *ri* of other words becomes *ar*.]

Sûtra 113.—**Tas' cha.*

Vritti.—*Kvachid rikârâdes'o bhavati* ।

Prayoga.—*Mândhâta, Mândhâtri* ।

[Sometimes *ta*.]

Sûtra 114.—*S'vâ-yuvâdhvanâm ânah.*

Vritti.—*S'van-yuvan-adhvan ity eteshâm ântasya âno bhavati* ।

Prayoga.—*S'vâ, s'vânam ; yuvâ, yuvânam ; adhvâ, adhvânam* । *s'vânangal, yuvânar, adhvânangal bahu-vachane* ।

[*S'van, yuvan, adhvan* obtain the termination *âna*.]

ಸೂತ್ರ ॥ ರಾನ್ತೋ ವೇಧಸಿ ವಿಧಾತುಃ ॥ ೧೧೧ ॥

ವೃತ್ತಿ ॥ ವಿಧಾತೃಶಬ್ದಸ್ಯ ವೇಧಸ್ಯರ್ಥೇ ರಾನ್ತೋ ಭವತಿ ॥

ಪ್ರಯೋಗ ॥ ವಿಧಾತ್ರಂ । ವಿಧಾತಂ ॥

ತಾತ್ಪರ್ಯ ॥ ಬ್ರಹ್ಮವಾಚಕವಾದ ವಿಧಾತೃ ಶಬ್ದಕ್ಕೆ ರಾನ್ತವಾಗುತ್ತದೆ.

ಸೂತ್ರ ॥ ಅರೋಽನ್ಯತ್ರ ॥ ೧೧೨ ॥

ವೃತ್ತಿ ॥ ಅನ್ಯತ್ರ ಕ್ರಿಯಾವಾಚಿನೋ ಧಾತೋ ಋಕಾರಾನ್ತಸ್ಯ ಅರಾದೇಶೋ ಭವತಿ ॥

ಪ್ರಯೋಗ ॥ ಪಿತರ, ಪಿತೃಗಳ । ಭ್ರಾತರಂ, ಭ್ರಾತೃಗಳ ॥

ತಾತ್ಪರ್ಯ ॥ ಕೆಲವು ಕಡೆ ಅಂದರೆ ಕ್ರಿಯಾ ಧಾತುವಲ್ಲದ ತೃ ಶಬ್ದಕ್ಕೆ ಅರ್ ಯಂಬದು ಬರುತ್ತದೆ.

ಸೂತ್ರ ॥ *ತಶ್ಚ ॥ ೧೧೩ ॥

ವೃತ್ತಿ ॥ ಕ್ವಚಿದೃಕಾರಾದೇಶೋ ಭವತಿ ॥

ಪ್ರಯೋಗ ॥ ಮಾಂಧಾತ, ಮಾಂಧಾತೃ ॥

ತಾತ್ಪರ್ಯ ॥ ಕೆಲವು ಕಡೆ ಋಕಾರವೇ ಬರುತ್ತದೆ, ಅಂದರೆ ೧೧೦ನೇ ಸೂತ್ರ ಪ್ರಕಾರ ಅರ ಯಂಬದಕ್ಕೆ ಬದಲಾಗಿ ವಿಧಾತೃ ಯಂಬದಾಗುತ್ತದೆಂಬುವದು.

ಸೂತ್ರ ॥ ಶ್ವಾಯುವಾಧ್ವನಾಮಾನಃ ॥ ೧೧೪ ॥

ವೃತ್ತಿ ॥ ಶ್ವನ್ ಯುವನ್ ಅಧ್ವನ್ ಇತ್ಯೇತೇಷಾಂ ಅನ್ತಸ್ಯ ಆನೋ ಭವತಿ ॥

ಪ್ರಯೋಗ ॥ ಶ್ವಾ, ಶ್ವಾನಂ । ಯುವಾ, ಯುವಾನಂ । ಅಧ್ವಾ, ಅಧ್ವಾನಂ ॥ ಶ್ವಾನಂಗಳ । ಯುವಾನರ । ಅಧ್ವಾನಂಗಳ ಬಹುವಚನೇ ॥

ತಾತ್ಪರ್ಯ ॥ ಶ್ವನ್, ಯುವನ್, ಅಧ್ವನ್ ಎಂಬ ಸಂಸ್ಕೃತ ಶಬ್ದಗಳ ಪ್ರಥಮಾ ವಿಭಕ್ತಿಗಳಾದ ಶ್ವಾ, ಯುವಾ, ಅಧ್ವಾ ಎಂಬ ಅನ್ತಗಳಿಗೆ ಆನ ಯಂಬದು ಬರುತ್ತದೆ.

---

* In B and C, 112 and 113 form one sûtra.

* ದ್ವಿ। ತೃ। ಪ್ರತಿಗಳಲ್ಲಿ ೧೧೨—೧೧೩ನೇ ಸೂತ್ರಗಳೆರಡೂ ಒಂದಾಗಿ ಸೇರಿಸಿ ಬರದು ಇದ್ದಾರೆ.

Sûtra 115.—*Sakhyur âyah.*

Vṛitti—*Sakhi-s'abdasya vibhaktishu para-bhûtâsu âya ity âdes'o bhavati* ।

Prayoga.—*Sakhâyam, sakhâyar* ।

[*Sakhi* takes *âya* before the case terminations.]

Sûtra 116.—*Vans-yansor upântyasya dîrgho vâ lopah.*

Vṛitti.—*Vans-yans-pratyayântayor upântyasya vâ dîrgho bhavati* । *krachid antyasya lopah* ।

Prayoga.—*Vidvans, vidvâmsam ; kanîyans, kanîyâmsam ; jyâyans, jyâyâmsam* ।

[*Vans* and *yans* lengthen the vowel or omit the last letter.]

Sûtra 117.—*Adantatâ cha.*

Vṛitti.—*Tat pratyayântayor upântyasya vâ dîrgho bhavati* । *krachid antyasya akârântatâ cha bhavati* ।

Prayoga.—*Kanîyâmsam, vidvâmsam* । *vâ grahaṇât krachid vikalpena tad antyasya lopas syât* । *yathâ :—s'reyam, s'reyâmsam, jñâyam, jñâyâmsam* ।

[Sometimes they terminate in *a*.]

ಸೂತ್ರ॥ ಸಖ್ಯುರಾಯಃ ॥೧೧೫॥

ವೃತ್ತಿ ॥ ಸಖಿಶಬ್ದಸ್ಯ ವಿಭಕ್ತಿಷು ಪರಭೂತಾಸು ಆಯ ಇತ್ಯಾದೇಶೋ ಭವತಿ ॥

ಪ್ರಯೋಗ ॥ ಸಖಾಯಂ । ಸಖಾಯರ್ ॥

ತಾತ್ಪರ್ಯ ॥ ಸಖಿ ಶಬ್ದಕ್ಕೆ ವಿಭಕ್ತಿಗಳು ಪರವಾದಾಗ ಆಯ ಎಂಬದು ಆದೇಶವಾಗುತ್ತದೆ.

ಸೂತ್ರ ॥ ವನ್ಸ್-ಯನ್ಸೋರುಪಾನ್ತ್ಯಸ್ಯ ದೀರ್ಘೋ ವಾ ಲೋಪಃ ॥೧೧೬॥

ವೃತ್ತಿ ॥ ವನ್ಸ್ ಯನ್ಸ್-ಪ್ರತ್ಯಯಾನ್ತಯೋರುಪಾನ್ತ್ಯಸ್ಯ ವಾ ದೀರ್ಘೋ ಭವತಿ। ಕ್ವಚಿದನ್ತ್ಯಸ್ಯ ಲೋಪಃ ॥

ಪ್ರಯೋಗ ॥ ವಿದ್ವನ್ಸ್, ವಿದ್ವಾಂಸಂ। ಕನೀಯನ್ಸ್, ಕನೀಯಾಂಸಂ। ಜ್ಯಾಯನ್ಸ್, ಜ್ಯಾಯಾಂಸಂ ॥

ತಾತ್ಪರ್ಯ॥ ವನ್ಸ್ ಯನ್ಸ್ ಪ್ರತ್ಯಯಾನ್ತಗಳಾದ ಸಂಸ್ಕೃತ ಪ್ರಥಮಾ ವಿಭಕ್ತಿಗಳ ಉಪಾನ್ತ್ಯಾಕ್ಷರಕ್ಕೆ ದೀರ್ಘವಾಗಲಿ ಅನ್ತ್ಯಕ್ಕೆ ಲೋಪವಾಗಲಿ ಆಗುತ್ತದೆ.

ಸೂತ್ರ ॥ ಅದನ್ತತಾ ಚ ॥೧೧೭॥

ವೃತ್ತಿ ॥ ತತ್ಪ್ರತ್ಯಯಾನ್ತಯೋರುಪಾನ್ತ್ಯಸ್ಯ ವಾ ದೀರ್ಘೋ ಭವತಿ। ಕ್ವಚಿದನ್ತ್ಯಸ್ಯ ಅಕಾರಾನ್ತತಾ ಚ ಭವತಿ ॥

ಪ್ರಯೋಗ ॥ ಕನೀಯಾಂಸಂ। ವಿದ್ವಾಂಸಂ ॥ ವಾ ಗ್ರಹಣಾತ್ ಕ್ವಚಿದ್ವಿಕಲ್ಪೇನ ತದನ್ತ್ಯಸ್ಯ ಲೋಪಸ್ಸ್ಯಾತ್ ॥ ಯಥಾ ॥ ಶ್ರೇಯಂ। ಶ್ರೇಯಾಂಸಂ । ಜ್ಞಾಯಂ। ಜ್ಞಾಯಾಂಸಂ ॥

ತಾತ್ಪರ್ಯ ॥ ಯನ್ಸ್ ವನ್ಸ್ ಪ್ರತ್ಯಯಾನ್ತ ಶಬ್ದಗಳ ಪ್ರಥಮಾ ವಿಭಕ್ತಿಗೆ ಅದರ ಉಪಾನ್ತ್ಯಾಕ್ಷರಕ್ಕೆ ದೀರ್ಘವೂ ಅಥವಾ ಅನ್ತ್ಯಾಕ್ಷರಕ್ಕೆ ಲೋಪವೂ ಸಂಭವಿಸುತ್ತಿರಲಾಗಿ ಇದಕ್ಕೆ ಅಕಾರಾನ್ತವೆಂಬದು ನಿಶ್ಚಯವು. ಲೋಪದಲ್ಲಿ ಶ್ರೇಯಂ ಎಂದು ಸಕಾರ ಲೋಪವಾಗಿದೆ.

Sûtra 118.—*Virâme vyañjanasyâpi.*

Vṛitti.—*Virâme vartamânasya vyañjanasyâpi akârântatâ bhavati* ।

Prayoga.—*Sampadam, marutam, vihâyasam* ।

[A final consonant takes a terminal *a*.]

Sûtra 119.—*Lopo vibhâshayâ.*

Vṛitti.—*Virâme vartamânasya vyañjanasya kvachid vikalpena lopas syât* ।

Prayoga.—*Nabhas, nabham; manas, manam;* râjan, râjam* ।

Kvachid dritva-yuktokârântatâ cha । *Prayoga* । *vâk, vâkku; ushas, ushassu; dik, dikku; parishat, parishattu* ।

[Or is dropped.]

Sûtra 120.—*Varge tad-vargântyah.*

Vṛitti.—*Vargâksharesbu pareshu tad-varga-pañchamâksharam anusvârâdes'as syât* ।

Prayoga.—*Bimkam geṭṭam, tâm chañchaḷa-chittam, suṭṭ-eṇṭakkum, mêlvattante tôrkkum, bilvambettam* । *kvachid vikalpah* । *bimkam geṭṭam*† ।

[*Anusvâra* before a *varga* consonant, becomes the fifth (or nasal) of the same varga.]

ಸೂತ್ರ ॥ ವಿರಾಮೇ ವ್ಯಂಜನಸ್ಯಾಪಿ ॥ ೧೧೮ ॥

ವೃತ್ತಿ ॥ ವಿರಾಮೇ ವರ್ತಮಾನಸ್ಯ ವ್ಯಂಜನಸ್ಯಾಪಿ ಅಕಾರಾನ್ತತಾ ಭವತಿ ॥

ಪ್ರಯೋಗ ॥ ಸಂಪದಂ । ಮರುತಂ । ವಿಹಾಯಸಂ ॥

ತಾತ್ಪರ್ಯ ॥ ವಿರಾಮದಲ್ಲಿ ವರ್ತಿಸುವ ವ್ಯಂಜನಕ್ಕೂ ಕೆಲವೆಡೆಯಲ್ಲಿ ಅಕಾರಾನ್ತತೆ ಬರುತ್ತದೆ. ಇಲ್ಲಿ ವಿರಾಮವೆಂದರೆ ಅಂತ್ಯಾಕ್ಷರ.

ಸೂತ್ರ ॥ ಲೋಪೋ ವಿಭಾಷಯಾ ॥ ೧೧೯ ॥

ವೃತ್ತಿ ॥ ವಿರಾಮೇ ವರ್ತಮಾನಸ್ಯ ವ್ಯಂಜನಸ್ಯ ಕ್ವಚಿದ್ವಿಕಲ್ಪೇನ ಲೋಪಸ್ಸ್ಯಾತ್ ॥

ಪ್ರಯೋಗ ॥ ನಭಸ್, ನಭಂ । ಮನಸ್, ಮನಂ* । ರಾಜನ್, ರಾಜಂ ॥

ಕ್ವಚಿದ್ದ್ವಿತ್ವಯುಕ್ತೋಕಾರಾನ್ತತಾ ಚ ॥ ಪ್ರಯೋಗ ॥ ವಾಕ್, ವಾಕ್ಕು । ಉಷಸ್, ಉಷಸ್ಸು । ದಿಕ್, ದಿಕ್ಕು । ಪರಿಷತ್, ಪರಿಷತ್ತು ॥

ತಾತ್ಪರ್ಯ ॥ ವಿರಾಮದಲ್ಲಿ ವರ್ತಿಸುವ ವ್ಯಂಜನಕ್ಕೆ ಕೆಲವುಕಡೆ ವಿಕಲ್ಪವಾಗಿ ಲೋಪವಾಗುತ್ತದೆ. ಕೆಲವುಕಡೆ ಆ ವಿರಾಮದ ವ್ಯಂಜನಕ್ಕೆ ದ್ವಿತ್ವ ಯುಕ್ತ ಉಕಾರಾನ್ತತೆಯೂ ಬರುತ್ತದೆ. ದಿಕ್ ದಿಕ್ಕು ಯೆಂಬುದಾಹರಣೆಗಳಿಂ ತಿಳಿಯುವದು.

ಸೂತ್ರ ॥ ವರ್ಗೇ ತದ್ವರ್ಗಾನ್ತ್ಯಃ ॥ ೧೨೦ ॥

ವೃತ್ತಿ ॥ ವರ್ಗಾಕ್ಷರೇಷು ಪರೇಷು ತದ್ವರ್ಗಪಂಚಮಾಕ್ಷರಮನುಸ್ವಾರಾದೇಶಸ್ಸ್ಯಾತ್ ॥

ಪ್ರಯೋಗ ॥ ಬಿಙ್ಕಂ ಗೆಟ್ಟಂ । ತಾಂ ಚಞ್ಚಳಚಿತ್ತಂ । ಸುತ್ತೆಣ್ಟಕ್ಕುಂ । ಮೇಲ್ವತ್ತನ್ತೆ ತೋರ್ಕ್ಕುಂ । ಬಿಲ್ವಮ್ಬೆತ್ತಂ । ಕ್ವಚಿದ್ವಿಕಲ್ಪಃ । ಬಿಂಕಂ ಗೆಟ್ಟಂ ॥

ತಾತ್ಪರ್ಯ ॥ ವರ್ಗಾಕ್ಷರಗಳು ಪರವಾದರೆ ಆಯಾ ವರ್ಗದ ಪಂಚಮಾಕ್ಷರವು ಅನುಸ್ವಾರಾದೇಶವಾಗುವದು.

---

* C ends here.

† That is, the anusvâra is used for the nasal, which is the common method of writing.

* ತೃ । ಯಲ್ಲಿ ಮನ ಎಂಬ ಉದಾಹರಣೆಗೆ ನಿಂತು ಇವೆ.

Sûtra 121.—*No nasya ṇena.*

Vṛitti—*Nakârasya ṇakâreṇa saha yoge ṇatvam bhavati* ।

Prayoga—*Kaṇ-neḷal, kaṇṇeḷal ; kaṇ-nîr, kaṇṇîr ; taṇ-nîr, taṇṇîr* ।

[When *ṇ* follows *n*, the latter becomes *ṇ*.]

Sûtra 122.—*Po ho vâ.*

Vritti—*S'abdeshu hakârasya pakâro vâ syât* ।

Prayoga—*Halam, palam ; halage, palage ; hâsu, pâsu ; maigâhu, maigâpu; kaigâhu, kaigâpu* ।

[*H* in a word may become p.]*

Sûtra 123.—*S'a-shayos sah.*

Vritti—*Atra s'akâra-shakârayoh sakârâdes'as syât* ।

Prayoga—*S'as'i, sasi ; s'is'u, sisu ; mashi, masi ; ṛishi, risi ; s'êshe, sêse* ।

[*S'* and *sh* become *s*.]

Sûtra 124.—*Sa-repha-samyoge tad-antare tv-ih.*

Vritti—*Shakâre repha-samyoga-yukte sati repha-shakârayor madhye ikâro bhavati* ।

Prayoga—*Harsham, harisam; varsham, varisam; sarshapam, sarisapam* ।

[When *r* precedes them, *i* comes between.]

ಸೂತ್ರ ॥ ಣೋ ನಸ್ಯ ಣೇನ ॥ ೧೨೧ ॥

ವೃತ್ತಿ ॥ ನಕಾರಸ್ಯ ಣಕಾರೇಣ ಸಹ ಯೋಗೇ ಣತ್ವಂ ಭವತಿ ॥

ಪ್ರಯೋಗ ॥ ಕಣ್-ನೆಳಲ್, ಕಣ್ಣೆಳಲ್ । ಕಣ್-ನೀರ್, ಕಣ್ಣೀರ್ । ತಣ್-ನೀರ್, ತಣ್ಣೀರ್ ॥

ತಾತ್ಪರ್ಯ ॥ ನಕಾರಕ್ಕೆ ಣಕಾರದ ಸಹಿತವಾಗಿ ಯೋಗವಾದರೆ ಣತ್ವ ಬರುತ್ತದೆ.

ಸೂತ್ರ ॥ ಪೋ ಹೋ ವಾ ॥ ೧೨೨ ॥

ವೃತ್ತಿ ॥ ಶಬ್ದೇಷು ಹಕಾರಸ್ಯ ಪಕಾರೋ ವಾ ಸ್ಯಾತ್ ॥

ಪ್ರಯೋಗ ॥ ಹಲಂ, ಪಲಂ । ಹಲಗೆ, ಪಲಗೆ । ಹಾಸು, ಪಾಸು । ಮೈಗಾಹು, ಮೈಗಾಪು । ಕೈಗಾಹು, ಕೈಗಾಪು ॥

ತಾತ್ಪರ್ಯ ॥ ಶಬ್ದಗಳಲ್ಲಿ ಹಕಾರಕ್ಕೆ ವಿಕಲ್ಪವಾಗಿ ಪಕಾರವಾಗತ್ತದೆ.

ಸೂತ್ರ ॥ ಶಷಯೋಸ್ಸಃ ॥ ೧೨೩ ॥

ವೃತ್ತಿ ॥ ಅತ್ರ ಶಕಾರಷಕಾರಯೋಃ ಸಕಾರಾದೇಶಸ್ಸ್ಯಾತ್ ॥

ಪ್ರಯೋಗ ॥ ಶಶಿ, ಸಸಿ । ಶಿಶು, ಸಿಸು । ಮಷಿ, ಮಸಿ । ಋಷಿ, ರಿಸಿ । ಶೇಷೆ, ಸೇಸೆ ॥

ತಾತ್ಪರ್ಯ ॥ ಶಕಾರ ಷಕಾರಗಳಿಗೆ ಸಕಾರಾದೇಶವಾಗುತ್ತದೆ.

ಸೂತ್ರ ॥ ಸರೇಫಸಂಯೋಗೇ ತದನ್ತರೇ ತ್ವಿಃ ॥ ೧೨೪ ॥

ವೃತ್ತಿ ॥ ಷಕಾರೇ ರೇಫಸಂಯೋಗಯುಕ್ತೇ ಸತಿ ರೇಫಷಕಾರಯೋರ್ಮಧ್ಯೇ ಇಕಾರೋ ಭವತಿ ॥

ಪ್ರಯೋಗ ॥ ಹರ್ಷಂ, ಹರಿಸಂ । ವರ್ಷಂ, ವರಿಸಂ । ಸರ್ಷಪಂ, ಸರಿಸಪಂ ।

ತಾತ್ಪರ್ಯ ॥ ರೇಫಯುಕ್ತವಾದ ಷಕಾರಕ್ಕೆ ಆ ರೇಫ ಷಕಾರಗಳ ಮಧ್ಯದಲ್ಲಿ ಇಕಾರ ಬರುತ್ತದೆ.

---

* In the literature of the language *p* marks the more ancient form, *h* the more modern: so much so that the respective periods have sometimes been named the *p* and *h* periods. Thus *posa* is now *hosa*; *paḷe* is *haḷe*; *peṇṇu* is *heṇṇu*; *pôgu* is *hôgu*; *ṗattu* is *hattu*, &c.

Sûtra 125.—*Hakârasyot.*

Vritti.—*Hakârasya repha-samyoge tayor madhye ukâras syât* ।

Prayoga.—*Arham, aruham ; barham, baruham ; gârhapatyam, gâruhapatyam ; arhantam, aruhantam** ।

[When *r* precedes *h*, then *u* comes between.]

Sûtra 126.—*Ḷakâraḥ pada-vidhau ḍasya vyñjaneshu.*

Vritti.—*Samâsa-vidhau vyañjaneshu pareshu ḍasya ḷas syât* ।

Prayoga.—*Kâḍu-purisam, kâḷvurisam ; kâḍu-kichchu, kâḷkichchu;† nâḍu-paragaṇam, nâḷvaragaṇam ; nâḍu-kaḍe, nâḷkaḍe ; kôḍu-koṭṭu, kôḷkoṭṭu* । *ity eteshâm prayogasya samâsa-vidhau pûrva-padopântya-svara-lopâd evam rûpam siddham* ।

[In compound words, *ḍ* followed by a consonant becomes *ḷ*.]

Sûtra 127.—*Ati ṭaḥ.*

Vritti.—*Ḍakârasya ati pratyaye pare ṭakâro bhavati* ।

Prayoga.—*Âḍ, âṭam ; nôḍ, nôṭam ; bêḍ, bêṭam ; mâḍ, mâṭam*।‡

[*Ḍ* before *ati* becomes *ṭ*.]

ಸೂತ್ರ ॥ ಹಕಾರಸ್ಯೋತ್ ॥ ೧೨೫ ॥

ವೃತ್ತಿ ॥ ಹಕಾರಸ್ಯ ರೇಫಸಂಯೋಗೇ ತಯೋರ್ಮಧ್ಯೇ ಉಕಾರಸ್ಸ್ಯಾತ್ ॥

ಪ್ರಯೋಗ ॥ ಅರ್ಹಂ, ಅರುಹಂ । ಬರ್ಹಂ, ಬರುಹಂ । ಗಾರ್ಹಪತ್ಯಂ, ಗಾರುಹಪತ್ಯಂ । ಅರ್ಹಂತಂ, ಅರುಹಂತಂ ॥*

ತಾತ್ಪರ್ಯ ॥ ರೇಫಯುಕ್ತವಾಗಿ ಹಕಾರವಿದ್ದರೆ ಆ ಹಕಾರ ರೇಫಗಳ ನಡುವೆ ಉಕಾರ ಬರುತ್ತದೆ.

ಸೂತ್ರ ॥ ಳಕಾರಃ ಪದವಿಧೌ ಡಸ್ಯ ವ್ಯಂಜನೇಷು ॥ ೧೨೬ ॥

ವೃತ್ತಿ ॥ ಸಮಾಸವಿಧೌ ವ್ಯಂಜನೇಷು ಪರೇಷು ಡಸ್ಯ ಳಸ್ಸ್ಯಾತ್ ॥

ಪ್ರಯೋಗ ॥ ಕಾಡು-ಪುರಿಸಂ, ಕಾಳ್ವುರಿಸಂ। ಕಾಡು-ಕಿಚ್ಚು, ಕಾಳ್ಕಿಚ್ಚು†। ನಾಡು-ಪರಗಣಂ, ನಾಳ್ವರಗಣಂ। ನಾಡು-ಕಡೆ, ನಾಳ್ಕಡೆ। ಕೋಡು-ಕೊಟ್ಟು, ಕೋಳ್ಕೊಟ್ಟು ॥ ಇತ್ಯೇತೇಷಾಂ ಪ್ರಯೋಗಸ್ಯ ಸಮಾಸವಿಧೌ ಪೂರ್ವಪದೋಪಾನ್ತ್ಯಸ್ವರಲೋಪಾದೇವಂ ರೂಪಂ ಸಿದ್ಧಂ ॥

ತಾತ್ಪರ್ಯ ॥ ಸಮಾಸಮಾಡುವದರಲ್ಲಿ ವ್ಯಂಜನಗಳು ಪರವಾದಾಗ ಡಕಾರಕ್ಕೆ ಳಕಾರ ಬರುತ್ತದೆ. ಹೀಗಾಗುವ ಸಮಾಸದ ಪೂರ್ವಪದೋಪಾನ್ತ್ಯ ಸ್ವರಲೋಪವಾಗಿ ಈ ರೂಪವು ಸಿದ್ಧವಾಗುತ್ತದೆ.

ಸೂತ್ರ ॥ ಅತಿ ಟಃ ॥ ೧೨೭ ॥

ವೃತ್ತಿ ॥ ಡಕಾರಸ್ಯ ಅತಿಪ್ರತ್ಯಯೇ ಪರೇ ಟಕಾರೋ ಭವತಿ ॥

ಪ್ರಯೋಗ ॥ ಆಡ್, ಆಟಂ। ನೋಡ್, ನೋಟಂ। ಬೇಡ್, ಬೇಟಂ। ಮಾಡ್, ಮಾಟಂ ॥ ‡

ತಾತ್ಪರ್ಯ ॥ ಸಮಾಸ ಮಾಡುವದರಲ್ಲಿ ಡಕಾರಕ್ಕೆ ಅತಿ ಪ್ರತ್ಯಯ ಪರವಾದರೆ ಟಕಾರವಾಗುತ್ತದೆ.

---

* Not in C. † C. ends here. ‡ In C the examples are *naḍu, naṭṭam ; paḍu, paṭṭam.*

* ತ್ರ ॥ ಯಲ್ಲಿ ಅರ್ಹಂತಂ ಎಂಬುದು ಇಲ್ಲ, † ತ್ರ ॥ ಯಲ್ಲಿ ಇಲ್ಲಿಗೆ ನಿಂತು ಇದೆ.
‡ ॥ ತ್ರ ॥ ನಡು, ನಟ್ಟಂ । ಪಡು, ಪಟ್ಟಂ ಎಂಬವು ಇವೆ.

Sûtra 128.—*Rakârasya rephah.*

Vṛitti.—*Samâse rakârasya repho bhavati* ।

Prayoga.—*Mâr-koral, mârkoral; mâr-balam, mârbalam; nûr-maḍi, nûrmaḍi; nûr-sâsiram, nûrchhâsiram* ।

[*R* becomes *repha.*] *

Sûtra 129.—*Âde ṛi-riḥ.*

Vṛitti.—*S'abdeshv âdi-bhûtasya ṛikârasya ritvam bhavati* ।

Prayoga.—*Tṛitîyam, tritîyam; ṛiṇam, riṇam; ṛitu, ritu; ṛishi, risi* ।

[An initial *ṛi* becomes *ri.*]

Sûtra 130.—*Ya-rayor anâdisthayor ai-au svareṇa vâ.*

Vṛitti.—*Anâdau vartamânayor yakâra-vakârayos svareṇa saha yathâsaṅkhyam aikâr-aukârau bhavataḥ* ।

Prayoga.—*Kayirâram, kairâram; hârayisidam, hâraisidam; kerayisidam, keraisidam; pûrayisidam, pûraisidam; kavadale, kaudale; kavuṅkuḷ, kauṅkuḷ; kâvuṅgu, kauṅgu; avuṅkidam, auṅkidam* ।†

[Medial *y* and *v*, uniting with a vowel, become *ai* and *au.*]

Iti Karṇâṭaka-vyâkaraṇa-vṛittau ‡ Bhâshâ-bhûshaṇe S'abda-rîti-vidhânam nâma pañchamaḥ parichchhedaḥ ।

ಸೂತ್ರ ॥ ರಕಾರಸ್ಯ ರೇಫಃ ॥ ೧೨೮ ॥

ವೃತ್ತಿ ॥ ಸಮಾಸೇ ರಕಾರಸ್ಯ ರೇಫೋ ಭವತಿ ॥

ಪ್ರಯೋಗ ॥ ಮಾರ್-ಕೊರಲ್, ಮಾರ್ಕೊರಲ್ । ಮಾರ್-ಬಲಂ, ಮಾರ್ಬಲಂ । ನೂರ್-ಮಡಿ, ನೂರ್ಮಡಿ । ನೂರ್-ಸಾಸಿರಂ, ನೂರ್ಛಾಸಿರಂ ॥

ತಾತ್ಪರ್ಯ ॥ ಸಮಾಸದಲ್ಲಿ ರಕಾರಕ್ಕೆ ರೇಫವಾಗುತ್ತದೆ. ರೇಫವೆಂದರೆ ಇಲ್ಲಿ ಅರಕಾವತ್ತೆಂಬರ್ಥವು.

ಸೂತ್ರ ॥ ಆದೇಋಋಃ ॥ ೧೨೯ ॥

ವೃತ್ತಿ ॥ ಶಬ್ದೇಷ್ವಾದಿಭೂತಸ್ಯ ಋಕಾರಸ್ಯ ರಿತ್ವಂ ಭವತಿ ॥

ಪ್ರಯೋಗ ॥ ತೃತೀಯಂ, ತ್ರಿತೀಯಂ । ಋಣಂ, ರಿಣಂ । ಋತು, ರಿತು । ಋಷಿ, ರಿಸಿ ॥

ತಾತ್ಪರ್ಯ ॥ ಶಬ್ದಗಳಲ್ಲಿ ಆದಿಭೂತವಾದ ಋಕಾರಕ್ಕೆ ರಿತ್ವ ಬರುತ್ತದೆ.

ಸೂತ್ರ ॥ ಯವಯೋರನಾದಿಸ್ಥಯೋ ರೈಚ್ ಔಚ್ ಸ್ವರೇಣ ವಾ ॥೧೩೦ ॥

ವೃತ್ತಿ ॥ ಅನಾದೌ ವರ್ತಮಾನಯೋರ್ಯಕಾರವಕಾರಯೋಸ್ಸ್ವರೇಣ ಸಹ ಯಥಾಸಙ್ಖ್ಯಮೈಕಾರೌಕಾರೌ ಭವತಃ ॥

ಪ್ರಯೋಗ ॥ ಕಯಿವಾರಂ, ಕೈವಾರಂ। ಹಾರಯಿಸಿದಂ, ಹಾರೈಸಿದಂ। ಕೇರಯಿಸಿದಂ, ಕೇರೈಸಿದಂ। ಪೂರಯಿಸಿದಂ, ಪೂರೈಸಿದಂ। ಕವದಲೆ, ಕೌದಲೆ। ಕವುಂಕುಳ್, ಕೌಂಕುಳ್। ಕಾವುಂಗು, ಕೌಂಗು। ಅವುಂಕಿದಂ, ಔಂಕಿದಂ ॥†

ತಾತ್ಪರ್ಯ ॥ ಆದಿಯಲ್ಲದ ಯಕಾರ ವಕಾರಗಳಿಗೆ ಸ್ವರದೊಡನೆ ಕೂಡಿ ಯಥಾ ಕ್ರಮವಾಗಿ ಐಕಾರ ಔಕಾರಗಳಾಗುವವು.

ಇತಿ ಕರ್ಣಾಟಕ ವ್ಯಾಕರಣ ವೃತ್ತೌ ‡ ಭಾಷಾ ಭೂಷಣೇ ಶಬ್ದರೀತಿ ವಿಧಾನಂ ನಾಮ ಪಂಚಮಃ ಪರಿಚ್ಛೇದಃ ॥

---

* In old written compositions the consonant is invariably doubled after *r.* Thus *nûrmmaḍi, pêrmmaḍi, pannirchchhâsiram,* &c. No exception has been found to this practice.

† C has only the first and last. ‡ See note p. 7.

† ತೃ ॥ ಪ್ರತಿಯಲ್ಲಿ ಮೊದಲನೇ ಉದಾಹರಣೆಯೂ ಕಡೇ ಉದಾಹರಣೆಯೂ ಇದೆ.

‡ ೭ನೇ ಪುಟವನ್ನು ನೋಡಬೇಕು.

(VI. Compound Words.)

Samâsa Vidhânam.

Sûtra 131.—*Nâmnâm samâsas saṅgatârthah.*

Vṛitti.—*Nâma-vâchinâm s'abdânâm parasparam anvaya-siddho'rthas samâsa-samjñas syât* ।

[A compound word is formed of a noun combined with the words united to it.]

Sûtra 132.—*Tatrântar-vartinyo vibhaktayo lopyâh.*

Vṛitti.—*Tatra samâsa-padeshu madhya-vartinyo vibhaktayo lupyante* ।

[The words thus united to it drop their case terminations.]

Sûtra 133.—*Uttara-padârtha-pravṛittis tatpurushah.*

Vṛitti.—*Uttara-padârtha eva pradhâno yasmin sa samâsah tatpurusha-samjñas syât* ।

Prayoga.—*Sûleyara kêri, sûlegêri* । *ity atra vibhakti-lopâd eka-rûpatvam* । *evam eva* । *arasu mane, aramane ; mâvina kâyi, mâṅgâyi ; pasiya ole, pach-chole* ।

[When the final word is the chief in meaning, the compound is a *tatpurusha*.]

---

೬. ಸಮಾಸ ವಿಧಾನಂ.

ಸೂತ್ರ ॥ ನಾಮ್ನಾಂ ಸಮಾಸಸ್ಸಙ್ಗತಾರ್ಥಃ ॥ ೧೩೧ ॥

ವೃತ್ತಿ ॥ ನಾಮವಾಚಿನಾಂ ಶಬ್ದಾನಾಂ ಪರಸ್ಪರಮನ್ವಯಸಿದ್ಧೋಽರ್ಥಸ್ಸಮಾಸಸಂಜ್ಞಸ್ಸ್ಯಾತ್ ॥

ತಾತ್ಪರ್ಯ ॥ ನಾಮ ಪದವನ್ನು ಕೂಡಿ ನುಡಿಯುವರ್ಥವು ಸಮಾಸವೆನ್ನಲ್ಪಡುವದು. ಇದಕ್ಕೆ ಸಮಾಸ ಸಂಜ್ಞೆ.

ಸೂತ್ರ ॥ ತತ್ರಾನ್ತರ್ವರ್ತಿನ್ಯೋ ವಿಭಕ್ತಯೋ ಲೋಪ್ಯಾಃ ॥ ೧೩೨ ॥

ವೃತ್ತಿ ॥ ತತ್ರ ಸಮಾಸಪದೇಷು ಮಧ್ಯವರ್ತಿನ್ಯೋ ವಿಭಕ್ತಯೋ ಲುಪ್ಯನ್ತೇ ॥

ತಾತ್ಪರ್ಯ ॥ ಆ ಸಮಾಸ ಪದಗಳ ಮಧ್ಯದಲ್ಲಿರುವ ವಿಭಕ್ತಿಗಳು ಲೋಪಿಸುತ್ತವೆ.

ಸೂತ್ರ ॥ ಉತ್ತರಪದಾರ್ಥಪ್ರವೃತ್ತಿಸ್ತತ್ಪುರುಷಃ ॥ ೧೩೩ ॥

ವೃತ್ತಿ ॥ ಉತ್ತರಪದಾರ್ಥ ಏವ ಪ್ರಧಾನೋ ಯಸ್ಮಿನ್ ಸ ಸಮಾಸಃ ತತ್ಪುರುಷಸಂಜ್ಞಸ್ಸ್ಯಾತ್ ॥

ಪ್ರಯೋಗ ॥ ಸೂಳೆಯರ ಕೇರಿ, ಸೂಳೆಗೇರಿ ಇತ್ಯತ್ರ ವಿಭಕ್ತಿಲೋಪಾದೇಕರೂಪತ್ವಂ ॥ ಏವಮೇವ । ಅರಸು ಮನೆ, ಅರಮನೆ । ಮಾವಿನಕಾಯಿ, ಮಾಂಗಾಯಿ । ಪಸಿಯ ಒಲೆ, ಪಚ್ಚೊಲೆ ॥

ತಾತ್ಪರ್ಯ ॥ ಪರಪದದ ಅರ್ಥವನ್ನೇ ಮುಖ್ಯವಾಗಿವುಳ್ಳದ್ದು ತತ್ಪುರುಷ ಸಮಾಸವೆಂಬುವದು. ಪರ ಪದವೆಂದರೆ ಮುಂದಣ ಪದ.

Sûtri 134.—*Sa-evaikâs'rayah karmadhârayah.*

Vṛitti.—*Tatpurusha-samâsa-evâdhikaraṇas' chet karmadhâraya-samjñas syât* ।

Prayoga.—*Kempina târare, kendârare ; kempina daḷam, kendaḷam ; teḷitappa basul, teḷvasul ; piriya mole, permole ; kariya naidil, kannaidil ; kaḍiya-tapam, kaḍitapam ; kaḍiya âḷ, kaṭṭâḷ ; naḷiya tôḷ, naḷidôḷ* ।

[If a *tatpurusha* has only one qualifying word, the compound is a *karmadhâraya.*]

Sûtra 135.—*Saṅkhyâdis' ched dviguh.*

Vṛitti.—*Sa cha karmadhârayas saṅkhyâ-pûrvas' ched dvigu-samjñas syât* ।

Prayoga.—*Eraḍu bâḷ, irbbâḷ ; eraḍu kai, irkkai ; ondu piḍi, ôrppiḍi ; ondu tale, ôrttale ; eraḍu kaṇ, irkkaṇ ; mûru lokam, mûlokam* ।

[If the qualifying word of the *karmadhâraya* is a numeral, the compound is a *dvigu.*]

Sûtra 136.—*Pûrva-padârtha-pradhâno'vyayîbhâvah.*

Vṛitti.—*Spashṭo'rthah* ।

Prayoga.—*Keḷagaṇa kere, kîḷkere ; keḷagaṇa poḍe, kîḷpoḍe ; poragaṇa aḍi, poraḍi ; poragaṇa mai, poramai ; mêgaṇa kâl, mêgâl* ।

[When the qualifying word is the chief in meaning, the compound is an *avyayîbhâva.*]

ಸೂತ್ರ ॥ ಸಏವೈಕಾಶ್ರಯಃ ಕರ್ಮಧಾರಯಃ ॥ ೧೩೪ ॥

ವೃತ್ತಿ ॥ ತತ್ಪುರುಷಸಮಾಸ ಏವೈಕಾಧಿಕರಣಶ್ಚೇತ್ ಕರ್ಮಧಾರಯಸಂಜ್ಞಸ್ಸ್ಯಾತ್ ॥

ಪ್ರಯೋಗ ॥ ಕೆಂಪಿನ ತಾವರೆ, ಕೆಂದಾವರೆ । ಕೆಂಪಿನ ದಳಂ, ಕೆಂದಳಂ । ತೆಳಿತಪ್ಪ ಬಸುಲ್, ತೆಳ್ವಸುಲ್ । ಪಿರಿಯ ಮೊಲೆ, ಪೇರ್ಮೊಲೆ । ಕರಿಯ ನೈದಿಲ್, ಕನ್ನೈದಿಲ್ । ಕಡಿಯ ತಪಂ, ಕಡಿತಪಂ । ಕಡಿಯ ಆಳ್, ಕಟ್ಟಾಳ್ । ನೞಿಯ ತೋಳ್, ನೞಿದೋಳ್ ॥

ತಾತ್ಪರ್ಯ ॥ ಆತತ್ಪುರುಷ ಸಮಾಸವೇ ಏಕಾಧಿಕರಣವುಳ್ಳದ್ದಾದರೆ ಕರ್ಮಧಾರಯವೆನ್ನಿಸಿಕೊಳ್ಳುವದು. ಏಕಾಧಿಕರಣವೆಂದರೆ ಒಂದೇ ಮುಖ್ಯ ಪದವನ್ನುಳ್ಳದ್ದು.

ಸೂತ್ರ ॥ ಸಂಖ್ಯಾದಿಶ್ಚೇದ್ದ್ವಿಗುಃ ॥ ೧೩೫ ॥

ವೃತ್ತಿ ॥ ಸ ಚ ಕರ್ಮಧಾರಯಸ್ಸಂಖ್ಯಾಪೂರ್ವಶ್ಚೇದ್ದ್ವಿಗು ಸಂಜ್ಞಸ್ಸ್ಯಾತ್ ॥

ಪ್ರಯೋಗ ॥ ಎರಡು ಬಾಳ್, ಇರ್ಬ್ಬಾಳ್ । ಎರಡು ಕೈ, ಇರ್ಕ್ಕೈ । ಒಂದು ಪಿಡಿ, ಓರ್ಪ್ಪಿಡಿ । ಒಂದು ತಲೆ, ಓರ್ತ್ತಲೆ । ಎರಡು ಕಣ್, ಇರ್ಕ್ಕಣ್ । ಮೂರು ಲೋಕಂ, ಮೂಲೋಕಂ ॥

ತಾತ್ಪರ್ಯ ॥ ಆಕರ್ಮಧಾರಯವೇ ಸಂಖ್ಯಾಪೂರ್ವದ್ದಾದರೆ ದ್ವಿಗುಸಮಾಸವೆನ್ನಿಸಿಕೊಳ್ಳುವದು.

ಸೂತ್ರ ॥ ಪೂರ್ವಪದಾರ್ಥಪ್ರಧಾನೋಽವ್ಯಯೀಭಾವಃ ॥ ೧೩೬ ॥

ವೃತ್ತಿ ॥ ಸ್ಪಷ್ಟೋಽರ್ಥಃ ॥

ಪ್ರಯೋಗ ॥ ಕೆಳಗಣ ಕೆರೆ, ಕೀಳ್ಕೆರೆ ॥ ಕೆಳಗಣ ಪೊಡೆ, ಕೀಳ್ಪೊಡೆ । ಪೊರಗಣ ಅಡಿ, ಪೊರಡಿ । ಪೊರಗಣ ಮೈ ಪೊರಮೈ । ಮೇಗಣ ಕಾಲ್, ಮೇಗಾಲ್ ॥

ತಾತ್ಪರ್ಯ ॥ ಪೂರ್ವ ಪದವರ್ಥವೇ ಮುಖ್ಯವಾಗಿಉಳ್ಳದ್ದು ಅವ್ಯಯೀಭಾವ ಸಮಾಸವೆನ್ನಿಸಿಕೊಳ್ಳುವದು.

Sûtra 137.—*Sarva-padârtha-pradhâno dvandvah.*

Vritti.—*Spashto'rthah* ।

Prayoga.—*Kai-vanegaḷ, karu-marigaḷ, nâḍu-biḍugaḷ, kere-toregaḷ, beṭṭa-ghaṭṭaṅgaḷ, kai-kâlgaḷ* ।

[When all the words are co-ordinate in meaning, the compound is a *dvandva*.]

Sûtra 138.—*Anya-padârtha-pradhâno bahuvrîhih.*

Vritti.—*Spashto'rthah* ।

Prayoga.—*Kaḍu-villam, keṅgaṇim, nuchchakki, kallerddeyam, kusi-goralam, kem-misegam* ।

[Compounds which qualify another word are *bahuvrîhi*.]

Sûtra 139.—*Sama-Samskritam desiya-padena samasyate.*

Vritti.—*Atra Karṇâṭaka-bhâshâyâm Samskrita-sama-s'abdam Karṇâṭaka-padena saha samâsah kriyate** ।

Prayoga.—*Nârada-daṇḍige, para-kottaḷam, arasu-daḷam, kûr-asi, mâ-janam, mâ-pâtakam, turaga-daḷam* ।

[Karṇâṭaka words form compounds with Sanskrit words.]

ಸೂತ್ರ ॥ ಸರ್ವಪದಾರ್ಥಪ್ರಧಾನೋ ದ್ವನ್ದ್ವಃ ॥ ೧೩೭ ॥

ವೃತ್ತಿ ॥ ಸ್ಪಷ್ಟೋऽರ್ಥಃ ॥

ಪ್ರಯೋಗ ॥ ಕೈವನೆಗಳ್ । ಕರುಮರಿಗಳ್ । ನಾಡುಬೀಡುಗಳ್ । ಕೆರೆತೊರೆಗಳ್ । ಬೆಟ್ಟಘಟ್ಟಂಗಳ್ । ಕೈಕಾಲ್ಗಳ್ ॥

ತಾತ್ಪರ್ಯ ॥ ಎಲ್ಲಾ ಪದಗಳೂ ಮುಖ್ಯವಾಗಿವುಳ್ಳದ್ದು ದ್ವಂದ್ವಸಮಾಸವೆನ್ನಿಸಿ ಕೊಳ್ಳುವದು.

ಸೂತ್ರ ॥ ಅನ್ಯಪದಾರ್ಥಪ್ರಧಾನೋ ಬಹುವ್ರೀಹಿಃ ॥ ೧೩೮ ॥

ವೃತ್ತಿ ॥ ಸ್ಪಷ್ಟೋऽರ್ಥಃ ॥

ಪ್ರಯೋಗ ॥ ಕಡುವಿಲ್ಲಂ। ಕೆಂಗಣಿಂ। ನುಚ್ಚಕ್ಕಿ। ಕಲ್ಲೆರ್ದ್ದೆಯಂ। ಕುಸಿಗೊರಲಂ। ಕೆಮ್ಮೀಸೆಗಂ॥

ತಾತ್ಪರ್ಯ ॥ ಮತ್ತೊಂದು ಪದಾರ್ಥವೇ ಮುಖ್ಯವಾಗ್ಯುಳ್ಳದ್ದು ಬಹುವ್ರೀಹಿ ಸಮಾಸವೆಂದೆನ್ನಿಸಿ ಕೊಳ್ಳುವದು.

ಸೂತ್ರ ॥ ಸಮಸಂಸ್ಕೃತಂ ದೇಶ್ಯಪದೇನ ಸಮಸ್ಯತೇ ॥ ೧೩೯ ॥

ವೃತ್ತಿ ॥ ಅತ್ರ ಕರ್ಣಾಟಕಭಾಷಾಯಾಂ ಸಂಸ್ಕೃತಸಮಶಬ್ದಂ ಕರ್ಣಾಟಕಪದೇನ ಸಹ ಸಮಾಸಃ ಕ್ರಿಯತೇ* ॥

ಪ್ರಯೋಗ ॥ ನಾರದ ದಂಡಿಗೆ । ಪರಕೊತ್ತಳಂ । ಅರಸುದಳಂ । ಕೂರಸಿ । ಮಾಜನಂ । ಮಾ ಪಾತಕಂ । ತುರಗದಳಂ ॥

ತಾತ್ಪರ್ಯ ॥ ತತ್ಸಮ ಪದಗಳು ದೇಶ್ಯ ಪದಗಳ ಸಂಗಡ ಕೂಡಿಸಿ ಸಮಾಸ ಮಾಡಲ್ಪಡುತ್ತವೆ.

---

* B in this place introduces Sama—Samskrita-lakshaṇam anyatra, with the following quotation from S'abdamaṇidarpaṇa II. 9, regarding which see *supra* Introd. ii.

Samudita saṅkhyâvyaya rahi । tam enisi vartipa nighaṇṭuvina nâma-pado ।
ttama varṇa prakritigaḷam । sama-Samskrita vesaran iṭṭu liṅgam mâḷvar ॥

*ದ್ವಿ॥ ಪ್ರತಿಯಲ್ಲಿ ಮಾತ್ರವೇ ಸಮಸಂಸ್ಕೃತಲಕ್ಷಣಮನ್ಯತ್ರವೆಂದು ಶಬ್ದಮಣಿದರ್ಪಣದ ೨ನೇ ಅಧ್ಯಾಯದ ೯ನೇ ಸೂತ್ರವನ್ನು ಉದಾಹರಿಸುತ್ತದೆ. ಹ್ಯಾಗಂದರೆ,

ಕಂ ॥ ಸಮುದಿತ ಸಂಖ್ಯಾವ್ಯಯ ರಹಿ। ತಮೆನಿಸಿ ವರ್ತಿಪ ನಿಘಂಟುವಿನ ನಾಮಪದೋ।
ತ್ತಮವರ್ಣ ಪ್ರಕೃತಿಗಳಂ। ಸಮಸಂಸ್ಕೃತವೆಸರನಿಟ್ಟು ಲಿಂಗಂ ಮಾಳ್ವರ್ ॥

Sûtra 140.—*Kârakam pareṇa samartha-kriyôpadena.*

Vritti.—*Karma-pûrvam kârakañ-cha pareṇa prasiddha-kriyâpadena samam samasyate* ।

Prayoga.—*Terad-ittam, ettu-goṇḍam, serey-iddam, okkal-pôdam* ।

[Words which are governed, form compounds with the governing verb.]

Sûtra 141.—*Akârântân-maḥ.*

Vritti.—*Akârântât kârakât param makâras syât* ।

Prayoga.—*Manam-golgum, suṇṇam-goṇḍam*, besam-bagedam, kasam-iṭṭam, manam-perchidam, jasam-badedam* ।

[If ending in *a*, they take *m* in forming the compound.]

Sûtra 142.—*Vis'eshyottara-pade pûrva-padasyopântya-svarâder lopaḥ.*

Vritti.—*Vis'eshya-bhûtottara-pade sati pûrva-pada-sambandhinâm upântya-svarâdyânâm avayava-lopas syât* ।

Prayoga.—*Kariya maḍu, kârmaḍu ; ini mâvu, immâvu ; kuritu bâḷ, kûrvâḷ ; initu uṇisu, innuṇisu ; nuṇitu saram, nuṇjaram ; jâṇa mâtu, jaṇmâtu ; oḷḷitu mânasam, oḷmânasam ; oḷḷitu guṇam, oḷguṇam* ।

[In forming a compound with a noun in the nominative, the qualifying word drops the suffixes of its root.]

ಸೂತ್ರ ॥ ಕಾರಕಂ ಪರೇಣ ಸಮರ್ಥಕ್ರಿಯಾಪದೇನ ॥ ೧೪೦ ॥

ವೃತ್ತಿ ॥ ಕರ್ಮಪೂರ್ವಂ ಕಾರಕಞ್ಚ ಪರೇಣ ಪ್ರಸಿದ್ಧ ಕ್ರಿಯಾಪದೇನ ಸಮಂ ಸಮಸ್ಯತೇ ॥

ಪ್ರಯೋಗ ॥ ತೆರದಿತ್ತಂ । ಎತ್ತುಗೊಂಡಂ । ಸೆರೆಯಿದ್ದಂ । ಒಕ್ಕಲ್ಪೋದಂ ॥

ತಾತ್ಪರ್ಯ ॥ ಕರ್ಮ ಮೊದಲಾದ ಕಾರಕ ಪದಗಳು ಮುಂದಣ ಪದದೊಡನೆ ಪ್ರಸಿದ್ಧ ಕ್ರಿಯಾಪದ ದೊಡನೆ ಸಮಾಸಿಸಲ್ಪಡುತ್ತದೆ.

ಸೂತ್ರ ॥ ಅಕಾರಾನ್ತಾನ್ಮಃ ॥ ೧೪೧ ॥

ವೃತ್ತಿ ॥ ಅಕಾರಾನ್ತಾತ್ಕಾರಕಾತ್ಪರಂ ಮಕಾರಸ್ಸ್ಯಾತ್ ॥

ಪ್ರಯೋಗ ॥ ಮನಂಗೊಳ್ಗಂ । ಸುಣ್ಣಂಗೊಂಡಂ* । ಬೆಸಂಬಗೆದಂ । ಕಸಮಿಟ್ಟಂ । ಮನಂ ಪೇರ್ಚಿದಂ । ಜಸಂಬಡೆದಂ ॥

ತಾತ್ಪರ್ಯ ॥ ಅಕಾರಾಂತವಾದ ಕಾರಕದ ಮುಂದೆ ಸಮಾಸದ ಮುಂದೆ ಮಕಾರವಾಗುವದು, ಅಂದರೆ ಸೊನ್ನೆ ಬರುವದೆಂಬದು.

ಸೂತ್ರ ॥ ವಿಶೇಷ್ಯೋತ್ತರಪದೇ ಪೂರ್ವಪದಸ್ಯೋಪಾನ್ತ್ಯಸ್ವರಾದೇರ್ಲೋಪಃ ॥ ೧೪೨ ॥

ವೃತ್ತಿ ॥ ವಿಶೇಷ್ಯ ಭೂತೋತ್ತರಪದೇ ಸತಿ ಪೂರ್ವಪದಸಮ್ಬನ್ಧಿನಾಂ ಉಪಾನ್ತ್ಯ ಸ್ವರಾದ್ಯಾನಾಂ ಅವಯವಲೋಪಸ್ಸ್ಯಾತ್ ॥

ಪ್ರಯೋಗ ॥ ಕರಿಯ ಮಡು, ಕಾರ್ಮಡು । ಇನಿ ಮಾವು, ಇಮ್ಮಾವು । ಕುರಿತು ಬಾಳ್, ಕೂರ್ವಾಳ್ । ಇನಿತು ಉಣಿಸು, ಇನ್ನುಣಿಸು । ನುಣಿತು ಸರಂ, ನುಣ್ಜರಂ । ಜಾಣ ಮಾತು, ಜಾಣ್ಮಾತು । ಒಳ್ಳಿತು ಮಾನಸಂ, ಒಳ್ಮಾನಸಂ । ಒಳ್ಳಿತು ಗುಣಂ, ಒಳ್ಗುಣಂ ॥

ತಾತ್ಪರ್ಯ ॥ ಪರಪದವು ವಿಶೇಷ್ಯವಾಗಿದ್ದು ಸಮಾಸವಾಗುವದಾದರೆ ಪೂರ್ವಪದದಲ್ಲಿನ ಕಡೇ ಅಕ್ಷರಕ್ಕೆ ಮೊದಲಿನ ಅಕ್ಷರವಾದ ಸ್ವರಾದಿಗಳಿಗೆ ಅವಯವ ಲೋಪವಾಗುತ್ತದೆ. ವಿಶೇಷ್ಯವಂದರೆ. ಕರ್ತೃಪದ ಅಥವಾ ಆಖ್ಯೆ.

---

*C ends here.

* ತೃ ॥ ಯಲ್ಲಿ ಇಷ್ಟೇ ಇದೆ.

Sûtra 143.—*Ikârasyaiddhrasvah.*

Vritti.—*Prâguktavad upântya-svarâdi-lope krite pûrvasyekârasya hrasvaekâras syât* ।

Prayoga.—*Piriya maram, permaram ; piriya pâvu, perbâvu ; biḷiya mugil, beḷmugil* ।

[Moreover an *i* in the root becomes *e* short.]

Sûtra 144.—*Na cha kvachit.*

Vritti.—*Na cha kvachid ity anena ikârasya hrasva-ekârah kvachin-na bhavatîti* ।

Prayoga.—*Biṇṇitu kone, biṇgone ; biṇṇitu pore, biṇpore ; biḷupu mone, biḷmone* ।

[But in some cases not.]

Sûtra 145.—*Svarâdau dîrghas tv-aguroh.*

Vritti.—*Svarâdau pare pade sati aguroh pûrva-padasya dîrgho bhavati* । *tu-s'abdas' chârthah* ।

Prayoga.—*Kariya aḍavi, kâraḍavi ;* piriya oḍal, pêroḍal ; kariya iruḷ, kâriruḷ* ।

Atra sûtre aguror ity apara-svara-dirghe sati pûrva-varṇasya dirgho na bhavati । *Prayoga* । *pasiya ôle, pachchôle; iniya rasam, iñcharasam*† ।

[When the final word begins with a vowel, the vowel of the preceding word is lengthened: but not when the initial vowel of the final word is long.]

ಸೂತ್ರ ॥ ಇಕಾರಸ್ಯೈದ್ಧ್ರಸ್ವಃ ॥ ೧೪೩ ॥

ವೃತ್ತಿ ॥ ಪ್ರಾಗುಕ್ತವದುಪಾನ್ತ್ಯಸ್ವರಾದಿಲೋಪೇ ಕೃತೇ ಪೂರ್ವಸ್ಯೇಕಾರಸ್ಯ ಹ್ರಸ್ವಏಕಾರಸ್ಸ್ಯಾತ್ ॥

ಪ್ರಯೋಗ ॥ ಪಿರಿಯ ಮರಂ, ಪೆರ್ಮರಂ । ಪಿರಿಯ ಪಾವು, ಪೆರ್ಬಾವು । ಬಿಳಿಯ ಮುಗಿಲ್, ಬೆಳ್ಮುಗಿಲ್ ॥

ತಾತ್ಪರ್ಯ ॥ ಪೂರ್ವದಲ್ಲಿ ಹೇಳಿದಂತೆ ಕಡೆಯಕ್ಷರ ಮೊದಲಿನ ಸ್ವರಾದಿಗಳಿಗೆ ಲೋಪವಾಗಲು ಪೂರ್ವ ಪದದ ಇಕಾರಕ್ಕೆ ಹ್ರಸ್ವ ಏಕಾರವಾಗುತ್ತದೆ.

ಸೂತ್ರ ॥ ನ ಚ ಕ್ವಚಿತ್ ॥ ೧೪೪ ॥

ವೃತ್ತಿ ॥ ನ ಚ ಕ್ವಚಿದಿತ್ಯನೇನ ಇಕಾರಸ್ಯ ಹ್ರಸ್ವ ಏಕಾರಃ ಕ್ವಚಿನ್ನ ಭವತೀತಿ ॥

ಪ್ರಯೋಗ ॥ ಬಿಣ್ಣಿತು ಕೊನೆ, ಬಿಣ್ಗೊನೆ । ಬಿಣ್ಣಿತು ಪೊರೆ, ಬಿಣ್ಪೊರೆ । ಬಿಳುಪು ಮೊನೆ, ಬಿಳ್ಮೊನೆ ॥

ತಾತ್ಪರ್ಯ ॥ ನಚ ಕ್ವಚಿತ್ ಅಂದರೆ ಕೆಲವು ಕಡೆಗಳಲ್ಲಿ ಇಕಾರಕ್ಕೆ ಹ್ರಸ್ವ ಏಕಾರವಾಗುವದಿಲ್ಲವೆಂಬುದು.

ಸೂತ್ರ ॥ ಸ್ವರಾದೌ ದೀರ್ಘಸ್ತ್ವಗುರೋಃ ॥ ೧೪೫ ॥

ವೃತ್ತಿ ॥ ಸ್ವರಾದೌ ಪರೇ ಪದೇ ಸತಿ ಅಗುರೋಃ ಪೂರ್ವಪದಸ್ಯ ದೀರ್ಘೋ ಭವತಿ । ತುಶಬ್ದಶ್ಚಾರ್ಥಃ ॥

ಪ್ರಯೋಗ ॥ ಕರಿಯ ಅಡವಿ, ಕಾರಡವಿ* । ಪಿರಿಯ ಒಡಲ್, ಪೇರೊಡಲ್ । ಕರಿಯ ಇರುಳ್, ಕಾರಿರುಳ್ ॥

ಅತ್ರ ಸೂತ್ರೇ ಅಗುರೋರಿತ್ಯಪರಸ್ವರ ದೀರ್ಘೇ ಸತಿ ಪೂರ್ವವರ್ಣಸ್ಯ ದೀರ್ಘೋ ನ ಭವತಿ ॥

ಪ್ರಯೋಗ ॥ ಪಸಿಯ ಓಲೆ, ಪಚ್ಚೋಲೆ । ಇನಿಯ ರಸಂ ಇಂಚರಸಂ† ॥

ತಾತ್ಪರ್ಯ ॥ ಪರಪದವು ಸ್ವರಾದಿಯಾಗಿದ್ದರೆ ಪೂರ್ವಪದದ ಹ್ರಸ್ವಕ್ಕೆ ದೀರ್ಘವಾಗುತ್ತದೆ, ಆದರೆ ಪರಪದದ ಸ್ವರವು ದೀರ್ಘವಾಗಿದ್ದರೆ ಪೂರ್ವಪದದ ವರ್ಣಕ್ಕೆ ದೀರ್ಘವಾಗುವದಿಲ್ಲ.

---

* A and B have instead of this—kariya mugil, kârmugil, which seems not to belong here.

* ಪ್ರ । ದ್ವಿ । ಪ್ರತಿಗಳಲ್ಲಿ ಕರಿಯ ಮುಗಿಲ್, ಕಾರ್ಮುಗಿಲ್ ಎಂದಿದೆ. ಈ ಉದಾಹರಣೆಯು ಸೂತ್ರಕ್ಕೆ ಸೇರಿದ್ದಲ್ಲವೆಂದು ಕಾಣುತ್ತದೆ.

† This example is not in C.

† ತೃ । ಪ್ರತಿಯಲ್ಲಿ ಇಲ್ಲ.

Sûtra 146.—*Ṇa-ṭa-ḷa-na-tânâm dvirbhâvaḥ.*

Vṛitti.—*Ṇâdînâm pañcha-varṇânâm svarâdau pare upântyâvayava-lopa-pûrvakam dvitvam bhavati* ।

Prayoga.—*Taṇ elar, taṇṇelar ; kaḍu âyam, kaṭṭâyam ; oḷitu uṇisu, oḷḷuṇisu ; in uṇisu, innuṇisu ; kit aḍi, kittaḍi ; kit iḷe, kittiḷe** ।

[When the final word begins with a vowel, and the preceding word in its radical form ends in *ṇ*, *ṭ*, *ḷ*, *n* or *t*, this letter is doubled.]

Sûtra 147.—*Kaḍidu-niḍidu-dvayasyâdyeka-svara-parasya ṭaḥ.*

Vṛitti.—*Anayos' s'abdayor âdi-svarât parasya svarâdau pade pare pûrvâvayava-lopo bhûtvâ ṭakâra âpadyate* ।

Prayoga.—*Kaḍidu âḷ, kaṭṭâḷ ; niḍidu oḍal, niṭṭoḍal ; niḍidu aḍakil, niṭṭaḍakil†* ।

[In forming a compound with a word beginning with a vowel, *kaḍidu* and *niḍidu* change the *ḍ* of their roots to *ṭ*.]

Sûtra 148.—*Naḍos' cha.*

Vṛitti.—*Naḍu-s'abdastha-ḍakârasya cha ṭakâras syât* ।

Prayoga.—*Naḍu iruḷ, naṭṭiruḷ ; naḍu aḍavi, naṭṭaḍavi* ।

[So also with *naḍu*.]

ಸೂತ್ರ । ಣಟಳನತಾನಾಂ ದ್ವಿರ್ಭಾವಃ ।೧೪೬।

ವೃತ್ತಿ । ಣಾದೀನಾಂ ಪಂಚವರ್ಣಾನಾಂ ಸ್ವರಾದೌ ಪರೇ ಉಪಾನ್ತ್ಯಾವಯವಲೋಪಪೂರ್ವಕಂ ದ್ವಿತ್ವಂ ಭವತಿ ।

ಪ್ರಯೋಗ । ತಣ್ ಎಲರ್, ತಣ್ಣೆಲರ್ । ಕಡು ಆಯಂ, ಕಟ್ಟಾಯಂ । ಒಳಿತು ಉಣಿಸು, ಒಳ್ಳುಣಿಸು । ಇನ್ ಉಣಿಸು, ಇನ್ನುಣಿಸು । ಕಿತ್ ಅಡಿ, ಕಿತ್ತಡಿ । ಕಿತ್ ಇಳೆ, ಕಿತ್ತಿಳೆ* ।

ತಾತ್ಪರ್ಯ । ಣ ಟ ಳ ನ ತ ಯಂಬೀಯೈದು ವರ್ಣಗಳಿಗೆ ಪರಪದವು ಸ್ವರಾದಿಯಾಗಿದ್ದರೆ ಉಪಾನ್ತ್ಯಾವಯವ ಲೋಪ ಸಹಿತವಾಗಿ ದ್ವಿತ್ವವಾಗುತ್ತದೆ.

ಸೂತ್ರ । ಕಡಿದುನಿಡಿದುದ್ವಯಸ್ಯಾದ್ಯೇಕಸ್ವರಪರಸ್ಯ ಟಃ ।೧೪೭।

ವೃತ್ತಿ । ಅನಯೋಶ್ಶಬ್ದಯೋರಾದಿ ಸ್ವರಾತ್ಪರಸ್ಯ ಸ್ವರಾದೌ ಪದೇ ಪರೇ ಪೂರ್ವಾವಯವ ಲೋಪೋ ಭೂತ್ವಾ ಟಕಾರ ಆಪದ್ಯತೇ ।

ಪ್ರಯೋಗ । ಕಡಿದು ಆಳ್, ಕಟ್ಟಾಳ್ । ನಿಡಿದು ಒಡಲ್, ನಿಟ್ಟೊಡಲ್ । ನಿಡಿದು ಅಡಕಿಲ್, ನಿಟ್ಟಡಕಿಲ್† ।

ತಾತ್ಪರ್ಯ । ಕಡಿದು ನಿಡಿದು ಎಂಬ ಶಬ್ದಗಳಿಗೆ ಸ್ವರಾದಿಯಾದ ಪದ ಪರವಾದರೆ ಪೂರ್ವಾವಯವ ಲೋಪವಾಗಿ ಟಕಾರ ಬರುತ್ತದೆ.

ಸೂತ್ರ । ನಡೋಶ್ಚ ।೧೪೮।

ವೃತ್ತಿ । ನಡುಶಬ್ದಸ್ಥ ಡಕಾರಸ್ಯ ಚ ಟಕಾರಸ್ಸ್ಯಾತ್ ।

ಪ್ರಯೋಗ । ನಡು ಇರುಳ್, ನಟ್ಟಿರುಳ್ । ನಡು ಅಡವಿ, ನಟ್ಟಡವಿ ।

ತಾತ್ಪರ್ಯ । ನಡು ಎಂಬ ಶಬ್ದವೂ ಮೇಲಂತೆಯೇ.

---

* Not in C. † Not in C.

* ತೃ । ಯಲ್ಲಿ ಈ ಉದಾಹರಣೆ ಇಲ್ಲ. † ತೃ । ಯಲ್ಲಿ ಈ ಉದಾಹರಣೆ ಇಲ್ಲ.

Sûtra 149.—*Kiridos tah.*

Vritti.—*Kiridu-s'abde âdi-svarât parasya akârasya svarâdi-pade pare sâvayava-lopam takâro bhavati* ।

Prayoga.—*Kiriya âtam, kittâtam ; kiriya adi, kittadi ; kiriya iḷi, kittiḷi* ।

[In forming a compound with a word beginning with a vowel, *kiridu* drops its termination and changes the final letter of its root to *t*.]

Sûtra 150.—*Teshâm udantatvam vyañjaneshu.*

Vritti.—*Kadidu-nididu-kiridu-ity-eteshâm vyañjaneshu pareshu ukârântatâ syât* ।

Prayoga.—*Kadiya kudure, kadugudure ; kiridu gejje, kirugejje ; kiridu gâṇa, kirugâṇa* ।

[In forming a compound with a word beginning with a consonant, *kadidu, nididu,* and *kiridu* drop their termination and add *u* to their root.]

Sûtra 151.—*Posatv-âdinâm adantatvam nipâtyate.*

Vritti.—*Posatu-paḷadu-yaḷadu-poragu-vaḷagu-ity-âdinâm padânâm akârântatvam upântyâvayava-lopapûrvam nipâtyate* ।

Prayoga.—*Posatu suggi, posasuggi ; posatu des'e, posades'e; haḷadu kaḷave, haḷagaḷave ; poḷadu alagu, poḷa-alagu ; eḷadu mâvu, eḷamâvu ; eḷadu taḷir, eḷadaḷir ; poragu vâru, poravâru ; oḷagu kai, oḷagai ; oḷu aṭṭam, oḷa-aṭṭam** ।

[In forming a compound with a word beginning with a consonant, *posatu, paḷadu, eḷadu, poragu* and *oḷagu* drop their termination and add *a* to their root.]

ಸೂತ್ರ ॥ ಕಿರಿದೋಸ್ತಃ ॥ ೧೪೯ ॥

ವೃತ್ತಿ ॥ ಕಿರಿದುಶಬ್ದೇ ಆದಿಸ್ವರಾತ್ಪರಸ್ಯ ಅಕಾರಸ್ಯ ಸ್ವರಾದಿಪದೇ ಪರೇ ಸಾವಯವಲೋಪಂ ತಕಾರೋ ಭವತಿ ॥

ಪ್ರಯೋಗ ॥ ಕಿರಿಯ ಆತಂ, ಕಿತ್ತಾತಂ । ಕಿರಿಯ ಅಡಿ, ಕಿತ್ತಡಿ । ಕಿರಿಯ ಇಳಿ, ಕಿತ್ತಿಳಿ ॥

ತಾತ್ಪರ್ಯ ॥ ಕಿರಿದು ಶಬ್ದವು ಸ್ವರಾದಿಪದ ಪರವಾದರೆ ಅವಯವ ಲೋಪವಾಗಿ ತಕಾರವಾಗುತ್ತದೆ.

ಸೂತ್ರ ॥ ತೇಷಾಮುದನ್ತತ್ವಂ ವ್ಯಞ್ಜನೇಷು ॥ ೧೫೦ ॥

ವೃತ್ತಿ ॥ ಕಡಿದು ನಿಡಿದು ಕಿರಿದು ಇತ್ಯೇತೇಷಾಂ ವ್ಯಞ್ಜನೇಷು ಪರೇಷು ಉಕಾರಾನ್ತತಾ ಸ್ಯಾತ್ ॥

ಪ್ರಯೋಗ ॥ ಕಡಿಯ ಕುದುರೆ, ಕಡುಗುದುರೆ । ಕಿರಿದು ಗೆಜ್ಜೆ, ಕಿರುಗೆಜ್ಜೆ । ಕಿರಿದು ಗಾಣ, ಕಿರುಗಾಣ ॥

ತಾತ್ಪರ್ಯ ॥ ಕಡಿದು ನಿಡಿದು ಕಿರಿದು ಯೆಂಬೀಶಬ್ದಗಳಿಗೆ ವ್ಯಂಜನಗಳು ಪರವಾದರೆ ಉಪಾನ್ತ್ಯಾವಯವಕ್ಕೆ ಉಕಾರಾನ್ತತ್ವವೂ ಅನ್ತ್ಯಾವಯವಕ್ಕೆ ಲೋಪವೂ ಆಗುವದು.

ಸೂತ್ರ ॥ ಪೊಸತ್ವಾದೀನಾಮದನ್ತತ್ವಂ ನಿಪಾತ್ಯತೇ ॥ ೧೫೧ ॥

ವೃತ್ತಿ ॥ ಪೊಸತು ಪಳದು ಯಳದು ಪೊರಗು ವಳಗು ಇತ್ಯಾದೀನಾಂ ಪದಾನಾಂ ಅಕಾರಾನ್ತತ್ವಮುಪಾನ್ತ್ಯಾವಯವಲೋಪಪೂರ್ವಂ ನಿಪಾತ್ಯತೇ ॥

ಪ್ರಯೋಗ ॥ ಪೊಸತು ಸುಗ್ಗಿ, ಪೊಸಸುಗ್ಗಿ । ಪೊಸತು ದೆಸೆ, ಪೊಸದೆಸೆ । ಹಳದು ಕಳವೆ, ಹಳಗಳವೆ । ಪೊಳದು ಅಲಗು, ಪೊಳಅಲಗು । ಎಳದು ಮಾವು, ಎಳಮಾವು । ಎಳದು ತಳಿರ, ಎಳದಳಿರ ಪೊರಗು ವಾರು, ಪೊರವಾರು । ಒಳಗು ಕೈ, ಒಳಗೈ । ಒಳು ಅಟ್ಟಂ, ಒಳಅಟ್ಟಂ* ॥

ತಾತ್ಪರ್ಯ ॥ ಪೊಸತು ಮುಂತಾದ ಶಬ್ದಗಳಿಗೆ ವ್ಯಂಜನಗಳು ಪರವಾದರೆ ಉಪಾನ್ತ್ಯಾವಯವ ಲೋಪವೂ ಉಂಟಾಗಿ ಈ ಶಬ್ದಗಳಿಗೆ ಅಕಾರಾನ್ತತ್ವವೂ ಬರುತ್ತದೆ.

---

* Not in C.

* ತೃ ॥ ಪ್ರತಿಯಲ್ಲಿ ಕಡೇ ಉದಾಹರಣೆ ಇಲ್ಲ.

Sûtra 152.—*Kechchane-pechchane-bechchane-s'abdânâm châder matvam.*

Vṛitti.—*Eteshâm trayâṇâm châder vyañjane pare makârâdes'as syât* ।

Prayoga.—*Kechchaneya taḻir, kendaḻir ; kechchaneya mugil, kemmugil ; kechchaneya kuḍi, keṅguḍi ; kechchaneya nîr, kennîr ; bechchaneya nîr, bennîr ; pachchaneya tale, pandale ; pachchaneya taḻir, pandaḻir* ।

[In forming a compound with a word beginning with a consonant, *kechchane, pechchane* and *bechchane* drop their termination and change the last letter of their root to *m.*]

Sûtra 153.—*Sv-antatâ cha.*

Vṛitti.—*Kechchane-ity-âdînâm cha vyañjane pare sukârâdes'as' cha bhavati* ।

Prayoga.—*Kechchaneya kallu, kisugallu ; kechchaneya kâḍu, kisugâḍu ; bechchaneya suy, bisusuy ; bechchaneya kadir, bisugadir ; pachchaneya vandal, pasuvandal* ।
Yoga-vibhâgâd ishṭa-pravṛitteh kvachit sukâro na bhavati । *Prayoga* । *pachchaneya ôle, pachchôle ; pachchaneya aḍike, pachchaḍike ; bechchaneya aḍi, bechchaḍi* ।

[Also to *su*. (But sometimes not.)]

ಸೂತ್ರ ॥ ಕೆಚ್ಚನೆ ಪೆಚ್ಚನೆ ಬೆಚ್ಚನೆ ಶಬ್ದಾನಾಂ ಚಾದೇರ್ಮತ್ವಂ ॥ ೧೫೨ ॥

ವೃತ್ತಿ ॥ ಏತೇಷಾಂ ತ್ರಯಾಣಾಂ ಚಾದೇರ್ವ್ಯಞ್ಜನೇ ಪರೇ ಮಕಾರಾದೇಶಸ್ಸ್ಯಾತ್ ॥

ಪ್ರಯೋಗ ॥ ಕೆಚ್ಚನೆಯ ತೞಿರ್, ಕೆಂದೞಿರ್। ಕೆಚ್ಚನೆಯ ಮುಗಿಲ್, ಕೆಂಮುಗಿಲ್। ಕೆಚ್ಚನೆಯ ಕುಡಿ, ಕೆಂಗುಡಿ। ಕೆಚ್ಚನೆಯ ನೀರ್, ಕೆನ್ನೀರ್। ಬೆಚ್ಚನೆಯ ನೀರ್, ಬೆನ್ನೀರ್। ಪಚ್ಚನೆಯ ತಲೆ, ಪಂದಲೆ। ಪಚ್ಚನೆಯ ತೞಿರ್, ಪಂದೞಿರ್ ॥

ತಾತ್ಪರ್ಯ ॥ ಕೆಚ್ಚನೆ ಪಚ್ಚನೆ ಬೆಚ್ಚನೆ ಯೆಂಬೀ ಮೂರು ಶಬ್ದಗಳಿಗೆ ವ್ಯಂಜನ ಪರವಾದರೆ ಆದಿಯಲ್ಲಿ ಮಕಾರಾದೇಶವಾಗುತ್ತದೆ.

ಸೂತ್ರ ॥ ಸ್ವನ್ತತಾ ಚ ॥ ೧೫೩ ॥

ವೃತ್ತಿ ॥ ಕೆಚ್ಚನೆ ಇತ್ಯಾದೀನಾಂ ಚ ವ್ಯಂಜನೇ ಪರೇ ಸುಕಾರಾದೇಶಶ್ಚ ಭವತಿ ॥

ಪ್ರಯೋಗ॥ ಕೆಚ್ಚನೆಯ ಕಲ್ಲು, ಕಿಸುಗಲ್ಲು। ಕೆಚ್ಚನೆಯ ಕಾಡು, ಕಿಸುಗಾಡು। ಬೆಚ್ಚನೆಯ ಸುಯ್, ಬಿಸುಸುಯ್। ಬೆಚ್ಚನೆಯ ಕದಿರ್, ಬಿಸುಗದಿರ್। ಪಚ್ಚನೆಯ ವಂದಲ್, ಪಸುವಂದಲ್ ॥
ಯೋಗವಿಭಾಗಾದಿಷ್ಟಪ್ರವೃತ್ತೇಃ ಕ್ವಚಿತ್ಸುಕಾರೋ ನ ಭವತಿ ॥ ಪ್ರಯೋಗ ॥ ಪಚ್ಚನೆಯ ಓಲೆ, ಪಚ್ಚೋಲೆ। ಪಚ್ಚನೆಯ ಅಡಿಕೆ, ಪಚ್ಚಡಿಕೆ। ಬೆಚ್ಚನೆಯ ಅಡಿ ಬೆಚ್ಚಡಿ ॥

ತಾತ್ಪರ್ಯ ॥ ಕೆಚ್ಚನೆ ಇತ್ಯಾದಿಗಳಿಗೆ ವ್ಯಂಜನ ಪರವಾದರೆ ಸುಕಾರಾದೇಶವಾಗುವದೂ ವುಂಟು. ಯೋಗವಿಭಾಗದಿಂದ ಇಷ್ಟಪ್ರವೃತ್ತಿಯಾದ್ದರಿಂದ ಕೆಲವುಕಡೆ ಸುಕಾರವಾಗುವದೂ ಇಲ್ಲ.

Sûtra **154.**—*Ekâre vibhâsha ikâraḥ.*

Vṛitti.—*Teshv asmin sukârâdes'e sati vikalpâd ekârasya ikâras syât* ।

Prayoga.—*Kechchaneya sañje, kisu sañje*; kechchaneya kaṇigile, kisugaṇigile* ।

Krachinn-ekâraḥ । *Prayoga* । *kechchaneya uri, kêsuri ; kechchaneya aḍi, kêsaḍi ; kechchaneya akki, kêsakki* ।

[At the same time the *e* of their root becomes *i*. (But sometimes *ê*.)]

Sûtra **155.**—*Tatpurushe pûrvà-padântya-lopaḥ prâyo yathochit-âgamas' cha.*

Vṛitti.—*Asmin samâse prâk-padântya-lopa-pûrvam vikalpâd yathochit-âgamas' cha bhavati* ।

Prayoga.—*Arasu nêril, aranêril ; arasu giṇi, aragiṇi ; arasu mane, aramane* ।

[In forming a *tatpurusha* compound, the preceding word, dropping its last syllable, generally undergoes one or other of the foregoing changes.]

Sûtra **156.**—*Ellasya.*

Vṛitti.—*Atra lakârasya dîrgham syât* ।

Prayoga.—*Ella ratnangaḷ, ellâ-ratnangaḷ ; ella mâvu, ellâ-mâvu* । *prâyo-grahaṇât krachin-na* । *ella dhanam, ella kere* ।

[*Ella* lengthens its final vowel. (But sometimes not.)]

ಸೂತ್ರ ॥ ಏಕಾರೇ ವಿಭಾಷ ಇಕಾರಃ ॥ ೧೫೪ ॥

ವೃತ್ತಿ ॥ ತೇಷ್ವಸ್ಮಿನ್ ಸುಕಾರಾದೇಶೇ ಸತಿ ವಿಕಲ್ಪಾದೇಕಾರಸ್ಯ ಇಕಾರಸ್ಸ್ಯಾತ್ ।

ಪ್ರಯೋಗ ॥ ಕೆಚ್ಚನೆಯ ಸಂಜೆ, ಕಿಸುಸಂಜೆ* । ಕೆಚ್ಚನೆಯ ಕಣಿಗಿಲೆ, ಕಿಸುಗಣಿಗಿಲೆ ॥

ಕ್ವಚಿನ್ನೇಕಾರಃ ॥ ಪ್ರಯೋಗ ॥ ಕೆಚ್ಚನೆಯ ಉರಿ, ಕೇಸುರಿ । ಕೆಚ್ಚನೆಯಅಡಿ, ಕೇಸಡಿ । ಕೆಚ್ಚನೆಯ ಅಕ್ಕಿ, ಕೇಸಕ್ಕಿ ॥

ತಾತ್ಪರ್ಯ ॥ ಈ ಸುಕಾರಾದೇಶವಾಗುತ್ತಿರಲಾಗಿ ವಿಕಲ್ಪದಿಂದ ಎಕಾರಕ್ಕೆ ಇಕಾರವಾಗುತ್ತದೆ. ಕೆಲವು ಕಡೆ ಏಕಾರವಾಗುವದು.

ಸೂತ್ರ ॥ ತತ್ಪುರುಷೇ ಪೂರ್ವಪದಾನ್ತ್ಯಲೋಪಃ ಪ್ರಾಯೋ ಯಥೋಚಿತಾಗಮಶ್ಚ ॥ ೧೫೫ ॥

ವೃತ್ತಿ ॥ ಅಸ್ಮಿನ್ ಸಮಾಸೇ ಪ್ರಾಕ್ಪದಾನ್ತ್ಯಲೋಪಪೂರ್ವಂ ವಿಕಲ್ಪಾದ್ಯಥೋಚಿತಾಗಮಶ್ಚ ಭವತಿ ॥

ಪ್ರಯೋಗ ॥ ಅರಸು ನೇರಿಲ್, ಅರನೇರಿಲ್ । ಅರಸು ಗಿಣಿ, ಅರಗಿಣಿ । ಅರಸು ಮನೆ, ಅರಮನೆ ॥

ತಾತ್ಪರ್ಯ ॥ ತತ್ಪುರುಷ ಸಮಾಸದಲ್ಲಿ ಪೂರ್ವಪದಾನ್ತ್ಯಲೋಪವೂ ವಿಕಲ್ಪವಾಗಿ ಯಥೋಚಿತಾಗಮವೂ ಆಗುತ್ತದೆ.

ಸೂತ್ರ ॥ ಎಲ್ಲಸ್ಯ ॥ ೧೫೬ ॥

ವೃತ್ತಿ ॥ ಅತ್ರ ಲಕಾರಸ್ಯ ದೀರ್ಘಂ ಸ್ಯಾತ್ ॥

ಪ್ರಯೋಗ ॥ ಎಲ್ಲ ರತ್ನಂಗಳ್, ಎಲ್ಲಾ ರತ್ನಂಗಳ್ । ಎಲ್ಲ ಮಾವು, ಎಲ್ಲಾಮಾವು ॥ ಪ್ರಾಯೋಗ್ರಹಣಾತ್ಕ್ವಚಿನ್ನ ॥ ಎಲ್ಲಧನಂ, ಎಲ್ಲಕೆರೆ ॥

ತಾತ್ಪರ್ಯ ॥ ಎಲ್ಲ ಶಬ್ದದ ಲಕಾರಕ್ಕೆ ದೀರ್ಘ ಬರುತ್ತದೆ. ಪ್ರಾಯಶ್ಶಬ್ದಗ್ರಹಣದಿಂದ ಕೆಲವುಕಡೆ ದೀರ್ಘ ಬರುವದಿಲ್ಲ

---

* C ends here.

* ತೃ ॥ ಯಲ್ಲಿ ಮೊದಲನೇ ಉದಾಹರಣೆ ಮಾತ್ರವಿದೆ.

Sûtra 157.—*Bahuvrîhâv ad ante.*

Vṛitti.—*Asmin samâse ante akârântatâ* ।

Prayoga.—*Baṭṭadoḍeyam, keṅgaṇṇam, nalda-kiviyam* । *kvachin-na bhavati* । *kalyerde, aḷarde* ।

[*Bahuvrîhi* compounds generally have the termination *a.* (Sometimes not.)]

Sûtra 158.—*Illasyeliḥ.*

Vṛitti.—*Bahuvrîhau illa-ityasya ily-âdes'as syât* ।

Prayoga.—*Nâṇ illada mânasam, nâṇili-mânasam ; pal illada bâyam, pallili-vâyam ; kûr illada katti, kûrili-gatti* ।

[*Illa* in them becomes *ili.*]

Sûtra 159.—*Dvigau saṅkhyâ-vâchinâm upântya-vyañjanâder lopaḥ.*

Vṛitti.—*Dvigu-samâse saṅkhyâ-vâchaka-padânâm upântya vyañjanâder lopo bhavati* ।

Prayoga.—*Nâlku gêṇ, nâlgêṇ ; nâlku des'e, nâlde s'e ; aidu kaṇḍagam, aigaṇḍagam ; aidu saram, aisaram ; êḷu gâvudam, êḷgâvudam ; êḷu moḷam, êḷmoḷam ; mûru lokam, mûlokam* ।

[In *dvigu* compounds, the numerals drop their last syllable.]

ಸೂತ್ರ ॥ ಬಹುವ್ರೀಹಾವದನ್ತೇ ॥ ೧೫೭ ॥

ವೃತ್ತಿ ॥ ಅಸ್ಮಿನ್ ಸಮಾಸೇ ಅನ್ತೇ ಅಕಾರಾನ್ತತಾ ॥

ಪ್ರಯೋಗ ॥ ಬಟ್ಟಬೊಡೆಯಂ । ಕೆಂಗಣ್ಣಂ।, ನಲ್ದಕಿವಿಯಂ ॥ ಕ್ವಚಿನ್ನ ಭವತಿ ॥ಕಲ್ಯೆರ್ದೆ । ಅಳರ್ದೆ ॥

ತಾತ್ಪರ್ಯ ॥ ಬಹುವ್ರೀಹಿ ಸಮಾಸದಲ್ಲಿ ಅಂತದೊಳಗೆ ಅಕಾರಾನ್ತತ್ವವಾಗುತ್ತದೆ, ಕೆಲವುಕಡೆಯಿಲ್ಲ.

ಸೂತ್ರ ॥ ಇಲ್ಲಸ್ಯೇಲಿಃ ॥ ೧೫೮ ॥

ವೃತ್ತಿ ॥ ಬಹುವ್ರೀಹೌ ಇಲ್ಲಇತ್ಯಸ್ಯ ಇಲ್ಯಾದೇಶಸ್ಸ್ಯಾತ್ ॥

ಪ್ರಯೋಗ ॥ ನಾಣ್ ಇಲ್ಲದ ಮಾನಸಂ, ನಾಣಿಲಿಮಾನಸಂ। ಪಲ್ ಇಲ್ಲದ ಬಾಯಂ, ಪಲ್ಲಿಲಿವಾಯಂ । ಕೂರ್ ಇಲ್ಲದ ಕತ್ತಿ, ಕೂರಿಲಿಗತ್ತಿ ॥

ತಾತ್ಪರ್ಯ ॥ ಬಹುವ್ರೀಹಿ ಸಮಾಸದಲ್ಲಿ ಇಲ್ಲ ಯಂಬದಕ್ಕೆ ಇಲಿಯಂಬದಾದೇಶವಾಗುತ್ತದೆ.

ಸೂತ್ರ ॥ ದ್ವಿಗೌ ಸಙ್ಖ್ಯಾವಾಚಿನಾಮುಪಾನ್ತ್ಯವ್ಯಞ್ಜನಾದೇರ್ಲೋಪಃ ॥ ೧೫೯ ॥

ವೃತ್ತಿ ॥ ದ್ವಿಗುಸಮಾಸೇ ಸಙ್ಖ್ಯಾವಾಚಕಪದಾನಾಮುಪಾನ್ತ್ಯವ್ಯಞ್ಜನಾದೇರ್ಲೋಪೋ ಭವತಿ ॥

ಪ್ರಯೋಗ ॥ ನಾಲ್ಕು ಗೇಣ್, ನಾಲ್ಗೇಣ್ । ನಾಲ್ಕು ದೆಸೆ, ನಾಲ್ದೆಸೆ । ಐದು ಕಂಡಗಂ, ಐಗಂಡಗಂ । ಐದು ಸರಂ, ಐಸರಂ । ಏಳು ಗಾವುದಂ, ಏಳ್ಗಾವುದಂ । ಏಳು ಮೊಳಂ, ಏಳ್ಮೊಳಂ । ಮೂರು ಲೋಕಂ, ಮೂಲೋಕಂ ॥

ತಾತ್ಪರ್ಯ ॥ ದ್ವಿಗುಸಮಾಸದಲ್ಲಿ ಸಂಖ್ಯಾವಾಚಕ ಪದಗಳ ಉಪಾನ್ತ್ಯ ವ್ಯಂಜನಾದಿಗಳಿಗೆ ಲೋಪವಾಗುತ್ತದೆ.

Sûtra 160.—*Ekârtha-vâchikasyaurantah.*

Vritti.—*Ekârtha-vâchi-s'abdasya ôr-âdes'as syât* |

Prayoga.—*Ondu nuḍi, ôrmuḍi ; ondu tale, ôrttale ; ondu piḍi, ôrppiḍi* |

[The word for one becomes *ôr*.]

Sûtra 161.—*Ir-âdes'o dvy-arthasya.*

Vritti.—*Dvigu-samâse dvi-saṅkhyâ-vâchi-s'abdasya ir-âdes'o bhavati* |

Prayoga.—*Irvvakkam ganḍar, irmmai* |

Atra kvachit svâbhâvikah | *eraḷmûru, eraḷmâtu, eraḷkai** |

Keshâñchin-mate nyûna-sthale îr-âdes'as syât | *îraidu* |

[The word for two becomes *ir*. (But sometimes not.) According to the teaching of some it becomes *îr* when used in a subordinate sense.]

Sûtra 162.—*Ka-pa-vargayos trayâkhyasya tâv-âgamau bahuḷam hrasvah pûrvasya cha.*

Vritti.—*Tri-saṅkhyâ-vâchi-padasya ka-pa-vargayoh paratah tâv-âgamau bhavatah* | *prathama-varṇasya hrasvah parâder dvitvam cha bhavati* |

Prayoga.—*Mûru koḍe, mukkoḍe ; mûru guḍḍe, mugguḍḍe ; mûru puri, muppuri ; mûru maḍi, mummaḍi* |

Kvachit prâg-varṇa-hrasvatvam parâdy-akshara-dvitvam cha na stah |

Prayoga | *mûru gêṇ, mûgêṇ ; mûru gâvudam, mûgâvudam* |

[The word for three, in forming a compound with a word beginning with a letter of the *ka* or *pa varga*, shortens its own vowel and doubles the initial consonant of the other word. (But sometimes not)]

ಸೂತ್ರ | ಏಕಾರ್ಥವಾಚಿಕಸ್ಯೌರನ್ತಃ | ೧೬೦ |

ವೃತ್ತಿ | ಏಕಾರ್ಥವಾಚಿಶಬ್ದಸ್ಯ ಓರಾದೇಶಸ್ಸ್ಯಾತ್ |

ಪ್ರಯೋಗ | ಒಂದು ನುಡಿ, ಓರ್ನ್ನುಡಿ | ಒಂದು ತಲೆ, ಓರ್ತ್ತಲೆ | ಒಂದು ಪಿಡಿ, ಓರ್ಪ್ಪಿಡಿ |

ತಾತ್ಪರ್ಯ | ಏಕಾರ್ಥವಾಚಕವಾದ ಶಬ್ದಕ್ಕೆ ಓರ್ ಯಂಬಾದೇಶವಾಗುತ್ತದೆ. ಏಕಾರ್ಥವಾಚಕವಂದರೆ ಒಂದೆಂಬರ್ಥವಾದದ್ದು.

ಸೂತ್ರ | ಇರಾದೇಶೋ ದ್ವ್ಯರ್ಥಸ್ಯ | ೧೬೧ |

ವೃತ್ತಿ | ದ್ವಿಗುಸಮಾಸೇ ದ್ವಿಸಙ್ಖ್ಯಾವಾಚಿಶಬ್ದಸ್ಯ ಇರಾದೇಶೋ ಭವತಿ |

ಪ್ರಯೋಗ | ಇರ್ವ್ವಕ್ಕಂ ಗಂಡರ್ | ಇರ್ಮ್ಮೆ | ಅತ್ರ ಕ್ವಚಿತ್ಸ್ವಾಭಾವಿಕಃ | ಎರಳ್ಮೂರು | ಎರಳ್ಮಾತು | ಎರಳ್ಕೈ |

*ಕೇಷಾಂಚಿನ್ಮತೇ ನ್ಯೂನಸ್ಥಲೇ ಈರಾದೇಶಸ್ಸ್ಯಾತ್ | ಈರೈದು |

ತಾತ್ಪರ್ಯ | ದ್ವಿಗುಸಮಾಸದಲ್ಲಿ ಸಂಖ್ಯಾವಾಚಿ ಶಬ್ದಕ್ಕೆ ಇರಾದೇಶವಾಗುತ್ತದೆ. ದ್ವಿಸಂಖ್ಯಾವಾಚಿ ಅಂದರೆ ಯೆರಡೆಂಬುವದು.

ಸೂತ್ರ | ಕಪವರ್ಗಯೋಸ್ತ್ರಯಾಖ್ಯಸ್ಯ ತಾವಾಗಮೌ ಬಹುಳಂ ಹ್ರಸ್ವಃ ಪೂರ್ವಸ್ಯ ಚ | ೧೬೨ |

ವೃತ್ತಿ | ತ್ರಿಸಙ್ಖ್ಯಾವಾಚಿಪದಸ್ಯ ಕಪವರ್ಗಯೋಃ ಪರತಃ ತಾವಾಗಮೌ ಭವತಃ | ಪ್ರಥಮವರ್ಣಸ್ಯ ಹ್ರಸ್ವಃ ಪರಾದೇರ್ದ್ವಿತ್ವಂ ಚ ಭವತಿ |

ಪ್ರಯೋಗ | ಮೂರು ಕೊಡೆ, ಮುಕ್ಕೊಡೆ | ಮೂರು ಗುಡ್ಡೆ, ಮುಗ್ಗುಡ್ಡೆ | ಮೂರು ಪುರಿ, ಮುಪ್ಪುರಿ | ಮೂರು ಮಡಿ, ಮುಮ್ಮಡಿ | ಕ್ವಚಿತ್ಪ್ರಾಗ್ವರ್ಣ ಹ್ರಸ್ವತ್ವಂ ಪರಾದ್ಯಕ್ಷರದ್ವಿತ್ವಂ ಚ ನ ಸ್ತಃ |

ಪ್ರಯೋಗ | ಮೂರು ಗೇಣ್, ಮೂಗೇಣ್ | ಮೂರು ಗಾವುದಂ, ಮೂಗಾವುದಂ |

ತಾತ್ಪರ್ಯ | ದ್ವಿಗು ಸಮಾಸದಲ್ಲಿ ತ್ರಿಸಂಖ್ಯಾವಾಚಿ ಪದಗಳ ಕವರ್ಗ ಪವರ್ಗಗಳಿಗೆ ಪರದಲ್ಲಿ ಪೂರ್ವ ಪದವರ್ಣಕ್ಕೆ ಹ್ರಸ್ವವೂ ಪರಪದಾದಿ ವರ್ಣಕ್ಕೆ ದ್ವಿತ್ವವೂ ಆಗುತ್ತದೆ. ಕೆಲವು ಕಡೆ ಈ ಯೆರಡೂ ಆಗುವದಿಲ್ಲ.

---

* C ends here.

* ತೃ | ಪ್ರತಿಯಲ್ಲಿ ಈ ವಿಶೇಷ ಇಲ್ಲ.

Sûtra 163.—*Tryâdînâm vyañjaneshv eva.*

Vṛitti.—*Tri-prabhṛitînâm saṅkhyâ-vâchinâm upântya-vyañjanasya vyñja-neshu pareshv eva tad-upântyâvayavasya lopas syât* ǀ

Prayoga.—*Mûru lokam, mûlôkam* ǀ *vyañjaneshv iti kim* ǀ *svarâdau pare na lopa iti* ǀ *mûraḍi, mûroḍḍu, mûrane, mûroḷ, mûrâne* ǀ

[The words for three and the remaining numerals drop their last syllable in forming a compound with a word beginning with a consonant. (And not with one beginning with a vowel).]

Sûtra 164.—*Na shaḍartha-vâchakasyâder hrasvaḥ.*

Vṛitti.—*Shaṭ-saṅkhyâ-vâchina upântyasya pûrvaval-lopo na bhavati* ǀ *api-tu âder âkârasya hrasvas syât* ǀ

Prayoga.— *Âru tiṅgaḷ, aruḍiṅgaḷ ; âru gêṇ, arugêṇ* ǀ

[But not the word for six : this shortens its initial *â*.]

Sûtra 165.—*Saptârthâbhidhâyinas' cha.*

Vṛitti.—*Sapta-saṅkhyâ-vâchinas' chopântya-svara-lope sati pûrva-svarasya hrasvas syât* ǀ

Prayoga.—*Êḷu modal, eḷmodal ; êḷu pore, eḷvore ; êḷu varakkaṅgaḷ, eḷvarakkaṅgaḷ* ǀ

[The word for seven, while dropping its final vowel, shortens its initial vowel.]

ಸೂತ್ರ ‖ ತ್ರ್ಯಾದೀನಾಂ ವ್ಯಞ್ಜನೇಷ್ವೇವ ‖ ೧೬೩ ‖

ವೃತ್ತಿ ‖ ತ್ರಿಪ್ರಭೃತೀನಾಂ ಸಙ್ಖ್ಯಾವಾಚಿನಾಂ ಉಪಾನ್ತ್ಯವ್ಯಞ್ಜನಸ್ಯ ವ್ಯಞ್ಜನೇಷು ಪರೇಷ್ವೇವ ತದುಪಾನ್ತ್ಯಾವಯವಸ್ಯ ಲೋಪಸ್ಸ್ಯಾತ್ ‖

ಪ್ರಯೋಗ ‖ ಮೂರು ಲೋಕಂ, ಮೂಲೋಕಂ। ವ್ಯಞ್ಜನೇಷ್ವಿತಿ ಕಿಂ। ಸ್ವರಾದೌ ಪರೇ ನ ಲೋಪ ಇತಿ। ಮೂರಡಿ। ಮೂರೊಡ್ಡು। ಮೂರನೆ। ಮೂರೊಳ್। ಮೂರಾನೆ ‖

ತಾತ್ಪರ್ಯ ‖ ಮೂರು ಮೊದಲಾದ ಸಂಖ್ಯಾ ವಾಚಿಗಳ ಉಪಾನ್ತ್ಯ ವ್ಯಂಜನಕ್ಕೆ ವ್ಯಂಜನಗಳು ಪರವಾದರೆ ಮಾತ್ರವೇ ಆ ಉಪಾನ್ತ್ಯಾವಯವಕ್ಕೆ ಲೋಪವು ಆಗುತ್ತದೆ. ಸ್ವರಪರವಾದರೆ ಲೋಪವಿಲ್ಲ.

ಸೂತ್ರ ‖ ನ ಷಡರ್ಥವಾಚಕಸ್ಯಾದೇರ್ಹ್ರಸ್ವಃ ‖ ೧೬೪ ‖

ವೃತ್ತಿ ‖ ಷಟ್ಸಙ್ಖ್ಯಾವಾಚಿನ ಉಪಾನ್ತ್ಯಸ್ಯ ಪೂರ್ವವಲ್ಲೋಪೋ ನ ಭವತಿ। ಅಪಿತು ಆದೇರಾಕಾರಸ್ಯ ಹ್ರಸ್ವಸ್ಸ್ಯಾತ್ ‖

ಪ್ರಯೋಗ ‖ ಆರು ತಿಂಗಳ್, ಅರುದಿಂಗಳ್। ಆರು ಗೇಣ್, ಅರುಗೇಣ್ ‖

ತಾತ್ಪರ್ಯ ‖ ಷಟ್ಸಂಖ್ಯಾವಾಚಕ ಶಬ್ದದ ಉಪಾನ್ತ್ಯಕ್ಕೆ ಪೂರ್ವ ಹೇಳಿದಂತೆ ಲೋಪವಾಗದು. ಆದರೆ ಮೊದಲಿನ ಆಕಾರಕ್ಕೆ ಹ್ರಸ್ವವಾಗುತ್ತದೆ.

ಸೂತ್ರ ‖ ಸಪ್ತಾರ್ಥಾಭಿಧಾಯಿನಶ್ಚ ‖ ೧೬೫ ‖

ವೃತ್ತಿ ‖ ಸಪ್ತಸಙ್ಖ್ಯಾವಾಚಿನಶ್ಚೋಪಾನ್ತ್ಯ ಸ್ವರಲೋಪೇ ಸತಿ ಪೂರ್ವಸ್ವರಸ್ಯ ಹ್ರಸ್ವಸ್ಸ್ಯಾತ್ ‖

ಪ್ರಯೋಗ ‖ ಏಳು ಮೊದಲ್, ಎಳ್ಮೊದಲ್। ಏಳು ಪೊರೆ, ಎಳ್ವೊರೆ। ಏಳು ವರಕ್ಕಂಗಳ್, ಎಳ್ವರಕ್ಕಂಗಳ್ ‖

ತಾತ್ಪರ್ಯ ‖ ಸಪ್ತಸಂಖ್ಯಾವಾಚಕ ಶಬ್ದದ ಉಪಾನ್ತ್ಯಸ್ವರ ಲೋಪವಾಗುತ್ತಿರೆ ಪೂರ್ವಸ್ವರಕ್ಕೆ ಹ್ರಸ್ವವಾಗುವದು.

Sûtra 166.—*Navâkhyâyâs tombha samjñi hattau.*

Vritti.—*Nava-vâchaka-padasya das'ârthe hattv iti s'abde pare tombha ity âdes'o bhavati* ।

Prayoga.—*Tombhattu* । *nava das'akam ity arthah* ।

[The word for nine, in forming a compound with the word for ten, becomes *tombha.*]

Sûtra 167.—*Ombhai s'ate.*

Vritti.—*Navâkhyâyâs' s'ata-vâchaka-s'abde pare ombhai ity ayam âdes'as syât* ।

Prayoga.—*Ombhainûru* ।

[With the word for hundred, it becomes *ombhai.*]

Sûtra 168.—*Sahasre cha.*

Vritti.—*Nava-vâchaka-s'abdasya sahasra-sankhyâ-vâchini-pade pare ombhai ity âdes'as syât* ।

Prayoga.—*Ombhaisâsiram* ।

[Also with the word for thousand.]

Sûtra 169.—*Das'âkhyâyâh payin.*

Vritti.—*Das'a-vâchi-s'abdasya cha sahasra vâchake parato'vasthite sati payin ity âdes'o bhavati* ।

Prayoga.—*Payinsâsiram* ।

[The word for ten, in forming a compound with the word for thousand, becomes *payin.*]

ಸೂತ್ರ ॥ ನವಾಖ್ಯಾಯಾಸ್ತೊಂಭ ಸಂಜ್ಞಿ ಹತ್ತೌ ॥ ೧೬೬ ॥

ವೃತ್ತಿ ॥ ನವವಾಚಕಪದಸ್ಯ ದಶಾರ್ಥೇ ಹತ್ತ್ವಿತಿ ಶಬ್ದೇ ಪರೇ ತೊಂಭ ಇತ್ಯಾದೇಶೋ ಭವತಿ ॥

ಪ್ರಯೋಗ ॥ ತೊಂಭತ್ತು । ನವದಶಕಮಿತ್ಯರ್ಥಃ ॥

ತಾತ್ಪರ ॥ ನವವಾಚಕ ಪದಕ್ಕೆ ದಶಾರ್ಥಕವಾದ ಹತ್ತೆಂಬ ಶಬ್ದವು ಪರವಾದರೆ ತೊಂಭ ಯೆಂಬದಾದೇಶವಾಗುತ್ತದೆ.

ಸೂತ್ರ ॥ ಒಂಭೈ ಶತೇ ॥ ೧೬೭ ॥

ವೃತ್ತಿ ॥ ನವಾಖ್ಯಾಯಾಶ್ಶತವಾಚಕಶಬ್ದೇ ಪರೇ ಒಂಭೈ ಇತ್ಯಯಮಾದೇಶಸ್ಸ್ಯಾತ್ ॥

ಪ್ರಯೋಗ ॥ ಒಂಭೈನೂರು ॥

ತಾತ್ಪರ್ಯ ॥ ನವವಾಚಕ ಪದಕ್ಕೆ ಶತವಾಚಕ ಶಬ್ದವು ಪರವಾದರೇ ಒಂಭೈ ಯೆಂಬದಾದೇಶವಾಗುತ್ತದೆ.

ಸೂತ್ರ ॥ ಸಹಸ್ರೇ ಚ ॥ ೧೬೮

ವೃತ್ತಿ ॥ ನವವಾಚಕಶಬ್ದಸ್ಯ ಸಹಸ್ರಸಙ್ಖ್ಯಾವಾಚಿನಿ ಪದೇ ಪರೇ ಒಂಭೈ ಇತ್ಯಾದೇಶಸ್ಸ್ಯಾತ್ ॥

ಪ್ರಯೋಗ ॥ ಒಂಭೈಸಾಸಿರಂ ॥

ತಾತ್ಪರ್ಯ ॥ ನವವಾಚಕ ಪದಕ್ಕೆ ಸಹಸ್ರ ಸಂಖ್ಯಾವಾಚಕವಾದ ಶಬ್ದವು ಪರವಾದರೆ ಒಂಭೈ ಯೆಂಬದಾದೇಶವಾಗುತ್ತದೆ.

ಸೂತ್ರ ॥ ದಶಾಖ್ಯಾಯಾಃ ಪಯಿನ್ ॥ ೧೬೯ ॥

ವೃತ್ತಿ ॥ ದಶವಾಚಿಶಬ್ದಸ್ಯ ಚ ಸಹಸ್ರವಾಚಕೇ ಪರತೋऽವಸ್ಥಿತೇ ಸತಿ ಪಯಿನ್ ಇತ್ಯಾದೇಶೋ ಭವತಿ ॥

ಪ್ರಯೋಗ ॥ ಪಯಿನಸಾಸಿರಂ ॥

ತಾತ್ಪರ್ಯ ॥ ದಶವಾಚಿ ಶಬ್ದಕ್ಕೆ ಸಹಸ್ರವಾಚಕ ಶಬ್ದವು ಪರವಾದರೆ ಪಯಿನ್ ಯೆಂಬದಾದೇಶವಾಗುತ್ತದೆ.

Sûtra 170.—*Pann-aika-dvy-arthayoh.*

Vṛitti.—*Das'âkhyâyâh eka-dvi-saṅkhyâ-vâchi-s'abdayoh parayoh pann ity âdes'as syât.*

Prayoga.—*Pannondu, pannerаḍu* ।

[The word for ten, followed by the word for one or two, becomes *pann*.*]

Sûtra 171.—*Anyatra padih.*

Vṛitti.—*Anyatrânyayoh tri-chatur-vâchaka-s'abdayoh parayoh das'a-vâchinah padîty âdes'o bhavati* ।

Prayoga.—*Padimûru, padinâlku* ।

[Followed by the remaining numerals, it becomes *padi*.*]

Sûtra 172.—*Svarâdau nâgamah.*

Vṛitti.—*Das'âkhyâyâh svarâdi-saṅkhyâ-vâchake pare padîty âdes'as tat param nakârâgamas' cha bhavati* ।

Prayoga.—*Padinaidu, padinâru, padinêḷu, padineṇṭu* ।

Bahuḷâdhikârât kvachit prakṛityaiva tishṭhati । *yathâ* । *pattombhattu* ।

[But if the following word begins with a vowel, *n* comes between. (In some cases, however, it keeps its radical form).]

Iti Karṇâṭaka-vyâkaraṇa-vṛittau † Bhâshâ-bûshaṇe S'amâsa-vidhânam nâma shashṭhah parichchhedah ।

ಸೂತ್ರ ॥ ಪನ್ನೈಕದ್ವ್ಯರ್ಥಯೋಃ ॥ ೧೭೦ ॥

ವೃತ್ತಿ ॥ ದಶಾಖ್ಯಾಯಾಃ ಏಕದ್ವಿಸಙ್ಖ್ಯಾವಾಚಿಶಬ್ದಯೋಃ ಪರಯೋಃ ಪನ್ನಿತ್ಯಾದೇಶಸ್ಸ್ಯಾತ್ ॥

ಪ್ರಯೋಗ ॥ ಪನ್ನೊಂದು, ಪನ್ನೆರಡು ॥

ತಾತ್ಪರ್ಯ ॥ ದಶವಾಚಕ ಶಬ್ದಕ್ಕೆ ಏಕದ್ವಿ ಸಂಖ್ಯಾವಾಚಿ ಶಬ್ದಗಳು ಪರವಾದರೆ ಪನ್ನ ಯೆಂಬುದಾದೇಶವಾಗುತ್ತದೆ.

ಸೂತ್ರ ॥ ಅನ್ಯತ್ರ ಪಡಿಃ ॥ ೧೭೧ ॥

ವೃತ್ತಿ ॥ ಅನ್ಯತ್ರಾನ್ಯಯೋಃ ತ್ರಿಚತುರ್ವಾಚಕಶಬ್ದಯೋಃ ಪರಯೋಃ ದಶವಾಚಿನಃ ಪಡೀತ್ಯಾದೇಶೋ ಭವತಿ ॥

ಪ್ರಯೋಗ ॥ ಪಡಿಮೂರು । ಪಡಿನಾಲ್ಕು ॥

ತಾತ್ಪರ್ಯ ॥ ಅನ್ಯತ್ರ ಅಂದರೆ ತ್ರಿಚತುರ್ವಾಚಕ ಶಬ್ದಗಳು ಪರವಾದರೆ ದಶವಾಚಕ ಶಬ್ದಕ್ಕೆ ಪಡಿ ಯೆಂಬುದಾದೇಶವಾಗುತ್ತದೆ.

ಸೂತ್ರ ॥ ಸ್ವರಾದೌ ನಾಗಮಃ ॥ ೧೭೨ ॥

ವೃತ್ತಿ ॥ ದಶಾಖ್ಯಾಯಾಃ ಸ್ವರಾದಿಸಙ್ಖ್ಯಾವಾಚಕೇ ಪರೇ ಪಡೀತ್ಯಾದೇಶಸ್ತತ್ಪರಂ ನಕಾರಾಗಮಶ್ಚ ಭವತಿ ॥

ಪ್ರಯೋಗ ॥ ಪಡಿನೈದು । ಪಡಿನಾರು । ಪಡಿನೇಳು । ಪಡಿನೆಂಟು ॥

ಬಹುಳಾಧಿಕಾರಾತ್ ಕ್ವಚಿತ್ ಪ್ರಕೃತ್ಯೈವ ತಿಷ್ಠತಿ । ಯಥಾ । ಪತ್ತೊಂಭತ್ತು ॥

ತಾತ್ಪರ್ಯ ॥ ದಶವಾಚಕ ಶಬ್ದಕ್ಕೆ ಸ್ವರಾದಿಯಾದ ಸಂಖ್ಯಾವಾಚಕವು ಪರವಾದರೆ ಪಡಿ ಯೆಂಬಾದೇಶವೂ ಅದರ ಮೇಲೆ ನಕಾರಾಗಮವೂ ಬರುತ್ತದೆ. ಬಹುಳಾಧಿಕಾರದಿಂದ ಕೆಲವು ಕಡೆ ಪ್ರಕೃತಿಯಾಗಿಯೇ ನಿಲ್ಲುತ್ತದೆ.

ಇತಿಕರ್ಣಾಟಕ ವ್ಯಾಕರಣ ವೃತ್ತೌ † ಭಾಷಾ ಭೂಷಣೇ ಸಮಾಸ ವಿಧಾನಂ
ನಾಮ ಷಷ್ಠಃ ಪರಿಚ್ಛೇದಃ ॥

---

* The current forms are *haṇṇ* and *hadi*; see note to Sûtra 122.

† See note p. 7. † ೭ನೇ ಪುಟವನ್ನು ನೋಡಬೇಕು.

(VII. Derivatives.)

Taddhita Vidhânam.

Sûtra 173.—***Tad asya paṇyam-s'ilpam-niyogas' chety asminn-igah.***

Vṛitti.—***Asya punsah tad-vastu paṇyam-vyavahârah-silpam-krityam-niyogah-adhikâras' chety asminn-arthe liṅgât paratah iga-pratyayo bhavati*** ।

Prayoga.—***Paṇye :—tambuligam, gandigam, davasigam*** । ***s'ilpe :—paṭasâligam, paḍavandigam, paṭṭaḷigam, telligam*** । ***niyoge :—banḍârigam, bâṇasigam, koṭârigam*** ।

[The affix *iga* is used to form words denoting one's trade, art, or office.]

Sûtra 174.—***Tad vetty-adhîte vâ.***

Vṛitti.—***Tad vastu jânâty-abhyasyatîty-arthe chordhvam' iga-pratyayas syât*** ।

Prayoga.—***Jôyisigam, gaṇitigam, siddhântigam*** । ***kvachid âchârârthe cha dṛis'yate*** । ***Prayoga*** । ***suṅkam âcharatîti suṅkigam ity âdi*** ।

[Also one's profes-ion or pursuit. (Sometimes one's control or authority.)]

ತದ್ಧಿತ ವಿಧಾನಂ.

ಸೂತ್ರ ॥ ತದಸ್ಯ ಪಣ್ಯಂ ಶಿಲ್ಪಂ ನಿಯೋಗಶ್ಚೇತ್ಯಸ್ಮಿನ್ನಿಗಃ ॥ ೧೭೩ ॥

ವೃತ್ತಿ ॥ ಅಸ್ಯ ಪುಂಸಃ ತದ್ವಸ್ತು ಪಣ್ಯಂ ವ್ಯವಹಾರಃ ಶಿಲ್ಪಂ ಕೃತ್ಯಂ ನಿಯೋಗಃ ಅಧಿಕಾರಶ್ಚೇತ್ಯಸ್ಮಿನ್ನರ್ಥೇ ಲಿಂಗಾತ್ಪರತಃ ಇಗಪ್ರತ್ಯಯೋ ಭವತಿ ॥

ಪ್ರಯೋಗ ॥ ಪಣ್ಯೇ ॥ ತಂಬುಲಿಗಂ । ಗಂದಿಗಂ । ದವಸಿಗಂ ॥ ಶಿಲ್ಪೇ ॥ ಪಟುಸಾಲಿಗಂ । ಪಡವಂದಿಗಂ । ಪತ್ತಳಿಗಂ । ತೆಲ್ಲಿಗಂ ॥ ನಿಯೋಗೇ ॥ ಬಂಡಾರಿಗಂ । ಬಾಣಸಿಗಂ । ಕೊಟಾರಿಗಂ ॥

ತಾತ್ಪರ್ಯ ॥ ಅದು ಈತನಿಗೆ ವ್ಯವಹಾರವೆಂತಲೂ ಕೃತ್ಯವೆಂತಲೂ ಅಧಿಕಾರವೆಂತಲೂ ಹೇಳಬೇಕಾದರ್ಥದಲ್ಲಿ ಲಿಂಗಕ್ಕೆ ಪರವಾಗಿ ಇಗ ಪ್ರತ್ಯಯ ಬರುವದು.

ಸೂತ್ರ ॥ ತದ್ವೇತ್ತ್ಯಧೀತೇ ವಾ ॥ ೧೭೪ ॥

ವೃತ್ತಿ ॥ ತದ್ವಸ್ತು ಜಾನಾತ್ಯಭ್ಯಸ್ಯತೀತ್ಯರ್ಥೇ ಚೋರ್ಧ್ವಮಿಗಪ್ರತ್ಯಯಸ್ಸ್ಯಾತ್ ॥

ಪ್ರಯೋಗ ॥ ಜೋಯಿಸಿಗಂ । ಗಣಿತಿಗಂ । ಸಿದ್ಧಾಂತಿಗಂ । ಕ್ವಚಿದಾಚಾರಾರ್ಥೇ ಚ ದೃಶ್ಯತೇ ॥

ಪ್ರಯೋಗ ॥ ಸುಂಕಮಾಚರತೀತಿ ಸುಂಕಿಗಮಿತ್ಯಾದಿ ॥

ತಾತ್ಪರ್ಯ ॥ ಅದು ಅವನಿಗೆ ತಿಳಿಯುತ್ತದೆಂಬರ್ಥದಲ್ಲಿಯೂ ಅದನ್ನು ಅವನಭ್ಯಸಿಸುತ್ತಾನೆಂಬರ್ಥದಲ್ಲಿಯೂ ಕೂಡ ಕಡೇಲಿ ಇಗ ಪ್ರತ್ಯಯ ಬರುತ್ತದೆ. ಕೆಲವು ಕಡೆ ಅದನ್ನು ಆಚರಿಸುತ್ತಾನೆಂಬರ್ಥದಲ್ಲಿಯೂ ಇಗ ಪ್ರತ್ಯಯವು ಕಾಣಲ್ಪಡುತ್ತದೆ.

Sûtra 175.—*Ichas tatra jâte bhâve vâ.*

Vṛitti.—*Taj-janita ity arthe icha-pratyayo vâ syât* ।

Prayoga.—*Poḷalôḷ puṭṭidâtam Poḷalicham, Kâlûrôḷ puṭṭidâtam Kâlûricham, Karahaḍa des'adôḷ puṭṭidâtam Karahaḍicham* । *atra yathâ lakshyam vaktavyam* । *kvachid iyantatvam cha* । *Poḷaligam, Kâlûrigam ity âdi* ।

[The affix *icha* denotes one's native place: *iga* is also used for this.]

Sûtra 176.—*Vaḷa-vaḷḷau tatrâdhikṛiti.**

Vṛitti.—*Atrâyam adhikârity arthe vaḷa-vaḷḷâv itîmau pratyayau bhavataḥ* ।

Prayoga.—*Maḍivaḷam, maḍivaḷḷam; aḍapavaḷam, aḍapavaḷḷam; sejjevaḷam, sejjevaḷḷam*† ।

[*Vaḷa* and *vaḷḷa* denote one's jurisdiction.]

Sûtra 177.—*Vyâpṛite pravaṇe cha kâraḥ.*

Vṛitti.—*Kvachid vyâpte vyâsakte cha vâchye kâra-pratyayaḥ* ।

Prayoga.—*Naḍivaḷikâram, âṭagâram, muṇḍukâram, aramanekâram, bilkâram* ‡ ।

[*Kâra* denotes one's nature or work (employment).]

ಸೂತ್ರ ॥ ಇಚಸ್ತತ್ರ ಜಾತೇ ಭಾವೇ ವಾ ॥ ೧೭೫ ॥

ವೃತ್ತಿ ॥ ತಜ್ಜನಿತ ಇತ್ಯರ್ಥೇ ಇಚಪ್ರತ್ಯಯೋ ವಾ ಸ್ಯಾತ್ ॥

ಪ್ರಯೋಗ ॥ ಪೊಳಲೋಳ್ ಪುಟ್ಟಿದಾತಂ ಪೊಳಲಿಚಂ । ಕಾಲೂರೋಳ್ ಪುಟ್ಟಿದಾತಂ ಕಾಲೂರಿಚಂ । ಕರಹಡ ದೇಶದೋಳ್ ಪುಟ್ಟಿದಾತಂ ಕರಹಡಿಚಂ । ಅತ್ರ ಯಥಾಲಕ್ಷ್ಯಂ ವಕ್ತವ್ಯಂ । ಕ್ವಚಿದಿಗನ್ತತ್ವಂ ಚ । ಪೊಳಲಿಗಂ । ಕಾಲೂರಿಗಮಿತ್ಯಾದಿ ॥

ತಾತ್ಪರ್ಯ ॥ ಅಲ್ಲಿ ಪುಟ್ಟಿದನೆಂಬರ್ಥದಲ್ಲಿ ವೈಕಲ್ಪಿಕವಾಗಿ ಇಚ ಪ್ರತ್ಯಯವಾಗುತ್ತದೆ. ವೈಕಲ್ಪಿಕವೆಂಬದರಿಂದ ಕೆಲವು ಕಡೆ ಪೊಳಲಿಗವೆಂದು ಇಗ ಪ್ರತ್ಯಯವೂ ಬರುತ್ತದೆ.

ಸೂತ್ರ ॥ ವಳವಳ್ಳೌ ತತ್ರಾಧಿಕೃತಿ * ॥ ೧೭೬ ॥

ವೃತ್ತಿ ॥ ಅತ್ರಾಯಮಧಿಕಾರೀತ್ಯರ್ಥೇ ವಳವಳ್ಳಾವಿತೀಮೌ ಪ್ರತ್ಯಯೌ ಭವತಃ ॥

ಪ್ರಯೋಗ ॥ ಮಡಿವಳಂ, ಮಡಿವಳ್ಳಂ । ಅಡಪವಳಂ, ಅಡಪವಳ್ಳಂ । ಸೆಜ್ಜೆವಳಂ, ಸೆಜ್ಜೆವಳ್ಳಂ† ॥

ತಾತ್ಪರ್ಯ ॥ ಇಲ್ಲಿ ಈತನಧಿಕಾರಿಯೆಂಬರ್ಥದಲ್ಲಿ ವಳ ವಳ್ಳ ಯೆಂಬೀ ಪ್ರತ್ಯಯಗಳು ಬರುತ್ತವೆ.

ಸೂತ್ರ ॥ ವ್ಯಾಪೃತೇ ಪ್ರವಣೇ ಚ ಕಾರಃ ॥ ೧೭೭ ॥

ವೃತ್ತಿ ॥ ಕ್ವಚಿದ್ವ್ಯಾಪ್ತೇ ವ್ಯಾಸಕ್ತೇ ಚ ವಾಚ್ಯೇ ಕಾರಪ್ರತ್ಯಯಃ ॥

ಪ್ರಯೋಗ ॥ ನಡಿವಳಿಕಾರಂ । ಆಟಗಾರಂ । ಮುಂಡುಕಾರಂ । ಅರಮನೆಕಾರಂ । ಬಿಲ್ಕಾರಂ ‡ ॥

ತಾತ್ಪರ್ಯ ॥ ವ್ಯಾಪ್ತಿಯಲ್ಲಿಯೂ ಪವಣಿನಲ್ಲಿಯೂ ಕಾರ ಪ್ರತ್ಯಯ ಬರುವದು.

---

* In B *tatrâdhikṛitau*; In C *tatrâdhikṛite*. † Not in C.

* ದ್ವಿ ॥ ಯಲ್ಲಿ ಕೃತೌ ಎಂದಿದೆ. ತೃ ॥ ಯಲ್ಲಿ ಕೃತೇ ಎಂದಿದೆ. † ತೃ ॥ ಯಲ್ಲಿ ಇಲ್ಲ.

‡ C. Adds *mâlegâram*. ‡ ತೃ ॥ ಯಲ್ಲಿ ಮಾಲೆಗಾರಂ ಇದೆ.

Sûtra 178.—*Tud asyâstiti vantah.*

Vritti.—*Vais'ishtyârthe vanta-pratyayas syât* ।

Prayoga.—*Sirivantam, guṇavantam, âyuvantam* ।

[*Vanta* denotes one's characteristic.]

Sûtra 179.—*Upamânârthe vôl.*

Vritti.—*Vôl susthiram* ।

Prayoga.—*Manuvôl yajñam* । *kvachid anteti* । *kariyante bhadra-guṇam* ।

[*Vôl* expresses comparison. (Sometimes *ante* is used.)]

Sûtra 180.—*Hrasvo vâ.*

Vritti.—*Vôl pratyayo vikalpâddhrasvo bhavati* ।

Prayoga.—*Harivôl, harivol ; karivôl, karivol* ।

[*Vôl* is sometimes short.]

Sûtra 181.—*Akârântân-nâgamo ba-s'rutis' cha.*

Vritti.—*Adantâch-chhabdât parasya vôl ity asya pûrvam nâgamah svasya bakâra-s'rutis' cha bhavati* ।

Prayoga.—*Nigaḷambôl, chaṇḍrambôl beḷagitu* ।

When *vôl* is affixed to a word ending in *a*, the latter adds *n*, and *vôl* becomes *bôl.*]

ಸೂತ್ರ । ತದಸ್ಯಾಸ್ತೀತಿ ವನ್ತಃ । ೧೭೮ ।

ವೃತ್ತಿ । ವೈಶಿಷ್ಟ್ಯಾರ್ಥೇ ವನ್ತಪ್ರತ್ಯಯಸ್ಸ್ಯಾತ್ ।

ಪ್ರಯೋಗ । ಸಿರಿವನ್ತಂ । ಗುಣವನ್ತಂ । ಆಯುವನ್ತಂ ।

ತಾತ್ಪರ್ಯ । ಅದು ಈತಂಗೆ ವುಂಟೆಂದು ಹೇಳುವರ್ಥದಲ್ಲಿ ವನ್ತ ಪ್ರತ್ಯಯವಾಗುತ್ತದೆ.

ಸೂತ್ರ । ಉಪಮಾನಾರ್ಥೇ ವೊಲ್ । ೧೭೯ ।

ವೃತ್ತಿ । ವೊಲ್ ಸುಸ್ಥಿರಂ ।

ಪ್ರಯೋಗ । ಮನುವೊಲ್ ಯಜ್ಞಂ । ಕ್ವಚಿದನ್ತೇತಿ । ಕರಿಯನ್ತೆ ಭದ್ರಗುಣಂ ॥

ತಾತ್ಪರ್ಯ । ಉಪಮಾನಾರ್ಥದಲ್ಲಿ ವೊಲ್ ಪ್ರತ್ಯಯವು ಬರುವದು.

ಸೂತ್ರ । ಹ್ರಸ್ವೋ ವಾ । ೧೮೦ ।

ವೃತ್ತಿ । ವೊಲ್ ಪ್ರತ್ಯಯೋ ವಿಕಲ್ಪಾದ್ಧ್ರಸ್ವೋ ಭವತಿ ।

ಪ್ರಯೋಗ । ಹರಿವೊಲ್, ಹರಿವೊಲ್ । ಕರಿವೊಲ್, ಕರಿವೊಲ್ ।

ತಾತ್ಪರ್ಯ । ವೊಲ್ ಪ್ರತ್ಯಯವು ವಿಕಲ್ಪದಿಂದ ಹ್ರಸ್ವವಾಗುತ್ತದೆ.

ಸೂತ್ರ । ಅಕಾರಾನ್ತಾನ್ನಾಗಮೋ ಬಶ್ರುತಿಶ್ಚ । ೧೮೧ ।

ವೃತ್ತಿ । ಅದನ್ತಾಚ್ಛಬ್ದಾತ್ ಪರಸ್ಯ ವೊಲಿತ್ಯಸ್ಯ ಪೂರ್ವಂ ನಾಗಮಃ ಸ್ವಸ್ಯ ಬಕಾರಶ್ರುತಿಶ್ಚ ಭವತಿ ।

ಪ್ರಯೋಗ । ನಿಗಳಂಬೊಲ್ । ಚಂದ್ರಂಬೊಲ್ ಬೆಳಗಿತು ।

ತಾತ್ಪರ್ಯ । ಅಕಾರಾನ್ತ ಶಬ್ದಕ್ಕೆ ಪರವಾದ ವೊಲ್ ಯೆಂಬದಕ್ಕೆ ಪೂರ್ವದಲ್ಲಿ ನಕಾರಾಗಮವೂ ವೊಲ್ ಯೆಂಬದಕ್ಕೆ ಬಕಾರವೂ ಆಗುತ್ತದೆ.

Sûtra 182.—*Saṅkhyâyâh pûraṇe aneyah.*

Vṛitti.—*Saṅkhyâ-pûrty-arthe aneya-pratyayo bhavati* ।

Prayoga.—*Padinâlkaneyavam, padinaidaneyavam, padinâraneyavam; Tîrthaṅkaram S'ântinâtham Jinaroḷage padinâlkaneyavam; chakravartigaḷoḷ aidaneyan-ene puṇyam pûjârchanakke S'ântis'an-antu nôntavaroḷ ere* ।

[*Aneya* denotes numeral order.]

Sûtra 183.—*Vârârthe me vâ.*

Vṛitti.—*Ekavâram dvivâram ity âdy arthe me-pratyayo syât* ।

Prayoga.—*Orme, irme, mûme, mume* । *ity atah* । *ondu sûḷ, eraḍu sûḷ* ।

[*Me* denotes number of times.]

Sûtra 184.—*Bhâvârthe ke pu.*

Vṛitti.— *Tasya bhâva ity-arthe ke-pu-iti dvau pratyayau bhavatah* ।

Prayoga.—*Kâṇke, pûṇke, poraḷke, teraḷke; nuṇpu, taṇpu, kempu, sompu* ।

[*Ke* and *pu* denote abstract quality.]

ಸೂತ್ರ ॥ ಸಙ್ಖ್ಯಾಯಾಃ ಪೂರಣೇ ಅನೆಯಃ ॥ ೧೮೨ ॥

ವೃತ್ತಿ ॥ ಸಙ್ಖ್ಯಾಪೂರ್ತ್ಯರ್ಥೇ ಅನೆಯಪ್ರತ್ಯಯೋ ಭವತಿ ॥

ಪ್ರಯೋಗ ॥ ಪದಿನಾಲ್ಕನೆಯವಂ । ಪದಿನೈದನೆಯವಂ । ಪದಿನಾರನೆಯವಂ । ತೀರ್ಥಂಕರಂ ಶಾಂತಿನಾಥಂ ಜಿನರೊಳಗೆ ಪದಿನಾಲ್ಕನೆಯವಂ । ಚಕ್ರವರ್ತಿಗಳೊಳೈದನೆಯನೆನೆ ಪುಣ್ಯಂ ಪೂಜಾರ್ಚನಕ್ಕೆ ಶಾಂತೀಶನಂತು ನೋಂತವರೊಳೆರೆ ॥

ತಾತ್ಪರ್ಯ ॥ ಸಂಖ್ಯಾ ಪೂರಣಾರ್ಥದಲ್ಲಿ ಅನೆಯ ಪ್ರತ್ಯಯವಾಗುತ್ತದೆ. ಸಂಖ್ಯಾ ಪೂರಣವೆಂದರೆ ಸಂಖ್ಯಾ ನಿರ್ದಿಷ್ಟವಾಚಕ.

ಸೂತ್ರ ॥ ವಾರಾರ್ಥೆ ಮೆ ವಾ ॥ ೧೮೩ ॥

ವೃತ್ತಿ ॥ ಏಕವಾರಂ ದ್ವಿವಾರಮಿತ್ಯಾದ್ಯರ್ಥೇ ಮೆಪ್ರತ್ಯಯೋ ಸ್ಯಾತ್ ॥

ಪ್ರಯೋಗ ॥ ಓರ್ಮೆ । ಇರ್ಮೆ । ಮೂಮೆ, ಮುಮೆ ॥ ಇತ್ಯತಃ ॥ ಒಂದು ಸೂಳ್ । ಎರಡು ಸೂಳ್ ಇತ್ಯಾದಿ ॥

ತಾತ್ಪರ್ಯ ॥ ಒಂದು ಸಾರಿ ಯೆರಡು ಸಾರಿ ಯೆಂಬರ್ಥದಲ್ಲಿ ವಿಕಲ್ಪವಾಗಿ ಮೆ ಪ್ರತ್ಯಯವಾಗುತ್ತದೆ.

ಸೂತ್ರ ॥ ಭಾವಾರ್ಥೇ ಕೆ ಪು ॥ ೧೮೪ ॥

ವೃತ್ತಿ ॥ ತಸ್ಯ ಭಾವ ಇತ್ಯರ್ಥೇ ಕೆ ಪು ಇತಿ ದ್ವೌ ಪ್ರತ್ಯಯೌ ಭವತಃ ॥

ಪ್ರಯೋಗ ॥ ಕಾಣ್ಕೆ । ಪೂಣ್ಕೆ । ಪೊರಳ್ಕೆ । ತೆರಳ್ಕೆ । ನುಣ್ಪು । ತಣ್ಪು । ಕೆಂಪು । ಸೊಂಪು ॥

ತಾತ್ಪರ್ಯ ॥ ಭಾವಾರ್ಥದಲ್ಲಿ ಕೆ-ಪು ಯೆಂಬ ಯೆರಡು ಪ್ರತ್ಯಯಗಳಾಗುತ್ತವೆ. ಭಾವಾರ್ಥವೆಂದರೆ ಭಾವನಾಮವಾಚಕ ಪ್ರತ್ಯಯವೆಂದರಿಯುವದು.

Sûtra 185.—*Chetaneshv ike-rku-me-tanâni.*

Vritti.—*Chetana-vishaye bhâvârtha-vivakshâyâm satyâm ike-rku-me-tana-iti chatvârah pratyayâ bhavanti* ।

Prayoga.—*Mânasike, âyatike ; urku, sorku ; kûrme, pêrme ; kalitanam, ballâḷtanam,* baḍatanam, chôratanam* ।

[*Ike, rku, me, tana,* denote an abstract quality of animate objects.]

Sûtra 186.—*Kriyârthâd dhâtor at.*

Vritti.—*Kriyâ-vâchinas' s'abdât param a-pratyayo bhavati* । *kiñcha ati ṭa iti prâgukta-sûtrât* † *ṭakâras' cha* ।

Prayoga.—*Âḍ, âṭam ; nôḍ, nôṭam ; kûḍ, kûṭam ; sôl, sôlam ; sâl, sâlam* ।

[Verbal nouns have the affix *a* ; sometimes *ḍ* preceding becomes *ṭ*.]

Sûtra 187.—*Adu-idu-ênbhyah pramâṇe nitu.*

Vritti.—*Ebhyas tribhyah param pramâṇârthe nitu-pratyayo bhavati* ।

Prayoga.—*Adu, anitu ; idu, initu ; ên, enitu* ।

Atra tat-takârasya dvitvam kechid ichchhanti । *Prayoga* । *Anittu, inittu, enittu* ।

[*Adu, idu, ên,* take the affix *nitu* when expressing how much. (Sometimes the *t* is doubled.)]

ಸೂತ್ರ ॥ ಚೇತನೇಷ್ವಿಕೇರ್ಕುಮೆತನಾನಿ ॥ ೧೮೫ ॥

ವೃತ್ತಿ ॥ ಚೇತನವಿಷಯೇ ಭಾವಾರ್ಥವಿವಕ್ಷಾಯಾಂ ಸತ್ಯಾಂ ಇಕೆ ರ್ಕು ಮೆ ತನ ಇತಿ ಚತ್ವಾರಃ ಪ್ರತ್ಯಯಾ ಭವನ್ತಿ ॥

ಪ್ರಯೋಗ ॥ ಮಾನಸಿಕೆ, ಆಯತಿಕೆ । ಉರ್ಕು, ಸೊರ್ಕು । ಕೂರ್ಮೆ, ಪೇರ್ಮೆ । ಕಲಿತನಂ, ಬಲ್ಲಾಳ್ತನಂ,* ಬಡತನಂ, ಚೋರತನಂ ॥

ತಾತ್ಪರ್ಯ ॥ ಚೇತನವನ್ನು ಹೇಳುವ ಭಾವಾರ್ಥದಲ್ಲಿ ಇಕೆ ರ್ಕು ಮೆ ತನ ಯೆಂಬ ನಾಲ್ಕು ಪ್ರತ್ಯಯಗಳು ಬರುವವು.

ಸೂತ್ರ ॥ ಕ್ರಿಯಾರ್ಥಾದ್ಧಾತೋರತ್ ॥ ೧೮೬ ॥

ವೃತ್ತಿ ॥ ಕ್ರಿಯಾವಾಚಿನಶ್ಶಬ್ದಾತ್ಪರಮಪ್ರತ್ಯಯೋ ಭವತಿ । ಕಿಂಚ ಅತಿಟ ಇತಿ ಪ್ರಾಗುಕ್ತ ಸೂತ್ರಾತ್† ಟಕಾರಶ್ಚ ॥

ಪ್ರಯೋಗ ॥ ಆಡ್, ಆಟಂ । ನೋಡ್, ನೋಟಂ । ಕೂಡ್, ಕೂಟಂ । ಸೋಲ್, ಸೋಲಂ । ಸಾಲ್, ಸಾಲಂ ॥

ತಾತ್ಪರ್ಯ ॥ ಕ್ರಿಯೆಯಿಂದ ಬಂದ ಶಬ್ದಕ್ಕೆ ಅ ಪ್ರತ್ಯಯ ಬರುವದು. ಅತಿಟಯೆಂಬ ಮೊದಲಿನ ಸೂತ್ರ ಪ್ರಕಾರ † ಟಕಾರವೂ ಬರುವದು.

ಸೂತ್ರ ॥ ಅದು ಇದು ಏನ್ಭ್ಯಃ ಪ್ರಮಾಣೇ ನಿತು ॥ ೧೮೭ ॥

ವೃತ್ತಿ ॥ ಏಭ್ಯಸ್ತ್ರಿಭ್ಯಃ ಪರಂ ಪ್ರಮಾಣಾರ್ಥೇ ನಿತುಪ್ರತ್ಯಯೋ ಭವತಿ ॥

ಪ್ರಯೋಗ ॥ ಅದು, ಅನಿತು । ಇದು, ಇನಿತು । ಏನ್, ಎನಿತು ॥

ಅತ್ರತತ್ತಕಾರಸ್ಯ ದ್ವಿತ್ವಂ ಕೇಚಿದಿಚ್ಛನ್ತಿ ॥ ಪ್ರಯೋಗ ॥ ಅನಿತ್ತು । ಇನಿತ್ತು । ಎನಿತ್ತು ॥

ತಾತ್ಪರ್ಯ ॥ ಅದು, ಇದು, ಏನ ಎಂಬ ಈ ಮೂರು ಶಬ್ದಗಳ ಪರದಲ್ಲಿ ನಿತು ಪ್ರತ್ಯಯವಾಗುತ್ತದೆ. ಕೆಲವರು ಆತಕಾರಕ್ಕೆ ದ್ವಿತ್ವವನ್ನೂ ಹೇಳುತ್ತಾರೆ.

---

* Not in C. — * ತ್ರ ॥ ಯಲ್ಲಿ ಈ ಉದಾಹರಣೆ ಇಲ್ಲ.

† See sûtra 127. — † ೧೨೭ನೇ ಸೂತ್ರ.

Sûtra 188.—*Prakâra-kâlârthe tu-du.*

Vṛitti.—*Prakârârthe kâlârthe cha yathâ kramam tu du ity etau bhavataḥ* ।

Prayoga.—*Antu, intu, entu* ; *andu, indu, endu* ।

[To express in what manner or time, they take *tu* and *du* respectively.]

Sûtra 189.—*Âḷis tâchchhîlye.*

Vṛitti.—*Tad asya s'îlam ity arthe âḷiḥ syât* ।

Prayoga.—*Odâḷi, mârâḷi, siggâḷi,* kêḍâḷi* ।

[*Âḷi* denotes one's nature or character.]

Sûtra 190.—*Kuḷis' cha.*

Vṛitti.—*Tâchchhîlye teshâm eva s'abdânâm kuḷir iti cha sambhavati* ।

Prayoga.—*Ôdukuḷi, añjukuḷi, âṭakuḷi* ।

[Also *kuḷi.*]

Sûtra 191.—*Tat karotîty asmâd gârah.*

Vṛitti.—*Tat karotîty ataḥ param gâra-pratyayas syât* ।

Prayoga.—*Maṇiyam mâḍuva âtam maṇigâram*† । *evam, kañchugâram, baḷegâram, kumbhagâram, suṇṇagâram* ।

[*Gâra* denotes a maker.]

ಸೂತ್ರ ॥ ಪ್ರಕಾರಕಾಲಾರ್ಥೇ ತು ದು ॥ ೧೮೮ ॥

ವೃತ್ತಿ ॥ ಪ್ರಕಾರಾರ್ಥೇ ಕಾಲಾರ್ಥೇ ಚ ಯಥಾ ಕ್ರಮಂ ತು ದು ಇತ್ಯೇತೌ ಭವತಃ ॥

ಪ್ರಯೋಗ ॥ ಅಂತು, ಇಂತು, ಎಂತು । ಅಂದು, ಇಂದು, ಎಂದು ॥

ತಾತ್ಪರ್ಯ ॥ ಪ್ರಕಾರಾರ್ಥದಲ್ಲಿಯೂ ಕಾಲಾರ್ಥದಲ್ಲಿಯೂ ಕ್ರಮವಾಗಿ ತು ದು ಎಂಬ ಪ್ರತ್ಯಯಗಳಾಗುತ್ತವೆ. ಪ್ರಕಾರವೆಂದರೆ ಅಂತೆ ಯೆಂಬರ್ಥ.

ಸೂತ್ರ ॥ ಆಳಿಸ್ತಾಚ್ಛೀಲ್ಯೇ ॥ ೧೮೯ ॥

ವೃತ್ತಿ ॥ ತದಸ್ಯ ಶೀಲಮಿತ್ಯರ್ಥೇ ಆಳಿಸ್ಸ್ಯಾತ್ ॥

ಪ್ರಯೋಗ ॥ ಓದಾಳಿ । ಮಾರಾಳಿ । ಸಿಗ್ಗಾಳಿ* । ಕೇಡಾಳಿ ॥

ತಾತ್ಪರ್ಯ ॥ ಅದು ಅವನಿಗೆ ಶೀಲವೆಂಬರ್ಥದಲ್ಲಿ ಆಳಿ ಪ್ರತ್ಯಯವಾಗುತ್ತದೆ.

ಸೂತ್ರ ॥ ಕುಳಿಶ್ಚ ॥ ೧೯೦ ॥

ವೃತ್ತಿ ॥ ತಾಚ್ಛೀಲ್ಯೇ ತೇಷಾಮೇವ ಶಬ್ದಾನಾಂ ಕುಳಿರಿತಿ ಚ ಸಮ್ಭವತಿ ॥

ಪ್ರಯೋಗ ॥ ಓದುಕುಳಿ । ಅಂಜುಕುಳಿ । ಆಟಕುಳಿ ॥

ತಾತ್ಪರ್ಯ ॥ ಶೀಲವೆಂಬರ್ಥದಲ್ಲಿ ಕುಳಿ ಯೆಂಬ ಪ್ರತ್ಯಯವೂ ಬರುವದುಂಟು.

ಸೂತ್ರ ॥ ತತ್ಕರೋತೀತ್ಯಸ್ಮಾದ್ಗಾರಃ ॥ ೧೯೧ ॥

ವೃತ್ತಿ ॥ ತತ್ಕರೋತೀತ್ಯತಃ ಪರಂ ಗಾರಪ್ರತ್ಯಯಸ್ಸ್ಯಾತ್ ॥

ಪ್ರಯೋಗ ॥ ಮಣಿಯಂ ಮಾಡುವ ಆತಂ ಮಣಿಗಾರಂ †। ಏವಂ । ಕಂಚುಗಾರಂ । ಬಳೆಗಾರಂ । ಕುಂಬಗಾರಂ । ಸುಣ್ಣಗಾರಂ ॥

ತಾತ್ಪರ್ಯ ॥ ಅದನ್ನು ಮಾಡುತ್ತಾನೆಂಬದರಲ್ಲಿ ಗಾರಪ್ರತ್ಯಯವಾಗುತ್ತದೆ.

---

* Not in B and C. — * ದ್ವಿ-ತೃ ॥ ಗಳಲ್ಲಿ ಸಿಗ್ಗಾಳಿ ಇಲ್ಲ.

† C ends here. — † ತೃ ॥ ಮೊದಲನೇದು ಮಾತ್ರವಿದೆ.

Sutra 192.—*Udantân-nâgamo bahulam.*

Vritti.—*Ukârânta-s'abdâd gâra-pratyaye pare nâgamo vâ syât* ।

Prayoga.—*Pempugâram, pempuṅgâram ; sompugâram, sompuṅgâram ; jûjugâram, bêhugâram** ।

Atra Kâvyâvalokanoktam sûtram :—

Niratam gâra pratyaya ।
muru mudadim kumbha kamma s'abdakk idum ।
param âgire gârakkum ।
tara lopam bahuḷa vidhiyamam dore-koḷgum ॥

Asya Guru-Hampa-Devokta prayogah :—

Kari-yugada puchchha-yugamum ।
kara-yugadind otti piḍiye tan-mukha-yugadin ।
daruṇa jala-muṇme tidigaḷa ।
nirad ottuva kammaram bolirdam Bhîmam ॥

Kammagâram, kammaram, kumbagâram, kumbaram ।
Bahuḷâdhikârât kummâram kumbâram iti cha ।
athaivam prochuh prâñchah । *koṅkugôl, kuḍugôl ; koṅkumiñchu, kuḍu-miñchu* ।

[When *gâra* is affixed to a word ending in *u*, then *n* is generally inserted between.]

ಸೂತ್ರ ॥ ಉದನ್ತಾನ್ನಾಗಮೋ ಬಹುಳಂ ॥ ೧೯೨ ॥

ವೃತ್ತಿ ॥ ಉಕಾರಾನ್ತಶಬ್ದಾದ್ಗಾರಪ್ರತ್ಯಯೇ ಪರೇ ನಾಗಮೋ ವಾ ಸ್ಯಾತ್ ॥

ಪ್ರಯೋಗ ॥ ಪೆಂಪುಗಾರಂ, ಪೆಂಪುಂಗಾರಂ । ಸೊಂಪುಗಾರಂ, ಸೊಂಪುಂಗಾರಂ । ಜೂಜುಗಾರಂ । ಬೇಹುಗಾರಂ ॥

*ಅತ್ರ ಕಾವ್ಯಾವಲೋಕನೋಕ್ತಂ ಸೂತ್ರಂ ॥

ನಿರತಂ ಗಾರ ಪ್ರತ್ಯಯ ।
ಮುರು ಮುದದಿಂ ಕುಂಭಕಮ್ಮ ಶಬ್ದಕ್ಕಿದುಂ ।
ಪರಮಾಗಿರೆ ಗಾರಕ್ಕುಂ ।
ತರ ಲೋಪಂ ಬಹುಳ ವಿಧಿಯಮಂ ದೊರೆಕೊಳ್ಗುಂ ॥

ಅಸ್ಯ ಗುರುಹಂಪದೇವೋಕ್ತಪ್ರಯೋಗಃ ॥

ಕರಿಯುಗದ ಪುಚ್ಛಯುಗಮುಂ ।
ಕರಯುಗದಿಂದೊತ್ತಿ ಪಿಡಿಯೆ ತನ್ಮುಖಯುಗದಿಂ ।
ದರುಣಜಲಮುಣ್ಮೆ ತಿದಿಗಳ ।
ನಿರದೊತ್ತುವ ಕಮ್ಮರಂ ಬೊಲಿರ್ದಂ ಭೀಮಂ ॥

ಕಮ್ಮಗಾರಂ, ಕಮ್ಮರಂ । ಕುಂಬಗಾರಂ, ಕುಂಬರಂ ॥

ಬಹುಳಾಧಿಕಾರಾತ್ ಕುಮ್ಮಾರಂ ಕುಂಬಾರಮಿತಿ ಚ ॥

ಅಥೈವಂ ಪ್ರೋಚುಃ ಪ್ರಾಞ್ಚಃ । ಕೊಂಕುಗೋಲ್, ಕುಡುಗೋಲ್ । ಕೊಂಕು ಮಿಂಚು । ಕುಡುಮಿಂಚು ॥

ತಾತ್ಪರ್ಯ ॥ ಉಕಾರಾನ್ತ ಶಬ್ದಕ್ಕೆ ಗಾರಪ್ರತ್ಯಯ ಪರವಾದಲ್ಲಿ ಬಹುಳವಾಗಿ ನಾಗಮವಾಗುತ್ತದೆ.

---

* B and C end here.

* ದ್ವಿ-ತೃ ॥ ಪ್ರತಿಗಳಲ್ಲಿ ಇದು ಇಲ್ಲ.

Sûtra 193.—*Apabhrams'epy evam kârasya.*

Vṛitti.—*Samskṛitokta-kâra-pratyayasya asyâm Karṇâṭaka-bhâshâyâm apy evam eva* ǀ

[*Gâra* also denotes the Sanskrit *kâra.*]

Sûtra 194.—*Striyâm iti cha.*

Vṛitti.—*Atra strî-vishayârthe vaktavye pûrva-padânte iti-pratyayas' cha syât* ǀ

Prayoga.—*Jâṇagiti, baḷegâriti, bâṇasigiti* ǀ
Kvachid ikâra lopah ǀ *maṇegârti, âḷugârti, suṇṇagârti, maḍivaḷti, gaṭṭivaḷti* ǀ *kvachid ubhayathâpi* ǀ *vakkaliti, vakkaligiti* ǀ

[To express the name of a woman, the affix *iti* is used. (Sometimes the first *i* is dropped, sometimes both forms are used.)]

Sûtra 195.—*Aḷ e cha guṇavachanebhyah.*

Vṛitti.—*Strî-liṅge guṇavâchibhyah param aḷ-e-kâras' cha yathâ prayogam bhavatah* ǀ

Prayoga.—*Nallaḷ, mollaḷ, baḷḷidaḷ, iniyaḷ ; sîtage, chature, pâṇve* ǀ *evam âdi* ǀ

[Feminine adjectives have the affix *aḷ* or *e.*]

ಸೂತ್ರ ॥ ಅಪಭ್ರಂಶೇಪ್ಯೇವಂ ಕಾರಸ್ಯ ॥ ೧೯೩ ॥

ವೃತ್ತಿ ॥ ಸಂಸ್ಕೃತೋಕ್ತಕಾರಪ್ರತ್ಯಯಸ್ಯ ಅಸ್ಯಾಂ ಕರ್ಣಾಟಕಭಾಷಾಯಾಮಪ್ಯೇವಮೇವ ॥
ತಾತ್ಪರ್ಯ ॥ ಸಂಸ್ಕೃತದ ಕಾರ ಪ್ರತ್ಯಯದ ತದ್ಭವದಲ್ಲಿಯೂ ಹೀಗೆಯೇ ಗಾರಪ್ರತ್ಯಯ ಬರುತ್ತದೆ.

ಸೂತ್ರ ॥ ಸ್ತ್ರೀಯಾಮಿತಿ ಚ ॥ ೧೯೪ ॥

ವೃತ್ತಿ ॥ ಅತ್ರ ಸ್ತ್ರೀ ವಿಷಯಾರ್ಥೇ ವಕ್ತವ್ಯೇ ಪೂರ್ವಪದಾನ್ತೇ ಇತಿಪ್ರತ್ಯಯಶ್ಚ ಸ್ಯಾತ್ ॥
ಪ್ರಯೋಗ ॥ ಜಾಣಗಿತಿ । ಬಳೆಗಾರಿತಿ । ಬಾಣಸಿಗಿತಿ ॥
ಕ್ವಚಿದಿಕಾರ ಲೋಪಃ । ಮಣೆಗಾರ್ತಿ । ಆಳುಗಾರ್ತಿ । ಸುಣ್ಣಗಾರ್ತಿ । ಮಡಿವಳ್ತಿ । ಗಟ್ಟಿವಳ್ತಿ ।
ಕ್ವಚಿದುಭಯಥಾಪಿ । ವಕ್ಕಲಿತಿ । ವಕ್ಕಲಿಗಿತಿ ॥
ತಾತ್ಪರ್ಯ ॥ ಸ್ತ್ರೀಯರನ್ನು ಹೇಳುವ ಈ ಪ್ರತ್ಯಯ ಸ್ಥಾನದಲ್ಲಿ ಇತಿ ಯೆಂಬ ಪ್ರತ್ಯಯ ಬರುತ್ತದೆ.

ಸೂತ್ರ ॥ ಅಳೇ ಚ ಗುಣವಚನೇಭ್ಯಃ ॥ ೧೯೫ ॥

ವೃತ್ತಿ ॥ ಸ್ತ್ರೀಲಿಙ್ಗೇ ಗುಣವಾಚಿಭ್ಯಃ ಪರಂ ಅಳ್ ಏಕಾರಶ್ಚ ಯಥಾ ಪ್ರಯೋಗಂ ಭವತಃ ॥
ಪ್ರಯೋಗ ॥ ನಲ್ಲಳ್, ಮೊಲ್ಲಳ್, ಬಳ್ಳಿದಳ್, ಇನಿಯಳ್ । ಸೀತಗೆ, ಚತುರೆ, ಪಾಣ್ವೆ । ಏವಮಾದಿ ॥

ತಾತ್ಪರ್ಯ ॥ ಸ್ತ್ರೀಲಿಂಗದಲ್ಲಿ ಗುಣವಾಚಕಗಳ ಪರವಾಗಿ ಅಳ್ ಮತ್ತು ಎ ಯೆಂಬ ಪ್ರತ್ಯಯಗಳು ಬರುತ್ತವೆ.

Sûtra 196.—*Id-ud-antah pumsi vâ.*

Vritti.—*Ikârânta-ukârântas' cha s'abdah pulliṅge striliṅge cha samâna-rûpo vâ syât* ।

Prayoga.—*Nâṇili, sondi, soraṭi, mâtâḷi, sâdu, gâḷu, pâru* ।

Kvachid vyañjanântaṅ cha bhavati । *maruḷ* ।

[Words ending in *i* and *u* have the same form for feminine and neuter. (Sometimes the final vowel is dropped.)]

Sûtra 197.—*Vîpsânukaraṇâbhîkshṇya-kriyâsamabhihâra-sâmîpya-châpalyâdau.*

Vritti.—*Eshv artheshu nâmavâchinah parasya dvir-vachanam bhavati* ।

Prayoga.—*Vîpsâyâm:—ûr-ûru, mane-vane, nâḍu-nâḍu* । *anukaraṇe:—bhôr-bhôrane, ghaḷi-ghaḷilane* । *âbhîkshṇye:—nôḍu-nôḍu, tiḷisu-tiḷisu* । *kriyâ-samabhihâre:—naḍe naḍe-yendu nuḍivar* । *sâmîpye:—keḷa-keḷage, kela-keladôḷ* । *châpalye:—oppis-oppisu, poy-poy, mâṇ-mâṇ** ।

kutrachid anukaraṇe tri prayogas' cha । *baḷegaḷ ghal-ghal-ghalkene* ।

âdi grahaṇâd anyatraiva bhavati । *ene-ene, nuḍiye-nuḍiye, antante* ।

[To express ardent desire, imitation of a sound, eagerness, urgency, nearness, changeableness, a word is repeated. (Sometimes thrice: also to express other meanings.)]

ಸೂತ್ರ ॥ ಇದುದನ್ತಃ ಪುಂಸಿ ವಾ ॥ ೧೯೬ ॥

ವೃತ್ತಿ ॥ ಇಕಾರಾನ್ತ ಉಕಾರಾನ್ತಶ್ಚ ಶಬ್ದಃ ಪುಲ್ಲಿಙ್ಗೇ ಸ್ತ್ರೀಲಿಙ್ಗೇ ಚ ಸಮಾನರೂಪೋ ವಾ ಸ್ಯಾತ್ ॥

ಪ್ರಯೋಗ ॥ ನಾಣಿಲಿ । ಸೊಂದಿ । ಸೊರಟಿ । ಮಾತಾಳಿ । ಸಾದು । ಗಾಳು । ಪಾರು ॥

ಕ್ವಚಿದ್ವ್ಯಂಜನಾನ್ತಂ ಚ ಭವತಿ । ಮರುಳ್ ॥

ತಾತ್ಪರ್ಯ ॥ ಇಕಾರಾನ್ತ ಉಕಾರಾನ್ತ ಶಬ್ದಗಳು ಸ್ತ್ರೀಲಿಂಗದಲ್ಲಿಯೂ ಪುಲ್ಲಿಂಗದಲ್ಲಿಯೂ ವಿಕಲ್ಪವಾಗಿ ಸಮಾನ ರೂಪಗಳನ್ನುಳ್ಳವುಗಳೇ ಆಗುತ್ತವೆ.

ಸೂತ್ರ ॥ ವೀಪ್ಸಾನುಕರಣಾಭೀಕ್ಷ್ಣ್ಯಕ್ರಿಯಾಸಮಭಿಹಾರಸಾಮೀಪ್ಯ ಚಾಪಲ್ಯಾದೌ ॥ ೧೯೭ ॥

ವೃತ್ತಿ ॥ ಏಷ್ವರ್ಥೇಷು ನಾಮವಾಚಿನಃ ಪರಸ್ಯ ದ್ವಿರ್ವಚನಂ ಭವತಿ ॥

ಪ್ರಯೋಗ ॥ ವೀಪ್ಸಾಯಾಂ । ಊರೂರು । ಮನೆವನೆ । ನಾಡು ನಾಡು ॥ ಅನುಕರಣೇ । ಭೋರ್ಭೋರನೆ । ಘಳಿಘಳಿಲನೆ ॥ ಆಭೀಕ್ಷ್ಣ್ಯೇ । ನೋಡುನೋಡು । ತಿಳಿಸುತಿಳಿಸು ॥ ಕ್ರಿಯಾಸಮಭಿಹಾರೇ । ನಡೆನಡೆಯೆಂದು ನುಡಿವರ ॥ ಸಾಮೀಪ್ಯೇ । ಕೆಳಕೆಳಗೆ । ಕೆಲಕೆಲದೊಳ್ ॥ ಚಾಪಲ್ಯೇ । ಒಪ್ಪಿಸೊಪ್ಪಿಸು । ಪೊಯ್ಪೊಯ್ । ಮಾಣ್ಮಾಣ್ ॥

* ಕುತ್ರಚಿದನುಕರಣೇ ತ್ರಿ ಪ್ರಯೋಗಶ್ಚ । ಬಳೆಗಳ್ ಘಲ್ಘಲ್ಘಲ್ಕೆನೆ ।

ಆದಿಗ್ರಹಣಾದನ್ಯತ್ರೈವ ಭವತಿ । ಎನೆಎನೆ । ನುಡಿಯೆ ನುಡಿಯೆ । ಅಂತಂತೆ ॥

ತಾತ್ಪರ್ಯ ॥ ವಿಪ್ಸಾದಿಗಳಲ್ಲಿ ನಾಮವಾಚಕಕ್ಕೆ ಪರವಾಗಿ ದ್ವಿರುಕ್ತಿಯಾಗುತ್ತವೆ.

---

* B ends here.

* ದ್ವಿ ॥ ಯಲ್ಲಿ ಮುಂದಿನ ಉದಾಹರಣೆ ಇಲ್ಲ.

Sûtra 198.—*Atrâdi-lopâdi kâryam samâsavat.*

Vṛitti.—*Asmin taddhitâdhikaraṇe lopâdikam samâsoktavat kâryam pûrvavad ity arthaḥ* ।

[In forming derivatives, the rules for insertion and elision of letters in the chapter on compound words to be observed.]

*Iti Karṇâṭaka-vyâkaraṇa-vṛittau * Bhâshâ-bûshaṇe Taddhita-vidhânam nâma saptamaḥ parichchhedaḥ.*

(VIII. Verbs.)

Âkhyâta-niyama Vidhânam.

Sûtra 199.—*Kriyârtho dhâtuḥ.*

Vṛitti.—*Kriyaivârtho yasya sa dhâtu-saṁjño bhavati* ।

[A verbal root is one expressing action.]

Sûtra 200.—*Tasmâd am-ar-ay-ir-en-evo vibhaktayaḥ.*

Vṛitti.—*Dhâtoḥ paraḥ pratyaya-rûpâḥ am-ar-ay-ir-en-ev iti vibhaktayo bhavanti* ।

[Verbal roots take the inflections *am, ar, ay, ir, en* and *ev.*]

ಸೂತ್ರ ॥ ಅತ್ರಾದಿ ಲೋಪಾದಿಕಾರ್ಯಂ ಸಮಾಸವತ್ ॥ ೧೯೮ ॥

ವೃತ್ತಿ ॥ ಅಸ್ಮಿನ್ ತದ್ಧಿತಾಧಿಕರಣೇ ಲೋಪಾದಿಕಂ ಸಮಾಸೋಕ್ತವತ್ಕಾರ್ಯಂ ಪೂರ್ವವದಿತ್ಯರ್ಥಃ ॥

ತಾತ್ಪರ್ಯ ॥ ಈ ತದ್ಧಿತಾಧಿ ಕರಣದಲ್ಲಿ ಲೋಪಾದಿಗಳು ಪೂರ್ವದಲ್ಲಿ ಸಮಾಸದೊಳಗೆ ಹೇಳಿರುವ ವಿಧಿಗಳಂತೆ ಮಾಡತಕ್ಕದ್ದು.

ಇತಿ ಕರ್ಣಾಟಕ ವ್ಯಾಕರಣವೃತ್ತೌ * ಭಾಷಾ ಭೂಷಣೇ
ತದ್ಧಿತ ವಿಧಾನಂ ನಾಮ ಸಪ್ತಮಃ ಪರಿಚ್ಛೇದಃ ॥

ಆಖ್ಯಾತ ನಿಯಮ ವಿಧಾನಂ.

ಸೂತ್ರ ॥ ಕ್ರಿಯಾರ್ಥೋ ಧಾತುಃ ॥ ೧೯೯ ॥

ವೃತ್ತಿ ॥ ಕ್ರಿಯೈವಾರ್ಥೋ ಯಸ್ಯ ಸ ಧಾತುಸಂಜ್ಞೋ ಭವತಿ ॥

ತಾತ್ಪರ್ಯ ॥ ಕ್ರಿಯೆಯೇ ಅರ್ಥವಾಗಿ ವುಳ್ಳದ್ದು ಧಾತುವೆನ್ನಿಸಿಕೊಳ್ಳುವದು.

ಸೂತ್ರ ॥ ತಸ್ಮಾದಮರಯಿರೆನೆವೊ ವಿಭಕ್ತಯಃ ॥ ೨೦೦ ॥

ವೃತ್ತಿ ॥ ಧಾತೋಃ ಪರಾಃ ಪ್ರತ್ಯಯರೂಪಾಃ ಅಮ್ ಅರ್ ಅಯ್ ಇರ್ ಎನ್ ಎವ್ ಇತಿ ವಿಭಕ್ತಯೋ ಭವನ್ತಿ ॥

ತಾತ್ಪರ್ಯ ॥ ಧಾತುಗಳಿಗೆ ಅಮ್-ಅರ್-ಅಯ್-ಇರ್-ಎನ್-ಎವ್ ಯೆಂಬ ವಿಭಕ್ತಿಗಳು ಬರುತ್ತವೆ.

---

* See note p. 7.

* ೭ನೇ ಪುಟ ನೋಡು.

Sûtra 201.—*Da-dapa-va-kârâdyâ bhûta-vartamâna-bhavishyant-yah.*

Vritti.—*Tâs' cha shad-vibhaktayo da-dapa-va-ity aksharâdyâs satyo yathâ-kramam bhûtâdy arthakâ bhavanti* । *tad yathâ* । *dam, dar, day, dir, den, dev ity ete bhûtavantyah* । *dapam, dapar, dapay, dapir, dapen, dapev ity ete vartamânâh* । *vam, var, vay, vir, ven, vev ity ete bhavishyantyah* ।

[These six inflections, preceded by *d*, *dap*, or *v*, form the past, present and future tenses respectively.]

Sûtra 202.—*Naiva nañ-arthe.*

Vritti.—*Pratishedhârthe ime da-dapa-va-kârâ vibhaktyâdau naiva bhavanti* ।

Prayoga.—*Mâdam, mâdar, mâday, mâdir, mâden, mâdev* ।

[But in the negative mood the inflections are used without inserting these letters.]

Sûtra 203.—*Tâs tu dve-dve prathama-madhyamottama-purushâh.*

Vritti.—*Tâ vibhaktayas tu dve dve eka-vachana-bahu-vachana-rûpâh prathamâdi purusha-samjñâs syuh* । *tat katham* । *am, ar, ity etau prathama-purushah* । *en, ev, ity etau uttama-purushah* । *ay, ir, ity etau madhyama-purushah* । *atra kâla-traya-gamaka-varnâ yojyâh* ।

[Each pair of these inflections expresses, one the singular and the other the plural, of the first, second and third * persons respectively.]

ಸೂತ್ರ ॥ ದದಪವಕಾರಾದ್ಯಾ ಭೂತವರ್ತಮಾನಭವಿಷ್ಯನ್ತ್ಯಃ ॥ ೨೦೧ ॥

ವೃತ್ತಿ ॥ ತಾಶ್ಚ ಷಡ್ವಿಭಕ್ತಯೋ ದದಪವಇತ್ಯಕ್ಷರಾದ್ಯಾಸ್ಸತ್ಯೋ ಯಥಾಕ್ರಮಂ ಭೂತಾದ್ಯರ್ಥಕಾ ಭವನ್ತಿ । ತದ್ಯಥಾ । ದಮ್ । ದರ್ । ದಯ್ । ದಿರ್ । ದೆನ್ । ದೆವ್ ಇತ್ಯೇತೇ ಭೂತವನ್ತ್ಯಃ । ದಪಮ್ । ದಪರ್ । ದಪಯ್ । ದಪಿರ್ । ದಪೆನ್ । ದಪೆವ್ ಇತ್ಯೇತೇ ವರ್ತಮಾನಾಃ । ವಮ್ । ವರ್ । ವಯ್ । ವಿರ್ । ವೆನ್ । ವೆವ್ ಇತ್ಯೇತೇ ಭವಿಷ್ಯನ್ತ್ಯಃ ॥

ತಾತ್ಪರ್ಯ ॥ ಆ ಆರು ವಿಭಕ್ತಿಗಳು ದ-ದಪ-ವ ಯೆಂಬೀ ಅಕ್ಷರಗಳನ್ನಾದಿಯಲ್ಲಿ ವುಳ್ಳದ್ದಾಗಿ ಯಥಾಕ್ರಮದಲ್ಲಿ ಭೂತ ವರ್ತಮಾನ ಭವಿಷ್ಯದರ್ಥಕಗಳಾಗುವವು.

ಸೂತ್ರ ॥ ನೈವ ನಞರ್ಥೇ ॥ ೨೦೨ ॥

ವೃತ್ತಿ ॥ ಪ್ರತಿಷೇಧಾರ್ಥೇ ಇಮೇ ದದಪವಕಾರಾ ವಿಭಕ್ತ್ಯಾದೌ ನೈವ ಭವನ್ತಿ ॥

ಪ್ರಯೋಗ ॥ ಮಾಡಮ್ । ಮಾಡರ್ । ಮಾಡಯ್ । ಮಾಡಿರ್ । ಮಾಡೆನ್ । ಮಾಡೆವ್ ॥

ತಾತ್ಪರ್ಯ ॥ ಪ್ರತಿಷೇಧಾರ್ಥದಲ್ಲಿ ಈ ದ-ದಪ-ವ ಕಾರಗಳು ವಿಭಕ್ತಿಗಳ ಆದಿಯಲ್ಲಿ ಬರುವದಿಲ್ಲ.

ಸೂತ್ರ ॥ ತಾಸ್ತು ದ್ವೇದ್ವೇ ಪ್ರಥಮಮಧ್ಯಮೋತ್ತಮಪುರುಷಾಃ ॥ ೨೦೩ ॥

ವೃತ್ತಿ ॥ ತಾ ವಿಭಕ್ತಯಸ್ತು ದ್ವೇದ್ವೇ ಏಕವಚನಬಹುವಚನರೂಪಾಃ ಪ್ರಥಮಾದಿಪುರುಷಸಂಜ್ಞಾಸ್ಸ್ಯುಃ । ತತ್ಕಥಂ । ಅಮ್ । ಅರ್ ಇತ್ಯೇತೌ ಪ್ರಥಮ ಪುರುಷಃ । ಎನ್ । ಎವ್ ಇತ್ಯೇತೌ ಉತ್ತಮ ಪುರುಷಃ । ಅಯ್ । ಇರ್ ಇತ್ಯೇತೌ ಮಧ್ಯಮ ಪುರುಷಃ । ಅತ್ರ ಕಾಲತ್ರಯಗಮಕವರ್ಣಾ ಯೋಜ್ಯಾಃ ॥

ತಾತ್ಪರ್ಯ ॥ ಆವಿಭಕ್ತಿಗಳು ಯೆರಡೆರಡು ಏಕವಚನ ಬಹುವಚನ ರೂಪಗಳುಳ್ಳವುಗಳಾಗಿ ಪ್ರಥಮ ಮಧ್ಯಮ ಉತ್ತಮ ಪುರುಷ ಸಂಜ್ಞೆಗಳನ್ನು ಹೊಂದುವವು.

---

* These terms will be used in the European sense: in Hindu languages the first person is our third, while our first is their chief or principal person, and our second their middle person.

Sûtra 204.—*Anyârthe prathamah.*

Vṛitti.—*Tvam-aham-ity arthau vinâ anyârthe tân-iti-vachane prathama-purushas syât* |

Prayoga.—*Tâm mâḍidam, tâv mâḍidar** |

[The third person is expressed by *tân*, meaning all besides thou and I.]

Sûtra 205.—*Yushmad-asmador madhyamottamau.*

Vṛitti.—*Yushmad-arthe nîn-iti-vachane asmad-arthe ân-iti-vachane cha yathâ-kramam madhyamottama-purushau bhavatah* |

Prayoga.—*Nîm mâḍiday, nîv mâḍidir* | *uttame:—âm mâḍidem, âv mâḍidev* | *evam kâla-trayârthâs' cha vaktavyâh* |

[The second and first persons are expressed by *nîn*, and *ân* respectively, meaning thou and I.]

Sûtra 206.—*Yugapat-prayoge paras teshâm.*

Vṛitti.—*Anyad-yushmad-asmadâm yaugapadyena prayoge teshâm purushâṇâm madhye kartṛishu parânurûpah purushas syât* |

Prayoga.—*Âtanum nînum mâḍidir* | *âtanum ânum mâḍidev* | *evam anyonya prayogepi tri-kâla-bhedo jñeyah* |

[When two persons are used together (with one verb) the second includes the third, and the first the second (*i. e.* the verb agrees in person with the former).]

ಸೂತ್ರ ॥ ಅನ್ಯಾರ್ಥೇ ಪ್ರಥಮಃ ॥ ೨೦೪ ॥

ವೃತ್ತಿ ॥ ತ್ವಮಹಮಿತ್ಯರ್ಥೌ ವಿನಾ ಅನ್ಯಾರ್ಥೇ ತಾನಿತಿ ವಚನೇ ಪ್ರಥಮಪುರುಷಸ್ಸ್ಯಾತ್ ॥

ಪ್ರಯೋಗ ॥ ತಾಮ್ ಮಾಡಿದಂ । ತಾವ್ ಮಾಡಿದರ್ * ॥

ತಾತ್ಪರ್ಯ ॥ ನೀನು ನಾನೆಂಬರ್ಥದಲ್ಲಿ ವಿನಾಯಿಸಿ ಅನ್ಯಾರ್ಥವಾದ ತಾನೆಂಬ ವಚನದಲ್ಲಿ ಪ್ರಥಮ ಪುರುಷವಾಗುತ್ತದೆ.

ಸೂತ್ರ ॥ ಯುಷ್ಮದಸ್ಮದೋರ್ಮಧ್ಯಮೋತ್ತಮೌ ॥ ೨೦೫ ॥

ವೃತ್ತಿ ॥ ಯುಷ್ಮದರ್ಥೇ ನೀನಿತಿ ವಚನೇ ಅಸ್ಮದರ್ಥೇ ಆನಿತಿ ವಚನೇ ಚ ಯಥಾಕ್ರಮಂ ಮಧ್ಯಮೋತ್ತಮ ಪುರುಷೌ ಭವತಃ ॥

ಪ್ರಯೋಗ ॥ ನೀಮ್ ಮಾಡಿದಯ್ । ನೀವ್ ಮಾಡಿದಿರ್ । ಉತ್ತಮೇ । ಆಮ್ ಮಾಡಿದೆಂ । ಆವ್ ಮಾಡಿದೆವ್ । ಏವಂ ಕಾಲತ್ರಯಾರ್ಥಾಶ್ಚ ವಕ್ತವ್ಯಾಃ ॥

ತಾತ್ಪರ್ಯ ॥ ಯುಷ್ಮದರ್ಥಕವಾದ ನೀನೆಂಬ ವಚನದಲ್ಲಿಯೂ ಅಸ್ಮದರ್ಥವಾದ ಆನೆಂಬ ವಚನದಲ್ಲಿಯೂ ಕ್ರಮವಾಗಿ ಮಧ್ಯಮ ಪುರುಷ ಉತ್ತಮ ಪುರುಷಗಳಾಗುವವು.

ಸೂತ್ರ ॥ ಯುಗಪತ್ಪ್ರಯೋಗೇ ಪರಸ್ತೇಷಾಂ ॥ ೨೦೬ ॥

ವೃತ್ತಿ ॥ ಅನ್ಯದ್ಯುಷ್ಮದಸ್ಮದಾಂ ಯೌಗಪದ್ಯೇನ ಪ್ರಯೋಗೇ ತೇಷಾಂ ಪುರುಷಾಣಾಂ ಮಧ್ಯೇ ಕರ್ತೃಷು ಪರಾನುರೂಪಃ ಪುರುಷಸ್ಸ್ಯಾತ್ ॥

ಪ್ರಯೋಗ ॥ ಆತನುಂ ನೀನುಂ ಮಾಡಿದಿರ್ । ಆತನುಮಾನುಂ ಮಾಡಿದೆವ್ ॥

ಏವಮನ್ಯೋನ್ಯ ಪ್ರಯೋಗೇಪಿ ತ್ರಿಕಾಲಭೇದೋ ಜ್ಞೇಯಃ ॥

ತಾತ್ಪರ್ಯ ॥ ಅನ್ಯದರ್ಥ ಯುಷ್ಮದರ್ಥ ಅಸ್ಮದರ್ಥಗಳು ಏಕಕಾಲದಲ್ಲಿ ಪ್ರಯೋಗಿಸಿದರೆ ಅವುಗಳಲ್ಲಿ ಪ್ರಥಮಕ್ಕೆ ಮಧ್ಯಮ ಪುರುಷವೂ ಮಧ್ಯಮಕ್ಕೆ ಉತ್ತಮ ಪುರುಷವೂ ಮುಖ್ಯವಾಗಿ ಪ್ರಯೋಗಿಸಲ್ಪಡುವವು.

---

* Instead of these C has Devam mâḍidam, Devar mâḍidar

* ತೃ ॥ ಯಲ್ಲಿ ಇದಕ್ಕೆ ಬದಲಾಗಿ ದೇವಂ ಮಾಡಿದಂ ಎಂಬುದಿದೆ.

Sûtra 207.—*Svârthe kâle.*

Vṛitti.—*Tâs' cha shaḍ-vibhaktayas svârthe sva-sva-kâle cha bhavanti* । *yathâ atîta-kâle bhûtavatyaḥ* ।

Prayoga.—*Prathama :—mâḍidam, mâḍidar* । *madhyama:—mâḍiday, mâḍidir* । *uttama :—mâḍidem, mâḍidev* । *adyatane vartamânâḥ* । *pra :—mâḍidapam, mâḍidapar* । *ma :—mâḍidapay, mâḍidavir* । *utta :—mâḍidapem, mâḍidapev* । *eshya kâle bhavishyantyaḥ* । *pra :—mâḍuvam, mâḍuvar* । *ma :—mâḍuvay, mâḍuvir* । *utta :—mâḍuvem, mâḍuvev* । *ittham kâla-trayârthâḥ purusha-trayepi boddhavyâḥ* ।

[Those six inflections are used for each tense.]

Sûtra 208.—*Ekasminn eka-vachanam.*

Vṛitti.—*Ekârtha-vishaye eka-vachanam syât* ।

Prayoga.—*Âtan ôrvane mâḍidam, mâḍidapam, mâḍuvam* । *nîn ôrvane mâḍiday, mâḍidapay, mâḍuvay* । *ân ôrvane mâḍidem, mâḍuvem* ।

[The singular expresses the act of one.]

ಸೂತ್ರ ॥ ಸ್ವಾರ್ಥೇ ಕಾಲೇ ॥ ೨೦೭ ॥

ವೃತ್ತಿ ॥ ತಾಶ್ಚ ಷಡ್ವಿಭಕ್ತಯಸ್ಸ್ವಾರ್ಥೇ ಸ್ವಸ್ವಕಾಲೇ ಚ ಭವನ್ತಿ । ಯಥಾ ಅತೀತಕಾಲೇ ಭೂತವತ್ಯಃ ॥

ಪ್ರಯೋಗ ॥ ಪ್ರ ॥ ಮಾಡಿದಂ । ಮಾಡಿದರ್ ॥ ಮ ॥ ಮಾಡಿದಯ್ । ಮಾಡಿದಿರ್ ॥ ಉ ॥ ಮಾಡಿದೆಂ । ಮಾಡಿದೆವ್ ॥ ಅದ್ಯತನೇ ವರ್ತಮಾನಾಃ ॥ ಪ್ರ ॥ ಮಾಡಿದಪಂ । ಮಾಡಿದಪರ್ ॥ ಮ ॥ ಮಾಡಿದಪಯ್ । ಮಾಡಿದಪಿರ್ ॥ ಉ ॥ ಮಾಡಿದಪೆಂ । ಮಾಡಿದಪೆವ್ । ಏಷ್ಯಕಾಲೇ ಭವಿಷ್ಯನ್ತ್ಯಃ ॥ ಪ್ರ ॥ ಮಾಡುವಂ । ಮಾಡುವರ್ ॥ ಮ ॥ ಮಾಡುವಯ್ । ಮಾಡುವಿರ್ ॥ ಉ ॥ ಮಾಡುವೆಂ । ಮಾಡುವೆವ್ ॥ ಇತ್ಥಂ ಕಾಲತ್ರಯಾರ್ಥಾಃ ಪುರುಷತ್ರಯೇಪಿ ಬೋದ್ಧವ್ಯಾಃ ॥

ತಾತ್ಪರ್ಯ ॥ ಆ ಆರು ವಿಭಕ್ತಿಗಳು ತಂತಮ್ಮ ಕಾಲಗಳಲ್ಲಿ ಸರಿಯಾಗಿ ಪ್ರಯೋಗಿಸಲಾಗುವವು. ಹ್ಯಾಗಂದರೆ, ಕಳೆದ ಕಾಲದಲ್ಲಿ ಭೂತ ವಿಭಕ್ತಿಗಳೂ ಆಕಾಲದಲ್ಲಿ ವರ್ತಮಾನದವುಗಳೂ ಬರುವ ಕಾಲದಲ್ಲಿ ಭವಿಷ್ಯದ್ವಿಭಕ್ತಿಗಳೂ ಆಗುವವು.

ಸೂತ್ರ ॥ ಏಕಸ್ಮಿನ್ನೇಕವಚನಂ ॥ ೨೦೮ ॥

ವೃತ್ತಿ ॥ ಏಕಾರ್ಥವಿಷಯೇ ಏಕವಚನಂ ಸ್ಯಾತ್ ॥

ಪ್ರಯೋಗ ॥ ಆತನೋರ್ವನೆ ಮಾಡಿದಂ, ಮಾಡಿದಪಂ, ಮಾಡುವಂ । ನೀನೋರ್ವನೆ ಮಾಡಿದಯ್, ಮಾಡಿದಪಯ್, ಮಾಡುವಯ್ । ಆನೋರ್ವನೆ ಮಾಡಿದೆಂ, ಮಾಡುವೆಂ ॥

ತಾತ್ಪರ್ಯ ॥ ಏಕಾರ್ಥ ವಿಷಯದಲ್ಲಿ ಏಕವಚನವಾಗುತ್ತದೆ. ಏಕಾರ್ಥವೆಂದರೆ ಒಬ್ಬ-ಒಂದೆಂಬರ್ಥ.

Sûtra 209.—*Dvitva-bahutvayor anyat.*

Vṛitti.—*Dvitve bahutve cha bahu-vachanam eva syât* ।

Prayoga.—*Avar mâḍidar, mâḍidapar, mâḍuvar* । *nîvu mâḍidir, mâḍidapir, mâḍuvir* । *âvu mâḍidev, mâḍidapev, mâḍuvev* ।

[The plural expresses the act of two or more.]

Sûtra 210.—*Udu uvu napumsaka-prathamasya.*

Vṛitti.—*Prathama-purushaika-vachana-bahu-vachanayoḥ kartṛi-vâchi-s'ab-dasya napumsaka-liṅge sati udu-uvu-ity-âdes'au yathâ-kramam bhavataḥ* ।

Prayoga.—*Âdudu, âduvu, âdapudu, âdapuvu, appudu, appuvu* ।

[*Udu* and *uvu* are the neuter terminations of the third person singular and plural respectively.]

Sûtra 211.—*Bhâve cha.*

Vṛitti.—*Bhâvârtha-prathama-vachanayos' cha udu-uvu bhavataḥ* ।

Prayoga.—*Mâḷpudu, mâḷpuvu, kûrpudu, kûrpuvu* ।

[Also of gerunds.]

ಸೂತ್ರ ॥ ದ್ವಿತ್ವಬಹುತ್ವಯೋರನ್ಯತ್ ॥ ೨೦೯ ॥

ವೃತ್ತಿ ॥ ದ್ವಿತ್ವೇ ಬಹುತ್ವೇ ಚ ಬಹುವಚನಮೇವ ಸ್ಯಾತ್ ॥

ಪ್ರಯೋಗ ॥ ಅವರ್ ಮಾಡಿದರ್, ಮಾಡಿದಪರ್, ಮಾಡುವರ್। ನೀವು ಮಾಡಿದಿರ್, ಮಾಡಿದಪಿರ್, ಮಾಡುವಿರ್ । ಆವು ಮಾಡಿದೆವ್, ಮಾಡಿದಪೆವ್, ಮಾಡುವೆವ್ ॥

ತಾತ್ಪರ್ಯ ॥ ದ್ವಿತ್ವ ಬಹುತ್ವಗಳಲ್ಲಿ ಬಹುವಚನವಾಗುತ್ತದೆ. ದ್ವಿತ್ವ ಯೆರಡೆಂಬರ್ಥ ಬಹುತ್ವವೆಂದರೆ ಅನೇಕಾರ್ಥಕ.

ಸೂತ್ರ ॥ ಉದು ಉವು ನಪುಂಸಕಪ್ರಥಮಸ್ಯ ॥ ೨೧೦ ॥

ವೃತ್ತಿ ॥ ಪ್ರಥಮಪುರುಷೈಕವಚನಬಹುವಚನಯೋಃ ಕರ್ತೃವಾಚಿಶಬ್ದಸ್ಯ ನಪುಂಸಕಲಿಂಗೇ ಸತಿ ಉದು ಉವು ಇತ್ಯಾದೇಶೌ ಯಥಾಕ್ರಮಂ ಭವತಃ ॥

ಪ್ರಯೋಗ ॥ ಆದುದು । ಆದುವು । ಆದಪುದು । ಆದಪುವು । ಅಪ್ಪುದು । ಅಪ್ಪುವು ॥

ತಾತ್ಪರ್ಯ ॥ ನಪುಂಸಕ ಲಿಂಗದ ಪ್ರಥಮ ಪುರುಷೈಕ ವಚನ ಬಹುವಚನಗಳಿಗೆ ಕ್ರಮವಾಗಿ ಉದು ಉವು ಯೆಂಬಾದೇಶಗಳಾಗುತ್ತವೆ.

ಸೂತ್ರ ॥ ಭಾವೇ ಚ ॥ ೨೧೧ ॥

ವೃತ್ತಿ ॥ ಭಾವಾರ್ಥಪ್ರಥಮವಚನಯೋಶ್ಚ ಉದು ಉವು ಭವತಃ ॥

ಪ್ರಯೋಗ ॥ ಮಾಳ್ಪುದು, ಮಾಳ್ಪುವು । ಕೂರ್ಪುದು, ಕೂರ್ಪುವು ॥

ತಾತ್ಪರ್ಯ ॥ ಭಾವಾರ್ಥ ಪ್ರಥಮೈಕವಚನ ಬಹುವಚನಗಳಿಗೆ ಉದು ಉವು ಯೆಂಬಾದೇಶಗಳಾಗುತ್ತವೆ.

Sûtra **212**.—*Tad eka-vachanasya tu-ttûv ânyeshâm.*

Vṛitti.—*Prathama-purushaika-vachanasya anyeshâm mate tu-ttu-ity-âdes'au bhavataḥ* ।

Prayoga.—*Puṭṭitu, puṭṭittu ; keṭṭitu, keṭṭittu ; aṭṭitu, aṭṭittu* ।

[According to the teaching of others, the termination of the singular should be *tu* or *ttu.*]

Sûtra **213**.—*Striyâm aḷ tad ante.*

Vṛitti.—*Strî-liṅge prathamaika-vachanânte aḷ-pratyayas syât* ।

Prayoga.—*Âḍidaḷ, âḍidapaḷ, âḍuvaḷ ; janiyisidaḷ, janiyisidapaḷ, janiyisuvaḷ* ।

[The feminine third person singular has the termination *aḷ.*]

Sûtra **214**.—*Gum-kumau sarvatra-bhavishyantyâḥ.*

Vṛitti.—*Eshyârthe prathama-purushasya sarva-vibhakti-liṅgeshu gum-kum-ity-âdes'au bhavataḥ* ।

Prayoga.—*Mâtam mîgum âtam, mâtam mîgum âke, adarim mîrugum idu, âtam barkum, âke barkum, adu barkum* ।

[*Gum* and *kum* are the terminations of the future for all cases and genders of the third person.]

ಸೂತ್ರ ॥ ತದೇಕವಚನಸ್ಯ ತುತ್ತೂ ವಾನ್ಯೇಷಾಂ ॥ ೨೧೨ ॥

ವೃತ್ತಿ ॥ ಪ್ರಥಮಪುರುಷೈಕವಚನಸ್ಯ ಅನ್ಯೇಷಾಂ ಮತೇ ತು ತ್ತು ಇತ್ಯಾದೇಶೌ ಭವತಃ ॥

ಪ್ರಯೋಗ ॥ ಪುಟ್ಟಿತು । ಪುಟ್ಟಿತ್ತು । ಕೆಟ್ಟಿತು, ಕೆಟ್ಟಿತ್ತು । ಅಟ್ಟಿತು, ಅಟ್ಟಿತ್ತು ॥

ತಾತ್ಪರ್ಯ ॥ ಪ್ರಥಮ ಪುರುಷೈಕವಚನಕ್ಕೆ ಅನ್ಯಾಚಾರ್ಯರ ಮತದಲ್ಲಿ ತು ತ್ತು ಯೆಂಬಾದೇಶಗಳಾಗುತ್ತವೆ.

ಸೂತ್ರ ॥ ಸ್ತ್ರಿಯಾಮಳ್ತದನ್ತೇ ॥ ೨೧೩ ॥

ವೃತ್ತಿ ॥ ಸ್ತ್ರೀ ಲಿಙ್ಗೇ ಪ್ರಥಮೈಕವಚನಾನ್ತೇ ಅಳ್ಪ್ರತ್ಯಯಸ್ಸ್ಯಾತ್ ॥

ಪ್ರಯೋಗ ॥ ಆಡಿದಳ್, ಆಡಿದಪಳ್, ಆಡುವಳ್ । ಜನಿಯಿಸಿದಳ್, ಜನಿಯಿಸಿದಪಳ್, ಜನಿಯಿಸುವಳ್ ॥

ತಾತ್ಪರ್ಯ ॥ ಸ್ತ್ರೀ ಲಿಂಗದ ಪ್ರಥಮೈಕವಚನಾನ್ತದಲ್ಲಿ ಅಳ್ ಪ್ರತ್ಯಯವಾಗುತ್ತದೆ.

ಸೂತ್ರ ॥ ಗುಂಕುಮೌ ಸರ್ವತ್ರ ಭವಿಷ್ಯನ್ತ್ಯಾಃ ॥ ೨೧೪ ॥

ವೃತ್ತಿ ॥ ಏಷ್ಯಾರ್ಥೇ ಪ್ರಥಮಪುರುಷಸ್ಯ ಸರ್ವವಿಭಕ್ತಿಲಿಙ್ಗೇಷು ಗುಂ ಕುಂ ಇತ್ಯಾದೇಶೌ ಭವತಃ ॥

ಪ್ರಯೋಗ ॥ ಮಾತಂ ಮೀಗುಮಾತಂ । ಮಾತಂ ಮೀಗುಮಾಕೆ । ಅದಱಿಂ ಮೀರುಗುಮಿದು । ಆತಂ ಬರ್ಕುಂ । ಆಕೆ ಬರ್ಕುಂ । ಅದು ಬರ್ಕುಂ ॥

ತಾತ್ಪರ್ಯ ॥ ಭವಿಷ್ಯತ್ಕಾಲದಲ್ಲಿ ಪ್ರಥಮ ಪುರುಷದ ಸರ್ವ ವಿಭಕ್ತಿಗಳಿಗೂ ಗುಂ ಕುಂ ಯೆಂಬಾದೇಶಗಳಾಗುತ್ತವೆ.

Sûtra 215.—*Dâdâv id-âgamo bahuḷam.*

Vṛitti.—*Purusha-traya-vachaneshu da-dapos satoh dakârât prâg-vikalpâd id-âgamas syât* ।

Prayoga.—*Mechchidam, mechchidapam, mechchidar, mechchidapar* ।

Kiñcha tukârâdau cha idâgamo bhavati । *Prayoga* । *ujjittu, bechchittu, meṭṭittu* । *bahuḷatvât* । *keṭṭattu, sattuttu, hiḍidam, paḍedam, ôḷidam, kaḷidam, paḷidam* ।

[*D* and *dap* (see 201) are often preceded by *i*. (Also *tu*; but sometimes not).]

Sûtra 216.—*Y-us' cha ve.*

Vṛitti.—*Vakârâdau vibhakti-gaṇe pare is' cha us' cha yuh ikârokârâgamau bhavatah* ।

Prayoga.—*Nuḍivam, jaḍivam, mâḍuvam, kûḍuvam, âḍuvam, koḍuvam* ।

Cha-s'abda-svîkârâd anyopi bhavati । *beḷevem, kaḷevem, s'aḷavem, yaḷivem* । *kvachid itvam cha na syât* । *îvem, kâḍuvem ity âdi* ।

[*Va* by *i* and *u*. (Sometimes they have a different form. Sometimes they are not preceded by *i*).]

Sûtra 217.—*Ra-ḷâbhyâm vasya pah.*

Vṛitti.—*Repha ḷakârâbhyâm parasya vakârasya pakâras syât* ।

Prayoga.—*Barpar, irpar, barpam, irpam, beḷpam, beḷpar, nôḷpam, nôḷpar* ।

[*V* following upon *r* or *l*, becomes *p*.]

ಸೂತ್ರ ॥ ದಃದಾವಿದಾಗಮೋ ಬಹುಳಂ ॥ ೨೧೫ ॥

ವೃತ್ತಿ ॥ ಪುರುಷತ್ರಯವಚನೇಷು ದದಪೋಸ್ಸತೋಃ ದಕಾರಾತ್ಪ್ರಾಗ್ವಿಕಲ್ಪಾದಿದಾಗಮಸ್ಸ್ಯಾತ್ ॥

ಪ್ರಯೋಗ ॥ ಮೆಚ್ಚಿದಂ । ಮೆಚ್ಚಿದಪಂ । ಮೆಚ್ಚಿದರ್ । ಮೆಚ್ಚಿದಪರ್ ॥

ಕಿಂಚ ತುಕಾರಾದೌ ಚ ಇದಾಗಮೋಭವತಿ ॥ ಪ್ರಯೋಗ ॥ ಉಜ್ಜಿತ್ತು । ಬೆಚ್ಚಿತ್ತು । ಮೆಟ್ಟಿತ್ತು ॥ ಬಹುಳತ್ವಾತ್ ॥ ಕೆಟ್ಟತ್ತು । ಸತ್ತುತ್ತು । ಹಿಡಿದಂ । ಪಡೆದಂ । ಓಳಿದಂ । ಕಳಿದಂ । ಪೞಿದಂ ॥

ತಾತ್ಪರ್ಯ ॥ ದದಪಂಗಳಲ್ಲಿ ದಕಾರದ ಹಿಂದೆ ಪುರುಷತ್ರಯ ವಚನದ್ವಯಗಳಲ್ಲಿಯೂ ವಿಕಲ್ಪವಾಗಿ ಇಕಾರಾಗಮು ಬರುತ್ತದೆ.

ಸೂತ್ರ ॥ ಯುಶ್ಚ ವೇ ॥ ೨೧೬ ॥

ವೃತ್ತಿ ॥ ವಕಾರಾದೌ ವಿಭಕ್ತಿಗಣೇ ಪರೇ ಇಶ್ಚ ಉಶ್ಚ ಯುಃ ಇಕಾರೋಕಾರಾಗಮೌ ಭವತಃ ॥

ಪ್ರಯೋಗ ॥ ನುಡಿವಂ । ಜಡಿವಂ । ಮಾಡುವಂ । ಕೂಡುವಂ । ಆಡುವಂ । ಕೋಡುವಂ ॥

ಚಶಬ್ದಸ್ವೀಕಾರಾದನ್ಯೋಪಿ ಭವತಿ । ಬೆಳೆವೆಂ । ಕಳೆವೆಂ । ಶಳವೆಂ । ಯಳಿವೆಂ ॥ ಕ್ವಚಿದಿತ್ವಂ ಚ ನ ಸ್ಯಾತ್ । ಈವೆಂ । ಕಾಡುವೆಂ । ಇತ್ಯಾದಿ ॥

ತಾತ್ಪರ್ಯ ॥ ವಕಾರಾದಿ ವಿಭಕ್ತಿ ಗಣ ಪರವಾದರೆ ಇಕಾರ ಉಕಾರಾಗಮಗಳು ಬರುತ್ತವೆ. ಚ ಶಬ್ದ ಸ್ವೀಕಾರದಿಂದ ಅನ್ಯಾದೃಕ್ಷರಾಗಮವೂ ಬರುವದು.

ಸೂತ್ರ ॥ ರಳಾಭ್ಯಾಂ ವಸ್ಯ ಪಃ ॥ ೨೧೭ ॥

ವೃತ್ತಿ ॥ ರೇಫಳಕಾರಾಭ್ಯಾಂ ಪರಸ್ಯ ವಕಾರಸ್ಯ ಪಕಾರಸ್ಸ್ಯಾತ್ ॥

ಪ್ರಯೋಗ ॥ ಬರ್ಪರ್ । ಇರ್ಪರ್ । ಬರ್ಪಂ । ಇರ್ಪಂ । ಪೆಳ್ಪಂ । ಬೆಳ್ಪರ್ । ನೋಳ್ಪಂ । ನೋಳ್ಪರ್ ॥

ತಾತ್ಪರ್ಯ ॥ ರೇಫಳಕಾರಗಳಿಗೆ ಪರವಾದ ವಕಾರಕ್ಕೆ ಪಕಾರವು ಬರುವದು.

Sûtra 128.—*Okârâd api vaktavyah.*

Vritti.—*Okârât parasyâpi vakârasya pakâro vâchyah* ।

Prayoga.—*Pôpam, pôpar,* ôpam, ôpar* ।

[Also when it follows *ô*.]

Sûtra 219.—*Dhâtor anekâksharâd isuh.*

Vritti.—*Aneka-varṇâd dhâtor vibhakti-gaṇe pare isu ity âgamas syât* ।

Prayoga.—*Pogayisugam, sogayisidam, sogayisidaḷ,* rañjisidam, rañjisidaḷ* ।

[Polysyllabic roots take *isu* before the inflections.]

Sûtra 220.—*Prayojake cha.*

Vritti.—*Dhâtoh prayojakârthepi isu ity âgamas syât* ।

Prayoga.—*Âḍisidam, pâḍisidam, sârisidam, pôrisidam, kaṇgoḷisidam* ।

[Also causals.]

Sûtra 221.—*Ge-ke vâ prathamasyâs'ishi vidhy-âdishu.*

Vritti.—*Âs'ir-arthe vidhy-âdy-artheshu cha ge-ke ity âdes'au vâ stah* ।

Prayoga.—*Yavag-ishṭârthamam mâḍuge, Jinam namag-ishṭârthamam mâḷke, nôḍuge, mâḷke* ।

[In blessing or commanding the termination of the first (third) person becomes *ge* or *ke*.]

ಸೂತ್ರ ॥ ಓಕಾರಾದಪಿ ವಕ್ತವ್ಯಃ ॥ ೨೧೮ ॥

ವೃತ್ತಿ ॥ ಓಕಾರಾತ್ಪರಸ್ಯಾಪಿ ವಕಾರಸ್ಯ ಪಕಾರೋ ವಾಚ್ಯಃ ॥

ಪ್ರಯೋಗ ॥ ಪೋಪಂ, ಪೋಪರ್* । ಓಪಂ, ಓಪರ್ ॥

ತಾತ್ಪರ್ಯ ॥ ಓಕಾರಕ್ಕೆ ಪರವಾದ ವಕಾರಕ್ಕೆ ಸಹ ಪಕಾರವಾಗುತ್ತದೆ.

ಸೂತ್ರ ॥ ಧಾತೋರನೇಕಾಕ್ಷರಾದಿಸುಃ ॥ ೨೧೯ ॥

ವೃತ್ತಿ ॥ ಅನೇಕವರ್ಣಾದ್ಧಾತೋರ್ವಿಭಕ್ತಿಗಣೇ ಪರೇ ಇಸುಇತ್ಯಾಗಮಸ್ಸ್ಯಾತ್ ॥

ಪ್ರಯೋಗ ॥ ಪೊಗಯಿಸುಗಂ । ಸೊಗಯಿಸಿದಂ । ಸೊಗಯಿಸಿದಳ್ । *ರಂಜಿಸಿದಂ । ರಂಜಿಸಿದಳ್ ॥

ತಾತ್ಪರ್ಯ ॥ ಅನೇಕಾಕ್ಷರಗಳುಳ್ಳ ಧಾತುಗಳಿಗೆ ವಿಭಕ್ತಿಗಣವು ಪರವಾದರೆ ಇಸು ಯೆಂಬುದಾದೇಶವಾಗುವದು.

ಸೂತ್ರ ॥ ಪ್ರಯೋಜಕೇ ಚ ॥ ೨೨೦ ॥

ವೃತ್ತಿ ॥ ಧಾತೋಃ ಪ್ರಯೋಜಕಾರ್ಥೇಪಿ ಇಸು ಇತ್ಯಾಗಮಸ್ಸ್ಯಾತ್ ॥

ಪ್ರಯೋಗ ॥ ಆಡಿಸಿದಂ । ಪಾಡಿಸಿದಂ । ಸಾರಿಸಿದಂ । ಪೋರಿಸಿದಂ । ಕಣ್ಗೊಳಿಸಿದಂ ॥

ತಾತ್ಪರ್ಯ ॥ ಧಾತುವಿನ ಪ್ರೇರಣಾರ್ಥಕದಲ್ಲಿಯೂ ಸಹ ಇಸು ಎಂಬುದಾದೇಶವಾಗುತ್ತದೆ.

ಸೂತ್ರ ॥ ಗೆ ಕೆ ವಾ ಪ್ರಥಮಸ್ಯಾಶಿಷಿ ವಿಧ್ಯಾದಿಷು ॥ ೨೨೧ ॥

ವೃತ್ತಿ ॥ ಆಶೀರರ್ಥೇ ವಿಧ್ಯಾದ್ಯರ್ಥೇಷು ಚ ಗೆ ಕೆ ಇತ್ಯಾದೇಶೌ ವಾ ಸ್ತಃ ॥

ಪ್ರಯೋಗ ॥ ಯವಗಿಷ್ಟಾರ್ಥಮಂ ಮಾಡುಗೆ । ಜಿನಂ ನಮಗಿಷ್ಟಾರ್ಥಮಂ ಮಾಳ್ಕೆ । ನೋಡುಗೆ । ಮಾಳ್ಕೆ ॥

ತಾತ್ಪರ್ಯ ॥ ಆಶೀರರ್ಥದಲ್ಲಿಯೂ ವಿಧ್ಯಾದ್ಯರ್ಥಗಳಲ್ಲಿಯೂ ಪ್ರಥಮಪುರುಷಕ್ಕೆ ವಿಕಲ್ಪವಾಗಿ ಗೆ ಕೆ ಯೆಂಬಾದೇಶಗಳು ಬರುವವು.

---

* C ends here.

* ತೃ ॥ ಪ್ರತಿಯಲ್ಲಿ ರಂಜಿಸು ಎಂಬುದಿಲ್ಲ.

Sûtra 222.—*Madhyamaika-vachanasyed-ud-etah.*

Vṛitti.—*Madhyama-purushaika-vachanasya* **it-ut-et** *iti traya âdes'âs syuh* |

Prayoga.—*Uḍi, baḍi, bigi, kaḍi, jaḍi, kûḍu, pûḍu, mâḍu, ôḍu, nôḍu, pâḍu, kaḷe, tege, bage* |

[That of the middle (second) person singular becomes *i*, *u* and *e*.)

Sûtra 223.—*Prâyo lopas' cha.*

Vṛitti.—*Prâchuryeṇa prâguktâdes'ânâm lopas' cha bhavati* |

Prayoga.—*Nil, pêḷ, bây, laiy, kaḷ, kêḷ* *|

[Often they are dropped.]

Sûtra 224.—*Kriyâ-samabhihâre cha.*

Vṛitti.—*Vyavahâra-paunahpunyepi madhyama-purushaika-vachanasya* **i-u-e** *ity âdes'âs syuh* |

Prayoga.—*Kuḍi-kuḍi-yendu kuḍisidar, piḍi-piḍi-yendu piḍisidar, koḍu-koḍu-yendu koḍisidar*,† *pogu-pogu-yendu pogisidar* |

Prâyo-grahaṇât kvachil-lopah | *nil, kêḷ* |

[In repeating a command, the termination of the middle (second) person singular becomes *i*, *u* and *e*. (Sometimes it is dropped.)]

ಸೂತ್ರ ॥ ಮಧ್ಯಮೈಕವಚನಸ್ಯೇದುದೇತಃ ॥ ೨೨೨ ॥

ವೃತ್ತಿ ॥ ಮಧ್ಯಮಪುರುಷೈಕವಚನಸ್ಯ ಇತ್ ಉತ್ ಎತ್ ಇತಿ ತ್ರಯ ಆದೇಶಾಸ್ಸ್ಯುಃ ॥

ಪ್ರಯೋಗ ॥ ಉಡಿ । ಬಡಿ । ಬಿಗಿ । ಕಡಿ । ಜಡಿ । ಕೂಡು । ಪೂಡು । ಮಾಡು । ಓಡು । ನೋಡು । ಪಾಡು । ಕಳೆ । ತೆಗೆ । ಬಗೆ ॥

ತಾತ್ಪರ್ಯ ॥ ಮಧ್ಯಮ ಪುರುಷೈಕವಚನಕ್ಕೆ ಇತ್ ಉತ್ ಎತ್ ಯೆಂಬೀ ಮೂರು ಆದೇಶಗಳಾಗುತ್ತವೆ. ಇತ್ ಅಂದರೆ ಇ ಯೆಂಬರ್ಥವು. ಹೀಗೆಯೇ ಸರ್ವತ್ರ ಊಹಿಸುವದು.

ಸೂತ್ರ ॥ ಪ್ರಾಯೋ ಲೋಪಶ್ಚ ॥ ೨೨೩ ॥

ವೃತ್ತಿ ॥ ಪ್ರಾಚುರ್ಯೇಣ ಪ್ರಾಗುಕ್ತಾದೇಶಾನಾಂ ಲೋಪಶ್ಚ ಭವತಿ ॥

ಪ್ರಯೋಗ ॥ ನಿಲ್ । ಪೇಳ್ । ಬಾಯ್ । ಬೈಯ್ । ಕಳ್ * । ಕೇಳ್ ॥

ತಾತ್ಪರ್ಯ ॥ ಪ್ರಾಯಕವಾಗಿ ಹಿಂದೆ ಹೇಳಿದ ಆದೇಶಗಳಿಗೆ ಲೋಪವೂ ಕೆಲವೆಡೆಗಳಲ್ಲಿ ಆಗುತ್ತದೆ.

ಸೂತ್ರ ॥ ಕ್ರಿಯಾಸಮಭಿಹಾರೇ ಚ ॥ ೨೨೪ ॥

ವೃತ್ತಿ ॥ ವ್ಯವಹಾರಪೌನಃಪುನ್ಯೇಪಿ ಮಧ್ಯಮಪುರುಷೈಕವಚನಸ್ಯ ಇ ಉ ಎ ಇತ್ಯಾದೇಶಾಸ್ಸ್ಯುಃ ॥

ಪ್ರಯೋಗ ॥ ಕುಡಿ ಕುಡಿಯೆಂದು ಕುಡಿಸಿದರ್ । ಪಿಡಿ ಪಿಡಿಯೆಂದು ಪಿಡಿಸಿದರ್ । ಕೊಡು ಕೊಡು ಯೆಂದು ಕೊಡಿಸಿದರ್ । ಪೋಗು ಪೋಗು ಯೆಂದು ಪೋಗಿಸಿದರ್ * ॥

ಪ್ರಾಯೋಗ್ರಹಣಾತ್ಕ್ವಚಿಲ್ಲೋಪಃ । ನಿಲ್ । ಕೇಳ್ ॥

ತಾತ್ಪರ್ಯ ॥ ಕ್ರಿಯಾವ್ಯವಹಾರವನ್ನು ಮರಳಿ ಮರಳಿ ಮಾಡೆಂಬಲ್ಲಿ ಮಧ್ಯಮ ಪುರುಷೈಕವಚನಕ್ಕೆ ಇ ಉ ಎ ಎಂಬುದೇಶಗಳಾಗುವವು.

---

* C has only *niḷ, pêḷ, kêḷ.* † C stops here.

* ತೃ ॥ ಯಲ್ಲಿ ಬಾಯ್ ಬೈಯ್ ಕಳ್ ಎಂಬವು ಇಲ್ಲ. † ತೃ ॥ ಪೋಗು ಪೋಗು ಎಂಬದಿಲ್ಲ.

Sutra 225.—*Dvitva-bahutvayor im.*

Vṛitti.—*Madhyama-purusha-dvi-vachana-bahu-vachanayoh im âdes'as syât* ।

Prayoga.—*Nuḍim, nôḍim, irisim* ।

[In the dual and plural, the termination of the middle (second) person becomes *im.*]

Sûtra 226.—*Am-uttamasyaika-vachanâd anyatra.*

Vṛitti—*Uttama-purushaika-vachanâd anyayoh dvitva-bahutvayoh vidhyâdy artheshu am âdes'as syât* । *âdi-padena nimantraṇ-âmantraṇ-ânveshaṇa-sampras'na-prârthana-prabhṛitayo jñâtavyâh* ।

Prayoga.—*Mâḷpam, mâḍuvam, nôḷpam, nôḍuvam,* bêḷpam, bêḍuvam, âḍuvam, kûḍuvam, pôpam, bappam* ।

[From the chief (first) person singular, the dual and plural of the imperative and of moods expressing invitation, address, inquiry, entreaty, &c. are formed by adding *am.*]

Sûtra 227.—*Hetâv isuh.*

Vṛitti.—*Karaṇa-prayojakârthe vidheya-vyâpârârthavad dhâtoh parata isu ity âdes'as syat* ।

Prayoga.—*Mâḍisidam, pâḍisidam,* irisidam, tarisidam, baḍisidam, kavi-yisidam* ।

[The causal by adding *isu.*]

ಸೂತ್ರ ॥ ದ್ವಿತ್ವಬಹುತ್ವಯೋರಿಮ್ ॥ ೨೨೫ ॥

ವೃತ್ತಿ ॥ ಮಧ್ಯಮಪುರುಷದ್ವಿವಚನ ಬಹುವಚನಯೋಃ ಇಮಾದೇಶಸ್ಸ್ಯಾತ್ ॥

ಪ್ರಯೋಗ ॥ ನುಡಿಂ । ನೋಡಿಂ । ಇರಿಸಿಂ ॥

ತಾತ್ಪರ್ಯ ॥ ಮಧ್ಯಮ ಪುರುಷ ದ್ವಿವಚನ ಬಹುವಚನಗಳಲ್ಲಿ ಇಮ್ ಯೆಂಬಾದೇಶವಾಗುವದು.

ಸೂತ್ರ ॥ ಅಮುತ್ತಮಸ್ಯೈಕವಚನಾದನ್ಯತ್ರ ॥ ೨೨೬ ॥

ವೃತ್ತಿ ॥ ಉತ್ತಮಪುರುಷೈಕವಚನಾದನ್ಯಯೋಃ ದ್ವಿತ್ವಬಹುತ್ವಯೋಃ ವಿಧ್ಯಾದ್ಯರ್ಥೇಷು ಅಮಾದೇಶಸ್ಸ್ಯಾತ್ । ಆದಿಪದೇನ ನಿಮನ್ತ್ರಣಾಮನ್ತ್ರಣಾನ್ವೇಷಣಸಮ್ಪ್ರಶ್ನಪ್ರಾರ್ಥನಪ್ರಭೃತಯೋ ಜ್ಞಾತವ್ಯಾಃ ॥

ಪ್ರಯೋಗ॥ ಮಾಳ್ಪಂ, ಮಾಡುವಂ। ನೋಳ್ಪಂ, ನೋಡುವಂ। *ಬೇಳ್ಪಂ, ಬೇಡುವಂ। ಆಡುವಂ। ಕೂಡುವಂ। ಪೋಪಂ। ಬಪ್ಪಂ ॥

ತಾತ್ಪರ್ಯ ॥ ಉತ್ತಮಪುರುಷೈಕವಚನದ ದೆಸೆಯಿಂದ ಇತರವಾದ ದ್ವಿವಚನ ಬಹುವಚನಗಳಿಗೆ ವಿಧ್ಯಾದ್ಯರ್ಥಗಳಲ್ಲಿ ಅಮ್ ಯೆಂಬಾದೇಶವಾಗುತ್ತದೆ.

ಸೂತ್ರ ॥ ಹೇತಾವಿಸುಃ ॥ ೨೨೭ ॥

ವೃತ್ತಿ ॥ ಕರಣಪ್ರಯೋಜಕಾರ್ಥೇ ವಿಧೇಯವ್ಯಾಪಾರಾರ್ಥವದ್ಧಾತೋಃ ಪರತ ಇಸುರಿತ್ಯಾದೇಶಸ್ಸ್ಯಾತ್ ॥

ಪ್ರಯೋಗ ॥ ಮಾಡಿಸಿದಂ । ಪಾಡಿಸಿದಂ । * ಇರಿಸಿದಂ । ತರಿಸಿದಂ । ಬಡಿಸಿದಂ । ಕವಿಯಿಸಿದಂ ॥

ತಾತ್ಪರ್ಯ ॥ ಕರಣಪ್ರಯೋಜಕದಲ್ಲಿ ಮಾಡುವ ವ್ಯಾಪಾರಾರ್ಥಮುಳ್ಳ ಧಾತುವಿನ ದೆಸೆಯಿಂದ ಪರವಾಗಿ ಇಸು ಪ್ರತ್ಯಯವಾಗುತ್ತದೆ.

---

* C ends here.

* ತೃ ॥ ಯಲ್ಲಿ ಮೊದಲನೇ ಎರಡು ಉದಾಹರಣೆಗಳಿಲ್ಲ.

Sûtra 228.—*Kriyâyâm kriyârthâyâm al.*

Vṛitti.—*Vyâpâre vyâpârâthavad dhâtoḥ parataḥ al ity âdes'as syât* ।

Prayoga.—*Mâḍal bagedam, nôḍal udbharisidam,* kûḍal eḷasidam, pâḍal toḍagidam, pôgal oḍarchidam, bêgal sârdam* ।

[The infinitive by adding *al.*]

Sûtra 229.—*Pratishedhe cha.*

Vṛitti.—*Nishedhârthavad dhâtos' cha param al syât* ।

Prayoga.—*Pôgal bâradu, usaral bêḍa, nôḍal âgadu* ।

[Also the prohibitive.]

Sûtra 230.—*Saṅgatântare bahuḷam al-lopaḥ.*

Vṛitti.—*Yuktânyârthe kvachid al-âdes'a-lopas syât* ।

Prayoga.—*Sandipud allam** ।

Pratishedha-vidhi-vyâpti-pakshe । *nuḍiyal bâradu, nuḍiya bâradu, teravêḷ kariyam, baravêḷ padâtiyam* ।

[In some cases the *al* is dropped.]

ಸೂತ್ರ ॥ ಕ್ರಿಯಾಯಾಂ ಕ್ರಿಯಾರ್ಥಾಯಾಮಲ್ ॥ ೨೨೮ ॥

ವೃತ್ತಿ ॥ ವ್ಯಾಪಾರೇ ವ್ಯಾಪಾರಾರ್ಥವದ್ಧಾತೋಃ ಪರತಃ ಅಲಿತ್ಯಾದೇಸಸ್ಸ್ಯಾತ್ ॥

ಪ್ರಯೋಗ ॥ ಮಾಡಲ್ ಬಗೆದಂ । ನೋಡಲುದ್ಭವಿಸಿದಂ । *ಕೂಡಲೆಳಸಿದಂ । ಪಾಡಲ್ ತೊಡಗಿದಂ । ಪೋಗಲೊಡರ್ಚಿದಂ । ಬೇಗಲ್ ಸಾರ್ದಂ ॥

ತಾತ್ಪರ್ಯ ॥ ವ್ಯಾಪಾರದಲ್ಲಿ ವ್ಯಾಪಾರಾರ್ಥವುಳ್ಳ ಧಾತುವಿನ ದೆಸೆಯಿಂದ ಪರವಾಗಿ ಅಲ್ ಯೆಂಬದ್ಧಾದೇಶವಾಗುವದು.

ಸೂತ್ರ ॥ ಪ್ರತಿಷೇಧೇ ಚ ॥ ೨೨೯ ॥

ವೃತ್ತಿ ॥ ನಿಷೇಧಾರ್ಥವದ್ಧಾತೋಶ್ಚ ಪರಮಲ್ ಸ್ಯಾತ್ ॥

ಪ್ರಯೋಗ ॥ ಪೋಗಲ್ಬಾರದು । ಉಸುರಲ್ಬೇಡ । ನೋಡಲಾಗದು ॥

ತಾತ್ಪರ್ಯ ॥ ನಿಷೇಧಾರ್ಥವುಳ್ಳ ಧಾತುವಿಗೆ ಪರವಾಗಿ ಅಲ್ ಅದೇಶವಾಗುವದು.

ಸೂತ್ರ ॥ ಸಙ್ಗತಾನ್ತರೇ ಬಹುಳಮಲ್ಲೋಪಃ ॥ ೨೩೦ ॥

ವೃತ್ತಿ ॥ ಯುಕ್ತಾನ್ಯಾರ್ಥೇ ಕ್ವಚಿದಲಾದೇಶಲೋಪಸ್ಸ್ಯಾತ್ ॥

ಪ್ರಯೋಗ ॥ ಸಂದಿಪುದಲ್ಲಂ ॥

ಪ್ರತಿಷೇಧವಿಧಿವ್ಯಾಪ್ತಿಪಕ್ಷೇ । ನುಡಿಯಲ್ ಬಾರದು । ನುಡಿಯಬಾರದು । ತೆರವೇಳ್ ಕರಿಯಂ । ಬರವೇಳ್ ಪದಾತಿಯಂ ॥

ತಾತ್ಪರ್ಯ ॥ ವಿಕಲ್ಪವಾಗಿ ಕೆಲವೆಡೆಯೊಳಲ್ಲಿ ಅಲ್ ಯೆಂಬದು ಲೋಪವಾಗುವದು.

---

* C. ends here.

* ತೃ ॥ ಯಲ್ಲಿ ಎರಡು ಇವೆ.

Sûtra 231.—*Uttam-utam tad-ante.*

Vṛitti.—*Vartamâna-kriyârthe ante uttam-utam-ity etâv âdes'au stah* ।

Prayoga.—*Kedaruttam, kedarutam, naḍeruttam, naḍerutam, mâḍuttam, mâḍutam, noḍuttam, noḍutam—bandudu* ।

[The present progressive takes the termination *uttam* or *utam*.]

Sûtra 232.—*Pûrva-kâla-kriyâyâm id-utau yathâ-lakshyam.*

Vṛitti.—*Pûrva-kâlika-vyâpâra-vishaye vyañjane pare sati dhâtoḥ parataḥ it-ut-ity âdes'au yathâ-lakshyam bhavataḥ* ।

Prayoga.—*Nôḍi pôdam, baḷi vandam, mind-uṇḍum, kaṇḍu nindam* ।

[The past, followed by a word beginning with a consonant, takes the termination *i* and *u*.]

Sûtra 233.—*Dhâtor id-utor upântyayor êd-ôtau prâyah* ।

Vṛitti.—*Dhâtûnâm upântyayor ikâr-okârayoh ekâra okâras' cha prâyo bhavataḥ* ।

Prayoga.—*Kiḍ, keṭṭam ; is, echcham ; kuḍu, koṭṭam ; ugu, okkam* ।
Prâyo grahaṇât kvachin-na stah । *biḍu, biṭṭam ; suḍu, suṭṭam ; iḍu, iṭṭam ; uḍu, uṭṭam ; ity âdi* ।

[The medial *i* and *u* of a root often become *e* and *o* (in the past. Sometimes not).]

ಸೂತ್ರ ॥ ಉತ್ತಮುತಂ ತದನ್ತೇ ॥ ೨೩೧ ॥

ವೃತ್ತಿ ॥ ವರ್ತಮಾನ ಕ್ರಿಯಾರ್ಥೇ ಅನ್ತೇ ಉತ್ತಂ ಉತಂ ಇತ್ಯೇತಾವಾದೇಶೌ ಸ್ತಃ ॥

ಪ್ರಯೋಗ ॥ ಕೆದರುತ್ತಂ । ಕೆದರುತಂ । ನಡೆವುತ್ತಂ । ನಡೆವುತಂ । ಮಾಡುತ್ತಂ । ಮಾಡುತಂ । ನೋಡುತ್ತಂ । ನೋಡುತಂ —ಬಂದುದು ॥

ತಾತ್ಪರ್ಯ ॥ ಆವರ್ತಮಾನ ಕ್ರಿಯಾರ್ಥದಲ್ಲಿ ಕಡೆಯಲ್ಲಿ ಉತ್ತಂ ಉತಂ ಯೆಂಬೀ ಯೆರಡಾದೇಶ ಗಳು ಬರುವವು.

ಸೂತ್ರ ॥ ಪೂರ್ವಕಾಲಕ್ರಿಯಾಯಾಮಿದುತೌ ಯಥಾಲಕ್ಷ್ಯಂ ॥ ೨೩೨ ॥

ವೃತ್ತಿ ॥ ಪೂರ್ವಕಾಲಿಕವ್ಯಾಪಾರವಿಷಯೇ ವ್ಯಞ್ಜನೇ ಪರೇ ಸತಿ ಧಾತೋಃ ಪರತಃ ಇತ್ ಉತ್ ಇತ್ಯಾದೇಶೌ ಯಥಾಲಕ್ಷ್ಯಂ ಭವತಃ ॥

ಪ್ರಯೋಗ ॥ ನೋಡಿ ಪೋದಂ । ಬಳಿ ವಂದಂ । ಮಿಂದುಂಡಂ । ಕಂಡು ನಿಂದಂ ॥

ತಾತ್ಪರ್ಯ ॥ ಭೂತಕಾಲ ವ್ಯಾಪಾರದಲ್ಲಿ ವ್ಯಂಜನ ಪರವಾದರೆ ಧಾತುವಿಗೆ ಪರದಲ್ಲಿ ಇತ್ ಉತ್ ಯೆಂಬವಾದೇಶಗಳಾಗುವವು.

ಸೂತ್ರ ॥ ಧಾತೋರಿದುತೋರುಪಾನ್ತ್ಯಯೋರೇದೋತೌ ಪ್ರಾಯಃ ॥ ೨೩೩ ॥

ವೃತ್ತಿ ॥ ಧಾತೂನಾಮುಪಾನ್ತ್ಯಯೋರಿಕಾರೋಕಾರಯೋಃ ಏಕಾರ ಒಕಾರಶ್ಚ ಪ್ರಾಯೋ ಭವತಃ ॥

ಪ್ರಯೋಗ ॥ ಕಿಡ್, ಕೆಟ್ಟಂ । ಇಸ್, ಎಚ್ಚಂ । ಕುಡು, ಕೊಟ್ಟಂ । ಉಗು, ಒಕ್ಕಂ ।
ಪ್ರಾಯೋಗ್ರಹಣಾತ್ಕ್ವಚಿನ್ನಸ್ತಃ । ಬಿಡು, ಬಿಟ್ಟಂ । ಸುಡು, ಸುಟ್ಟಂ । ಇಡು, ಇಟ್ಟಂ । ಉಡು, ಉಟ್ಟಂ । ಇತ್ಯಾದಿ ॥

ತಾತ್ಪರ್ಯ ॥ ಧಾತುವಿನ ಉಪಾನ್ತ್ಯಗಳಾದ ಇಕಾರ ಉಕಾರಗಳಿಗೆ ಪ್ರಾಯಕವಾಗಿ ಏಕಾರ ಒಕಾರ ಗಳು ಬರುತ್ತವೆ. ಪ್ರಾಯೋಗ್ರಹಣದಿಂದ ಕೆಲವು ಕಡೆ ಯಿಲ್ಲ.

Sûtra 234.—*Ato dîrgho' nâgameshu.*

Vṛitti.—*Anâgameshu âgama-rahita-vibhaktishu para-bhûtâsu dhâtor akârasya dîrghas syât* ।

Prayoga.—*Bar, bâram, bâral ; tar, târam, târal* ।

[When terminations are added without augment, the medial *a* of a root is lengthened.]

Sûtra 235.—*Tṛitîyânâm vyañjanâdau prathamatvam.*

Vṛitti.—*Dhâtu-sambandhinâm varga-tṛitîya-varṇanâm pûrva-vyañjaneshu satsu kriyârthe tat-tad-varga-prathamâksharam syât* ।

Prayoga.—*Pôgu, pokkam ; neḍu, neṭṭam ; paḍu, paṭṭam* ।

[A root ending with a consonant the third of a *varga* (sonant), changes it in the past to the first of that *varga* (surd).]

Sûtra 236.—*Ra-ḍayos ta-ḷau.*

Vṛitti.—*Repha-ḍakârayoh vyañjanâdau pare yathâ-kramam takâra-ḷakârau bhavatah* ।

Prayoga.—*Peru, pettam; keru, kettam; teru, tettam; mâḍu, mâḷku; bêḍu, bêḷku* ।

[*R* and *ḍ* followed by a consonant become *t* and *ḷ*.]

ಸೂತ್ರ ॥ ಅತೋ ದೀರ್ಘೋ' ನಾಗಮೇಷು ॥ ೨೩೪ ॥

ವೃತ್ತಿ ॥ ಅನಾಗಮೇಷು ಆಗಮರಹಿತವಿಭಕ್ತಿಷು ಪರಭೂತಾಸು ಧಾತೋರಕಾರಸ್ಯ ದೀರ್ಘಸ್ಸ್ಯಾತ್ ॥

ಪ್ರಯೋಗ ॥ ಬರ್, ಬಾರಂ, ಬಾರಲ್ । ತರ್, ತಾರಂ, ತಾರಲ್ ॥

ತಾತ್ಪರ್ಯ ॥ ಆಗಮವಿಲ್ಲದ ವಿಭಕ್ತಿಗಳು ಪರವಾಗಲಾಗಿ ಧಾತುವಿನ ಅಕಾರಕ್ಕೆ ದೀರ್ಘವಕ್ಕುಂ ॥

ಸೂತ್ರ ॥ ತೃತೀಯಾನಾಂ ವ್ಯಞ್ಜನಾದೌ ಪ್ರಥಮತ್ವಂ ॥ ೨೩೫ ॥

ವೃತ್ತಿ ॥ ಧಾತುಸಮ್ಬನ್ಧಿನಾಂ ವರ್ಗತೃತೀಯವರ್ಣಾನಾಂ ಪೂರ್ವವ್ಯಞ್ಜನೇಷು ಸತ್ಸು ಕ್ರಿಯಾರ್ಥೇ ತತ್ತದ್ವರ್ಗಪ್ರಥಮಾಕ್ಷರಂ ಸ್ಯಾತ್ ॥

ಪ್ರಯೋಗ ॥ ಪೊಗು, ಪೊಕ್ಕಂ । ನೆಡು, ನೆಟ್ಟಂ । ಪಡು, ಪಟ್ಟಂ ॥

ತಾತ್ಪರ್ಯ ॥ ಧಾತುವಿನಲ್ಲಿನ ವರ್ಗ ತೃತೀಯ ವರ್ಣಗಳಿಗೆ ಕ್ರಿಯಾರ್ಥದಲ್ಲಿ ಅದರದರ ಪ್ರಥಮಾಕ್ಷರ ಬರುವದು.

ಸೂತ್ರ ॥ ರಡಯೋಸ್ತಳೌ ॥ ೨೩೬ ॥

ವೃತ್ತಿ ॥ ರೇಫಡಕಾರಯೋಃ ವ್ಯಞ್ಜನಾದೌ ಪರೇ ಯಥಾಕ್ರಮಂ ತಕಾರಳಕಾರೌ ಭವತಃ ॥

ಪ್ರಯೋಗ ॥ ಪೆರು, ಪೆತ್ತಂ । ಕೆರು, ಕೆತ್ತಂ । ತೆರು, ತೆತ್ತಂ । ಮಾಡು, ಮಾಳ್ಕು । ಬೇಡು ಬೇಳ್ಕು ॥

ತಾತ್ಪರ್ಯ ॥ ರೇಫ ಡಕಾರಗಳಿಗೆ ವ್ಯಂಜನಾದಿಗಳು ಪರವಾದರೆ ಕ್ರಮವಾಗಿ ತಕಾರ ಳಕಾರ ಬರುವವು.

Sûtra 237.—*Vakârasya pah.*

Vritti.—*Dhâtu-sambandhinor-vakârasya vyañjanâdau pare sati pakâro bhavati* ।

Prayoga.—*Tarpam, barpam* ।

[*V* becomes *p*.]

Sûtra 238.—*Â-pobhyâm dasya te yah.*

Vritti.—*Âkâra-pokârâbhyâm parasya dakârasya takâre pare yakâro bhavati* ।

Prayoga.—*Âytu, pôytu* ।

[If *d* after *â* and *pô* changes to *t*, *y* is inserted between.]

Sûtra 239.—*Himsâ-gaty-arthâl-lo nah.*

Vritti.—*Himsârthakât gaty-arthâch-cha dhâtoh parasya lakârasya vyañjane pare nakâro bhavati* ।

Prayoga.—*Kondam, sandam* ।

[In the roots for kill and pass, the *l* followed by a consonant becomes *n*.]

ಸೂತ್ರ ॥ ವಕಾರಸ್ಯ ಪಃ ॥ ೨೩೭ ॥

ವೃತ್ತಿ ॥ ಧಾತುಸಮ್ಬನ್ಧಿನೋರ್ವಕಾರಸ್ಯ ವ್ಯಞ್ಜನಾದೌ ಪರೇ ಸತಿ ಪಕಾರೋ ಭವತಿ ॥

ಪ್ರಯೋಗ ॥ ತರ್ಪಂ । ಬರ್ಪಂ ॥

ತಾತ್ಪರ್ಯ ॥ ಧಾತುವಿನ ವಕಾರಕ್ಕೆ ವ್ಯಂಜನಾದಿಗಳು ಪರವಾದರೆ ಪಕಾರಾದೇಶವಾಗುವದು.

ಸೂತ್ರ ॥ ಆಪೋಭ್ಯಾಂ ದಸ್ಯ ತೇ ಯಃ ॥ ೨೩೮ ॥

ವೃತ್ತಿ ॥ ಆಕಾರಪೋಕಾರಾಭ್ಯಾಂ ಪರಸ್ಯ ದಕಾರಸ್ಯ ತಕಾರೇ ಪರೇ ಯಕಾರೋ ಭವತಿ ॥

ಪ್ರಯೋಗ ॥ ಆಯ್ತು । ಪೋಯ್ತು ॥

ತಾತ್ಪರ್ಯ ॥ ಆಕಾರ ಪೋಕಾರಗಳಿಗೆ ಪರವಾದ ದಕಾರಕ್ಕೆ ತಕಾರ ಪರವಾದರೆ ಯಕಾರವಾಗುವದು.

ಸೂತ್ರ ॥ ಹಿಂಸಾಗತ್ಯರ್ಥಾಲ್ಲೋ ನಃ ॥ ೨೩೯ ॥

ವೃತ್ತಿ ॥ ಹಿಂಸಾರ್ಥಕಾತ್ ಗತ್ಯರ್ಥಾಚ್ಚ ಧಾತೋಃ ಪರಸ್ಯ ಲಕಾರಸ್ಯ ವ್ಯಞ್ಜನೇ ಪರೇ ನಕಾರೋ ಭವತಿ ॥

ಪ್ರಯೋಗ ॥ ಕೊನ್ದಂ । ಸನ್ದಂ ॥

ತಾತ್ಪರ್ಯ ॥ ಹಿಂಸಾರ್ಥಕ ಗತ್ಯರ್ಥಕ ಧಾತುಗಳಿಗೆ ಪರವಾದ ಲಕಾರಕ್ಕೆ ವ್ಯಂಜನ ಪರವಾದರೆ ನಕಾರವಾಗುತ್ತದೆ. ಹಿಂಸಾರ್ಥಕವೆಂದರೆ ಕೊಲ್ಲುವದು, ಗತ್ಯರ್ಥಕವೆಂದರೆ ಹೋಗುವದು.

Sûtra 240.—*Vâ sthity-arthakasya.*

Vṛitti.—*Sthity-artha-dhâtu-sambandhi-lakârasya nakâro vikalpena bhavati* ।

Prayoga.—*Nindam, nillam* ।

[In the root for stand, the *l* sometimes becomes *n.*]

Sûtra 241.—*Ânayanâgamârthe vartino rephasya.*

Vṛitti.—*Anayor arthayor vartamâna-dhâtu-rephasya nakâras syât* ।

Prayoga.—*Tandam, bandam* । *atra ḷakâra-ḍakârayoḥ ṇa-ḍau vaktavyau* । *yathâ:—koṇḍam, kêḷvam* ।

[In the roots for bring and come, the *r* becomes *n.*]

Sûtra 242.—*Nasya chaḥ.*

Vṛitti.—*Atra nakârasya chakâras syât* ।

Prayoga.—*Echcham, echchar ; bechcham, bechchar*

[*N* becomes *ch.*]

ಸೂತ್ರ ॥ ವಾ ಸ್ಥಿತ್ಯರ್ಥಕಸ್ಯ ॥ ೨೪೦ ॥

ವೃತ್ತಿ ॥ ಸ್ಥಿತ್ಯರ್ಥಧಾತುಸಮ್ಬನ್ಧಿಲಕಾರಸ್ಯ ನಕಾರೋ ವಿಕಲ್ಪೇನ ಭವತಿ ॥

ಪ್ರಯೋಗ ॥ ನಿನ್ದಂ । ನಿಲ್ಲಂ ॥

ತಾತ್ಪರ್ಯ ॥ ಸ್ಥಿತ್ಯರ್ಥಕ ಧಾತು ಸಂಬಂಧವಾದ ಲಕಾರಕ್ಕೆ ವಿಕಲ್ಪವಾಗಿ ನಕಾರ ಬರುತ್ತದೆ. ಸ್ಥಿತ್ಯರ್ಥಕವಂದರೆ ನಿಲ್ಲು ಯೆಂಬರ್ಥ.

ಸೂತ್ರ ॥ ಆನಯನಾಗಮಾರ್ಥೇ ವರ್ತಿನೋ ರೇಫಸ್ಯ ॥ ೨೪೧ ॥

ವೃತ್ತಿ ॥ ಅನಯೋರರ್ಥಯೋರ್ವರ್ತಮಾನಧಾತುರೇಫಸ್ಯ ನಕಾರಸ್ಸ್ಯಾತ್ ॥

ಪ್ರಯೋಗ ॥ ತನ್ದಂ। ಬನ್ದಂ। ಅತ್ರ ಳಕಾರಡಕಾರಯೋಃ ಣಡೌ ವಕ್ತವ್ಯೌ ॥

ಯಥಾ ॥ ಕೊಣ್ಡಂ। ಕೇಳ್ವಂ ॥

ತಾತ್ಪರ್ಯ ॥ ಆನಯನಾರ್ಥಕ ಆಗಮಾರ್ಥಕ ಧಾತುಗಳಲ್ಲಿನ ರೇಫಕ್ಕೆ ನಕಾರವಾಗುವದು. ಆನಯನ ವಂದರೆ ತರುವದು. ಆಗಮವಂದರೆ ಬರುವದು.

ಸೂತ್ರ ॥ ನಸ್ಯ ಚಃ ॥ ೨೪೨ ॥

ವೃತ್ತಿ ಅತ್ರ ನಕಾರಸ್ಯ ಚಕಾರಸ್ಸ್ಯಾತ್ ॥

ಪ್ರಯೋಗ ॥ ಎಚ್ಚಂ, ಎಚ್ಚರ। ಬೆಚ್ಚಂ, ಬೆಚ್ಚರ ॥

ತಾತ್ಪರ್ಯ ॥ ನಕಾರಕ್ಕೆ ಚಕಾರವಾಗುತ್ತದೆ.

Sûtra 243.—*Mriti-dânârthayor ante to hrasvas' cha.*

Vritti.—*Anayor arthayor ante takârah pûrva-svarasya hrasvas' cha bhavati* ।

Prayoga.—*Sattam, pettam, ittam** ।

Cha-s'abdâd anyatra na to nâpi hrasvah । *âḷdam, bâḷdam, êḷdam, bêḷdam* ।

[The roots for die and give add *t* and shorten the medial vowel. (Not so in other cases.)]

Sûtra 244.—*Tosh ṭunâ ṭuh.*

Vritti.—*Ta-vargasya ṭa-vargeṇa yoge ṭuh ṭa-vargo bhavati* । *anunâsiko bindus' cha* ।

Prayoga.—*Uṇḍam* ।

[When letters of the *ta* varga (dentals) unite with those of the *ṭa* varga (linguals), both become of the *ṭa* varga (linguals). The *anunâsika* becomes the *bindu*.]

Sûtra 245.—*Ka-cha-ṭa-ta-pebhyo dasya pûrva-rûpam.*

Vritti.—*Varga-prathamâksharebhyah parasya dasya pûrva-rûpam syât* ।

Prayoga.—*Pokkam, mikkam, pêrcham, biṭṭam, ittam, tôrpam, barpam* ।

[When *d* follows on the first letter of a varga, it takes the form of the latter.]

ಸೂತ್ರ ॥ ವೃತಿದಾನಾರ್ಥಯೋರನ್ತೇ ತೋ ಹ್ರಸ್ವಶ್ಚ ॥ ೨೪೩ ॥

ವೃತ್ತಿ ॥ ಅನಯೋರರ್ಥಯೋರನ್ತೇ ತಕಾರಃ ಪೂರ್ವಸ್ವರಸ್ಯ ಹ್ರಸ್ವಶ್ಚ ಭವತಿ ॥

ಪ್ರಯೋಗ ॥ ಸತ್ತಂ । ಪೆತ್ತಂ । ಇತ್ತಂ* ।

ಚಶಬ್ದಾದನ್ಯತ್ರ ನ ತೋ ನಾಪಿ ಹ್ರಸ್ವಃ । ಆಳ್ದಂ । ಬಾಳ್ದಂ । ಏಳ್ದಂ । ಬೇಳ್ದಂ ॥

ತಾತ್ಪರ್ಯ ॥ ವೃತ ರ್ಥ ದಾನಾರ್ಥದಲ್ಲಿ ಅಂತಕ್ಕೆ ತಕಾರ ಬರುತ್ತದೆ. ಪೂರ್ವ ಸ್ವರಕ್ಕೆ ಹ್ರಸ್ವವು ಬರುತ್ತದೆ. ವೃತ್ಯರ್ಥವೆಂದರೆ ಸಾಯುವದು, ದಾನಾರ್ಥವೆಂದರೆ ಈಯುವದು. ಚ ಶಬ್ದದಿಂದ ಕೆಲವು ಕಡೆ ತಕಾರವೂ ಇಲ್ಲ, ಪೂರ್ವ ಹ್ರಸ್ವವೂ ಇಲ್ಲ.

ಸೂತ್ರ ॥ ತೋಷ್ಟುನಾ ಟುಃ ॥ ೨೪೪ ॥

ವೃತ್ತಿ ॥ ತವರ್ಗಸ್ಯ ಟವರ್ಗೇಣ ಯೋಗೇ ಟುಃ ಟವರ್ಗೋ ಭವತಿ । ಅನುನಾಸಿಕೋ ಬಿನ್ದುಶ್ಚ ॥

ಪ್ರಯೋಗ ॥ ಉಣ್ಡಂ ॥

ತಾತ್ಪರ್ಯ ॥ ತವರ್ಗಕ್ಕೆ ಟವರ್ಗದೊಡನೆ ಯೋಗ ಬಂದರೆ ಟವರ್ಗವಾಗುತ್ತದೆ. ಅನುನಾಸಿಕವು ಬಿಂದುವಾಗುತ್ತದೆ.

ಸೂತ್ರ ॥ ಕಚಟತಪೇಭ್ಯೋ ದಸ್ಯ ಪೂರ್ವರೂಪಂ ॥ ೨೪೫ ॥

ವೃತ್ತಿ ॥ ವರ್ಗಪ್ರಥಮಾಕ್ಷರೇಭ್ಯಃ ಪರಸ್ಯ ದಸ್ಯ ಪೂರ್ವರೂಪಂ ಸ್ಯಾತ್ ॥

ಪ್ರಯೋಗ ॥ ಪೊಕ್ಕಂ । ಮಿಕ್ಕಂ । ಪೇರ್ಚಂ । ಬಿಟ್ಟಂ । ಇತ್ತಂ । ತೋರ್ಪಂ । ಬರ್ಪಂ ॥

ತಾತ್ಪರ್ಯ ॥ ವರ್ಗ ಪ್ರಥಮಾಕ್ಷರಗಳಿಗೆ ಪರವಾದ ದಕಾರಕ್ಕೆ ಪೂರ್ವ ರೂಪವಾಗುವದು.

---

* C ends here.

* ತೃ ॥ ಯಲ್ಲಿ ಇಷ್ಟೇ ಯಿರುವದು.

Sûtra 246.—*La-ḷa-kârâbhyâm dasya to vâ.*

Vṛitti.—*La-ḷâbhyâm parasya dasya takâro vâ syât* ।

Prayoga.—*Sôltam, kaḷṭam, biltam* ।

Kvachin na bhavati । *pôldam, jôḷdam, aḷaldam, baḷaldam*

[When it follows *l* or *ḷ* it becomes *t*. (Sometimes not).]

Sûtra 247.—*Abhidhânato vyavasthitâ siddhih.*

Vṛitti.—*Abhidhâna-s'abda-siddhir vyavasthitâ* ।

[Here end the rules for inflected (declinable) words.]

Sûtra 248.—*Tatas' chodâhṛitam.*

[From here (the indeclinables) are explained by examples.]

*Iti Karṇâṭaka-vyâkaraṇa-vṛittau * Bhâshâ-bhûshaṇe Âkhyâta-niyama-vidhânaṃ nâma ashṭamah parichchhedah.*

ಸೂತ್ರ ॥ ಲಳಕಾರಾಭ್ಯಾಂ ದಸ್ಯ ತೋ ವಾ ॥ ೨೪೬ ॥

ವೃತ್ತಿ ॥ ಲಳಾಭ್ಯಾಂ ಪರಸ್ಯ ದಸ್ಯ ತಕಾರೋ ವಾ ಸ್ಯಾತ್ ॥

ಪ್ರಯೋಗ ॥ ಸೋಲ್ತಂ । ಕಳ್ತಂ । ಬಿಲ್ತಂ ।

ಕ್ವಚಿನ್ನ ಭವತಿ । ಪೋಲ್ದಂ । ಜೋಳ್ದಂ । ಅಳಲ್ದಂ । ಬಳಲ್ದಂ ॥

ತಾತ್ಪರ್ಯ ॥ ಲಳಕಾರಗಳಿಗೆ ಪರವಾದ ದಕಾರಕ್ಕೆ ವಿಕಲ್ಪವಾಗಿ ತಕಾರವಾಗುತ್ತದೆ. ವಿಕಲ್ಪ ಸೂತ್ರದಿಂ ಕೆಲವೆಡೆಯೊಳಿಲ್ಲ.

ಸೂತ್ರ ॥ ಅಭಿಧಾನತೋ ವ್ಯವಸ್ಥಿತಾ ಸಿದ್ಧಿಃ ॥ ೨೪೭ ॥

ವೃತ್ತಿ ॥ ಅಭಿಧಾನಶಬ್ದಸಿದ್ಧಿರ್ವ್ಯವಸ್ಥಿತಾ ॥

ತಾತ್ಪರ್ಯ ॥ ಅಭಿಧಾನ ವ್ಯವಸ್ಥಿತಿಗಳಿಂದ ಶಬ್ದಗಳ ಸಿದ್ಧಿ ಹೇಳಿದ್ದಾಯಿತು.

ಸೂತ್ರ ॥ ತತಶ್ಚೋದಾಹೃತಂ ॥ ೨೪೮ ॥

ತಾತ್ಪರ್ಯ ॥ ಆ ಮೇರೆಗೆ ಉದಹರಿಸಲ್ಪಟ್ಟಿತು.

ಇತಿ ಕರ್ಣಾಟಕ ವ್ಯಾಕರಣವೃತ್ತೌ * ಭಾಷಾಭೂಷಣೇ ಆಖ್ಯಾತ ನಿಯಮ ವಿಧಾನಂ ನಾಮ ಅಷ್ಟಮಃ ಪರಿಚ್ಛೇದಃ ।

---

* See note, p. 7.

* ೭ನೇ ಪುಟ ನೋಡು.

[IX. Indeclinables.]

Avyaya-nirûpaṇa Vidhânam.

Sûtra 249.—*Asaṅkhyam avyayam.*

Vṛitti.—*Saṅkhyâ-vachana-bhinnam padam avyaya-samjñam syât* |

[An indeclinable is a word that undergoes no changes on account of number, &c.]

Sûtra 250.—*Âdam aty-arthe.*

Vṛitti.—*Aty-arthe âdam iti syât* |

Prayoga.—*Âdam appidam* |*

[*Âdam* denotes much.]

Sûtra 251.—*Êgam vinis'chayârthe.*

Vṛitti.—*Nis'chaye êgam iti bhavati* |

Prayoga.—*Ante êgam* |

[*Êgam* denotes certainty.]

Sûtra 252.—*Hum pṛichchhâ-vitarkâvadhâraṇa-nivâraṇeshu.*

Vṛitti.—*Hum iti pṛichchhâdy-arthe niyujyate* |

Prayoga.—*Hum adentendu sâlgum, hum âtane, hum nil* |

[*Hum* denotes inquiry, deliberation, emphasis, prohibition.]

ಅವ್ಯಯ ನಿರೂಪಣ ವಿಧಾನಂ.

ಸೂತ್ರ || ಅಸಙ್ಖ್ಯಮವ್ಯಯಂ || ೨೪೯ ||

ವೃತ್ತಿ || ಸಙ್ಖ್ಯಾವಚನಭಿನ್ನಂ ಪದಮವ್ಯಯಸಂಜ್ಞಂ ಸ್ಯಾತ್ ||

ತಾತ್ಪರ್ಯ || ಸಂಖ್ಯೆಯೂ ವಚನವೂ ಇಲ್ಲದ ಪದಗಳು ಅವ್ಯಯ ಸಂಜ್ಞೆಯನ್ನು ಹೊಂದುತ್ತವೆ.

ಸೂತ್ರ || ಆದಮತ್ಯರ್ಥೇ || ೨೫೦ ||

ವೃತ್ತಿ || ಅತ್ಯರ್ಥೇ ಆದಮಿತಿ ಸ್ಯಾತ್ ||

ಪ್ರಯೋಗ || ಆದಮಪ್ಪಿದಂ ||*

ತಾತ್ಪರ್ಯ || ಅತ್ಯರ್ಥದಲ್ಲಿ ಆದವೆಂಬದು ಪ್ರಯೋಗಿಸಲ್ಪಡುತ್ತದೆ.

ಸೂತ್ರ || ಏಗಂ ವಿನಿಶ್ಚಯಾರ್ಥೇ || ೨೫೧ ||

ವೃತ್ತಿ || ನಿಶ್ಚಯೇ ಏಗಮಿತಿ ಭವತಿ ||

ಪ್ರಯೋಗ || ಅಂತೆ ಏಗಂ ||

ತಾತ್ಪರ್ಯ || ನಿಶ್ಚಯಾರ್ಥದಲ್ಲಿ ಏಗವೆಂಬವ್ಯಯವು ಪ್ರಯೋಗಿಸಲಾಗುತ್ತದೆ.

ಸೂತ್ರ || ಹುಂ ಪೃಚ್ಛಾವಿತರ್ಕಾವಧಾರಣನಿವಾರಣೇಷು || ೨೫೨ ||

ವೃತ್ತಿ || ಹುಮಿತಿ ಪೃಚ್ಛಾದ್ಯರ್ಥೇ ನಿಯುಜ್ಯತೇ ||

ಪ್ರಯೋಗ || ಹುಂ ಅದೆಂತೆಂದು ಸಾಲ್ಗುಂ | ಹುಂ ಆತನೆ | ಹುಂ ನಿಲ್ ||

ತಾತ್ಪರ್ಯ || ಪೃಚ್ಛಾದ್ಯರ್ಥದಲ್ಲಿ ಹುಂ ಯೆಂಬದು ಪ್ರಯೋಗಿಸಲ್ಪಡುತ್ತದೆ. ಪೃಚ್ಛೆಯಂದರೆ ಕೇಳುವದು.

---

* C omits all the examples under this chapter.

* ತ್ರ || ಯಲ್ಲಿ ಉದಾಹರಣೆಯೇ ಇಲ್ಲ.

Sûtra 253.—*Chih kutsane.*

Vṛitti.—*Garhaṇârthe chir iti syât* ।

Prayoga.—*Chih polla keydam, chih kashṭam* ।*

[*Chih* denotes blame.]

Sûtra 254.—*Matte-s'abdah kaṇṭha-samîkṛitau.*

Vṛitti.—*Bhûri-s'abdâd anyatra matte iti syât* ।

Prayoga.—*Mattadentu, matte maguḷḍu* ।

[*Matte* denotes a pause for taking breath.]

Sûtra 255.—*Amamâtyante.*

Vṛitti.—*Atyantârthe amameti bhavati* ।

Prayoga.—*Amama* ।

[*Amama* denotes very much.]

Sûtra 256.—*Kennam tatvâkhyâne.*

Vṛitti.—*Tatva-kathane kennam iti syât* ।

Prayoga.—*Kennam enage* ।†

[*Kennam* denotes in reality.]

ಸೂತ್ರ ॥ ಚಿಃ ಕುತ್ಸನೇ ॥ ೨೫೩ ॥

ವೃತ್ತಿ ॥ ಗರ್ಹಣಾರ್ಥೇ ಚಿರಿತಿ ಸ್ಯಾತ್ ॥

ಪ್ರಯೋಗ ॥ ಚಿಃ ಪೊಲ್ಲಕೆಯ್ದಂ । ಚಿಃ ಕಷ್ಟಂ ॥ *

ತಾತ್ಪರ್ಯ ॥ ನಿಂದಾರ್ಥಕದಲ್ಲಿ ಚಿಃ ಯೆಂಬದು ವರ್ತಿಸುತ್ತದೆ.

ಸೂತ್ರ ॥ ಮತ್ತೆಶಬ್ದಃ ಕಣ್ಠಸಮೀಕೃತೌ ॥ ೨೫೪ ॥

ವೃತ್ತಿ ॥ ಭೂರಿಶಬ್ದಾದನ್ಯತ್ರ ಮತ್ತೆ ಇತಿ ಸ್ಯಾತ್ ॥

ಪ್ರಯೋಗ ॥ ಮತ್ತದೆಂತು । ಮತ್ತೆ ಮಗುಳ್ದು ॥

ತಾತ್ಪರ್ಯ ॥ ಕಂಠಸಮೀಕರಣದಲ್ಲಿ ಮತ್ತೆ ಯೆಂಬವ್ಯಯವು ಪ್ರಯೋಗಿಸಲ್ಪಡುತ್ತದೆ. ಕಂಠಸಮೀಕರಣವಂದರೆ ನಿಶ್ವಾಸಾವಕಾಶವು ಉಸುರು ಬಿಡುವದು.

ಸೂತ್ರ ॥ ಅಮಮಾತ್ಯನ್ತೆ ॥ ೨೫೫ ॥

ವೃತ್ತಿ ॥ ಅತ್ಯನ್ತಾರ್ಥೇ ಅಮಮೇತಿ ಭವತಿ ॥

ಪ್ರಯೋಗ ॥ ಅಮಮ ॥

ತಾತ್ಪರ್ಯ ॥ ಅತ್ಯಂತವೆಂಬಲ್ಲಿ ಅಮಮ ಯಂಬದು ಪ್ರಯೋಗಿಸಲ್ಪಡುತ್ತದೆ. ಅತ್ಯಂತವಂದರೆ ಬಹು ಹೆಚ್ಚು ಯೆಂಬರ್ಥ.

ಸೂತ್ರ ॥ ಕೆನ್ನಂ ತತ್ವಾಖ್ಯಾನೇ ॥ ೨೫೬ ॥

ವೃತ್ತಿ ॥ ತತ್ವಕಥನೇ ಕೆನ್ನಮಿತಿ ಸ್ಯಾತ್ ॥

ಪ್ರಯೋಗ ॥ ಕೆನ್ನಮೆನಗೆ ॥ †

ತಾತ್ಪರ್ಯ ॥ ತತ್ವವನ್ನು ಹೇಳುವದರಲ್ಲಿ ಕೆನ್ನವೆಂಬದಾಗುತ್ತದೆ.

---

* These examples only in A. † Not in B.

* ದ್ವಿ॥ ತೃ ॥ ಯಲ್ಲಿ ಈ ಉದಾಹರಣೆಗಳೇ ಇಲ್ಲ. † ದ್ವಿ ॥ಯಲ್ಲಿ ಉದಾಹರಣೆ ಇಲ್ಲ.

Sûtra 257.—*Ôl ivârthe.*

Vṛitti.—*Aupamye ôl iti syât* ।

Prayoga.—*Girivôl, avambôl* * ।

[*Ôl* denotes resemblance.]

Sûtra 258.—*Hrasvo'pi.*

Vṛitti.—*Ôl iti s'abdaḥ hrasvas' cha bhavati* ।

Prayoga.—*Harivol, guruvol* ।

[*Ôl* is also short, *ol*.]

Sûtra 259.—*Mêṇ vikalpe.*

Vṛitti.—*Anis'chite'rthe mêṇ iti prayujyate* ।

Prayoga.—*Adu mêṇ, avam mêṇ* ।

[*Mêṇ* denotes uncertainty.]

Sûtra 260.—*Veram-valam vispashṭârthe.*

Vṛitti.—*Sphuṭârthe veram-valam iti syât* ।

Prayoga.—*Adu veram, idu valam* ।

[*Veram, valam* denote what is clear or manifest.]

ಸೂತ್ರ ॥ ಓಲಿವಾರ್ಥೇ ॥ ೨೫೭ ॥

ವೃತ್ತಿ ॥ ಔಪಮ್ಯೇ ಓಲಿತಿ ಸ್ಯಾತ್ ॥

ಪ್ರಯೋಗ ॥ ಗಿರಿವೋಲ್ । ಅವಂಬೋಲ್ *॥

ತಾತ್ಪರ್ಯ ॥ ಉಪಮಾನಾರ್ಥದಲ್ಲಿ ಓಲ್ ಯೆಂಬದು ಪ್ರಯೋಗಿಸಲ್ಪಡುತ್ತದೆ.

ಸೂತ್ರ ॥ ಹ್ರಸ್ವೋಽಪಿ ॥ ೨೫೮ ॥

ವೃತ್ತಿ ॥ ಓಲಿತಿ ಶಬ್ದಃ ಹ್ರಸ್ವಶ್ಚ ಭವತಿ ॥

ಪ್ರಯೋಗ ॥ ಹರಿವೊಲ್ । ಗುರುವೊಲ್ ॥

ತಾತ್ಪರ್ಯ ॥ ಓಲ್ ಯೆಂಬೀಶಬ್ದವು ಹ್ರಸ್ವವಾಗಿ ಒಲ್ ಯೆಂತಲೂ ಉಪಮಾನಾರ್ಥದಲ್ಲಿ ಪ್ರಯೋಗಿಸಲ್ಪಡುವದುಂಟು.

ಸೂತ್ರ ॥ ಮೇಣ್ವಿಕಲ್ಪೇ ॥ ೨೫೯ ॥

ವೃತ್ತಿ ॥ ಅನಿಶ್ಚಿತೇಽರ್ಥೇ ಮೇಣ್ ಇತಿ ಪ್ರಯುಜ್ಯತೇ ॥

ಪ್ರಯೋಗ ॥ ಅದು ಮೇಣ್ । ಅವಂ ಮೇಣ್ ॥

ತಾತ್ಪರ್ಯ ॥ ಅನಿಶ್ಚಯವಾದ ಅರ್ಥದಲ್ಲಿ ಮೇಣ್ ಯೆಂಬದು ಪ್ರಯೋಗಿಸಲ್ಪಡುತ್ತದೆ.

ಸೂತ್ರ ॥ ವೆರಂ ವಲಂ ವಿಸ್ಪಷ್ಟಾರ್ಥೇ ॥ ೨೬೦ ॥

ವೃತ್ತಿ ॥ ಸ್ಫುಟಾರ್ಥೇ ವೆರಂ ವಲಮಿತಿ ಸ್ಯಾತ್ ॥

ಪ್ರಯೋಗ ॥ ಅದು ವೆರಂ । ಇದು ವಲಂ ॥

ತಾತ್ಪರ್ಯ ॥ ಸ್ಪಷ್ಟವಾದದ್ದೆಂಬರ್ಥದಲ್ಲಿ ವೆರಂ ವಲಂ ಯೆಂಬಿವುಗಳೆರಡೂ ಪ್ರಯೋಗಿಸಲ್ಪಡುವವು.

---

* Not in B.

* ದ್ವಿ ॥ ಅವಂಬೋಲ್ ಎಂಬದು ಇಲ್ಲ.

Sûtra 261.—*Gaḍa-gaḷa vârtâ-sambhâshaṇayoḥ.*

Vṛitti.—*Anayor arthayor gaḍa-gaḷau staḥ* |

Prayoga.—*Entu gaḍa, entu gaḷa* |

[*Gaḍa, gaḷa* denote a rumour or conversation.]

Sûtra 262.—*Am um samuchchaye.*

Vṛitti.—*Samuchchayârthe am-um-ity-ubhau bhavataḥ* |

Prayoga.—*Tannoḷam, âkegam, âtanum, îtanum* |

[*Am, um* signify and.]

Sûtra 263.—*Akaṭa s'abdo vishâdârthe vartate.*

Vṛitti.—*Spashṭam* |

Prayoga.—*Ayyô akaṭa* |

[*Akaṭa* denotes distress.]

Sûtra 264.—*Toṭṭane âkasmike.*

Vṛitti.—*Haṭât siddhe'rthe toṭṭane iti syât* |

Prayoga.—*Toṭṭane bandam* |

[*Toṭṭane* denotes suddenness.]

ಸೂತ್ರ ॥ ಗಡ ಗಳ ವಾರ್ತಾಸಮ್ಭಾಷಣಯೋಃ ॥ ೨೬೧ ॥

ವೃತ್ತಿ ॥ ಅನಯೋರರ್ಥಯೋರ್ಗಡಗಳೌ ಸ್ತಃ ॥

ಪ್ರಯೋಗ ॥ ಎಂತು ಗಡ । ಎಂತು ಗಳ ॥

ತಾತ್ಪರ್ಯ ॥ ವರ್ತಮಾನ ಕಥನದಲ್ಲಿಯೂ ಸಮ್ಭಾಷಣೆಯಲ್ಲಿಯೂ ಗಡ-ಗಳ ಯೆಂಬವು ಪ್ರಯೋಗಿಸಲ್ಪಡುತ್ತವೆ.

ಸೂತ್ರ ॥ ಅಮುಂ ಸಮುಚ್ಚಯೇ ॥ ೨೬೨ ॥

ವೃತ್ತಿ ॥ ಸಮುಚ್ಚಯಾರ್ಥೇ ಅಮ್ ಉಮ್ ಇತ್ಯುಭೌ ಭವತಃ ॥

ಪ್ರಯೋಗ ॥ ತನ್ನೊಳಂ । ಆಕೆಗಂ । ಆತನುಂ । ಈತನುಂ ॥

ತಾತ್ಪರ್ಯ ॥ ಸಮುಚ್ಚಯಾರ್ಥದಲ್ಲಿ ಅಮ್ ಉಮ್ ಯೆಂಬ ಪ್ರತ್ಯಯಗಳು ಬರುತ್ತವೆ. ಸಮುಚ್ಚಯಾರ್ಥವೆಂದರೆ ಮತ್ತು ಯೆಂಬರ್ಥ.

ಸೂತ್ರ ॥ ಅಕಟಶಬ್ದೋ ವಿಷಾದಾರ್ಥೇ ವರ್ತತೇ ॥ ೨೬೩ ॥

ವೃತ್ತಿ ॥ ಸ್ಪಷ್ಟಂ ॥

ಪ್ರಯೋಗ ॥ ಅಯ್ಯೋ ಅಕಟ ॥

ತಾತ್ಪರ್ಯ ॥ ವಿಷಾದಾರ್ಥದಲ್ಲಿ ಅಕಟ ಯೆಂಬವ್ಯಯವು ಪ್ರಯೋಗಿಸಲ್ಪಡುತ್ತದೆ. ವಿಷಾದವೆಂದರೆ ದುಃಖ.

ಸೂತ್ರ ॥ ತೊಟ್ಟನೆ ಆಕಸ್ಮಿಕೇ ॥ ೨೬೪ ॥

ವತ್ತಿ ॥ ಹಟಾತ್ಸಿದ್ಧೇ'ರ್ಥೇ ತೊಟ್ಟನೆ ಇತಿ ಸ್ಯಾತ್ ॥

ಪ್ರಯೋಗ ॥ ತೊಟ್ಟನೆ ಬಂದಂ ॥

ತಾತ್ಪರ್ಯ ॥ ಆಕಸ್ಮಿಕದಲ್ಲಿ ತೊಟ್ಟನೆ ಯೆಂಬವ್ಯಯವು ಪ್ರಯೋಗಿಸಲ್ಪಡುತ್ತದೆ.

Sûtra **265**.—*Neṭṭane parisphuṭârthe.*

Vṛitti.—*Spashṭam* ।

Prayoga.—*Neṭṭane âdam* ।

[*Neṭṭane* denotes what is quite evident.]

Sûtra **266**.—*Val vâkyâlaṅkâra-pâdapûraṇâd upari.*

Vṛitti.—*Eshv artheshu val-s'abdas syât* ।

Prayoga.—*Iduval manushya nidda maravaltu, tâmval vêḷgum, aduval nis'chayam, karamval chôdyam* ।

[*Val* is used to improve a sentence or complete a verse.]

Iti Karṇâṭaka-vyâkaraṇa-vṛittau Bhûshâ-bhûshaṇe Avyaya-nirûpaṇa-vidhânam nâma navamaḥ parichchhedaḥ.*

[X. Particles.]

Nipâta-nirûpaṇa Vidhânam.

Sûtra **267**.—*Ata ûrdhvam nipâtaḥ pravakshyate.*

Vṛitti.—*Ata ûrdhvam nipâto veditavyaḥ* ।

[From here begin particles.]

ಸೂತ್ರ ॥ ನೆಟ್ಟನೆ ಪರಿಸ್ಫುಟಾರ್ಥೇ ॥ ೨೬೫ ॥

ವೃತ್ತಿ ॥ ಸ್ಪಷ್ಟಂ ॥

ಪ್ರಯೋಗ ॥ ನೆಟ್ಟನೆ ಆದಂ ॥

ತಾತ್ಪರ್ಯ ॥ ಪರಿಸ್ಫುಟಾರ್ಥದಲ್ಲಿ ನೆಟ್ಟನೆ ಯೆಂಬವ್ಯಯವು ಪ್ರಯೋಗಿಸಲ್ಪಡುತ್ತದೆ.

ಸೂತ್ರ ॥ ವಲ್ ವಾಕ್ಯಾಲಙ್ಕಾರಪಾದಪೂರಣಾದುಪರಿ ॥ ೨೬೬ ॥

ವೃತ್ತಿ ॥ ಏಷ್ವರ್ಥೇಷು ವಲ್ ಶಬ್ದಸ್ಸ್ಯಾತ್ ॥

ಪ್ರಯೋಗ ॥ ಇದುವಲ್ ಮನುಷ್ಯನಿದ್ದ ಮರವಲ್ತು । ತಾಂವಲ್ವೇಳ್ಗುಂ । ಅದುವಲ್ ನಿಶ್ಚಯಂ । ಕರಂವಲ್ ಚೋದ್ಯಂ ॥

ತಾತ್ಪರ್ಯ ॥ ವಾಕ್ಯ ಅಲಂಕಾರ ಪಾದಪೂರಣಗಳಿಗಾಗಿ ವಲ್ ಯೆಂಬವ್ಯಯವು ಪ್ರಯೋಗಿಸಲ್ಪಡುತ್ತದೆ.

ಇತಿ ಕರ್ಣಾಟಕ ವ್ಯಾಕರಣ ವೃತ್ತೌ *ಭಾಷಾಭೂಷಣೇ ಅವ್ಯಯ ನಿರೂಪಣ ವಿಧಾನಂ ನಾಮ ನವಮಃ ಪರಿಚ್ಛೇದಃ ।

ನಿಪಾತ ನಿರೂಪಣ ವಿಧಾನಂ.

ಸೂತ್ರ ॥ ಅತ ಊರ್ಧ್ವಂ ನಿಪಾತಃ ಪ್ರವಕ್ಷ್ಯತೇ ॥ ೨೬೭ ॥

ವೃತ್ತಿ ॥ ಅತ ಊರ್ಧ್ವಂ ನಿಪಾತೋ ವೇದಿತವ್ಯಃ ॥

ತಾತ್ಪರ್ಯ ॥ ಇನ್ನು ಮೇಲೆ ಹೇಳುವ ಪದಗಳಿಗೆ ನಿಪಾತಗಳೆಂಬ ಹೆಸರು.

---

* See note, p. 7.

* ೭ನೇ ಪುಟ ನೋಡಬೇಕು.

Sûtra 268.—*Ê ity abhyupagame.*

Vṛitti.—*Aṅgîkârârthe dîrgha-ekâro bhavati* ।

Prayoga.—*Ê adentuṭe* ।

[*Ê* long denotes assent.]

Sûtra 269.—*E laghus' ched avadhâraṇe.*

Vṛitti.—*Laghur ekâro'vadhâraṇârthah* ।

Prayoga.—*Adu e, âtanu e* ।

[*E* short denotes certainty.]

Sûtra 270.—*Elê vitarka-nâma-bhâvan-âmantraṇeshu.*

Vṛitti.—*Bhâvanâdishu elê iti syât* ।

Prayoga.—*Elê idâvudu, elê adakku, elê aṇṇâ* ।

[*Elê* expresses surprise or discovery ; and is used in naming or calling.]

Sûtra 271.—*Hrasvânto'pi cha.*

Vṛitti.—*Ayam nipâto hrasvas syât* ।

Prayoga.—*Ele aṇṇâ* ।

[Also with the last vowel short, *ele.*]

ಸೂತ್ರ ॥ ಏ ಇತ್ಯಭ್ಯುಪಗಮೇ ॥ ೨೬೮ ॥

ವೃತ್ತಿ ॥ ಅಙ್ಗೀಕಾರಾರ್ಥೇ ದೀರ್ಘ ಏಕಾರೋ ಭವತಿ ॥

ಪ್ರಯೋಗ ॥ ಏ ಅದೆಂತುಟೇ ॥

ತಾತ್ಪರ್ಯ ॥ ಅಂಗೀಕಾರದಲ್ಲಿ ಏ ಯೆಂಬದು ಪ್ರಯೋಗಿಸಲ್ಪಡುತ್ತದೆ.

ಸೂತ್ರ ॥ ಏ ಲಘುಶ್ಚೇದವಧಾರಣೇ ॥ ೨೬೯ ॥

ವೃತ್ತಿ ॥ ಲಘುರೇಕಾರೋ'ವಧಾರಣಾರ್ಥಃ ॥

ಪ್ರಯೋಗ ॥ ಅದು ಎ । ಆತನು ಎ ॥

ತಾತ್ಪರ್ಯ ॥ ಅವಧಾರಣದಲ್ಲಿ ಲಘು ಎಕಾರವಾಗುತ್ತದೆ. ಲಘು ಎಕಾರವೆಂದರೆ ಹ್ರಸ್ವ ಎಕಾರ.

ಸೂತ್ರ ॥ ಎಲೇ ವಿತರ್ಕನಾಮಭಾವನಾಮನ್ತ್ರಣೇಷು ॥ ೨೭೦ ॥

ವೃತ್ತಿ ॥ ಭಾವನಾದಿಷು ಎಲೇ ಇತಿ ಸ್ಯಾತ್ ॥

ಪ್ರಯೋಗ ॥ ಎಲೇ ಇದಾವುದು । ಎಲೇ ಅದಕ್ಕು । ಎಲೇ ಅಣ್ಣಾ ॥

ತಾತ್ಪರ್ಯ ॥ ವಿತರ್ಕ ನಾಮ ಭಾವನ ಅಮನ್ತ್ರಣಗಳಲ್ಲಿ ಎಲೇ ಯೆಂಬ ನಿಪಾತವು ಪ್ರಯೋಗಿಸಲ್ಪಡುತ್ತದೆ.

ಸೂತ್ರ ॥ ಹ್ರಸ್ವಾನ್ತೋ'ಪಿ ಚ ॥ ೨೭೧ ॥

ವೃತ್ತಿ ॥ ಅಯಂ ನಿಪಾತೋ ಹ್ರಸ್ವಸ್ಸ್ಯಾತ್ ॥

ಪ್ರಯೋಗ ॥ ಎಲೆ ಅಣ್ಣಾ ॥

ತಾತ್ಪರ್ಯ ॥ ಈ ನಿಪಾತವು ಹ್ರಸ್ವವೂ ಆಗುತ್ತದೆ.

Sûtra 272.—*Aha sampraharshe s'obhane cha.*

Vṛitti.—*Anayoḥ aha ity uchyate* ।

Prayoga.—*Aha vaḷḷitâyitu, aha molladâyitu* ।

[*Aha* expresses delight or propitiousness.]

Sûtra 273.—*Aḥ duḥkha-sûchake.*

Vṛitti.—*Spashṭam* ।

Prayoga.—*Aḥ aḥ vidhâtrî* ।

[*Aḥ* denotes sorrow.]

Sûtra 274.—*Am bheda-vismayayor dṛis'yate.*

Vṛitti.—*Spashṭam* ।

Prayoga.—*Am pâtaka vidhiye am* ।

[*Am* expresses disagreement or surprise.]

Sûtra 275.—*Aḥ avajñâyâm.*

Vṛitti.—*Spashṭam* ।

Prayoga.—*Aḥ adarkke* ।

[*Aḥ* expresses contempt.]

ಸೂತ್ರ ॥ ಅಹ ಸಮ್ಪ್ರಹರ್ಷೇ ಶೋಭನೇ ಚ ॥ ೨೭೨ ॥

ವೃತ್ತಿ ॥ ಅನಯೋಃ ಅಹ ಇತ್ಯುಚ್ಯತೇ ॥

ಪ್ರಯೋಗ ॥ ಅಹ ವಳ್ಳಿತಾಯಿತು । ಅಹ ಮೊಲ್ಲದಾಯಿತು ॥

ತಾತ್ಪರ್ಯ ॥ ಸಂತೋಷದಲ್ಲಿಯೂ ಶುಭದಲ್ಲಿಯೂ ಅಹ ಯೆಂಬ ನಿಪಾತವು ಪ್ರಯೋಗಿಸಲ್ಪಡುತ್ತದೆ.

ಸೂತ್ರ ॥ ಅಃ ದುಃಖಸೂಚಕೇ ॥ ೨೭೩ ॥

ವೃತ್ತಿ ॥ ಸ್ಪಷ್ಟಂ ॥

ಪ್ರಯೋಗ ॥ ಅಃ ಅಃ ವಿಧಾತ್ರೀ ॥

ತಾತ್ಪರ್ಯ ॥ ದುಃಖ ಸೂಚಕದಲ್ಲಿ ಅಃ ಯೆಂಬ ನಿಪಾತವು ಪ್ರಯೋಗಿಸಲ್ಪಡುತ್ತದೆ.

ಸೂತ್ರ ॥ ಅಂ ಭೇದವಿಸ್ಮಯಯೋರ್ದೃಶ್ಯತೇ ॥ ೨೭೪ ॥

ವೃತ್ತಿ ॥ ಸ್ಪಷ್ಟಂ ॥

ಪ್ರಯೋಗ ॥ ಅಂ ಪಾತಕ ವಿಧಿಯೇ ಅಂ ॥

ತಾತ್ಪರ್ಯ ॥ ಭೇದದಲ್ಲಿಯೂ ಆಶ್ಚರ್ಯದಲ್ಲಿಯೂ ಅಂ ಯೆಂಬ ನಿಪಾತವು ಬರುತ್ತದೆ.

ಸೂತ್ರ ॥ ಅಃ ಅವಜ್ಞಾಯಾಂ ॥ ೨೭೫ ॥

ವೃತ್ತಿ ॥ ಸ್ಪಷ್ಟಂ ॥

ಪ್ರಯೋಗ ॥ ಅಃ ಅದರ್ಕ್ಕೆ ॥

ತಾತ್ಪರ್ಯ ॥ ಅವಮಾನದಲ್ಲಿ ಅಃ ಯೆಂಬದು ಪ್ರಯೋಗಿಸಲ್ಪಡುತ್ತದೆ.

7

Sûtra 276.—*Ayyô vishâd-âpahâsayoḥ.*

Vṛitti.—*Spashṭam* ।

Prayoga.—*Ayyô anyâyam* ।

[*Ayyô* denotes distress or ridicule.]

Sûtra 277.—*Sa-evânukampâyâm cha.*

Vṛitti.—*Dayâ-vishaye ' pi ayyô iti syât* ।

Prayoga.—*Ayyô prâṇi bîḷdam* ।

[Also compassion.]

Sûtra 278.—*Ôhô nivâraṇârthe.*

Vṛitti.—*Spashṭam* ।

Prayoga.—*Ôhô sâlgum, ôhô māṇu* ।

[*Ôhô* is used for preventing.]

Sûtra 279.—*Are arame kvachit-kadâchid-arthayoḥ.*

Vṛitti.—*Kvachid-arthe kadâchid-arthe ' pi are-arame ity ubhau staḥ* ।

Prayoga.—*Are-yuḷidam, arame yattânum ôrmme* ।

[*Are, arame* signify sometimes or at some time.]

ಸೂತ್ರ ॥ ಅಯ್ಯೋ ವಿಷಾದಾಪಹಾಸಯೋಃ ॥ ೨೭೬ ॥

ವೃತ್ತಿ ॥ ಸ್ಪಷ್ಟಂ ॥

ಪ್ರಯೋಗ ॥ ಅಯ್ಯೋ ಅನ್ಯಾಯಂ ॥

ತಾತ್ಪರ್ಯ ॥ ವಿಷಾದವಲ್ಲಿಯೂ ಅಪಹಾಸ್ಯದಲ್ಲಿಯೂ ಅಯ್ಯೋ ಯೆಂಬದು ಪ್ರಯೋಗಿಸಲ್ಪಡುತ್ತದೆ.

ಸೂತ್ರ ॥ ಸವಿವಾನುಕಮ್ಪಾಯಾಂ ಚ ॥ ೨೭೭ ॥

ವೃತ್ತಿ ॥ ದಯಾವಿಷಯೇ'ಪಿ ಅಯ್ಯೋ ಇತಿ ಸ್ಯಾತ್ ॥

ಪ್ರಯೋಗ ॥ ಅಯ್ಯೋ ಪ್ರಾಣಿ ಬೀಳ್ದಂ ॥

ತಾತ್ಪರ್ಯ ॥ ದಯಾವಿಷಯದಲ್ಲಿಯೂ ಕೂಡ ಅಯ್ಯೋ ಯೆಂಬದು ಪ್ರಯೋಗಿಸಲಾಗುವದು.

ಸೂತ್ರ ॥ ಓಹೋ ನಿವಾರಣಾರ್ಥೇ ॥ ೨೭೮ ॥

ವೃತ್ತಿ ॥ ಸ್ಪಷ್ಟಂ ॥

ಪ್ರಯೋಗ ॥ ಓಹೋ ಸಾಲ್ಗುಂ । ಓಹೋ ಮಾಣು ॥

ತಾತ್ಪರ್ಯ ॥ ಅಡ್ಡಗಿಸುವದರಲ್ಲಿ ಓಹೋ ಯೆಂಬದು ನಿಪಾತವು.

ಸೂತ್ರ ॥ ಅರೆ ಅರಮೆ ಕ್ವಚಿತ್ಕದಾಚಿದರ್ಥಯೋಃ ॥ ೨೭೯ ॥

ವೃತ್ತಿ ॥ ಕ್ವಚಿದರ್ಥೇ ಕದಾಚಿದರ್ಥೇ'ಪಿ ಅರೆ ಅರಮೆ ಇತ್ಯುಭೌ ಸ್ತಃ ॥

ಪ್ರಯೋಗ ॥ ಅರೆಯುಳಿದಂ । ಅರಮೆ ಯತ್ತಾನುಮೋರ್ಮೆ ॥

ತಾತ್ಪರ್ಯ ॥ ಕೆಲವು ಕಡೆ ಕೆಲವು ವೇಳೆ ಒಂದಾನೊಂದು ವೇಳೇ ಯೆಂಬರ್ಥದಲ್ಲಿ ಅರೆ ಅರಮೆ ಯೆಂಬವು ಬರುತ್ತವೆ.

Sûtra **280**.—*Alte sampras'n-ânumânayoh.*

Vṛitti.—*Prichchhâyâm anumâne cha alte iti s'abdah prayujyate* ।

Prayoga.—*Nîn adam pêḷdeyalte, idalte* । *ity âdy ûhyam* ।

[*Alte* denotes inquiry or conjecture.]

*Iti Karṇâṭaka-vyâkaraṇa-vrittau * Bhâshâ-bhûshaṇe*
Nipâta-nirûpaṇa-vidhânam nâma
das'amah parichchhedah.

ಸೂತ್ರ ॥ ಅಲ್ತೆ ಸಮ್ಪ್ರಶ್ನಾನುಮಾನಯೋಃ ॥ ೨೮೦ ॥

ವೃತ್ತಿ॥ ಪೃಚ್ಛಾಯಾಮನುಮಾನೇ ಚ ಅಲ್ತೆ ಇತಿ ಶಬ್ದಃ ಪ್ರಯುಜ್ಯತೇ ॥

ಪ್ರಯೋಗ ॥ ನೀನದಂ ಪೇಳ್ದೆಯಲ್ತೆ । ಇದಲ್ತೆ । ಇತ್ಯಾದ್ಯೂಹ್ಯಂ ॥

ತಾತ್ಪರ್ಯ ॥ ಪೃಚ್ಛೆಯಲ್ಲಿಯೂ ಅನುಮಾನದಲ್ಲಿಯೂ ಅಲ್ತೆ ಯೆಂಬದು ಬರುವದು.

ಇತಿ ಕರ್ಣಾಟಕ ವ್ಯಾಕರಣವೃತ್ತೌ * ಭಾಷಾಭೂಷಣೇ
ನಿಪಾತ ನಿರೂಪಣ ವಿಧಾನಂ ನಾಮ
ದಶಮಃ ಪರಿಚ್ಛೇದಃ ॥

---

* See note, p. 7. * ೭ನೇ ಪುಟ ನೋಡು.

[Colophon.]

Karṇâṭa-s'abda-sûtrâṇi loka-vyutpatti-hetave |
rachitâni sphuṭârthâni kritinâ Nâga-Varmmaṇâ ||

Karṇâṭa-sûtra-vrittau tad Bhâshâ-bhûshaṇa-nâmani |
samjñâ-sandhis-subvibhakti-kârakam-s'abdarîtayah ||

Samâsa-taddhit-âkhyâtâ-avyayâni-nipâtakâh |
kramâd das'a-parichchhedaih sphuṭârthâs samudâhritâh ||

Jîyâd asau mahân prokta Nâga-Varmma-budhottamah |
yat-prajñayâ jagaty uchchair yâti Karṇâṭa-lakshaṇam ||*

[In order that the world might be conversant therewith were the rules of the Karṇâṭa language plainly written by the wise Nâga Varmmâ. The Karṇâṭa sûtras and vrittis by the name of Bhâshâ-Bhûshaṇa did he clearly arrange in ten chapters in the following order,—the alphabet, *sandhi*, declension, uses of the cases, forms of words, compound words, derivatives, verbs, indeclinables and particles.

Success to him called the great, Nâga Varmmâ the most enlightened, by whose intelligence the character of (the) Karṇâṭa (language) is raised to the highest (estimation) in the world.]

ಕರ್ಣಾಟಶಬ್ದಸೂತ್ರಾಣಿ ಲೋಕವ್ಯುತ್ಪತ್ತಿಹೇತವೇ ।
ರಚಿತಾನಿ ಸ್ಫುಟಾರ್ಥಾನಿ ಕೃತಿನಾ ನಾಗವರ್ಮ್ಮಣಾ ॥

ಕರ್ಣಾಟಸೂತ್ರವೃತ್ತೌ ತದ್ಭಾಷಾಭೂಷಣನಾಮನಿ ।
ಸಂಜ್ಞಾ ಸನ್ಧಿಸ್ಸುಬ್ವಿಭಕ್ತಿ ಕಾರಕಂ ಶಬ್ದರೀತಯಃ ॥

ಸಮಾಸ ತದ್ಧಿತಾಖ್ಯಾತಾ ಅವ್ಯಯಾನಿ ನಿಪಾತಕಾಃ ।
ಕ್ರಮಾದ್ದಶಪರಿಚ್ಛೇದೈಃ ಸ್ಫುಟಾರ್ಥಾಸ್ಸಮುದಾಹೃತಾಃ ॥

ಜೀಯಾದಸೌ ಮಹಾನ್ಪ್ರೋಕ್ತ ನಾಗವರ್ಮ್ಮಬುಧೋತ್ತಮಃ ।
ಯತ್ಪ್ರಜ್ಞಯಾ ಜಗತ್ಯುಚ್ಚೈರ್ಯಾತಿ ಕರ್ಣಾಟಲಕ್ಷಣಂ ॥*

---

* This verse appears to be an addition by some disciple or admirer.

* ಈ ಕಡೇ ಶ್ಲೋಕವು ಅವನ ಶಿಷ್ಯಪರಿವಾರದಲ್ಲಿ ಯಾರಿಂದಲೋ ಹೊಸದಾಗಿ ಸೇರಿಸಲ್ಪಟ್ಟ ಹಾಗೆ ಕಾಣುತ್ತದೆ.

APPENDIX I.

VARIÆ LECTIONES.

[L denotes Lingâyit version: B, Brahman version.]

Invocation. L. Sarvajñam tvâm &c.

Vṛitti 1. „ atha s'abdo'yam âdau maṅgaḷârthah (*stops here*).

„ 4. B. atra tach-chhabdopâdânaṃ...... .....akarâdi-svarâ ity-uktâ eva varṇâs te khalv eka .... bhavanti (*stops here*).

„ 5. „ êkârah ôkâro'pi &c.

Prayoga. ele, êḷe, ... gole, gôle.

Sûtra. 7. L. vargâs tu mântâh pañchas'ah pañcha.

B. vargâs ....pañcha pañcha.

Pra. 9. L. (*after* seve) jamvam, javam; gâmve, gâve; omvam, ovam; kâmvam; kamlane kanaldu, kallane kanaldu; omlane yonaldu, ollane yonaldu; ity âdi.

B. samyutam, sayyutam; jamvam, javam; sâmve, sâve; ômvam, ôvam; bâmvam, bâvam; kâmvam, kâvam; sêmve, sêve; kallane kanalgum; kallane sârgum; ollane vonalgum; ity âdi.

Sû. 10. L. *ends with* prayatnâs'rayât.

Vṛ. „ B. prayatnâs'rayât la-ra-ḍâ ity ete varṇâh ḷa ṟa ḻâ api bhavanti I teshâm vibhâshayâ pṛithak pṛithak prayojana-darsanâd ayam ârambhah.

Pra. „ L. *omits examples after* kaḷe; *after* anilam *adds* ile, iḷe; bâle, bâḷe; *and then gives* more, moṟe; mare, maṟe; *and again* koḍakaṭṭu, koḻkaṭṭu; kâḍakichchu, kâḻkichchu. *Thence it continues with examples of* prâsa, as follows:—kilire hayâḷigaḷ carjise jalaḍa nibhangaḷ gajangaḷ; krama prayogam I desegaḷan uḷurdu saral kaḷardum iḷirdatt âgaḷ; repha ṟakârangaḷge I sura giri doṇgida birudara kuruḷam koṟe koṟedu maṟuḷ iṟuḷtim beḷeyoḷ; ḍakâra ḷa ṟangaḷge prayogam I kaḷale suḍid eḷaḷe bagisi ghaḷilane naḍe yandu jaḍidu sârathiyam.

But ḷa, *whether Sanskrit or Kannaḍa, must not be used for* lakâra prâsa || prayogam I, ôlagadoḷ orme nata narapâlaka chûḍâmaṇi dyutipputi charaṇam; neladoḷ paṟe phuṟe phaṇiyavoḷ ola pokkaḷ arisidan emba niyamam dûshyam; rephege I dhuradoḷ pari mariyâḍuva teṟadind aṟidaṟidan emba niyamam dûshyam || *also* taleyam kiḍti taraḷoḷ teṟeyade pesar intuṭ akkum I taleyam nerapam vams'am kareyam pott appuppud embudum I

Pra. 10. B. *introduces* mare, maṟe *after* moṟe.

„ 11. L. sankhyege:—irchhâsiram, eṇchhâsiram I anukaraṇege:—ghaḷilene, chhaṭilene, phaṭhilene, dhoppene, ghaṇmene, dhummene, bhonkene. *also* ghaḷige, jhalam, ḍhokaram, dhaḷam, bharam, ghoḷige.

B. sankhyeyalli:—ombhattu, eṇchhâsiram I anukaraṇadalli:—ghaṇṇene, chiṭhilene, dhummene, ḍhonkene, bhonkene. *also* ghaḷige, ṭhakku, dhore, bhâvi.

Vṛ. 14. „ .... svaras sannidhîyate.

„ 15. „ .... visarga-samjña syât.

„ 16. „ .... pada-samjñam syât.

Pra. 19. L. enna arasam, ennarasam; tanna âḷi, tannâḷi; munna irivam, munnirivam; kûrtu îvam, kûrtîvam; biṭṭu uḷivam, biṭṭuḷivam; keṭṭu ûḷvam, keṭṭûḷvam; biṭṭu ôḷvam, biṭṭôḷvam.

„ „ B. ....muttu uḷivam, muttuḷivam; biṭṭuḷvam; taltesevam; paḍadaiydugoḷvam; biṭṭolvam.

Pra. 20. L. ....nâḷige uḷḷane bâḷgum, nâḷiguḷḷane bâḷgum; pâḷige eṭṭadu karavâḷ, pâḷigeṭṭadu karavâḷ.

Vr. 21. B. yasmin nâma-bl âga-prasango &c.

Pra. „ L. paṭu ekavâkyam, paṭekavâkyam endu âgadu ; mâḍu idu, mâḍidu embal âgadu ; mûle ikkida', mûlikkidaḷ embad âgadu.

„ „ B. va'u ivam, vaḷuvivam ; gâ u ivaḷ, gâḷuvivaḷ ; âse oḷḍu, âseyoḷḍu ; kuduru ekk-tu'am, kudureyekkataḷam ; paḷe idu, paḍeyidu.

Sû. 22. L. ....pare yah.

B. âdi var.........................

Vr. „ „ âkârântâ var ântâd ekârântâch cha s'abdât tad antya svarasyetanthah svare pare ya-kâro vyavadhâya'o bhavati.

Pra. „ „ âye! yo' sangati ; S'riyoḷeyar salî irppa s'ayatiyirdam ; satiyirdaḷ ; bhai bhai yambinam gi tu.

B. â edeyo', 'y edeyo' ; î eḍeyo', îvedeyoḷ ; s'rî eḍe avu sale irpavu, s'rî eḍeyavu saleyirpavu.

„ 23. L. avaḷaye, adariye, nilal putriye, pavana tanûjanaye.

B. ....admave.

Sû. 24. L. vo vri-var âbyâm vah.

B. vo vri-var-âbhyâm.

Vr. „ „ ukârântât ri-var-ântâd api svare pare vakâro vyavadhâyako bhavati.

Pra. „ L. paṭu itam, paṭuvitam ; pit i ivam, pit ivivam ; mâtṛi e mânyaḷ, mâtṛive mânyaḷ, vidhuv illad iruḷ puv illada ko'ad ante.

„ „ B. vidhuv illad iruḷ puv illada ko'ad ant esedattu ; pitṛivivam ; mâtṛivivaḷ.

Here B introduces the following :—

Sû.—ô-varṇâch cha. *Vr.*—ôkâr-aukârântâch cha svare pare vakâro vyavadhâya syât. *Pra.*—gô endam, gôvendam ; nau endam, nauvendam.

Vr. 25. B. ....svare pare svabhâvatas santi.

Pra. „ L. ele idâudu, antuṭe ale, arame aralda, are eḍeyoḷ, ayyo akkaṭâ, ôho irali, intirddant irkkum.

B. ele idâvudu, antuṭe atte, arame aralda, ara edeyoḷ, ayyo akkaṭa, ôho iravim, iddante irkkum.

Sû. 26. „ vis ankâvadhâraṇârthayoh.

Pra. „ L. (*after* rajjuô) iyyanô, akkume, âgadô...
(*after* âptam) âtane ôḷḷidam.

B. (*after* rajjuô) îvvane, îyvam, akkume âguvudu, &c.

„ 27. L. ....kukku kû endu kôḷi kûgidav âgaḷ.

„ 28. „ paḷa Kannaḍam, paḷaGannaḍam ; alikabbum, aligabbam ; kempu taḷir, kendaḷir bân tore, bândore ; tan pu'il, tambuḷil.

„ „ B. ....manṭaral.

Vr. 29. „ ....paṛâdi bhâṭânâm varga prathamânâm sva tritiyâ &c.

Pra. „ L. mârkoral, chîrkôrkoḷavi, mârtale, ôrtale, ôrpiḍi, ôrkai.

B. ....mârpaḍe, ôrkai, ôrpiḍi.

Vr. 30. „ chavarga-ṭavargayoh .... na syât.

Pra. „ L. a'ichennam, kaḍuchâgi, ûrachalli, kanchallam, mâtuṭeppaṛam, &c.

„ „ B. a'ichannam, kaḍuchâgi, urachella, mâtuṭeppaṛam, posaṭankam.

„ 31. L. posapesar, posavesar ; kaipare ; balupaḍe ; e'e bidir .... kalvâḷe ; tâyi mane, tâyvane ; maramaṇu, maravaṇu ; (*bahula*) nadu bera, ûdu molam, kemmugil, pâlmosar, kaimareḍu, balmuguḷ, pulmaruḷ, kârmugil.

„ „ B. posavesar, â'evidir, maravaṇe, kaivare, maivesam. kâyvane, bilvade, kâlvoḷe, pulvane, nîrvâvu, nîrveḷasu, nîrvânisar : (*bahula*) kemmugil, pâlmosar, perbâgil, bâymâḍidam, kaimaredam, balmuguḷ, pulmaram.

Vr. 32. B. ....kvachid anyad eva.

Pra. „ L. (*alayât*) mêlsari, balsari, maysonku.

„ „ B. (*kvachit*) kenjoḍal, ponjeḷe : (*alayât*) mêlsari, bâysari.

Vr. 33. „ ....jatvam bhavati.

Pra. „ L. *omits* munsulige, munjulige.

„ „ B. (*alayât*) *Has* balsari *for* pô'sari.

Vr. 35. „ hrasvâkshara-pûrvaka-padânte vartamânâh &c.

Pra. „ L. *omits* nel-ellam, nellellam ; *for last has* muḷ uḷḷavê kedagigaḷ, muḷḷuḷḷavê kedagigaḷ.

Pra. 35. B. *omits* 1*st*, 3*rd*, 5*th*: *then has* pullellam, nellellam, kiyyalli, muḷḷuḷḷavu kêdagegaḷ : (*hrasva*) *or last has* kêḍidum.

Vr. 36. „ *omits* hrasva-pûrve'pi.

Pra. „ L. saran âr, sara âr ; paradellam muttu mâṇikam ; todaḷiḷada nuḍi.

„ „ B. paravunnu, koranella, para âdavu, todaḷiḷada nuḍi.

Sû. 37. L. avyaye'pi cha.

Pra. „ „ idu dala pûrvam, smaraṇa vôlitam.

„ „ B. iduḍal pûrvam, smaraṇa vôlitam.

Sû. 40. L. tâstu m-am-im-ke-ad-ad-ôḷ.

Vr. „ B. *stops at* iti.

Pra. „ L. (*after discussing the different forms of the terminations at great length, gives them thus*) maram, maramam, maranam, maradim, maradindam, maradinde, marade, marake, marakke, maradattaṇim, maradattaṇindam, maradattaṇinde, marada, maradâ, maradôḷ, maradalli, mara, marane, marame, marave.

Vibhakti sahajanitakam :—maram, maramam, maradim, marakke, maradattaṇim, marada, maradôḷ.

Î vibhaktiya lakshaṇada kandam :—
mara nirdu iu, maranam kaḍi, maradim mâḍâneyam,
marakke gê nîram, maradattaṇim eleyuderyadu,
marada darpaṇ, maradôḷ iru, taḷirtiru marane.

„ „ B. nelam, nelanam, neladim, &c.

„ 41. L. toḍegaḷ, toḍegaḷam, toḍegaḷim, toḍegaḷge, toḍegaḷattaṇim, toḍegaḷa, toḍegaḷôḷ. Dvivachanakke :—toḍegaḷ rambhâ stambhada giḍugaḷ, kaṇgaḷ manôja virana neṇpaḷ, niḍudôḷaḷ bikkaritira vaḍaḷaḷigaḷ enisi mêre udâtana rûpam. Bahuvachanakke :—koḷagaḷ, koḷagaḷam, koḷagaḷim, koḷagaḷge, koḷagaḷattaṇim, koḷagaḷa, koḷagaḷôḷ : koḷagaḷ daḷrt âbaṇgaḷ daḷtaḷjuṇgaḷ samṛiddha madhugaḷ madhugaḷ chaḷidaḷi kuḷâkuḷaṇgaḷ viḷasa daḷpratati madhura virutiye lanadôḷ. *Also* dvivachana prayoga :—Râma-Lakshmaṇar, Lakuḷa-Sahadêvar, Karṇ-Arjuṇar.

Pra. 41. B. *adds* bahuvachanakke :—kuruḷgaḷ, kuruḷgaḷam, kuruḷgaḷim, kuruḷgaḷge, kuruḷgaḷattaṇim, kuruḷgaḷa, kuruḷgaḷôḷ.

Vr. 42. „ ....avu iti bhavati.

Pra. „ L. (*After* beṭṭitu *adds*) teḷḷitu, basidasidu, kaḍidu, niḍidenidu. *Then* ellavu, ellavam, ellavaṛim, ellavakke, &c. Guṇavachana :—niḍiyavu, niḍiyavaṛim, niḍiyavakke, niḍiyavaṛattaṇim, niḍiyavara, niḍiyavaṛôḷ.

„ „ B. *omits* ên : *after* beṭṭitu *adds* kiḷḷitu. *Then* ellavu, ellavam, ellavarim, ellavakke, &c.

Sû. 43. L. Strî-purusha-vâchakeshv &c.

Vr. „ B. *omits* s'abdeshu.

Pra. „ L. penḍiṛ, tôḷtiṛ, nanṭaṛ, nallaṛ, tammandiṛ, magaḷdiṛ, tandeviṛ, tâyviṛ. *Also* ayyangaḷ, avveyar ; mâvangaḷ, mâvandiṛ, atteviṛ, attegaḷ.

ârârge penḍiṛ oḷa uṭṭidar enbar ârârge tandeviṛ ! priya putrarârârge tâyviṛ eraḍ illade kûrpaṛ ârârâr ayya tane tanagam neravallar ârumam ! miṛuguva tamman unḍoḍeya kântikav altud enippa piriyôḷ taṛam nava vidhṛim âdharade sûsida kântiye kangaḷ embinam turida runjey âbharaṇam uṇmiva pângam marichi mâlesuttiṛ andud enippa kêdagiya beḷ suḷiyole beḍangu vaḷdirâ !!

„ „ B. penḍir, tôḷtir, nanṭar, nallar, tâyidir, tammandir, tandevir, magaḷvir. *Also* aiyyangaḷ, makkaḷgaḷ &c.

Pra. 44. L. ....abhimâna pararkkaḷ &c.
B. *omits* vichâra pararkaḷ *and* kôḷkaḷ.

„ 45. L. ôrvar, îrvar, mûvvar, nâlvar, ayvar, âruvar

„ „ B. ôrvaḷ, îrvvar, mûvar, aiyvar.

Sû. 46. L. *omits* this.

Pra. 47. „ Hari, kari, bâli, nadi, vidhu, madhu, vadhu, maḍu, bhrâtṛi, mâtṛi, savitṛi, bere, bere, tore, bâle, mâle, tôḷ, bâḷ, kôḷ.

„ „ B. *omits* nari *and inserts* mâtṛi.

Vr. 48. „ .... upântyâsyâvadher &c.

Pra. „ L. kariyavu, asiyavu, doḍḍidavu, ôḷḷidavu, teḷḷidavu.

Pra. 4. B. kariyavu, hasiyavu, doḍḍavu.

„ 49. L. adu :—avu, avam, avarim, avakke, &c. : idu, ivu ; edu, evu ; piridu, piriyavu.

„ 50. „ gajangaḷ, hayangaḷ, moganngaḷ.
nadigaḷ, maḷugaḷ, pârgaḷ, sâlgaḷ.

Vr. 51. B. .... nakârâgamo vidhîyate.

Pra. „ L. arasange.

„ „ B. .... sachivanim, putranôḷ.

Sû. 52. L. *omits* sûtras 52 to 56.

Pra. „ B. man dim, maralattariyim bandam, jagadôḷ nindam.

Sû. 53. „ vibhâshayâm im-nau.

Vr. „ „ amab âdau dvitî-sik-vardhane &c.

Pra. 54. „ puramir indu, putranâlam, maravi 'dere kârya.

„ 55. „ (*after* manuva kulam) vidhuvatta im (nityam) maḷuvinôḷ, giḷuvinôḷ, &c.

„ 56. „ ondarim, eraḷarim, nûrna, nḍarind, ilaramle, voḷe'arim, doḷdadara keḷage.

„ 57. L. mûḷanum, mûḷange, mûḷagattaim, mûḷaṇa, mûḷaḍôḷ ; (*so*) tenkal, paḷuval
laḷagal ; (*also*) atta, attal ; itti, ittal.

„ „ B. mûḷanim, paḷuva atta im, tenka a deseyim, baḍagaṇa dikkige.

Vr. 58 „ atah &c.

Sû. 59. L. *combines* Sû. 59 and 60, thus :—saptamyâs'cha utvam.

Pra. „ B. .... atta'irdam, attirdam ; ittalirdam. ittirdam.

„ 60. L. oḷagu, oḷage ; poragu, porage ; mêgu, mêge.

„ „ B. (uta) baḍagalirdam.

Sû. 61. L. *omits* Sû. 61 to 65.

Vr. 62. B. .... kvachit kevalâd api.

Pra. „ „ adarinde, gandhadinde ; kramade kalyâṇa.

„ 65. „ matige, s'rîge, naḍuge, edege, gôvige, ûrge, nîrge

Sû. 63. L. sarvanâmno' lingâd o vâ.

Pra. „ „ adu, adam, adarim, adakke ; (*so*) idu.

Sû. 67. „ *omits* Sû. 67 and 68.

Pra. 68. B. nṛipêndranâ parijanam, pêrmc dharmadâ, saḍguṇamâ kânteyâ ; (na) madanana
kaidu, vellidan angana, kaiyḷiḷiy allidam.

„ 69. L. billan, billân. Guna Varmana prayogam &c., *for* baḷegaḷ *has* baḷegum, *and ends*
ante kîsuvam.

mattam s'ishṭa prayogam I nṛipanân abhinuta mananânupame taranânapâra kîrti-
dhvajanâ I vipula guṇajñânan uchitanan apagata dôshan anudâra charitôdayanam I
intu dvitîyye piridum dîrgha prayogam I pirasam sithila bandham enisugam I
nṛipan abhimâna dhananan anupamavan atis'aya vis'âla kîrti dhvajanân upachita
guṇanânushitanan apagata dôshanan udâra charitôdayanam.

„ „ B. *omits the words* kaver Bhuvanaika-vîrasya.

Sû. 70. L. *omits* Sû. 70 to 72.

Pra. 72. B. mâve, malligeye, elare, koḷane ; (*after* gṛihyate) atah kvachin na bhavati I elai dêvâ,
elai bhûpâ.

„ 73. L. daivangaḷira, dêvategaḷira, mâmarangaḷira, nanṭirira. anya prayoga :—suratara-
nandanagaḷira, ratna-pinaddha-vimâna-kuṭṭimântara-suratâlayangaḷira, châru-vilôla-
kaṭâksha-pâta-sundara-parivâra-dêvîvatirâ, kaḍu geydu kritânta nintu nirnerameḷa-
doyye bârisane kemmau upêkshisi nôḍu tirpude I

Sû. 74. L. *omits this here, but quotes it as a case under* 40.

Pra. „ B. ....suggî, suggi ; ....vanamê, vaname ; &c.

Vr. 75. „ *omits* kartṛi.

Pra. 76. L. lingakke :—naram, maram, vanite, nallaḷ, kulam I arthakke :—uchcham, nîcham,
uddhatam, biddham I vachana matrakke :—ondânum, eraḍânum.

„ „ B. *For* nallam, nallaḷ, *has* nallan, vallaḷ
vacha :—ondânum, eraḍum.

„ 77. L. .... kolane, basavre, basantame.
anya grantha lakshaṇam I nilâ'aki-manjuḷa-mṛidu-bâle lakshaṇe-tunga-kuche
sarôjâsyêla-sadbâla-gaja-gamane ninnanum âlôkisi sôladirpa gaṇḍarum oḷam.

„ „ B. elai narendra : bhûpane, kânte, koḷane

Pra. 78. L. ....vik̄ye :—paḷavam kaḍidam I ....
vais'eshitakke :—paṭṭaṇaman eydidam I ....
ishṭakke :—pûrvam koydam &c.
anishṭakke :—pâvam dânṭidam, &c.

" " B. .... vikâ :—paḷuvam kaḍidam I..
vais'e :—paṭṭaṇamam pondidam I ... .
Ipsi :—kûḷan aṭṭam, bâḍam koydam I ....
ends edavidam.

" 79. L. ondu varisum ir lam, îr tingaḷam nôḷidam, ondu gâvudamam paridam, nâ gâvudamam nadedam, mû gâvudamam pôlam, are jâvamam nidre gaidam.

" " B. .... ôr gâvudamam paridam, ara jâvamam nidde gaiydam.

Vr. 80. " .... tṛitîyâ vibhaktir bhavati.

Pra. " L. .... kuḷuḷôlim koydam, &c.

" " B. Devadattanim hêḷalpaṭṭitu, kuḷuḷôlim kûydam, paras'uvinim kaḍidam.

" 81. L. .... ôlugaḷinde bandam.

" " B. jaḷadindam irddam, ôlagind irddam.

Vr. 82. B. karmaṇâ karaṇa-bhûten-opâdher-niyatena vivakshitam &c.

Sâ. 83. L. *omits this, and combines* 84 *and* 85 *in one.*

Pra. " B. .... ruchiyâytu .... pûjyange s'aṇasugam &c.

" 84. " .... kashṭamâgi .... koḷgum.

" 85. L. Devadattange laḍḍuge ruchiy âytu, pas'uvinge tṛiṇa hitam, âryange durjanam seṇasuvam, pâpankk anjuvam takkam, avange pulge kashṭamâgi padevam, âtana mâtım oni adakene koḷam, Janêndrange namaskâram, arasinge svasti.

" " B. Devange namaskâram, aasang eragidam..
bhaḍram Brâhmaṇange, surarge svâhâkâram, pitṛigaḷge &c.

" 86. L. *(after* iḷidam) upâdhyâyadattaṇim s'ishyang âdâytu.

" " B. *stops at* iḷidam.

Vr. 87. " .... prayujyate.

Pra. " L. enn oḍeyam, nâ I ereyam, marada kombu, pulleya pinḍu, ponnan ejje.

" " B. enn oḍeyam, puliya pinḍu, marada kombu.

Vr. 88. " âdhâre'rthe &c.

Pra. " L. karbinôḷ arasam, eḷôḷ enne, neladôḷ paṭṭirddam, mareyôḷ adangirdam.

" " B. nuḍivarôḷ &c.

Sâ. 89. L. nirdhâraṇe cha.

Pra. " " purusharôḷ kshatriya s'ûram, bôgigaḷôḷ sulabhan aggaḷam, nararôḷ uttamam sadguṇâḍhyam, nuḍivarôḷ kaḍu-jâṇam kavis'varam, avanalli âkeyalli yanagâ vidye sahajam, châgigaḷa ballaham.

" " B. nararôḷ kshatriyam s'ûram, tiḷidavarôl ati jâṇam, kavigaḷôḷ uttamam, jâṇigaḷa ballaham.

Vr. 90. " .... bhâshâsu prâyo viparyâso bhavati.

Sâ. 91. L. *before this introduces* Sû :—saptamyarthe shashṭhi. Pra :—bôgigaḷa ballaham.

Vr. " B. panchamyarthe vivakshite kvachit tṛitîyâ vibhaktiḥ prayujyate.

Pra. " L. ôreyattaṇim durchidam, ôreyim durchidam; kareyattaṇim bandam, kareyim bandam.

" " B. oreyattaṇim durchidam, oreyim durchidam; maneyattaṇim &c.

Sâ. 93. L. *omits this.*

Pra. " B. bahu tâpakke &c.

" 94. L. ninna pôpudu, binnan irdaḷ, ninna bare Muramathanâ.

" " B. nîm bare Kṛishṇa, ninna bare Kṛishṇa.

Vr. 95. " tṛitîyârthe saptamî prayujyate.

Pra. " L. *begins with* koḷaliyim, *and adds* kaviyind avana doreyâdam, kaviteyôḷ avana doreyâdam.

Sâ. 96. L. .... ekavachchhabdo bahv &c.

Pra. " " .... karigaḷivu; kai baḷedavu, kaigaḷ baḷedavu.

Vr. 97. B. .... vartamânas' s'abdo bahutvâkhyâne ekavad bhavati.

Pra. " L. desegaḷ pattu; mûru nâlku, mûru nâlkangaḷ; padinenbar; padinaivar.

" " B. dese pattu, desegaḷ pattu; mûru, nâlku, padimbar, padinaiyvar.

Pra. 98. L. bilpu, karppu, guppu, bippu, kûrme, pêrme.
bilpugal, karpugal, kûrmegal, pêrmegal.

Vr. 99. B. .... prathamâyâm prathamâ vibhaktau nîn ân tân iti rûpâni krameṇa bhavanti.

Pra. „ L. nîn irday, âm bandem, &c.

„ „ B. .... âm bandem &c.

Sû. 101. L. dvitva-bahutvayor &c.

Pra. „ „ nîmum, âmum, tâmum, nimage, &c.

„ „ B. *omits* nîm, âm, tâm; *and adds* nimmalli, emmalli, tammalli.

„ 102. L. avam, ivam, uvam, âtam, itam, ûtam.

„ „ B. .... ûtam, âtana, itana.

Pra. 104. B. âke, ike, âtam, îtam.

„ 105. L. .... abhilâsham.

„ 106. B. *adds* idu pâtram.

Sû. 107. L. .... et id antah.

Pra. „ „ mâle, nidre, yâtre, mudre, vasudhe, vanite.

„ „ B. (*for* vasudhe *has*) ile.

Sû. 108. L. id-ûtau hrasvah.

Pra. „ „ nadi, nadi, Lakshmi, nâri, kinnari, kumâri, Kâvêri, Gôdâvari, vadhu, Sarayu, khalapu, kândalu. anya lakshaṇam :—lalitâlike tilanâsike lalitângi vis âla jaghane chandrâsye samujvalita rade Manasijam kaḍu-gaviyâdam ninna yavvanam perchalodam!

„ „ B. (*for* pakshi *has*) Lakshmi.

„ 109. L. jyâ, hrî, strî, srî, bhrû, bhû.

„ „ B. *omits* û; and *adds* bhû.

Vr. 111. „ ....Vadhasy arthe sati &c.

Pra. „ L. vidhâtram.

„ „ B. vidhâtram.

Vr. 112. „ .... dhâtor anyasya rikârântasya &c

Pra. „ L. pitar, pitarar, bhrâtar, bhrâtarar, pitrigal, bhrâtrigal.

„ „ B. *introduces* mâtaram, mâtrigal.

Sû. 113. L. *omits it.*

Vr. „ B. kvachit rikârasya takârâdes'as' cha bhavati.

Pra. „ „ dhâta, mândhâta.

Vr. 117. „ .... upântyasya dîrgha krite tadantasya akârântata cha bhavati.

Pra. „ L. vidvâmsam, vidvâmsar, kaniyâmsam, kaniyâmsar.
s'reyam, s'reyâmsam, jyâyam, jyâyâmsam.

„ „ B. .... s'reyâmsam, jyâyam, jyâyâmsam.

„ 119. „ *adds* sampat, sampattu.

„ 120. L. .... tân chala chittam, tân chittam, suttentakkum, melvan tôrkkum, balpam chittam, &c.

„ „ B. .... tân chalachittam, suttentakkum, mêlvan tôrkum, bilvam pittam, &c.

„ 121. L. *omits* kannîr.

„ „ B. tan neïal, tanneïal; tan nîr, tannîr.

Pra. 122. „ halage, palage; hâlu, pâlu; kaiygâhu, kaiygâpu.

Sû. 123. „ s'a-shoe sah.

Vr. 124. „ .... repha samyogayor madhye &c.

Pra. „ L. & B. .... varsham, barisam; &c.

Vr. 125. B. .... samyoge sati tayor &c.

Pra. 126. L. kâdu purusham, kâlpurusham; .... kôḍukattu, kôlkattu.

„ „ B. .... koḍu kattu, kolkattu.

Sû. 130. L. & B. *omit* ch.

Pra. „ „ „ .... hâraisidam; terayisidam, teraisidam; pûrayisidam, pûraisidam; tavadale, taulale; kavunkal, kaunkal; kavungu, kaungu; ôvajam, aujam; avunkidam, aunkidam.

Pra. 133. L. .... arasina mane, aramane; âneya bâlu, ânevâlu; mâvina &c.

„ „ B. *ditto, but for* ânevâlu *has* ânepâlu.

Vr. 134. B. .... evaikâdhikaraṇatvena karmadhâraya &c.
Pra. „ L. & B. .... te[illegible]itap[illegible]a basur, teḷvasur ; ....
kaḍiya tapam, ka[illegible]u tap[illegible]m ; &c.
Vr. 135. B. .... sankhyâ-pûrvakas'ched &c.
Pra. „ „ *adds* era[illegible]u kaiyi, irakai.
„ 136. L. & B. *add* mêga[illegible]a kai, mêgai.
„ 137. „ „ ku[illegible]u v[illegible]llum, kengaṇṇam, nuchchakki vallam, &c.
Sû. 138. B. .... pa[illegible]ena samam samasyate.
Pra. „ L. & B. Nârada-daṇḍi[illegible]e, soṇṇyisitu Râva[illegible]a-Lanke, s'ri-Râma-paṭṭaṇam, para-dês'am
para-ma[illegible]ḍa[illegible]ikam, para-ve[illegible], para-kotta[illegible]am, &c.
„ 139. „ „ ûrcral b[illegible]n am, teraḷ ittam, ettu goṇḍam, nâykaḍe oḍlam, serey irddam, &c.
Vr. 141. B. adantât kârakât &c.
Pra. „ L. & B. .... b[illegible]sum ba[illegible]ed[illegible]m, ka[illegible]asam iṭṭam, &c.
Vr. 142. B. .... pade pare sati pûrva pada sambandhina u[illegible] ântya svarâdy avayava &c.
Pra. „ L. & B. .... iniya mâvu .... inidu u[illegible]isu ....
jâ[illegible]u mâtu &c.
„ 143. „ „ *add* piri[illegible]a bâ[illegible], perbâḷ.
Vr. 144. B. kvachin na bhavati.
Pra. „ L. (*after* bi gone) bi[illegible]pu ore, bi[illegible]pore ; ni[illegible]idu ede, niṭṭede ; bi[illegible]mole.
„ „ B. (*after* bi[illegible]go[illegible]e) bi[illegible]pu ore, bi[illegible]pore ; [illegible]i[illegible]du ede, niṭṭede ; biṇpu mone, biḷmone.
Vr. 145. „ .... pûrva-var[illegible]asya dirgho &c.
(*after* chârthah) para svare dirgha hrasva eveti cha.
Pra. „ L. kariya osa[illegible]u, kârosaḍu ; kariya mugil, kârmugil ; piriya oḍal &c.
pas'iya ôle, pachcl ôle ; pasur ôti, pachchôti ; iniya saram, încharam ; iniya kôl, in-
gôl ; iniya kaḍal, inga[illegible]al.
„ „ B. kariya osaḍu, kârosaḍu ; piriya o[illegible]al &c.
pas'iya ôle, pachchôle ; pasur ôti, pachchôti ; iniya saram, încharam ; iniya kôl, in-
kôl ; iniya kaḍal, ingaḍal.
Vr. 146. „ .... sv[illegible]râdau pade pare &c.
Pra. „ L. taṇu elar, taṇṇelar ; kaḍidu âyam, kattâyam ; vaḷḷitu unisu, vaḷḷunisu ; vaḷ âḷ,
vaḷḷâḷ ; in uṇisu &c.
„ „ B. .... kaḍidu âyam .... oḷḷuṇisu ; oḷḷitu âḷ, oḷḷâḷ ; in uṇi-
su &c.
Sû. 147. L. & B. .... svarât parasya ṭah.
Vr. 149. B. .... parasya rikârasya &c.
Pra. „ L. kaḍiya gudure, kaḍuṛudure ; kaḍidu dôtam, kaḍudôṭam ; kaḍidu vâḷ, kaḍuvâḷ.
Vr. 151. B. *adds* atra kvchina Karṇâṭa pûrvâchâryâ uḷâdes'am nis'chinuyâh.
Pra. 151. B. *omits* poatu des'e, posades'e.
L. *adds* oḷagu uḷe, oḷḷuḍe ; oḷagu vakkam, oḷvakkam ; oḷagu ûr, oḷûr.
B. *adds* oḷagu uḍe, uḷḷuḍe ; oḷagu pakkam, uḷpakkam ; oḷagu ûr, uḷḷûr.
Vr. 152. B. ... . chasya vyanjane &c. .... sukâro nasyât.
Pra. 153. L. & B. .... pachchaneya pandal, pasupandal.
(*after* bechchaḍi) bechchaneya ôḷu, bechchôḷu.
Pra. 154. „ „ (*after* kisu ganigile) bechchaneya suy, bisusuy.
„ 155. „ „ (*after* sraẓini) pûvina ponchal, pûgonchal ; mêgaṇa kai, mêgai ; mundaṇa kai,
mungai ; channa miy, channai ; mâvina kâyi, mângâyi.
Vr. 156. B. atra [illegible]kârasyâtvam syât.
Pra. „ „ *adds* ella guṇangaḷ.
Vr. 157. „ .... akârântatâ syât.
Pra. „ L. & B. *for* nalda *has* nelda.
„ 161. L. îrvam gaṇḍar &c.
(*after* îraidu) îro[illegible]idar.
„ „ B. îrmai &c. *omits* era[illegible]kal.
(*after* îraidu) îroḷḷidar.
Vr. 162. „ .... vargayoh parayoh tau ka-pa-varṇâv evâgamau bhavatah.
Pra. „ L. & B. .... mûru buri, muppuri ; &c.
add mûlôkam.

Pra. 163. L. mûlôkam, mûjavaḷi, mûderam.
.... mûroḷḍu, mûreḍe, mûrêḷ, mûrâne.
„ „ B. ditto, *omitting* mûrâne.
„ 164. L. *adds* âru beral, aruberal.
„ „ B. *adds* âru beral, aruberal ; âru mogam, arumogam.
„ 165. „ *omits* eḷvarakkangaḷ.
Sû. 166. L. .... tombhattu pañti hattau.
„ „ B. .... tombha pañti hattau.
Vr. 168. „ nava vâchakasya .... pare satyapi ombhai &c.
Sû. 170. L. pann-eka &c.
Vr. „ B. .... pannety &c.
Pra. 178. L. .... paṭṭasâligam .... (*omits* telligam) bhanḍârigam &c.
„ „ B. tâmbûligam, gandhigam, ... paṭṭasâligam .... bhanḍârigam &c.
„ 174. L. jyôyisigam &c.
„ 175. „ *adds* Avalicham *and* Karahaḍigam.
„ „ B. *adds* Karahaḍigam.
Sû. 176. L. & B. .... tatrâdhi kṛit.
Vr. „ B. .... arthe imau &c.
Pra. 177. L. naḍavaḷikâram, âṭagâram, punḍukâram, &c.
„ „ B. naḍavaḷikâram, âṭagâram, munḍugâram, manegâram &c.
„ 178. L. *adds* putravantam.
„ „ B. *adds* putravantam, sûnumantam.
Vr. 179. „ aupamye vâchye vôl iti prayujyate.
Pra. „ L. karivôl bhadraguṇam, karivôl susthiram, manuvôl yajñam, &c.
„ „ B. karivôl bhadraguṇam, manuvôl nayajñam.
kariyante, hariyante, vidhuvante.
Sû. 180. L. & B. hrasvo'pi vâ.
Pra. „ L. harivol, karivol, hariyavol, kariyavol.
„ „ B. karivol, manuvol.
„ 181. L. & B. nigalambôl toḍardudu, chandrambôl beḷagitu.
S'rî râjâvartadim kanḍarasida antivôl kaustubham megha mâlâkarambôl s'ankhavam mangoḍaliya maḷevôl nâbhi kûpôpa jâtam nirejam nîḷda kannaidila vol ire tan uchhâyeyim mikka lôkâdhâram rakshippanakkî bhuvana bhavanamam gânga chakrâyudhânkam.
„ 182. L. .... Jinam adanaroḷage padinâraneyavam ; tat sakaḷa chakravartigaḷoḷ .... nôntavaroḷare.
„ „ B. .... Jinam adaroḷage padinâraneyavam, tat sakala chakravartigaḷôḷ .... nôntavaroḷare.
Pra. 183. L. ôrme, mûrme .... mûru sûḷ.
„ 184. „ .... teraḷke ; tirpu, nuṇpu, biṇpu, pempu, sompu.
„ „ B. .... nuṇpu, binpu, taṇpu, &c.
Sû. 185. L. & B. .... ike-u-me-tanâni.
Vr. „ „ „ .... ike-u-me-tana iti &c.
Pra. „ L. .... urkku, sorkku ; .... billâḷtanam &c.
„ „ B. âḷkke, mâḷke ; mânasike ; urku .... billâḷtana &c.
Sû. 186. L. & B. kriyârthâd at.
Pra. 187. „ „ *add the quotation given under Sûtra* 69.
„ 191. L. .... kanchugâram, ôregâram, kumbagâram, sammagâram, baḷegâram.
„ „ B. .... kumbagâram, sammagâram, balegâram,
Pra. 192. L. pâḍugâram, pâḍungâram ; jûdugâram, jûdungâram ; behukâram, behunkâram ; pempugâram, pempungâram ....
(*For* Guru Hampa Devokta prayogah *has*) Pampa kavi prayogah. ....
kuḍugôḷ ; konkudere, kuḍudere, konkuminchu, &c.
„ B. pâḍugâram, pâḍungâram ; jûdugâram, jûdungâram ; behungâram, pempungâram.
.... kuḍugôḷ ; konkuvere, kuduvere, konkuminchu, &c.

Vr. 194. B. .... pûrva siddhe padânte &c.

Pra. „ L. bâṇasigiti : maṇigârti, âḷikârti, sammagârti, maḍivaḷti, gaṭṭivaḷti : okkalati, okkaligiti.

„ „ B. bâṇasigiti, baḷegâriti : maṇigârti, âḷigârti, sammagârti, maḍivaḷti, gaṭivaḷti : vokkaliti, vokkaligiti.

„ 195. L & B. nallaḷ, pollaḷ, ôḷḷidaḷ, iniyaḷ, sitage, chadure, pâṇbe.

„ 197. L. ......nôḍu-nôḍu, diṭṭisu-diṭṭisu : naḍe-naḍe-yendu nuḍivar, koy-koy-yendu koydar : keḷa-keḷage iḷigum, keḷa-keladôḷ, ide-ide, ... baḷegaḷ ghal-ghal-ghalkene giḷi sovâkegaḷ in oppugum &c.

„ „ B. .... nuḍivar, koy-koy-yendu koyvar : keḷa-keḷage iḷigum, kela-keladôḷ, ide-ide .... baḷegaḷ ghal-ghal-ghalkene giḷi-sovâkegaḷ in oppugum : ene nuḍiye-nuḍiye antante.

Vr. 199. B. .... samjñako bhavati.

Sû. 201. L & B. .... kârâdyâs tâ bhûtavati-vartamâna &c.

Pra. 204. L. tâm mâḍidam, tâm mâḍidar, tâm mâḍidapam, tâm mâḍidapar, tâm mâḍuvam, tâm mâḍuvar.

„ 205. „ .... mâḍidir, nîm mâḍidapay, nîv mâḍidapar, nîm mâḍuvay, nîv mâḍuvir : .... mâḍidev, âm mâḍidapem, âv mâḍidapev, âm mâḍuvem, âv mâḍuvev.

„ 206. „ .... mâḍidir, âtanum nînum mâḍidapir, âtanum nînum mâḍuvir : .... mâḍidev, âtanum ânum mâḍidapev, âtanum ânum mâḍuvev.

„ 207. „ (*for* mâḍidam &c. *has*) puṭṭidam &c.

„ 208. B. âtanê mâḍidam, nîne mâḍiḍay, nâne mâḍuvem.

„ 209. „ avar mâḍidar, nîvu mâḍidir, nâvu mâḍidev.

Sû. 210. L & B. udu-uvu napumsi &c.

Pra. 211. L. *adds* irppudu, irppuvu ; barppudu, barppuvu.

„ „ B. *adds* irpudu, irpuvu.

Vr. 212. L & B. *add* vyavasthita vibhâshayâ kvachin nityam takâra dvitvam eva bhavati.

Pra. „ „ ....puṭṭittu ; meṭṭitu, meṭṭittu ; aṭṭitu &c. âdattu, pôdattu, bandattu, keṭṭittu, (L only) sattittu.

Vr. 213. B. .... prathama-purush-aika &c.

Pra. „ L. aridaḷ, aridapaḷ, arivaḷ ; janiyisidaḷ &c.

„ „ B. aridaḷ, aridapaḷ, arivaḷ ; janisidaḷ, janisidapaḷ, &c.

„ 215. L. .... uchchittu, meṭṭittu ; keṭṭittu, sattittu, hiḍidam, paḍedam, baḍedam, kaḷidam, baḷidam.

„ „ B. .... uchchittu &c. hiḍidam, paḍedam, baḍedam.

„ 216. L. .... seḷevem, eḷevem.

„ „ B. .... seḷivem, eḷivem.

„ 217. L & B. *insert* kûrpam, kûrpar.

Sû. 218. L & B. vâ okârâd &c.

Pra. „ L. pôpam, pôpar ; oppam, oppar.

„ 219. B. sogayisidam, sogayisidaḷ, ranjisidam, ranjisugum.

Vr. 220. „ .... prayojaka-kartr-arthe'pi &c.

Pra. „ L & B. .... pâḍisidam, sôrisidam &c.

Sû. 221. L. u ge ke .... âdishu vâ.

„ „ B. .... âdishu vâ.

Pra. „ L. yamag .... Jinapati nimag .... tân adan nôḍuge, tân adam mâḷke.

„ „ B. devar ishṭârthaman .... Janapati nimag .... tân adan nôḍuge, tân adam mâḷke.

„ 222. L. .... mâḍu, nôḍu .... tege, ôde, pêḷe, bage.

„ „ B. .... baḍi, kaḍi .... pûḍu, nôḍu .... kaḷe tege, boḍe naḍe.

„ 223. L & B. .... kôḷ, kêḷ.

„ 224. L. .. .. kuḍiyisidar, ... piḍiyisidar, ... pogisidar, tege-tege-yendu tegeyisidar, &c.

„ „ B. .... kuḍiyisidar, ... piḍiyisidar, ... koḍisidar, pôgu-pôgendu pôgisidar, naḍe-naḍe-yendu naḍeyisidar, &c.

Pra. 225. L & B. nuḍiyim, nôḍim, irisim, tarisim.
„ 227. L. .... irisidam, karasidam, baḍisidam, kavisidam, kaviyisidam.
„ 228. „ *wanting.*
„ „ B. .... nôḍal udyôgisidam .... bêḍal sârdam.
Sû. 229. L. *wanting.*
Pra. „ L & B. misu kaliyam, pôgal bârudu, usiraḷ bêḍa, &c.
Vr. 230. B. .... kvachid vikalpâd al âd sa syât atrânya lakshaṇam.
Pra. „ L. .... teravêḷ kaliyam, baravêḷ baḍâtiyam.
„ „ B. .... teravêḷ kaliyam &c.
Sû. 231. L & B. uttum-utum tad ante.
Vr. „ „ „ .... ante uttum-utum-ity &c.
Pra. „ „ „ kolaruttum, kolarutum, naḍevuttum, naḍevutum, mâḍuttum, mâḍutum, nôḍuttum, nôḍutum, banḍudu.
„ 233. L. (*after* okkam) koḍu, koṭṭam.
„ „ B. (*after* okkam) tuḷu, tôṭam .... *omits* uḍu, uttam.
Vr. 235. „ .... varṇânâm pûrvam vyañjaneshu &c.
Pra. „ L & B. pokkam, naṭṭam, paṭṭam.
„ 236. „ „ *omit* teru, tettam.
Sû. 238. L. â-pobhyâm parasya dasya &c.
Vr. „ B. .... pare sati yakâro &c.
Pra. 241. L. & B. .... koṇḍam, koḷvam.
Sû. 244. L. tosh tunâ dih (!)
Pra. 245. L. & B. .... ittam, tarpam, barpam.
„ 246. L. *omits* kaltam.
„ „ B. .... a'aldam, bilal'am.
„ 253. „ .... chih kash'am idu.
Vr. 254. „ kanṭha samîkaraṇe matte &c.
Pra. „ L. .... tem natte maguldam.
„ „ B. *wanting.*
Sû. 255. L. *wanting.*
„ „ B. amana bhayâs'charyayor api.
Vr. „ „ bhayâs'charyayoh anama iti syât.
Pra. „ L. amam attente.
„ „ B. amam attante.
Vr. 256. „ tatva vabhane &c.
Pra. „ L & B. kennam enage ballidar ârpare, kennam pannam jannam nuḍigum.
L. *here introduces* Sû. salasau bonkal. *Vr.* bonkal iti s'abda sahâkhye vartate. *Pra.* bonkal toṭṭane nuḍidam.
Sû. 257. L & B. vôl ivârthe.
Vr. „ B. aupamye vôl &c.
Pra. „ L. aduvôl, girivôl &c.
„ „ B. avambôl, karivôl, harivôl, aduvôl.
Vr. 258. „ vôl iti &c.
Pra. „ L. harivol.
„ „ B. harivol, karivol, girivol.
„ 259. L. adu mêṇ, idu mêṇ.
„ „ B. adu mêṇ.
„ 260. L & B. adu veram, valam.
Vr. 261. B. ... . gaḍa-gaḷa ity etau &c.
Pra. 262. L & B. tannoḍam âkeyoḍam, âtangam âkegam, enagam tanagam, âtanum ânum âkeyum kudureyum, (L only) eḷtum kaḷteyum.
Sû. 263. B. *omits* vartate.
Pra. 265. L. neṭṭane âdante, toṭṭane mâḍal.
„ „ B. *adds* toṭṭane mâḍal.
„ 266. L. iduval manushya viddham appuvaltu &c.
„ „ B. iduval manushya viddhav appuvaltu &c. .... *omits* karamval chôdyam,
Sû. 267. L. ata ûrdhvam pralakshante.

Sû.	267.	B.	*omits* pravakshyate.
Vṛ.	„	„	ata ûrdhvam prachakshante nipâta samjñâ veditavyâh.
Pra.	269.	„	.... âtane, avaḷe.
„	270.	L.	.... ele adakkam &c.
„	„	B.	.... ele adakkum &c.
„	271.	„	ele yên idu.
Sû.	272.	L.	ah sampraharshe &c.
„	„	B.	assamprahaarshe &c.
Vṛ.	„	„	harshe mangale cha ah ity &c.
Pra.	„	L.	ah vollidâytu, ah polladâytu.
„	„	B.	ah polladâytu, ah vollidâytu.
Sû.	273.	L & B.	ah ah duhkha-sûchane.
Vṛ.	„	„	„ duhkha-suchane'rthe ah ab iti bhavati.
Pra.	„	B.	ah ah vidhâtranê.
Sû.	274.	L & B.	am bheda vismaya dṛis'yate.
Vṛ.	„	„	„ bhedâscharyayoh am iti syât.
Pra.	„	L.	.... vidhiye, am chhodyam.
„	„	B.	.... vidhiye, am chodyam.
„	275.	L.	ah adakke.
„	„	B.	ah adakke higâyt allavê.
Vṛ.	276.	B.	duhkha-hâsyayoh ayyô iti syât.
Pra.	„	L.	ayayyô anyâyam.
„	„	B.	ayyô anyâyam allavê.
Sû.	277.	„	*omits* cha.
Vṛ.	„	„	.... ayyô'pi syât.
„	278.	„	nivâraṇe ôhô iti bhavati.
Pra.	„	L.	.... ôhô mâṇ.
„	„	B.	.... ôhô mâṇ idannu.
Vṛ.	279.	„	krâpy-arthe jâty-arthe cha are &c.
Pra.	„	L.	are yaḍeyoḷ, are yulidam &c.
„	„	B.	are yâva yeḍeyoḷô, are mulidam &c.
Vṛ.	280.	B.	.... s'abdah syât.
Colophon.		L.	verses 2 & 3 wanting.
„		B.	verses 2 & 3 are put at the beginning of the work, and vary thus:—
			....
			samjñâ-sandhir-vibhakty-âdi kârakam s'abdaritayah ǁ
			....
			kramâd das'a parichchhedâ vyâkhyâyante sphuṭârthakâh ǁ
			omits Jîyâd asau &c.

APPENDIX II.

INDEX

OF

WORDS USED IN THE EXAMPLES.

[*The figures refer to sûtras.*]

ADDENDA ET CORRIGENDA.

Introduction.—

p. iv, line 20. *Add.*—From sûtra 193 it is evident that he derives Kannada from the Apabhramsa.

„ vi, „ 21. *Add.*—The exact numbers according to the Census of 1881 are :—

Kannada.	Mysore	... ...	3,095,647	
	Bombay	... ...	2,600,160	
	Madras	... ...	1,300,555	
	Nizam's Dominions	...	1,238,519	
	Coorg	... ...	92,079	
	Central Provinces	...	4,766	
	Cochin	... ...	2,369	
	Berar	... ...	1,487	
	Bengal	... ...	134	
	Panjab	... ...	68	
	North West Provinces	...	18	
	Central India	... ...	1	
	British Burma	... ...	5	
	French Territories	...	56	
				8,335,859
Tulu.	Madras	... ...	427,000	
	Coorg	... ...	9,589	
	Mysore	... ...	8,941	
				445,530
Kodagu.	Coorg	... ...	28,535	
	Madras	... ...	36	
	Mysore	... ...	21	
				28,592
Kota.	Madras	... ...		1,062
Badaga.	„	... ...		1,019
Toda	„	... ...		673
			Total......	8,812,735

The total for Kannada requires the figures for Travancore and the Portuguese territories to be added. Moreover, owing to the famine, more than a million have been lost. The total for Badaga is as given in the Madras Census Report, but the number of Badagas is therein stated to be 24,398. So also the number of Todas is stated to be 689.

p. xvi, line 18. *For* Chamunḍa *read* Châmunḍa.
„ xx „ 26. *Omit* was - - - - - - 1068.
„ „ „ 28. „ may - - - - - - person.
„ xxii, „ 23. *Add.*—A possible reference to Manasija may be contained in the following quotation given in L under sûtra 108.

Lalitâlike tilanâsike !
Lalitângi-vis'âla-jaghane Chandrâsye samu- !
jvalita-rade Manasijam kaḍu- !
gavi yâdam ninna yavvanam perchaloḍam !!

Although the rhyme requires *gali* in the last line, the original is clearly *gavi*.
"Languishing, bud-nosed, shapely broad-hipped Chandrâsi, with shining teeth, Manasija grew to a great poet as your youthful beauty increased."

p. xxx, „ 16. *For* Nanjesa *read* Nanjes'a.
„ xxxv, after line 18. *Insert.*—1838. *Krishṇamâchâri*, College Munshi at Madras, wrote a grammar called *Hosa-Gannaḍa-nuḍi-gannaḍi*.
„ xxxvi, line 27. *Omit* Hosa - - - - - - Madras.

Text.—

p. 5, line 2. *For* daire va *read* dair eva.
„ 9, „ 4. „ gâḷu-ival, gâḷuyival *read* gâḷu-ivaḷ, gâḷuyivaḷ.
„ 14, „ 13. „ ckitrada *read* chitrada.
„ 16, „ 10. „ ar „ ad.
„ „ „ 11. „ ar „ at. *For* sapṭa *read* sapta.
„ „ „ 14. „ ar „ at.
„ 24, „ 10. „ ued „ used.
„ 33, „ 11. „ bhavatî „ bhavati.
„ 37, „ 6. „ bande „ bandem.
„ 45, „ 6. „ vyñjaneshu *read* vyañjaneshu.
„ „ „ 8. „ kâḷvurisam „ kâḷpurisam.
„ „ „ 9. „ nâḷvaraganam „ nâḷparagaṇam.
„ „ „ 15. „ nôd „ nôḍ.
„ 48, „ 11. „ lokam, mûlokam *read* lôkam, mûlôkam.
„ 49, „ 8. „ kenganim „ kengannam.
„ nuchchhakki „ nuchchhakkivallam.
„ 52, „ 4. „ oḷitu „ oḷḷitu.
„ 53, „ 9. „ kaḍugudare „ kaḍugudure.
„ „ „ 17. „ poḷadu alagu, poḷa-alagu *read* paḷadu alagu, paḷa-alagu.
„ 54, „ 1. „ pechchane-bechchane „ bechchane-pechchane.
„ 56, „ 4. „ kalyerde „ kallerde.
„ „ „ 17. „ lokam, mûlokam „ lôkam, mûlôkam.
„ 60, „ 18. „ bûshaṇe „ bhûshaṇe.
„ 62, „ 4. „ des'adôḷ „ dês'adôḷ.
„ 64, „ 5. *After* punyam *insert* a semicolon.
„ 66, „ 7. *For* odâḷi *read* ôdâḷi.
„ 67, „ 7. „ idum „ endum.
„ 69, „ 11. „ mane-vane „ mane-mane.
„ „ „ 12. „ ghaḷi „ ghaḷil.
„ 70, „ 6. „ bûshaṇe „ bhûshaṇe.
„ 73, „ 6. „ mâḍidavir „ mâḍidapir.
„ 77, „ 1. „ 128 „ 218.
„ 81, „ 4. „ neḍuttam, noḍutam *read* nôḍuttam, nôḍutam.
„ „ „ 17. „ medial „ radical, *and omit* of a root.
„ 85, „ 5. „ bêḷdam „ biḷdam.
„ 93, „ 5. „ ah „ ahah.